2014

GUIDE TO SELF-PUBLISHING

Robert Lee Brewer, Editor

WRITER'S DIGEST BOOKS
WritersDigest.com
Cincinnati, Ohio

Publisher & Editorial Director, Writing Community: Phil Sexton

Writer's Market website: www.writersmarket.com
Writer's Digest website: www.writersdigest.com
Writer's Digest Bookstore: www.writersdigestshop.com

Distributed In Canada by Fraser Direct
100 Armstrong Avenue
Georgetown, Ontario, Canada L7G 5S4
Tel: (905) 877-4411

Distributed in the U.K. and Europe by F&W Media International
Brunel House, Newton Abbot, Devon, TQ12 4PU, England
Tel: (+44) 1626-323200, Fax: (+44) 1626-323319
E-mail: postmaster@davidandcharles.co.uk

Distributed in Australia by Capricorn Link
P.O. Box 704, Windsor, NSW 2756 Australia
Tel: (02) 4577-3555

ISSN: 2330-281X
ISBN-13: 978-1-59963-727-3
ISBN-10: 1-59963-727-8

Attention Booksellers: This is an annual directory of F+W Media, Inc.
Return deadline for this edition is December 31, 2014.

Edited by: Robert Lee Brewer
Cover designed by: Claudean Wheeler
Interior designed by: Claudean Wheeler
Page layout by: Geoff Raker
Production coordinated by: Greg Nock

CONTENTS

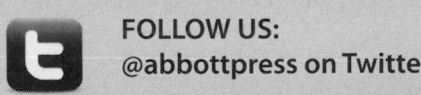

FROM THE EDITOR

Welcome to the inaugural edition of *Guide to Self-Publishing*! Whether it's done digitally or in print, the popularity of self-publishing has been one of the most exciting developments for writers to come out of the digital revolution in publishing and media.

Suddenly, the playing field has been leveled with cost-effective production options for smaller print runs (or none at all in the case of digital), and authors are able to sell directly to their readers without getting on the shelves of major bookstores. In fact, many self-published authors are finding they prefer the profit margins of DIY to going the traditional route.

In this first edition of the book, we've included instructional articles on how to produce books, deal with vendors, and put books up for sale. Further, this book includes important information on connecting with your target audience and promoting your work.

We've interviewed indie publishers who have already found success to tap into what they do and how they make it happen. Whether you write ficiton, nonfiction, or poetry, there's something of worth in these "been there, done that" articles.

Last but not least, the listings in this book are meant to help guide you through the sometimes overwhelming world of indie publishing. There are listings for self-publishing services, freelance editors, freelance designers, independent publicists, and more. Put together, we hope this book will help you find success as a self-publisher.

Until next time, keep publishing!

Robert Lee Brewer
Senior Content Editor, *Guide to Self-Publishing*
http://blog.writersmarket.com
http://twitter.com/robertleebrewer

GETTING STARTED

Guide to Self-Publishing is here to help you navigate the world of self-publishing your work. This article includes information about using this book, but it also covers some of the basics of creating your own books. In fact, this section of the book is labeled Production, because it covers the production of your indie products and services.

Other sections include Management, Promotion, and Interviews. In the Management section, there are articles covering topics like record keeping, self-publishing contracts, pay rates for freelancers you may wish to use, and even handling sales tax. The Promotion section is geared toward reaching your target audience and spreading the gospel about your indie books. Finally, the Interviews section shares stories from indie publishers who have found success self-publishing in a variety of genres.

Beyond the articles, there are plenty of listings for self-publishing companies, freelance editors, freelance designers, independent publicists, and conferences. Each listing section includes an introduction and overview about those specific listings, and the listings include contact information, rates, specialties, and more.

WHERE TO BEGIN

Any project, whether creating books or putting on an event, has to start somewhere—and usually that's with an idea. In book publishing, that idea hopefully turns into a manuscript and eventually a book. That's the simple explanation. Of course, book publishing, whether indie or traditional, is anything but simple.

Here's a better break down of what happens:

- **Writer gets idea.** The idea might start as the line in a poem or scene in a novel. But it starts as a spark, and that spark begins to catch other words and ideas on fire.
- **Writer pushes through a first draft.** For some writers, this might be a month-long novel writing challenge or years of research on a nonfiction book. It might even be collecting blog content to package and sell. Anyway, the writer gets from beginning to end.
- **Writer revises the first draft.** Well, writers who are serious about putting out a good product will revise their first drafts. Many books that fail can point to a lack of editing and production value as the main reason the book didn't catch on with readers. In traditional publishing, an editor and agent will work with a writer at this point.
- **Writer turns in final draft.** In traditional publishing, the writer is now pretty much done with creating the book. However, the indie publisher/writer still has plenty left to do in creating the book.
- **Designer lays out book.** Fonts are chosen (and licensed in some cases). Front matter, including title and copyright pages, and back matter, including glossaries and indexes, are designed. And don't forget the covers.
- **Publisher files a lot of paperwork.** Copyright is registered. ISBNs are secured (for print books, digital books—various versions). Budgets and marketing plans are set. Records are kept. Eventually, the book is sent to the printer.
- **Printer prints books.** For indie authors, this might mean sending to printer, or it could mean getting it loaded with a POD company. Also, it could mean loading a compatible electronic file for the digital platform of your choice (Kindle, Nook, iPad, etc.).
- **Publisher handles distribution.** For the indie publisher, distribution is going to be an uphill battle. But it's not impossible. Plus, successful indie publishers are good about getting creative with distribution and finding alternative routes to connecting with their target audience.
- **Publisher and writer promote the books.** Sometimes, the publisher does more; usually, the writer does more. In indie publishing, there's no question as to who shoulders most—if not all—of the work. That's right, the indie publisher/writer has to roll up her sleeves, make connections, and get her book in front of potential readers.
- **Next idea.** Successful writers and publishers are never finished with one book. If anything, they feel an even greater urge to figure out the next great idea and successful project. And so, the cycle continues.

KNOW YOUR OPTIONS

Indie publishers have more publishing options than ever. That can be a blessing and a curse. Do writers publish in print or electronic? Print-on-demand (POD) or print run? Local printer or self-publishing company? Writers have a lot of options to weigh.

Here are a few:

Vanity Publishing

Vanity publishers used to be the main game in town for self-publishing, and they accepted any project, regardless of its quality. In fact, the quality was often so bad that many contemporary indie publishers are still working their way out of that shadow.

> For some writers, these services are exactly what they're looking to find, and they're happy to pay a premium to receive them. However, many writers looking to 'make it' in indie publishing find vanity publishers are not the best (or most cost-effective) fit.

There's nothing wrong with vanity publishing if you know what you're getting into, but it's often not the most profitable enterprise. Vanity publishers often offer bundled services that might include producing a small print run of books, editing services, promotional services, ISBN registration, and more.

For some writers, these services are exactly what they're looking to find, and they're happy to pay a premium to receive them. However, many writers looking to "make it" in indie publishing find vanity publishers are not the best (or most cost-effective) fit.

Subsidy Publishing

Subsidy publishers are supposedly more selective than vanity publishers, but writers really need to do their homework to make sure this is the case. After all, subsidy publishing contracts and bundled offers are often nearly identical to vanity publishers. With the same money at stake, it's no secret that some subsidy publishers make more money from writers than readers.

Printers

Printing services don't typically screen writers at all and will print to order, but they are focused more on excellent printing than on upselling authors to bundled services. For ambitious indie publishers who aren't afraid to roll up their sleeves and handle everything from design to promotion, these are the folks that will help them get their words into print most effectively.

Some printing services will print a run of books all at once. Others offer POD options.

E-book Conversion Services

More than 20% of traditional book sales in 2012 were e-books. Many in the industry suspect that the ratio is much higher among indie authors. As a result of e-book success stories and multiple platforms, e-book conversion services have sprung up to service writers who need help getting their books digitally ready.

However, as with print publishing, the most ambitious indie publishers learn how to effectively convert their files without paying big fees to adapt to each new platform.

ACCESS YOUR EXCLUSIVE WEBINAR

To access the exclusive webinar that comes with this book, go to writersmarket.com/2014gtsp and learn how to build your brand.

BOOK COVER, COVER TEXT, INTERIOR

by Leslie Lee Sanders

A book is typically judged by its cover, its back cover description, and the quality of its interior text. Some readers still hold on to the once popular belief that all self-published books are of poor quality, filled with spelling and grammatical errors, and are no competition for the traditionally published books it shares the marketplace with. Here's how to self-publish with affordable traditionally published quality inside and out, so readers won't second guess taking a chance on your book.

WHAT YOU NEED

The first thing readers see when deciding to purchase a book is the cover. If the book's cover intrigues them, they move onto the back cover description. If the back cover description is well written and engaging, a skim of the interior pages will follow. Being in the digital age "skimming pages" can also refer to reading online excerpts and sample pages.

So it makes sense to appropriately implement these three suggestions when trying to self-publish a book with traditionally published quality:

- Professional-looking book cover
- Engaging back cover description
- Well-edited interior text

THE PERFECT BOOK COVER

When hiring a professional book cover designer there are certain things you need to look for. This will increase the likelihood you'll be happy with the final product.

Before hiring a cover artist, review their online portfolio for samples of past work. The best cover artists are those who are familiar with your particular genre, know exactly what book covers should look like for that genre, and possess the ability to create original art. Veteran cover artist, Mina Carter, advises to, "Always ask for a draft and whether alterations to the cover, and how many, are included in the price."

Book cover prices vary greatly depending on how detailed the design is, but a basic digital front cover design can start at $100.

- **Request high-resolution stock photos.** Using high-resolution photos and images can help you avoid a final product where the images are distorted, pixilated, or blurred. A professional cover artist is responsible for acquiring the photo art and usage license, and considers the price of the stock photos when providing you with a quote.
- **Make sure the typography on the cover matches the overall tone of the book and is legible.** Play around with different fonts and colors. The title of your book should be in a font that reflects the story's mood and should be easy to read on a thumbnail sized cover.

Use a compelling tagline that asks a question, or include a memorable line of the book that persuades the reader to find out more. Good shout lines are original, short, and are linked to the story's major conflict.

- **Add a one-line quote** from a respectable reader such as a top blogger, a bestselling author, or a well-known name or reviewer.
- **Add a shout line.** No quote? Use a compelling tagline that asks a question, or include a memorable line of the book that persuades the reader to find out more. Good shout lines are original, short, and are linked to the story's major conflict, e.g., *Fighting to live is easier when you have someone to live for.*
- **Add your credentials in a sentence or two.** Have you made it on a reputable bestsellers list? Have you won a prestigious literary award? A potential reader who sees this on your self-published book cover may be more likely to purchase.

PROFESSIONAL COVER ARTISTS

Here are some important things to know when looking for a cover artist.

According to veteran cover artist Mina Carter, "A cover artist should always be able to give you a quote and an idea of their workflow, as well as a lead time on the cover."

Cover artists also ask plenty of questions and require detailed answers regarding the look and feel you want to portray for your cover. Sometimes they ask you to fill out a cover art form, which is your chance to provide as much detail about the cover as you can. Details can range from a character's eye color to the exact name of the font for the title text.

The more in depth you are about what you want, the happier you'll be with the results.

- Get quotes and lead times from a few cover artists before getting too close to a deadline.
- Know the difference between print quality covers and sizes and e-covers and ensure you know what you're paying for (e.g., most cover artists charge more for a full cover, which includes the front and back covers and the spine).
- Cover artists may not purchase stock until the author gives the go ahead, so the draft may have stock site watermarks on them. However, the final cover should be free of watermarks.

THE PERFECT BACK COVER DESCRIPTION (BLURB)

After capturing the reader's attention with a great book cover, you need to hook them with an engaging back cover description also known as a "blurb." Here's how:

- **Restrict your blurb to around 200 words.** An average back cover description is about two or three paragraphs and around 200 words in length. You want to grab your reader quickly, using as few words as possible. Two hundred words broken into a couple paragraphs are easier to read. It's always best to write your blurb without word count in mind and edit later to tighten up the text.

Get to the meat of the story without giving too much away. What are the characters working, fighting, and striving for? Don't include twists and surprises, but hint at them.

- **Select the proper words.** Focus on the overall plot of the story while emphasizing the mood readers should expect from the book. To accomplish this, use certain words that convey the tone of the book. For example, if your book is a thriller, use words like: haunt, escape, and catch. If it's a romance, use words like: soul, warmth, longing, etc.

- **Introduce the main characters immediately**. The characters are the vehicles in which the reader travels through the conflict and experience the overall theme or message of the story. By introducing the main characters in the first few lines of your blurb, the reader quickly builds an interest in that character and their quest through conflict.
- **Indicate the major conflict**. Get to the meat of the story without giving too much away. What are the characters working, fighting and striving for? Don't include twists and surprises, but hint at them. Show them what they should expect from reading the book by enticing them with your blurb.

Entice readers by using the who-what-where-why-how system. This structure is similar to the Five Ws of journalism and could be used in a similar way to create an appealing book blurb.

Hook: Every great piece of writing should have a hook to reel the reader in. The hook should be something shocking, funny, or interesting enough to keep the reader engaged, and should tie into the overall tone of the story.

Construct your blurb by answering the five Ws.

Who: Introduce the main characters.

What: What are the characters fighting for? What is the major conflict of the story?

Where: Provide a brief description of the story's setting. Include a sentence describing the location, e.g., outer space, college, a battle field, etc.

When: When does the story take place and during what time? Here is a chance to mention the unique time period of your story, e.g., ninetieth century, medieval times, post-apocalypse, etc.

Why: Dedicate a sentence or a paragraph to answering or asking "why" in regards to the conflict or character's motives. Why are the characters in conflict? Why should the readers care? Tie in the conflict with what makes the situation relatable to your readers in order to make it more appealing. Use the very things that attract us to good storytelling, e.g., loss of something important, fighting for justice, finding courage, seeking understanding, or whatever makes your story's conflict relatable to your audience.

How: Always leave the reader wondering how the characters will get through the conflict. You can accomplish this by simply asking a question the reader would most likely ask. Or leave them with some sort of cliff hanger, e.g., *"How will they make it out and still stay strong?"* Or *"They must fight their way through the unknown, only then they'll know if it was worth it."*

> ## MORE EXAMPLES OF WORD USAGE BY GENRE:
>
> Use words to excite a mood or portray an idea that's related to your book's genre. Just like tropes in genres where the reader expects certain things to take place (e.g. wandering a wasteland in most post-apocalyptic fiction), certain words can set the mood or setting in specific genres. Examples are below. You would probably be able to guess the genre just by reading the list of words.
>
> **Thrillers:** Tension, uncertainty, gritty, rousing, anticipate.
>
> **Romance:** Emotional, ripen, satisfy, commitment, rouse.
>
> **Horror:** Dark, haunt, startle, induce, eerie, thrill, chill, presence.
>
> **Science Fiction:** Imagine, alternate, worldly, elements, speculate.
>
> **Humor:** Amuse, appeal, wit, absurd, wild.
>
> **Erotica:** Heat, moist, rushes, stir, indulge, desire, affair, indecent, stimulate, provoke.
>
> **Fantasy:** Phenomena, vibrant, super, imagery, fantastic, elements, grand.
>
> **Western:** Portray, desolate, settle, native, conquest, civil, honor, justice.
>
> **Historical:** Period, depict, record, regard, deviate, present, adhere.

WELL-EDITED INTERIOR TEXT

Well-edited interior text is important when making book samples and excerpts available to readers. This helps with a consumer's book-buying decision. Every good piece of writing has one thing in common. It is well edited. If you want interior text that is edited like a traditionally published book you can hire a freelance editor. If you decide not to hire an editor, here are ways to polish your interior text at little or no cost:

- **Red Ink.** Space your lines at 1.5 or 2.0, print out the pages of your manuscript, and mark revisions with a red ink pen. Editing on printed paper could give your eyes a much-needed break from staring at a computer screen for hours. Using red ink over black printed text can help you spot your revisions easier than black or blue ink which tends to get lost among all the dark print.
- **Get it critiqued**. Have someone else look over it. Get an author friend to critique it as well. Enlist as many people as possible to look over the final draft, fix errors and then have another person look over it again. Request honest comments and

embrace criticism about the book's content. Try not to focus only on typos, but on characterization, dialogue, motive, etc.

When red ink and several critiques are not enough, here are some tips for finding an editor.

- **Hire an editor.** Look for referrals and testimonials before committing, and ask for a test edit. An editor will usually edit the first few pages or up to a certain word count for free to give you an idea of what she can do for your entire manuscript. Keep in mind, many editors charge per word, per page, or per hour.
- **Know what kind of editing your story needs.** There are a few types of editors to choose from. Make sure you choose the ones you need for your story. *Copyeditors and Line editors* look for errors in spelling and grammar, small inconsistencies, and factual errors, etc. *Content Editors* edit the content for consistent characterization, point of view errors, plot issues, authentic-sounding dialogue, etc.

Utilize these tips and make your book shine among the average traditionally published books and even among the rare self-published gems.

LESLIE LEE SANDERS has self-published over a dozen erotic romance titles since 2005. She multi-published with romance publishers in 2011. Her blog was a finalist in the Goodreads' 2012 Independent Blogger Awards in the publishing category. Her website/blog (www.leslieleesanders.com) provides tips, advice, and information on writing and publishing for novice and indie authors..

TOP THREE TOOLS FOR PRODUCING GREAT BOOK COVERS

by Peggy DeKay

In the age of online book sites like Amazon.com and Barnes and Noble's online store, bn.com, the book cover has taken on a new significance. The burgeoning e-book market has created more stringent requirements and expectations for every book cover.

The growth of online book sales, and that 600-pound gorilla in the room, Amazon, demand that your book cover not only look great on a bookshelf, but also be enticing to online buyers in the form of a one-inch-by-one-inch icon displayed on a computer screen, an e-reader, or on a smart phone.

> The burgeoning e-book market has created more stringent requirements and expectations for every book cover.

For indie authors who hear the siren's call of DIY, there are some great resources available for creating your own book covers. Keep in mind that the best book covers are those that follow the P-A-R-C-S principle:

- P – Proper placement of graphics and text in a pleasing, uncluttered design
- A – Artistic in that you make sure your graphic symbolizes your story
- R – Readable fonts large enough to read on a book shelf or in a small icon online
- C – Contrast and clarity of each element
- S – Simplicity of design to engage online buyers

Since the graphic element is so important to creating a great book cover, obtaining great pictures that are properly licensed, or that you, as the author own, is important. My top three favorite sites for graphics are:

- www.dreamstime.com
- www.istockphoto.com
- www.bigstockphoto.com

While there are hundreds of other sites out there, these three are easy to use, reasonably priced, and have a large inventory of photos, and graphics. Always make sure that you have properly licensed your graphics since most downloadable graphics are licensed for use on websites, not book covers. Most copyright holders license their photographs or graphic designs according to the number of anticipated "views."

Make sure that your license is adequate for use as a book cover. If you are using clipart as an element in your book cover, be sure you have proper licensing.

Book covers, especially when sold online, can have hundreds of thousands of views. Read the fine print on these sites before you purchase and download the photo. Make sure that your license is adequate for use as a book cover. If you are using clipart as an element in your book cover, be sure that you have proper licensing.

Now that you have purchased and properly licensed your graphic element, it is time to design the cover. There are lots of tool out there to design book covers. They range from simple e-book cover creator programs to top of the line applications like Photoshop CS6 by Adobe, which retails for a whooping $689. You can purchase it online for less.

If you are not a professional designer, an application like Photoshop CS6 can be daunting, and come with an extended learning curve. Don't lose heart. There are three great alternatives to blowing up your book marketing budget while spending the next six months of your life learning Photoshop.

Adobe Photoshop CS6 by Adobe (DVD-ROM -May 7, 2012)
$699.00 $588.99 Windows 7 / XP *Prime
Order in the next 22 hours and get it by Thursday, Jan 31.
Only 7 left in stock - order soon.
More Buying Choices - Windows 7 / XP
$548.99 new (33 offers)
★★★★☆ ⊡ (46)
Software: See all 1,413 items

COVER CREATOR BY CREATESPACE.COM

If you are on a tight budget and need to design a great cover without spending *any* money…the answer is Cover Creator by Createspace. Cover Creator is a free online tool for designing a professional book cover using your own photos, text, and logos. Cover Creator automatically formats and sizes your cover based on your book's trim size and page count. You can choose between a limited set of templates and fonts. Once you have set-up your book title in CreateSpace.com, you can access Cover Creator from within their site.

I recently did a book cover for a client using Cover Creator with great results. Because you can upload your own photographs or artwork as the background, two book covers using the same template can look very different.

Figures 1 and 2 are samples of two templates I used for the book *The Other Side of Yesterday* by Kenn Grimes.

Figure 1 is the book cover we ultimately choose for Kenn's book. Figure 2 is the first template we tried. The photo on the front cover was taken by Kenn on his coffee table, using some old photographs and a

figure 1

figure 2

pendent, arranged in a collage. Save your photograph or graphic as a jpeg. High-resolution photographs work best.

Figure 2 is a different template. Notice that the photograph on this template covers both the front and back cover of the book. The color behind the text was changed. On most CreateSpace templates, you can change the background color, fonts, and the background photograph or graphic.

You can also add or delete the author photo and publisher's logo. The white block at the bottom of the back cover labeled "barcode area" is where the bar code and ISBN for your book will appear when the book is printed.

ADOBE PHOTOSHOP ELEMENTS 11

My second book cover tool of choice is a lighter version of Photoshop CS6 called Photoshop Elements 11. This is a great little program, and one that you can learn in less than an afternoon.

If you are stuck on a command, go to www.Youtube.com and watch a tutorial online. There are hundreds if not thousands of helpful videos on how to use Photoshop Elements 11 on Youtube.com.

Suggested retail for this product is $99. If you are into video editing, you can purchase a bundled package with Photoshop Elements 11 and Photoshop Premier for a suggested retail of $149.00. Again, both Photoshop Elements 11 and the bundle can be purchased online at a discount.

I like this software because it is versatile, and you can create a full-blown book cover or an e-book cover in an afternoon. Fair warning; for best results download a free book cover template from CreateSpace.com. You can do that for any book by clicking on this link: https://www.createspace.com/Help/Book/Artwork.do.

You will need to know your trim size (the dimensions of your book), and the total number of pages including the front and back matter.

Open Photoshop Elements 11 and then open the template that you just downloaded from CreateSpace. It should look like Figure 3. This will allow you to create a second layer and insert the background and graphic elements into the template.

BOOKCOVERPRO

The third tool for creating e-book and print book covers is BookCoverPro at www.bookcoverpro.com. BookCoverPro Standard retails for $97 and BookCoverPro Deluxe retails for $187. With this software, you can create any size book cover using a template from the galley or you can design your cover from scratch. It will work in either RGB or CMYK color mode.

figure 3

BookCoverPro also comes with an add-on for $59 that will allow you to turn your book cover art into brochures, postcards, fliers, mailers, bookmarks, bumper stickers, and more. This is a great feature for building your own promo kit. The software is easy to learn and with some experimentation, you should be creating exciting book covers in no time.

Now that you have the tools, go out and experiment. I am confident that you can, with tenacity, trial and error, and patience, create your own smashing book cover.

BONUS TOOL

For those of you who really want to go it alone, without spending any money, there is a bonus option. If you love all the features of Photoshop CS6 but hate the price, try www.gimp.org.

Gimp is the free alternative to Adobe Photoshop CS6 with about as stiff a learning curve. If you are serious about graphics and creating book covers from scratch, Gimp is a great choice.

PEGGY DEKAY is an author, blogger, podcaster, and book coach. She is a frequent speaker at writer's conferences, book fairs, and civic groups and is an adjunct instructor for the University of Louisville, Carnegie Center for Literacy, and Bellarmine University. She is a past director of Women Who Write, Inc., and the former editor of Writer's Wire. DeKay is the author of *Self-Publishing for Virgins: The first time author's guide to self-publishing*. Her podcast, The Business of Writing Today can be downloaded on iTunes or from her website at http://tbowt.com. DeKay is the co-organizer of The Business of Writing Today International Summit held annually in Louisville, Kentucky. E-mail her at peggy@tbowt.com.

WHY AND HOW TO HIRE A FREELANCE EDITOR

by Kit Cooley

Many writers don't feel they need to have a professional editor look at their work before they begin sending it out to an agent, a publisher, or to the printer. Even a well-written piece can contain some errors. As the author, you are quite intimate with your own work. You have read it so many times that you may not see the mistakes. You may not be aware of standards of usage and style.

An editor can help you to polish your manuscript no matter how you decide to publish, whether through traditional publishing or by self-publishing. An edited manuscript, free of typos, looks better to publishers and readers.

First impressions are important. When I worked on staff as an assistant editor for an independent publisher, I had the task of wading through the slush pile. The cover letter scribbled in red marker pen, the smudged copy, and the manuscripts full of typos were some of the first submissions to be discarded. I'm sure you've heard it said before: Most editors are busy people. Your story is much less likely to get a chance at publication if an editor can't read it. With two manuscripts in front of me, one polished and clean, and one full of errors in punctuation and grammar, I would be inclined to reject the sloppy one no matter how good the underlying story might be.

It is true that a publisher's staff editors will edit your manuscript once it is accepted for publication, but if you submit work riddled with errors, then it is unlikely to make it to a manuscript editor's desk. There certainly have been exceptions, and pieces have been accepted because the strength of the story shone through the mess, but with so much competition in the market today, it is worth the extra investment of hiring an editor to give your work the best chance to get published.

If you take the self-publishing route, please don't scrimp on editing. Writers who decide to self-publish often do so to retain more control over a manuscript. This independence also means that there will be no publisher or editorial staff behind you to clean up, so it is even more important that you enlist the support and expertise of an editor to help you apply the high standards needed to produce a quality publication.

A finished book or e-book with misspelled words, typos, and confusing sentence structure gives the impression that you don't care about what you have written. It lacks professionalism, and can cost you potential readers. You are paying to publish your hard work, so don't waste money on something that is not quite finished. A professional editor can help you to make your book a success. You should also be aware that there are print-on-demand publishers who are concerned with producing quality work, and who will not process a manuscript full of errors.

> Writers who decide to self-publish often do so to retain control over a manuscript. This independence also means that there will be no publisher or editorial staff behind you to clean up.

I was recently given a self-published novel to read. The flow of the story was interrupted with sections of text repeated word-for-word throughout the book. It seemed more like a rough draft than a finished piece. There were additional issues with the story, but for me, the disjointed scenes made the book unreadable. The author had gotten "good feedback" for the original stories from friends, family and writers' groups, and so these shorter vignettes (apparently unedited) were what became the published novel.

Writing groups and writing workshops are great venues for building your confidence as a writer. Working with other writers can offer a place to hone your skills, get constructive criticism for your work, and provide an opportunity to receive advice from others in your craft, including editors who also write. As beneficial as these activities are to your writing practice, none of them can replace what the undivided attention of a good editor can do for your manuscript.

WHAT AN EDITOR CAN DO FOR YOU

You can use the editing functions of word processing software programs to check spelling and grammar, but it is not sufficient, as computer programs cannot provide a careful reading of your work. A good editor will pick up on nuance in your writing, as well as pay attention to the mechanics of grammar, punctuation, syntax, usage, and style. The editor can also give an objective opinion, and point out parts of the text that may not make sense to a reader.

Professional editors will usually read through the entire manuscript first to get a sense of what the author is attempting to convey. The next step in the editing process is giving attention to the details of grammar and punctuation. Skillful application of the appropriate editorial style and determining if the text adheres to current usage is also part of what an editor can do for you. (For more information on the publishing process an excellent source is *The Chicago Manual of Style*. It also has a section describing editorial functions in detail.)

> The best time to hire an editor is when you have completed your manuscript, ... and when you feel it is ready to send to a publisher, agent or printer. The closer to finished the writing work is, the more thorough and cost-effective the editing process will be.

A good editor is not going to make heavy-handed changes to an author's work. During a close reading of your manuscript, he or she will point out inconsistencies and problem areas in the text, and make suggestions for additions, subtractions, or other changes. Some suggested changes may include alternative word usage, fixing problems in tense and person, advice on how to make seamless transitions from scene to scene, and rearranging sections of text to tighten narrative to help you improve the flow of the story. An editor with some publishing house experience can also bring a knowledge of book layout to your project that can be especially helpful to the author who is going the self-publishing route.

The best time to hire an editor is when you have completed your manuscript, whether it is a book, essay, short story, or group of poems, and when you feel it is ready to send to a publisher, agent or printer. The closer to finished the writing work is, the more thorough and cost-effective the editing process will be. There are reasons to hire an editor earlier in the writing process, but only if you require help in the development of the entire manuscript or project. (See a definition of developmental editing below.)

HOW TO CHOOSE AN EDITOR

When you are ready to have your manuscript polished and perfected, you want to make sure the editor that you hire for the job is a good match. How will you know if an editor is right for you? Here are some questions to ask potential manuscript editors and some guidelines to help you choose.

When you first interview an editor, find out what kind of experience he or she has had. If you are writing a novel, you want an editor who has worked with fiction writers. Are you writing a memoir? A technical manual? Make sure that the editor you hire has experience in your genre and has worked on similar projects. If the editing is to be done electronically, ask about software programs and platforms to confirm that these are compatible with what you are using. Most editors today must have some level of experience with electronic editing. Check to see if the editor's experience applies by being specific in describing the final format of your project.

Can you communicate with the editor that you choose? Your relationship with an editor is a professional partnership, and it is necessary to have clear communication. You must feel comfortable with discussing your work with the editor. Ask about expectations and what the editor needs from you. You will need to supply a word or page count and a printed paper manuscript or the electronic file. Ask for references from former clients or a list of completed projects to give you an idea of how the editor collaborates and what kind and quality of work she or he produces.

When you first interview an editor, find out what kind of experience he or she has had. If you are writing a novel, you want an editor who has worked with fiction writers. Are you writing a memoir? A technical manual? Make sure that the editor you hire has experience in your genre and worked on similar projects.

What style guides does the editor use (*The Chicago Manual of Style*, *AP Style Manual*)? Here is where knowledge of the guide used in your genre is helpful. If you don't know, a professional editor will be able to help you in that regard. The editor should also provide you with a style sheet (an alphabetical list designating unique usage of words in a particular manuscript) when the editing is complete.

What will it cost and what is included in the cost? What are the payment terms? Common arrangements are half of the money at the start of the project and the other half on completion, or a third paid at the start, middle and end of the project. A professional editor can provide you with an estimate of cost once you provide information on word count and subject matter. You get what you pay for, so be wary of low quotes. To determine a reasonable cost for your project, you can check the rates in the "How Much Should I Charge" section of this book.

Professional editing takes time. Discuss your desired submission or publication schedule to be sure the editor can fit you into the calendar.

Will the editor sign a letter of agreement or contract? A professional editor will have a standard form of one or the other (or both). Insist on memorializing the terms of your relationship with the editor you choose to hire. It can be as basic as a description of the scope of the project, when and in what format you will get your manuscript to the editor, and when and in what format you will get it back again.

Other important items to include are costs and payment terms, whether the author or the editor will be inserting changes into the text (this applies to both paper and electronic editing), and how to end the relationship in an equitable way if it is not working for either party.

KNOW WHAT KIND OF EDITOR YOU NEED

In these fluid days of change in the publishing world, editorial job functions can flow into one another. Job descriptions change. The flexible freelance editor will often be skilled in a variety of roles in the editorial process. The following definitions can help you in discussing your needs with a potential editor.

Copyediting (also called manuscript editing or line editing) involves reading a manuscript to correct spelling, punctuation, grammar, and syntax, improve style, and clarify inconsistencies or rearrange text for clarity and consistency of voice. Your finished novel or nonfiction manuscript will most likely require copyediting.

Developmental editing entails working with an author to develop a manuscript for submission and publication, deciding how material will be presented, and commenting on the content of the work, character flaws, or plot inconsistencies. This can include providing direction and helping to reorganize whole chapters, paragraphs or sections of the manuscript.

....

Your finished novel or nonfiction manuscript will most likely require copyediting.

....

Proofreading includes checking spelling, punctuation and formatting. Proofreading can also involve reading typeset galleys for typographical errors and inconsistencies against a copy of the final manuscript. This is usually the final step before a manuscript goes to the printer.

Substantive editing deals with the organization and presentation of content and can involve much rewriting and reorganizing. It is usually done through a combined effort of a publisher, an editor, and the author to improve the style of a book after it has been accepted for publication and before manuscript editing.

WHERE DO YOU FIND AN EDITOR?

By far the best way to find a good editor is through a recommendation from another writer. Ask at your writers' group meetings or at conferences and workshops for referrals. Classified ads in trusted writing publications, like *Writer's Digest*, are also a good place to look. Many editors have websites, so search online for someone in your area. If you are on LinkedIn or Facebook try making connections with other professionals in writing and editing groups.

As a writer you dig deep to bring raw ideas to the page. Using these guidelines will help you to find the right editor to work with you to make your words shine.

KIT COOLEY is a freelance editor and writer, who has been "making words shine" since 1999, and whose current business, Dream Lizard Creations, provides excellent service from research to ghostwriting, proofreading to content editing, and anything in between. Her freelance experience includes CNET, the *San Francisco Bay Guardian*, and Barrera Reporting, to name a few.

SELF-PUBLISHING CHECKLIST

Below is a checklist of essential hurdles to clear when self-publishing your book. This list makes the assumption that you've already completed and polished your manuscript. For even more information on self-publishing, check out *The Complete Guide to Self-Publishing*, by Tom and Marilyn Ross (Writer's Digest).

☐ **CREATE PRODUCTION SCHEDULE.** Put a deadline for every step of the process of self-publishing your book. A good rule of thumb is to double your estimates on how long each step will take. It's better to have too much time and hit your dates than constantly have to extend deadlines.

☐ **FIND EDITOR.** Don't skimp on your project and do all the editing yourself. Even editors need editors. Try to find an editor you trust, whether through a recommendation or a search online. Ask for references if the editor is new to you.

☐ **FIND DESIGNER.** Same goes here. Find a good designer to at least handle the cover. If you can have a designer lay out the interior pages too, that's even better.

☐ **DEFINE THE TARGET AUDIENCE.** In nonfiction this is an important step, because knowing the needs of the audience can help with the editing process. Even if you're writing fiction or poetry, it's a good idea to figure out who your audience is, because this will help you with the next few steps.

☐ **FIGURE OUT A PRINT AND DISTRIBUTION PLAN.** This plan should first figure out what the end product will be: printed book, e-book, app, or a combination of options. Then, the plan will define how the products will be created and distributed to readers.

☐ **SET PUBLICATION DATE.** The publication date should be set on your production schedule above. Respect this deadline more than all the others, because the marketing and distribution plans will most likely hinge on this deadline being met.

☐ **PLOT OUT YOUR MARKETING PLAN.** The smartest plan is to have a soft launch date of a week or two (just in case). Then, hard launch into your marketing campaign, which could be as simple as a book release party and social networking mentions, or as involved as a guest blog tour and paid advertising. With self-publishing, it's usually more prudent to spend energy and ideas than money on marketing—at least in the beginning.

☐ **HAVE AN EXCELLENT TITLE.** For nonfiction, titles are easy. Describe what your book is covering in a way that is interesting to your target audience. For fiction and poetry, titles can be a little trickier, but attempt to make your title easy to remember and refer.

☐ **GET ENDORSEMENT.** Time for this should be factored into the production schedule. Contact some authors or experts in a field related to your title and send them a copy of your manuscript to review. Ask them to consider endorsing your book, and if they do, put that endorsement on the cover. Loop in your designer to make this look good.

☐ **REGISTER COPYRIGHT.** Protect your work. Go to http://copyright.gov for more information on how to register your book.

☐ **SECURE ISBN.** An ISBN code helps booksellers track and sell your book. To learn more about securing an ISBN, go to www.isbn.org.

☐ **CREATE TABLE OF CONTENTS AND INDEX (FOR NONFICTION).** The table of contents (TOC) helps organize a nonfiction title and give structure for both the author and the reader. An index serves a similar function for readers, making it easier for them to find the information they want to find. While an index is usually not necessary for fiction or poetry, most poetry collections do use a table of contents to make it easy to locate individual poems.

☐ **INCLUDE AUTHOR BIO.** Readers want to know about the authors of the books they read. Make this information easy to find in the back of the book.

☐ **INCLUDE CONTACT INFORMATION.** In the front of the book, preferably on the copyright and ISBN page, include all contact information, including mailing address and website. E-mail address is optional, but the more options you give the better chance you'll be contacted.

❏ **EXECUTE MARKETING PLAN.** Planning is important, but execution is critical to achieving success. If you're guest posting, finish posts on time and participate in comments section of your blog post. If you're making bookstore appearances, confirm dates and show up a little early—plus invite friends and family to attend.

❏ **KEEP DETAILED ACCOUNTING RECORDS.** For tax purposes, you'll need to keep records of how much money you invest in your project, as well as how much you receive back. Keep accurate and comprehensive records from day one, and you'll be a much happier self-published author.

YOUR 2013–2014 SELF-PUBLISHING CALENDAR

The best way for writers to achieve success is by setting goals. Goals are usually met by writers who give themselves or are given deadlines. Something about having an actual date to hit helps create a sense of urgency in most writers (and editors for that matter). This writing calendar is a great place to keep your important deadlines.

Also, this writing calendar is a good tool for recording upcoming writing events you'd like to attend or contests you'd like to enter. Or use this calendar to block out valuable time for yourself—to just write.

Of course, you can use this calendar to record other special events, especially if you have a habit of remembering to write but of forgetting birthdays or anniversaries. After all, this calendar is now yours. Do with it what you will.

AUGUST 2013

SUN	MON	TUE	WED	THURS	FRI	SAT
				1	2	3
4	5	6	7	8	9	10
11	12	13	14	15	16	17
18	19	20	21	22	23	24
25	26	27	28	29	30	31

Think big. Establish large, long-term goals.

SEPTEMBER 2013

SUN	MON	TUE	WED	THU	FRI	SAT
1	2	3	4	5	6	7
8	9	10	11	12	13	14
15	16	17	18	19	20	21
22	23	24	25	26	27	28
29	30					

Break down what small steps you need to take to accomplish these long-term goals.

_____

_____

_____

_____

_____

OCTOBER 2013

SUN	MON	TUE	WED	THU	FRI	SAT
		1	2	3	4	5
6	7	8	9	10	11	12
13	14	15	16	17	18	19
20	21	22	23	24	25	26
27	28	29	30	31		

Set monthly writing goals for things such as word count or guest posts to submit.

NOVEMBER 2013

SUN	MON	TUE	WED	THU	FRI	SAT
					1	2
3	4	5	6	7	8	9
10	11	12	13	14	15	16
17	18	19	20	21	22	23
24	25	26	27	28	29	30

Write a novel during November as part of NaNoWriMo!

_____

_____

_____

_____

_____

DECEMBER 2013

SUN	MON	TUE	WED	THU	FRI	SAT
1	2	3	4	5	6	7
8	9	10	11	12	13	14
15	16	17	18	19	20	21
22	23	24	25	26	27	28
29	30	31				

Revise your novel, or get your manuscript ready to self-publish.

JANUARY 2014

SUN	MON	TUE	WED	THU	FRI	SAT
			1	2	3	4
5	6	7	8	9	10	11
12	13	14	15	16	17	18
19	20	21	22	23	24	25
26	27	28	29	30	31	

Evaluate your 2013 accomplishments and make 2014 goals.

_____

_____

_____

_____

_____

FEBRUARY 2014

SUN	MON	TUE	WED	THU	FRI	SAT
						1
2	3	4	5	6	7	8
9	10	11	12	13	14	15
16	17	18	19	20	21	22
23	24	25	26	27	28	

Make an effort to find writing friends and peers who can help you edit and/or share your work.

MARCH 2014

SUN	MON	TUE	WED	THU	FRI	SAT
						1
2	3	4	5	6	7	8
9	10	11	12	13	14	15
16	17	18	19	20	21	22
23	24	25	26	27	28	29
30	31					

Join a writing organization or small, local writers group.

APRIL 2014

SUN	MON	TUE	WED	THU	FRI	SAT
		1	2	3	4	5
6	7	8	9	10	11	12
13	14	15	16	17	18	19
20	21	22	23	24	25	26
27	28	29	30			

Try writing or self-publishing poetry for National Poetry Month.

MAY 2014

SUN	MON	TUE	WED	THU	FRI	SAT
				1	2	3
4	5	6	7	8	9	10
11	12	13	14	15	16	17
18	19	20	21	22	23	24
25	26	27	28	29	30	31

Plan to attend a writing conference this summer. Have work(s) ready to sell.

_____

_____

_____

_____

_____

JUNE 2014

SUN	MON	TUE	WED	THU	FRI	SAT
1	2	3	4	5	6	7
8	9	10	11	12	13	14
15	16	17	18	19	20	21
22	23	24	25	26	27	28
29	30					

Before your book is self-published, start pitching guest posts to top blogs.

JULY 2014

SUN	MON	TUE	WED	THU	FRI	SAT
		1	2	3	4	5
6	7	8	9	10	11	12
13	14	15	16	17	18	19
20	21	22	23	24	25	26
27	28	29	30	31		

Spend time considering the best cover possible. Think about what pulls you in to a great cover.

_____

_____

_____

_____

_____

AUGUST 2014

SUN	MON	TUE	WED	THU	FRI	SAT
					1	2
3	4	5	6	7	8	9
10	11	12	13	14	15	16
17	18	19	20	21	22	23
24	25	26	27	28	29	30
31						

Get involved in social media. Set goals. Start a blog now, and join Twitter next month.

SEPTEMBER 2014

SUN	MON	TUE	WED	THU	FRI	SAT
	1	2	3	4	5	6
7	8	9	10	11	12	13
14	15	16	17	18	19	20
21	22	23	24	25	26	27
28	29	30				

Keep a comprehensive file of all your writing ideas, from book concepts to character quirks.

OCTOBER 2014

SUN	MON	TUE	WED	THU	FRI	SAT
			1	2	3	4
5	6	7	8	9	10	11
12	13	14	15	16	17	18
19	20	21	22	23	24	25
26	27	28	29	30	31	

Remember to back up all your writing on disc or through e-mail.

NOVEMBER 2014

SUN	MON	TUE	WED	THU	FRI	SAT
						1
2	3	4	5	6	7	8
9	10	11	12	13	14	15
16	17	18	19	20	21	22
23	24	25	26	27	28	29
30						

Good writers read. Set a goal of reading at least two books a month.

DECEMBER 2014

SUN	MON	TUE	WED	THU	FRI	SAT
	1	2	3	4	5	6
7	8	9	10	11	12	13
14	15	16	17	18	19	20
21	22	23	24	25	26	27
28	29	30	31			

Reward yourself for good work. Celebrate successes, big and small.

HOW TO SWING BOTH WAYS

Writers who publish indie & traditional

by C. Hope Clark

Indie publishing is roaring and strong. Don't you love that name–Indie? It beats the worn-out, stigmatized *self-publishing*, as if producing our own books ranks with hand sewing clothes from burlap instead of buying them from the high-falutin department store catalog.

Traditional is no longer the kingpin. We do not need a publisher and do not have to give up the lion's share of royalties. We are no longer at the mercy of houses that move on only six weeks after the books hit the shelf. We have a louder voice. We call our own shots! Power to the people!

Some indie authors even proclaim New York dead. Some traditionals, holding tight to, um, tradition, still look down on the indies, gripping hard to a manifesto claiming a need for gatekeepers.

The squabbling reminds us of politics, with the left leading for a term, then the right, then the left again, leaving us craving a middle ground that could make everybody happy and put 24-hour cable news out of business.

Truth is authors can swing both ways. Many authors successfully use both publishing methods. Some enter the old-fashioned way first while some start with indie. Some use traditional for one series and indie with another. Our options are many.

C. HOPE CLARK: FICTION ONE WAY, NONFICTION ANOTHER

When I could not sell my mystery 15 years ago back when I entered the profession, I turned to nonfiction for my living. My platform grew through FundsforWriters.com , and I soon learned of the need for *The Shy Writer*, a guide for introverted writers in their painful efforts to earn an income. Needing the book quickly for conference appearances pushed me to self-publish in 2004 with a company called Booklocker, back when made-from-scratch self-publishing almost didn't exist, way before e-books were taken seriously.

But I continued with the mystery. A decade later I landed an agent and publisher for my novel *Lowcountry Bribe*, then a year later its sequel, *Tidewater Murder*. In my work promoting The Carolina Slade Mystery Series, however, I kept hearing accolades about *The Shy Writer*, a book now nine years old. I sold out of every one I had.

The interest prompted me to pen a sequel, *The Shy Writer Reborn*. When a conference asked me to teach a half-day class on the subject, I realized I needed this book in the hands of readers sooner than a traditional publisher could make it happen.

I now self-pub nonfiction in between my mystery books that take a year each to release. The more I promote one book, regardless the genre, regardless how it was printed, the more the others sell.

When a conference asked me to teach a half-day class on the subject, I realized I needed this book in the hands of readers sooner than a traditional publisher could make it happen.

Authors debate continuously about which method rules, which makes more sense, and which writers deserve the most respect. Why argue? The two worlds can co-exist. Readers don't care how a book comes to be, as long as it's a quality read.

J.A. KONRATH: TRADITIONAL SPRINGBOARD INTO INDIE HEAVEN

J.A. Konrath could be labeled the poster child for indie publishing. He began his career through Hyperion, with his Lt. Jacqueline "Jack" Daniels series. However, along the way he discovered a hunger for having more control over his books. He entered the indie arena back when the stigma was intense, and he excelled at cranking out more books, more series, more often, making much more money than he did as a conventional author.

He jumped into electronic publishing in its infancy and hit the ground running. His must-read blog is called A Newbie's Guide to Publishing, www.jakonrath.blogspot.com, and at the end of 2011 he announced he made $22,000 for the month of December from e-book sales. His success has only risen since then, not only due to a spiraling word-of-mouth platform, but also from his prolific production.

Konrath loves indie work and is an iron-clad indie author now. "I've worked with three major publishers. If the price was right, I'd work with them again. That said, I see no advantage to sending out queries and waiting to get an agent or a pub deal when it's possible to self-publish. If you do well self-publishing, you'll get offers, if that's your goal. But I believe holding out for a legacy publisher is silly when Kindle, Kobo, Apple, B&N, and Smashwords make self-pubbing so easy. Unless I was given a giant advance, I wouldn't give up the larger royalty and total control that self-pubbing offers. Writers should experiment, share information, and do a lot of research to figure out which path is best for them."

DEB STOVER: FROM DINOSAUR TO E-BOOK MAVEN

Digital rights weren't even mentioned in Deb Stover's first 11 contracts. She sold her initial book in December 1993 to Kensington, subsequently adding nine more single titles, plus one novella. Then she wrote a two-book series for Penguin's Jove imprint, and one book for Dorchester. In those days, *self-publishing* was a dirty word synonymous with vanity publishing, with stories of sub-standard product and stealing from authors. Still, she forecasted then that digital publishing could turn into a remarkable force in the industry.

And she found being a dinosaur has its advantages. In recent years she requested the reversion on all her books that went out of print. With the flourish of Kindle and iBooks, then the improvement of Nook, she saw her future. At first, she contracted a service that formatted and distributed her works for a percentage of her royalties. Now she produces the e-books herself.

In those days, self-publishing was a dirty word synonymous with vanity publishing, with stories of sub-standard product and stealing from authors.

She was asked whether she'd self-publish a new work. "I have never self-published a new project. These (her e-books) are novels and novellas that have been vetted and edited by a traditional publisher in the past. I have no plans to self-publish a new project. I actually prefer to work with traditional presses, even though I don't make as much money."

LISA SCOTT: TRADITIONAL FOR LONG WORKS AND INDIE FOR SHORTS

Lisa Scott had a bumpy start. She wrote women's fiction and a middle grade novel, but couldn't find an agent, a route she felt was her only choice at the time. So she turned to romance, but then couldn't find a publisher. So she uploaded her romance *No Foolin'* to Amazon, only for Harlequin to ask for the full manuscript for consideration. Harlequin ultimately said no, so she uploaded it again to Amazon.

Then Belle Books asked for the manuscript, and she landed a two-book deal to include *No Foolin'*, the first in her Willowdale Romance series. Having learned enough about self-publishing to feel cozy with it, she chose to write and upload collections of romantic short stories she called *Flirts!* since regular presses rarely show interest in collections.

When asked why she kept hoping for a traditional contract, she replied: "I'm definitely a believer in the 'more eggs in more baskets' theory. I felt they could offer some promotional opportunities for the books that I could not. And I felt that promotion in turn could help my self-published titles. So while I waited for *No Foolin's* release, I put out more *Flirts!* collections. Then a funny thing happened: My agent ended up selling my middle grade novel, *School of Charm* to HarperCollins for 2014 publication."

Scott admits the biggest obstacle for authors these days is getting noticed. The more avenues she uses, the better her chances of being seen by readers and industry professionals. But then she professes she has no backlist, so the power of a press empowers her a bit. "I might have a different opinion if I had already made a name for myself. I have a few writing friends who no longer feel they need the support of their traditional publisher and are self-publishing from here on out because they've got the fan base to support it. It's an exciting time to be a writer. I bring in a nice monthly four-figure income from my self-publishing that will help support me between royalty and advance checks from the traditional deals."

PUBLISHING IS WHAT WE MAKE IT

Finally, publishing has grown up to the point authors can dabble in and master both sides of the line that once divided the industry. Our indie books can establish our names while we seek representation, or our traditional image can sell our self-pubbed works. No longer an either/or dilemma, publishing is what we make it, however method we choose, with the grandest result often involving both.

C. HOPE CLARK is editor of FundsforWriters.com, chosen by *Writer's Digest* for its 101 Best Websites for Writers for over a dozen years. Hope also adores mysteries and is author of The Carolina Slade Mystery Series (Bell Bridge Books). She speaks often at events across the United States. www.fundsforwriters.com | www.chopeclark.com

WE LOVE SALES, BUT NOT SALES TAX

When and How to Charge Sales Tax

by Carol Topp, CPA

As indie publishers, we love sales and seeing our bank deposits grow, but with sales comes the challenge of understanding sales tax. The rules surrounding sales tax are changing and can be quite complex. Keeping records and paying sales tax are burdens we shoulder as a result of doing what we love—selling books.

WHEN TO CHARGE SALES TAX

The rules that govern when you must charge sales tax vary by state, but most depend on two important concepts:

Nexus means a connection or presence in a state, such as a physical location, property, employees, and sometimes affiliates. Attorney Martin I. Eisenstein explains, "Many publishers do business with third parties such as sales representatives, fulfillment houses, and platforms for the sale of e-books. Each of these relationships can create nexus for state tax purposes." If an indie publisher has nexus in a particular state, the publisher must collect and remit sales taxes in that state.

For example, Janice Campbell of Everyday Education based in Virginia sells and mails a copy of her book, *Get a Jump Start on College*, to a customer in Virginia. She must collect and remit sales tax to Virginia, where she has nexus. Campbell also sells and mails a book to a customer in Michigan. She does not have to collect Michigan sales tax because she does not have nexus in Michigan. Campbell travels to Pennsylvania and sells her books there. She created nexus (a physical presence, although temporary) and must collect sales tax and remit it to Pennsylvania.

Tangible personal property usually means physical property, other than real estate, that can be felt, touched, and moved, such as paperback books. Most sales of tangible personal property to the final purchaser are sales-taxable. However, some states have begun to tax the sale of electronic books and music downloads, even though they cannot be felt or touched. (See **Sales Tax on E-Books**.)

These concepts of nexus and tangible personal property will be important as you begin to understand your obligation to collect sales tax. Surprisingly, how you sell your books—in person, by mail, or over the Internet—is not as important as you might think when it comes to sales tax.

SALES TAX ON E-BOOKS

Most states charge sales tax on tangible personal property. What about digital items such as e-books? E-books are not tangible, but many states have expanded the definition of tangible goods to include anything that holds value. So far 23 states have enacted laws that charge sales tax on digital goods.

Michael Mazerov, a senior fellow at the Center on Budget and Public Policy Priorities, explains that digital goods can include computer software, games, music, video, and e-books. Research your state laws carefully. For example, North Dakota and Ohio tax software and games, but (so far) e-books, music, and film are exempt from sales tax there. A list of current state taxation of digital goods is available from CBPP.org here: http://www.cbpp.org/files/12-13-12sfp.pdf

SALES TAX AND THE INTERNET

Some people mistakenly believe that sales over the Internet are sales-tax-free, but this is not so. In 1998, President Clinton signed into law the Internet Tax Freedom Act (ITFA). Its purpose was to prevent state and local governments from imposing new taxes on Internet transactions and access. Contrary to popular belief, ITFA did not create a sales tax exemption for sales made over the Internet.

As SalesTaxSupport.com points out, "Sellers of items via the Internet must collect and remit applicable sales tax if the seller has nexus in the state of the destination of the sale. If the seller does not have nexus, the seller is not yet required to collect and remit the tax."

Some people mistakenly believe that sales over the Internet are sales-tax-free, but this is not so.

For an indie publisher, the method of conducting the sale (online, face-to-face, or catalog order) is not a determining factor for sales tax. Nexus is. If you have nexus in the destination state, you have to collect sales tax for that state. If not, then you do not have to collect sales tax for that state.

For example, I sell books on my website and ship them from my office in Ohio, so I have nexus in Ohio. When a buyer's destination address is in Ohio, my electronic shopping cart (Paypal) adds sales tax to that sale. I do not collect sales tax from purchasers in other states. Every six months, I remit the sales tax collected to the state of Ohio.

WHEN YOU DO NOT HAVE TO CHARGE SALES TAX

Sales tax is a record-keeping challenge for indie publishers, so it is important to understand when you do *not* have to collect sales tax. States vary in offering sales tax exemptions, but here are some common exemptions:

- Sales to a buyer who is not the final purchaser are exempt. If you sell your books to a bookstore, catalog, or other reseller, they collect the sales tax from the final purchaser. For example, Hal and Melanie Young sell their book, *Raising Real Men*, to Christian Book Distributors (CBD), an online bookseller. CBD collects sales tax on orders shipped to addresses where they have nexus (Massachusetts and Colorado). The Youngs neither collect nor pay sales tax on the books they sell to CBD.
- Sales to government agencies, nonprofit organizations, schools, and churches are frequently tax exempt. The exemption varies by state, but most states allow government agencies, especially public schools, to be exempt from paying sales tax. Many charities, which may include private schools and churches, may also receive sales tax exemption from their states. If you sell to a school, church, or charity, you should request a copy of their sales tax exemption certificate to keep in your files.
- Sales to out-of-state customers are exempt (for now). Typically, the seller does not have to collect sales tax on remote sales to out-of-state customers. This ruling was last clarified in 1992 under the landmark case *Quill v. North Dakota*. The Supreme Court ruled that no state may require a seller to collect tax on sales if the seller lacks a physical presence (nexus) in the state. The case left the door open for Congress to address the issue, particularly the burden on sellers to comply with over 6,000 taxing jurisdictions in the United States. Congress has been considering legislation to simplify sales tax collection and may allow states to require sales tax collection across state borders in the future. (See **Recent Legislation.**)

RECENT LEGISLATION

State governments are losing sales tax revenue as online shopping becomes more popular. Consumers who are not charged sales tax when purchasing online are supposed to report the sale and pay a use tax to their state but often do not. Because states found it difficult to obtain compliance from individuals, they turned to the federal government. Governors have been putting pressure on the federal government to allow the states to force remote sellers to collect and pay sales tax.

A number of recent federal bills like The Marketplace Equity Act, The Main Street Fairness Act, and The Marketplace Fairness Act promote simplification and fairness in collecting sales tax. These bills outline a centralized, one-stop, multistate registration system and uniform definitions of products and exemptions. The bills establish a small seller exemption, with a threshold of $500,000 or less in annual sales being exempt from mandatory collection of tax on remote sales.

If Congress passes sales tax legislation, many indie publishers will qualify as small sellers and be exempt from collecting sales tax on remote sales. For in-state sales, business would continue as usual: indie publishers would continue to collect sales tax in states where they have nexus. The proposed legislation could also benefit small sellers with a simplified, uniform system to manage sales tax obligations.

You can stay up to date on the status of sales tax legislation with the news feed at MarketplaceFairness.org/.

HOW TO COLLECT AND REMIT SALES TAX

All states except Alaska, Delaware, Montana, New Hampshire, and Oregon collect sales tax. When collecting and remitting sales tax, indie publishers should follow these steps:

1. Apply for a vendor's license (sometimes called a reseller registration or resale permit) from your state. Also apply for a temporary or transient vendors license if you travel and sell books in another state. Outright.com, an online accounting software program, provides sales tax information for each state at http://outright.com/blog/sales-tax-resources-for-online-sellers-in-every-state/
2. Research exemptions if your customers include schools, churches, or charities.

Some states allow each city or county to set its own sales tax rate in addition to the state sales tax rate. Accounting software such as QuickBooks allows you to set up several tax rates.

3. Set a reminder to remit the sales tax. It might be quarterly, biannually, or annually. If you reach a large dollar threshold, you may need to remit monthly.
4. Keep records of each sale and the applicable tax rate. Some states allow each city or county to set its own sales tax rate in addition to the state sales tax rate. Accounting software such as QuickBooks allows you to set up several tax rates.

5. Consider keeping the sales tax collected in a separate bank account so you will have the entire amount needed to remit to the state when it is due.

6. Determine if your state requires you to file a return even if you made no sales or owe no tax. For example, Ohio requires a report even if no sales were made. My client Alice received a $50 fine for failing to file a sales tax return even though she did not have any taxable sales for the period.

I tested how long would it take for me to gather information about sales tax in the state of Wisconsin. I researched answers to these specific questions:

- What is the sales tax rate? Can counties add onto the state rate? (The state sales tax rate is 5%, and counties can add up to .5% more.)
- Are e-book sales taxable? (Yes.)
- How frequently must I report and pay sales tax? (Report every quarter unless told by the state to submit monthly or annually.)
- How do I obtain a seller's permit? (Complete Wisconsin Form BTR-101 online. The fee is $20.)
- Am I required to file even if no sales tax is due? (Yes. Wisconsin requires reporting every quarter.)

I estimate it would take about two hours to research these questions and register my business in Wisconsin. I thought Wisconsin's information was fairly easy to follow. I considered myself a resident of Wisconsin for this example; finding information for a transient or temporary vendor may take more time.

For more help in collecting and remitting sales tax, visit The Sales Tax Institute's website SalesTaxInstitute.com. They offer helpful FAQs and links to more resources including sales tax software.

HOW TO SIMPLIFY YOUR SALES TAX

Sales tax involves tedious record keeping with little reward, so most indie publishers find legal ways to avoid the paperwork. Any or all of these suggestions might work to make sales tax compliance easier:

- Sell only to resellers, not to the final purchaser.
- If you live in a state that does not tax digital products, consider selling only e-books.
- Consider nontraditional sales avenues. Brian Jud, author of *How to Make Real Money Selling Books*, encourages sales to nonbookstore buyers. He explains, "One author sold over 5,000 copies of her dog care book to a dog food company. Not only did she make a bulk sale of books, but this smart author avoided collecting sales tax as well."

- Sell only online and let your merchant service provider (Paypal or Amazon, for example) collect the sales tax. Nina Roesner, author of *The Respect Dare*, does not directly sell her own books, even when she speaks. Buyers must purchase her book from a bookstore or online. Roesner admits that she may lose sales this way, but the simplicity appeals to her.
- Avoid traveling out of state to sell books. This limits your sales tax collection to only your home state, where you have nexus.
- If federal legislation is passed, keep sales below the $500 million threshold to be considered a small seller.
- If none of these options is viable, use software like QuickBooks to record all sales and the sales tax payable.

Sales tax is a complex and ever-changing topic. Indie publishers should stay abreast of their states' laws and the status of federal sales tax legislation. The concepts of nexus and tangible property are changing and will affect indie publishers in the future. Keeping detailed records and remitting sales tax are necessary, although unwelcome, burdens for everyone who loves to sell books.

CAROL TOPP, CPA is a Certified Public Accountant and author of *Business Tips and Taxes for Writers* (Media Angels). She has authored 10 books, both as an indie publisher and author for a small press. Learn more at CarolToppCPA.com and TaxesForWriters.com.

DISSECTING THE SELF-PUBLISHING CONTRACT

5 Key Issues for Authors

by Aimee Bissonette

Self-publishing can be a huge undertaking. There are so many issues to weigh. Different self-publishing service providers have different strengths and it can be hard to know which to use. Is your book primarily text or images? Do you plan to publish your book as an e-book, in print, or both? Do you need assistance with the entire self-publishing process or are you able to do some of the work yourself?

All of these are important considerations. But these aren't the only considerations. The contract terms offered by the Providers you are considering are important, as well. Provider contracts (often referred to as "Terms of Use" by online Providers) vary widely and some are more fair than others. Authors need to protect their creative works and their investment in the self-publishing process. Understanding the terms that govern the Author/Provider relationship is essential.

The following are 5 key contract issues for Authors evaluating self-publishing providers:

RIGHTS OWNERSHIP

Who "owns" the book and who controls its distribution and sale are key issues in all publishing contracts. Provider contracts should clearly state the Author is the sole owner of the text of the self-published book. In addition, the Author should own the book design, cover art, and formatting of the self-published book—even when these are created by the Provider. Plainly said, self-publishing should mean that you, the Author, own 100% of the rights to your book.

Instead of talking in terms of ownership, a Provider's contract language should discuss licensing of rights. The contract should enumerate the rights licensed, most commonly, the right to print, publish, distribute, and sell the book. The Author may also license the right to convert the book to one or more e-book formats and the right to house an electronic copy of the book on the Provider's server.

The Provider's contract should state whether the licenses are "exclusive" or "non-exclusive." If an Author grants an exclusive license to a Provider, the Provider is the only person or entity that may exercise that right while the contract is in place. The licensed right may not even be exercised by the Author during that time, so Authors should be careful about granting exclusive licenses. Exclusive licenses are appropriate when a Provider agrees to significant obligations beyond merely publishing and selling (e.g. warehousing, order fulfillment, marketing, publicity, catalog and website presence) but then only if the contract is easily terminated by the Author.

> If an Author grants an exclusive license to a Provider, the Provider is the only person or entity that may exercise that right while the contract is in place. The licensed right may not even be exercised by the Author during that time, so Authors should be careful about granting exclusive licenses.

Licensed rights should be limited only to those that are necessary for the Provider to fulfill the self-publishing services and the length of time those licenses remain in place should also be limited (licenses should either be for a specific period of time or terminable at will by the Author). Some Provider contracts require Authors to grant very expansive licenses that allow the Provider tremendous control. These Providers also may try to include "out of print" clauses, non-compete clauses, and option clauses in their contracts—none of which is appropriate in a self-publishing scenario. Steer clear of these Providers.

DESIGN SERVICES

Providers of self-publishing services offer a range of packages and services. Authors engage these Providers for their expertise in editing and design, as well as distribution and e-book conversion. It is important to compare and contrast these offerings to determine exactly what the various Providers include in terms of cover art, interior design, fonts, placement of bar codes, etc.

Provider contracts should be clear about the services offered and when additional fees will be charged. For instance, the contract should state whether an Author must pay additional fees for revisions of the designs created and whether the Provider will refund an Author's money should the Provider and the Author fail to see eye to eye on production issues.

When evaluating the many additional services offered by various Providers (and the attendant fees), Authors should consider what, if anything, they can do themselves. There is no need to buy what you don't need. For instance, many Providers will procure ISBNs as part of their services. Because it is expensive for an individual to purchase a single ISBN, it may make sense for the Author to have the Provider do so, unless the Author intends to issue the self-published book in multiple formats or editions. (Each version and format of a book requires a separate ISBN. If you anticipate that you will be issuing the book in multiple formats or that you may reissue your book in the future through someone other than your current provider, you may be better off purchasing a block of 10 ISBNs.)

By comparison, copyright registration is easily done online and requires payment only of a nominal filing fee to the US Copyright Office (the current fee is $35). Registering your copyright yourself is preferable to paying your provider a marked up fee to do so.

> Because it is expensive for an individual to purchase a single ISBN, it may make sense for the Author to have the Provider do so, unless the Author intends to issue the self-published book in multiple formats or editions.

As was noted above, ownership issues can arise with regard to design aspects of self-published books. Authors who engage Providers to design and format their books are encouraged to look for contract language along the lines of "Author owns 100% of the book cover, design and layout." If Authors supply their own images for their self-published books, they must be sure first to clear the rights to use those images.

Authors own the rights to images they create themselves (e.g. photos they take), but they are not free to use images pulled from the Internet without first obtaining permission. Even stock images obtained via Internet or subscription services are subject to restrictions. Authors must abide by the licensing terms and pay the appropriate fees to such services before including images on or in their self-published books.

If an Author retains a freelancer (an independent contractor) to provide cover art or other book design services, an agreement between the Author and freelancer should be crafted that specifically states, in writing, that the freelancer's work is a "work for hire" under US Copyright law and that the freelancer makes no claim of ownership in the Author's book. This will allow the Author to use the book's cover and design aspects in other ways as well, for example, on the Author's website, in print materials, and on social media.

HOW THE MONEY FLOWS

Providers take different approaches to pricing. Some dictate pricing and royalty terms, while others allow Authors to set their own retail price, author discount, and wholesale price (although sometimes subject to a minimum dollar amount to ensure the Provider can cover its administrative and credit card costs). Authors should seek arrangements that provide the Author with 100% of book royalties after deduction of production costs and third party service provider costs.

When it comes to tracking and getting paid for sales, self-publishing service Providers offer an advantage over traditional publishers. A number offer easily accessible sales information online and pay royalties on a monthly or quarterly basis, as opposed to the annual or semiannual payments provided by traditional publishers.

Compare Provider contracts based on how Providers track sales, how frequently they pay royalties, and the manner in which they pay. Many Providers set up Author accounts and establish a threshold amount above which funds are made available for electronic transfer. (If an Author prefers a physical check, a processing fee may be charged.) Look for contract language that establishes definite parameters and procedures for payment and provides a mechanism by which Authors can track sales and thus, judge the accuracy of payments made.

If funds owing the Author for book sales are not remitted to the Provider, the Provider has no obligation to pay the Author. The Author must undertake collection efforts agains the third party in such an instance.

With regard to payments, be aware that, as with traditional publishers, Providers will declare the right to withhold payments as an offset against any money the Author owes the Provider (e.g. payment for services, returns, refunds, customer credits). Providers will withhold payments if a claim is made against an Author for copyright infringement, defamation, or other violation of a third party's rights. Some Providers will also withhold payments for a period of time after termination of the contract (e.g. Amazon will hold funds for 3 months) so they are sure to have funds on hand to process refunds, credits, and returns accruing after the contract has ended.

In addition, be aware that the risk of non-payment of sales proceeds by a third party is borne solely by the Author. If funds owing the Author for book sales are not remitted to the Provider, the Provider has no obligation to pay the Author. The Author must undertake collection efforts against the third party in such an instance.

Lastly, Authors are responsible for paying income tax on the revenue they derive from book sales. Most Providers will require, at a minimum, that you provide them with a Social Security or Tax Identification number so they may fulfill their reporting obligations to the taxing authorities.

ENDING THE RELATIONSHIP

Self-publishing is changing rapidly. The services offered by Providers this year may be radically different from the services offered in the years to come. For that reason, it is important to have flexibility when it comes to terminating a contract with a Provider. Ideally, an Author should be able to terminate a Provider contract (in legal terms, "rescind" the Author's grant of rights) at any time. Provider contracts may require advance notice of termination, but such notice should not exceed 30 days.

Most Provider contracts allow for immediate termination followed by a short period within which the Provider may alert third party sellers and fulfill sales pending at the time of termination. Authors who have purchased additional services from their Providers (e.g. inclusion in an online or print catalog, premium distribution services) may have separate contracts for those services and may need to take additional steps to terminate those contracts.

....

Provider contracts may require advance notice of termination, but such notice should not exceed 30 days.

....

Be aware that Providers also have termination rights. Many Providers include contract language that allows the Provider to suspend an Author's access to its services, particularly if an Author engages in illegal or unethical behavior, or otherwise violates the rights of others. Authors are counseled to keep backup copies of their books and other content as protection in the unlikely event they are denied access to their Providers' services.

RESOLVING DISPUTES

As with any business relationship, the possibility exists for a dispute between Authors and Providers. Sometimes these disputes are about money, which highlights the importance of reviewing/auditing royalty statements, as mentioned above. Sometimes the disputes occur pre-publication and are resolved by a refund of some or all of the Author's money. Regardless of the dispute, Provider contracts will include dispute resolution provisions, which generally benefit the Provider.

Some provider contracts set a discrete and usually short (e.g. 6 months, 12 months) period of time within which an Author may bring a claim against the Provider for breach of contract. Authors are contractually bound by these time periods, even if state law provides a longer period of time within which a claim may be brought.

Providers also often include language that limits the issues on which an Author may base a claim, limits the Author's recovery to unpaid royalties only, or requires the Author to use arbitration rather than the courts to resolve disputes. These dispute resolution provisions are not likely to be negotiable but, because they dictate how and when an Author may bring legal claims against a Provider, they should not be disregarded.

BE A SMART CONSUMER

In conclusion, there are a multitude of issues for Authors to consider when evaluating self-publishing Provider contracts. The issues outlined above are particularly important, however, because they affect an author's ability to control the self-published work. There are many reputable Providers whose contracts offer even-handed terms.

In comparing provider contracts, trust your gut. Ask yourself: Does the contract seem fair? Is it written in language that is easy to understand? Am I able to negotiate any terms (or, at least, choose from a variety of packages)?

Be a smart consumer. Talk to others who have used the self-publishing Provider you are considering. And, above all, review contract terms so you can minimize the risk of problems and maximize all the benefits that can accrue from self-publishing.

AIMEE BISSONETTE has worked as a lawyer, teacher, and writer since 1987. Through Little Buffalo Law & Consulting, she helps her clients make smart decisions about licensing their creative works. She has negotiated publishing contracts with all of the major publishing houses and many small and medium size presses, as well. Aimée holds a J.D. from the University of Minnesota. She is the author of *Cyber Law: Maximizing Safety and Minimizing Risk in Classrooms* (Corwin Press 2009).

HOW MUCH SHOULD I CHARGE?

by Lynn Wasnak

If you're a beginning freelance writer, or don't know many other freelancers, you may wonder how anyone manages to earn enough to eat and pay the rent by writing or performing a mix of writing-related tasks. Yet, smart full-time freelance writers and editors annually gross $35,000 and up—sometimes into the $150,000-200,000 range. These top-earning freelancers rarely have names known to the general public. (Celebrity writers earn fees far beyond the rates cited in this survey.) But, year after year, they sustain themselves and their families on a freelance income, while maintaining control of their hours and their lives.

Such freelancers take writing and editing seriously—it's their business.

Periodically, they sit down and think about the earning potential of their work, and how they can make freelancing more profitable and fun. They know their numbers: what it costs to run their business; what hourly rate they require; how long a job will take. Unless there's a real bonus (a special clip, or a chance to try something new) these writers turn down work that doesn't meet the mark and replace it with a better-paying project.

If you don't know your numbers, take a few minutes to figure them out. Begin by choosing your target annual income—whether it's $25,000 or $100,000. Add in fixed expenses: social security, taxes, and office supplies. Don't forget health insurance and something for your retirement. Once you've determined your annual gross target, divide it by 1,000 billable hours—about 21 hours per week—to determine your target hourly rate.

Remember—this rate is flexible. You can continue doing low-paying work you love as long as you make up for the loss with more lucrative jobs. But you must monitor your rate of earning if you want to reach your goal. If you slip, remind yourself you're in charge. As a freelancer, you can raise prices, chase better-paying jobs, work extra hours, or adjust your spending.

"Sounds great," you may say. "But how do I come up with 1,000 billable hours each year? I'm lucky to find a writing-related job every month or two, and these pay a pittance."

That's where business attitude comes in: network, track your time, join professional organizations, and study the markets. Learn how to query, then query like mad. Take chances by reaching for the next level. Learn to negotiate for a fee you can live on—your plumber does! Then get it in writing.

You'll be surprised how far you can go, and how much you can earn, if you believe in your skills and act on your belief. The rates that follow are a guide to steer you in the right direction.

This report is based on input from sales finalized in 2009 and 2010 only. The data is generated from voluntary surveys completed by members of numerous professional writers' and editors' organizations and specialty groups. We thank these responding groups, listed below, and their members for generously sharing information. If you would like to contribute your input, e-mail lwasnak@fuse.net for a survey.

PARGICIPATING ORGANIZATIONS

Here are the organizations surveyed to compile the "How Much Should I Charge?" pay rate chart. You can also find Professional Organizations in the Resources.

- American Independent Writers (AIW), (202)775-5150. Website: www.amerindy writers.org.
- American Literary Translators Association (ALTA), (972)883-2093. Website: www. utdallas.edu/alta/.
- American Medical Writers Association (AMWA), (301)294-5303. Website: www. amwa.org.
- American Society of Journalists & Authors (ASJA), (212)997-0947. Website: www. asja.org.
- American Society of Media Photographers (ASMP), (215)451-2767. Website: www. asmp.org.
- American Society of Picture Professionals (ASPP), (703)299-0219. Website: www. aspp.com.
- American Translators Association (ATA), (703)683-6100. Website: www.atanet.org.
- Angela Hoy's Writers Weekly. Website: www.writersweekly.com.
- Association of Independents in Radio (AIR), (617)825-4400. Website: www.air media.org.
- Association of Personal Historians (APH). Website: www.personalhistorians.org.
- Educational Freelancers Association (EFA), (212)929-5400. Website: www.the-efa.org.

- Freelance Success (FLX), (877) 731-5411. Website: www.freelancesucess.com.
- International Association of Business Communicators (IABC), (415)544-4700. Website: www.iabc.com.
- Investigative Reporters & Editors (IRE), (573)882-2042. Website: www.ire.org.
- Media Communicators Association International (MCA-I), (888)899-6224. Website: www.mca-i.org.
- National Cartoonists Society (NCS), (407)647-8839. Website: www.reuben.org/main.asp.
- National Writers Union (NWU), (212)254-0279. Website: www.nwu.org.
- National Association of Science Writers (NASW), (510)647-9500. Website: www.nasw.org.
- Society of Professional Journalists (SPJ), (317)927-8000. Website: www.spj.org.
- Society for Technical Communication (STC), (703)522-4114. Website: www.stc.org.
- Women in Film (WIF). Website: www.wif.org.
- Writer's Guild of America East (WGAE), (212)767-7800. Website: www.wgaeast.org.
- Writer's Guild of America West (WGA), (323)951-4000. Website: www.wga.org.

LYNN WASNAK (www.lynnwasnak.com) was directed to the market for her first paid piece of deathless prose ("Fossils in Your Driveway" published by *Journeys* in 1968 for $4) by *Writer's Market*. In the 40 years since, she's made her living as a freelancer and has never looked back.

	PER HOUR			PER PROJECT			OTHER		
	HIGH	LOW	AVG	HIGH	LOW	AVG	HIGH	LOW	AVG
ADVERTISING & PUBLIC RELATIONS									
Advertising copywriting	$150	$35	$83	$9,000	$150	$2,752	$3/word	25¢/word	$1.56/word
Advertising editing	$125	$20	$64	n/a	n/a	n/a	$1/word	25¢/word	65¢/word
Advertorials	$180	$50	$92	$1,875	$200	$479	$3/word	75¢/word	$1.57/word
Business public relations	$180	$30	$84	n/a	n/a	n/a	$500/day	$200/day	$356/day
Campaign development or product launch	$150	$35	$95	$8,750	$1,500	$4,540	n/a	n/a	n/a
Catalog copywriting	$150	$25	$71	n/a	n/a	n/a	$350/item	$25/item	$116/item
Corporate spokesperson role	$180	$70	$107	n/a	n/a	n/a	$1,200/day	$500/day	$740/day
Direct-mail copywriting	$150	$35	$84	$8,248	$500	$2,839	$4/word $400/page	$1/word $200/page	$2.17/word $314/page
Event promotions/publicity	$125	$30	$75	n/a	n/a	n/a	n/a	n/a	$500/day
Press kits	$180	$30	$82	n/a	n/a	n/a	$850/60sec	$120/60sec	$456/60sec
Press/news release	$180	$30	$78	$1,500	$125	$700	$2/word $750/page	40¢/word $150/page	$1.17/word $348/page
Radio commercials	$99	$30	$72	n/a	n/a	n/a	$850/60sec	$120/60sec	$456/60sec

	PER HOUR			PER PROJECT			OTHER		
	HIGH	LOW	AVG	HIGH	LOW	AVG	HIGH	LOW	AVG
Speech writing/editing for individuals or corporations	$167	$35	$90	$10,000	$2,700	$5,036	$350/minute	$100/minute	$204/minute
BOOK PUBLISHING									
Abstracting and abridging	$125	$30	$74	n/a	n/a	n/a	$2/word	$1/word	$1.48/word
Anthology editing	$80	$23	$51	$7,900	$1,200	$4,588	n/a	n/a	n/a
Book chapter	$100	$35	$60	$2,500	$1,200	$1,758	20¢/word	8¢/word	14¢/word
Book production for clients	$100	$40	$67	n/a	n/a	n/a	$17.50/page	$5/page	$10/page
Book proposal consultation	$125	$25	$66	$1,500	$250	$788	n/a	n/a	n/a
Book publicity for clients	n/a	n/a	n/a	$10,000	$500	$2,000	n/a	n/a	n/a
Book query critique	$100	$50	$72	$500	$75	$202	n/a	n/a	n/a
Children's book writing	$75	$35	$50	n/a	n/a	n/a	$5/word $5,000/adv	$1/word $450/adv	$2.75/word $2,286/adv
Content editing (scholarly/textbook)	$125	$20	$51	$15,000	$500	$4,477	$20/page	$3/page	$6.89/page
Content editing (trade)	$125	$19	$54	$20,000	$1,000	$6,538	$20/page	$3.75/page	$8/page
Copyediting (trade)	$100	$16	$46	$5,500	$2,000	$3,667	$6/page	$1/page	$4.22/page

	PER HOUR			PER PROJECT			OTHER		
	HIGH	LOW	AVG	HIGH	LOW	AVG	HIGH	LOW	AVG
Encyclopedia articles	n/a	n/a	n/a	n/a	n/a	n/a	50¢/word $3,000/item	15¢/word $50/item	35¢/word $933/item
Fiction book writing (own)	n/a	n/a	n/a	n/a	n/a	n/a	$40,000/adv	$525/adv	$14,193/adv
Ghostwriting, as told to	$125	$35	$67	$47,000	$5,500	$22,892	$100/page	$50/page	$87/page
Ghostwriting, no credit	$125	$30	$73	n/a	n/a	n/a	$3/word $500/page	50¢/word $50/page	$1.79/word $206/page
Guidebook writing/editing	n/a	n/a	n/a	n/a	n/a	n/a	$14,000/adv	$10,000/adv	$12,000/adv
Indexing	$60	$22	$35	n/a	n/a	n/a	$12/page	$2/page	$4.72/page
Manuscript evaluation and critique	$100	$23	$66	$2,000	$150	$663	n/a	n/a	n/a
Manuscript typing	n/a	n/a	$20	n/a	n/a	n/a	$3/page	95¢/page	$1.67/page
Movie novelizations	n/a	n/a	n/a	$15,000	$5,000	$9,159	n/a	n/a	n/a
Nonfiction book writing (collaborative)	$125	$40	$80	n/a	n/a	n/a	$110/page $75,000/adv	$50/page $1,300/adv	$80/page $22,684/adv
Nonfiction book writing (own)	$125	$40	$72	n/a	n/a	n/a	$110/page $50,000/adv	$50/page $1,300/adv	$80/page $14,057/adv
Novel synopsis (general)	$60	$30	$45	$450	$150	$292	$100/page	$10/page	$37/page

	PER HOUR			PER PROJECT			OTHER		
	HIGH	LOW	AVG	HIGH	LOW	AVG	HIGH	LOW	AVG
Personal history writing/editing (for clients)	$125	$30	$60	$40,000	$750	$15,038	n/a	n/a	n/a
Proofreading	$75	$15	$31	n/a	n/a	n/a	$5/page	$2/page	$3.26/page
Research for writers or book publishers	$150	$15	$52	n/a	n/a	n/a	$600/day	$450/day	$525/day
Rewriting/structural editing	$120	$25	$67	$50,000	$2,500	$13,929	15¢/word	6¢/word	11¢/word
Translation—literary	n/a	n/a	n/a	$10,000	$7,000	$8,500	20¢/target word	6¢/target word	11¢/target word
Translation—nonfiction/technical	n/a	n/a	n/a	n/a	n/a	n/a	35¢/target word	8¢/target word	16¢/target word
BUSINESS									
Annual reports	$180	$45	$92	$15,000	$500	$5,708	$600	$100	$349
Brochures, booklets, flyers	$150	$30	$81	$15,000	$300	$4,215	$2.50/word $800/page	35¢/word $50/page	$1.21/word $341/page
Business editing (general)	$150	$25	$70	n/a	n/a	n/a	n/a	n/a	n/a
Business letters	$150	$30	$74	n/a	n/a	n/a	$2/word	$1/word	$1.47/word
Business plan	$150	$30	$82	$15,000	$200	$4,100	n/a	n/a	n/a

	PER HOUR			PER PROJECT			OTHER		
	HIGH	LOW	AVG	HIGH	LOW	AVG	HIGH	LOW	AVG
Business writing seminars	$200	$60	$107	$8,600	$550	$2,919	n/a	n/a	n/a
Consultation on communications	$180	$40	$95	n/a	n/a	n/a	$1,200/day	$500/day	$823/day
Copyediting for business	$125	$25	$60	n/a	n/a	n/a	$4/page	$2/page	$3/page
Corporate histories	$180	$35	$86	160,000	$5,000	$54,500	$2/word	$1/word	$1.50/word
Corporate periodicals, editing	$125	$35	$69	n/a	n/a	n/a	$2.50/word	75¢/word	$1.42/word
Corporate periodicals, writing	$135	$35	$78	n/a	n/a	$1,875	$3/word	$1/word	$1.71/word
Corporate profiles	$180	$35	$88	n/a	n/a	$3,000	$2/word	$1/word	$1.50/word
Ghostwriting for business execs	$150	$25	$84	$3,000	$500	$1,393	$2.50/word	50¢/word	$2/word
Ghostwriting for businesses	$250	$35	$109	$3,000	$500	$1,756	n/a	n/a	n/a
Newsletters, desktop publishing/production	$135	$35	$71	$6,600	$1,000	$3,480	$750/page	$150/page	$429/page
Newsletters, editing	$125	$25	$67	n/a	n/a	$3,600	$230/page	$150/page	$185/page
Newsletters, writing	$125	$25	$77	$6,600	$800	$3,567	$5/word $1,250/page	$1/word $150/page	$2.30/word $514/page

	PER HOUR			PER PROJECT			OTHER		
	HIGH	LOW	AVG	HIGH	LOW	AVG	HIGH	LOW	AVG
Translation services for business use	$75	$35	$52	n/a	n/a	n/a	$35/ target word $1.40/ target line	6¢/ target word $1/ target line	$2.30/ target word $1.20/ target line
Resume writing	$100	$60	$72	$500	$150	$287	n/a	n/a	n/a
COMPUTER, INTERNET & TECHNICAL									
Blogging—paid	n/a	n/a	$100	$2,000	$500	$1,240	$500/post	$6/post	$49/post
E-mail copywriting	$125	$35	$85	n/a	n/a	$300	$2/word	30¢/word	91¢/word
Educational webinars	$500	$0	$195	n/a	n/a	n/a	n/a	n/a	n/a
Hardware/Software help screen writing	$95	$60	$81	$6,000	$1,000	$4,000	n/a	n/a	n/a
Hardware/Software manual writing	$165	$30	$80	$23,500	$5,000	$11,500	n/a	n/a	n/a
Internet research	$95	$25	$55	n/a	n/a	n/a	n/a	n/a	n/a
Keyword descriptions	n/a	n/a	n/a	n/a	n/a	n/a	$200/page	$135/page	$165/page
Online videos for clients	$95	$60	$76	n/a	n/a	n/a	n/a	n/a	n/a

	PER HOUR			PER PROJECT			OTHER		
	HIGH	LOW	AVG	HIGH	LOW	AVG	HIGH	LOW	AVG
Social media postings for clients	$95	$30	$62	n/a	n/a	$500	n/a	n/a	$10/word
Technical editing	$150	$25	$65	n/a	n/a	n/a	n/a	n/a	n/a
Technical writing	$160	$30	$80	n/a	n/a	n/a	n/a	n/a	n/a
Web editing	$100	$25	$57	n/a	n/a	n/a	$10/page	$3/page	$5.67/page
Webpage design	$150	$35	$80	$4,000	$200	$1,278	n/a	n/a	n/a
Website or blog promotion	n/a	n/a	n/a	$650	$195	$335	n/a	n/a	n/a
Website reviews	n/a	n/a	n/a	$900	$50	$300	n/a	n/a	n/a
Website search engine optimization	$89	$60	$76	$50,000	$8,000	$12,000	n/a	n/a	n/a
White papers	$135	$25	$82	$10,000	$2,500	$4,927	n/a	n/a	n/a
EDITORIAL/DESIGN PACKAGES									
Desktop publishing	$150	$25	$67	n/a	n/a	n/a	$750/page	$30/page	$202/page
Photo brochures	$125	$65	$87	$15,000	$400	$3,869	$65/picture	$35/picture	$48/picture
Photography	$100	$50	$71	$10,500	$50	$2,100	$2,500/day	$500/day	$1,340/day

	PER HOUR			PER PROJECT			OTHER		
	HIGH	LOW	AVG	HIGH	LOW	AVG	HIGH	LOW	AVG
Photo research	$75	$25	$49	n/a	n/a	n/a	n/a	n/a	n/a
Picture editing	$100	$40	$64	n/a	n/a	n/a	$65/picture	$35/picture	$53/picture
EDUCATIONAL & LITERARY SERVICES									
Author appearances at national events	n/a	n/a	n/a	n/a	n/a	n/a	$500/hour $30,000/event	$100/hour $500/event	$285/hour $5,000/event
Author appearances at regional events	n/a	n/a	n/a	n/a	n/a	n/a	$1,500/event	$50/event	$615/event
Author appearances at local groups	$63	$40	$47	n/a	n/a	n/a	$400/event	$75/event	$219/event
Authors presenting in schools	$125	$25	$78	n/a	n/a	n/a	$350/class	$50/class	$183/class
Educational grant and proposal writing	$100	$35	$67	n/a	n/a	n/a	n/a	n/a	n/a
Manuscript evaluation for theses/dissertations	$100	$15	$53	$1,550	$200	$783	n/a	n/a	n/a
Poetry manuscript critique	$100	$25	$62	n/a	n/a	n/a	n/a	n/a	n/a
Private writing instruction	$60	$50	$57	n/a	n/a	n/a	n/a	n/a	n/a

	PER HOUR			PER PROJECT			OTHER		
	HIGH	LOW	AVG	HIGH	LOW	AVG	HIGH	LOW	AVG
Readings by poets, fiction writers	n/a	n/a	n/a	n/a	n/a	n/a	$3,000/event	$50/event	$225/event
Short story manuscript critique	$150	$30	$75	$175	$50	$112	n/a	n/a	n/a
Teaching adult writing classes	$125	$35	$82	n/a	n/a	n/a	$800/class $5,000/course	$150/class $500/course	$450/class $2,667/course
Writer's workshop panel or class	$220	$30	$92	n/a	n/a	n/a	$5,000/day	$60/day	$1,186/day
Writing for scholarly journals	$100	$40	$63	$450	$100	$285	n/a	n/a	n/a
FILM, VIDEO, TV, RADIO, STAGE									
Book/novel summaries for film producers	n/a	n/a	n/a	n/a	n/a	n/a	$34/page	$15/page	$23/page $120/book
Business film/video scriptwriting	$150	$50	$97	n/a	n/a	$600	$1,000/run min	$50/run min	$334/run min $500/day
Comedy writing for entertainers	n/a	n/a	n/a	n/a	n/a	n/a	$150/joke $500/group	$5/joke $100/group	$50/joke $283/group
Copyediting audiovisuals	$90	$22	$53	n/a	n/a	n/a	n/a	n/a	n/a
Educational or training film/video scriptwriting	$125	$35	$81	n/a	n/a	n/a	$500/run min	$100/run min	$245/run min

	PER HOUR			PER PROJECT			OTHER		
	HIGH	LOW	AVG	HIGH	LOW	AVG	HIGH	LOW	AVG
Feature film options	First 18 months, 10% WGA minimum; 10% minimum each 18-month period thereafter.								
TV options	First 180 days, 5% WGA minimum; 10% minimum each 180-day period thereafter.								
Industrial product film/video scriptwriting	$150	$30	$99	n/a	n/a	n/a	$500/run min	$100/run min	$300/run min
Playwriting for the stage	5-10% box office/Broadway; 6-7% box office/off-Broadway; 10% box office/regional theatre.								
Radio editorials	$70	$50	$60	n/a	n/a	n/a	$200/run min $400/day	$45/run min $250/day	$124/run min $325/day
Radio interviews	n/a	n/a	n/a	$1,500	$150	$683	n/a	n/a	n/a
Screenwriting (original screenplay-including treatment)	n/a	n/a	n/a	n/a	n/a	n/a	$117,602	$62,642	$90,122
Script synopsis for agent or film	$2,344/30 min, $4,441/60 min, $6,564/90 min								
Script synopsis for business	$75	$45	$62	n/a	n/a	n/a	n/a	n/a	n/a
TV commercials	$99	$60	$81	n/a	n/a	n/a	$2,500/30 sec	$150/30 sec	$1,204/30 sec
TV news story/feature	$1,455/5 min, $2,903/10 min, $4,105/15 min								
TV scripts (non-theatrical)	Prime Time: $33,681/60 min, $47,388/90 min Not Prime Time: $12,857/30 min, $23,370/60 min, $35,122/90 min								

	PER HOUR			PER PROJECT			OTHER		
	HIGH	LOW	AVG	HIGH	LOW	AVG	HIGH	LOW	AVG
TV scripts (teleplay/MOW)	$68,150/120 min								
MAGAZINES & TRADE JOURNALS									
Article manuscript critique	$125	$25	$64	n/a	n/a	n/a	n/a	n/a	n/a
Arts query critique	$100	$50	$75	n/a	n/a	n/a	n/a	n/a	n/a
Arts reviewing	$95	$60	$79	$325	$100	$194	$1.20/word	8¢/word	58¢/word
Book reviews	n/a	n/a	n/a	$900	$25	$338	$1.50/word	15¢/word	68¢/word
City magazine calendar	n/a	n/a	n/a	$250	$50	$140	$1/word	30¢/word	70¢/word
Comic book/strip writing	$200 original story, $500 existing story, $35 short script.								
Consultation on magazine editorial	$150	$30	$81	n/a	n/a	n/a	n/a	n/a	$100/page
Consumer magazine column	n/a	n/a	n/a	$2,500	$75	$898	$2.50/word	37¢/word	$1.13/word
Consumer front-of-book	n/a	n/a	n/a	$850	$350	$600	n/a	n/a	n/a
Content editing	$125	$25	$57	$6,500	$2,000	$3,819	15¢/word	6¢/word	11¢/word
Contributing editor	n/a	n/a	n/a	n/a	n/a	n/a	$156,000/ contract	$20,000/ contract	$51,000/ contract

	PER HOUR			PER PROJECT			OTHER		
	HIGH	LOW	AVG	HIGH	LOW	AVG	HIGH	LOW	AVG
Copyediting magazines	$100	$18	$50	n/a	n/a	n/a	$10/page	$2.90/page	$5.68/page
Fact checking	$125	$15	$46	n/a	n/a	n/a	n/a	n/a	n/a
Gag writing for cartoonists	$35/gag; 25% sale on spec.								
Ghostwriting articles (general)	$200	$30	$102	$3,500	$1,100	$2,229	$10/word	60¢/word	$2.25/word
Magazine research	$100	$15	$47	n/a	n/a	n/a	$500/item	$100/item	$200/item
Proofreading	$75	$15	$35	n/a	n/a	n/a	n/a	n/a	n/a
Reprint fees	n/a	n/a	n/a	$1,500	$20	$461	$1.50/word	10¢/word	73¢/word
Rewriting	$125	$20	$68	n/a	n/a	n/a	n/a	n/a	$50/page
Trade journal feature article	$122	$40	$80	$4,950	$150	$1,412	$3/word	20¢/word	$1.16/word
Transcribing interviews	$180	$90	$50	n/a	n/a	n/a	$3/min	$1/min	$2/min
MEDICAL/SCIENCE									
Medical/scientific conference coverage	$125	$50	$85	n/a	n/a	n/a	$800/day	$300/day	$600/day
Medical/scientific editing	$125	$21	$73	n/a	n/a	n/a	$12.50/page $600/day	$3/page $500/day	$4.40/page $550/day

	PER HOUR			PER PROJECT			OTHER		
	HIGH	LOW	AVG	HIGH	LOW	AVG	HIGH	LOW	AVG
Medical/scientific writing	$250	$30	$95	$5,000	$1,000	$3,354	$2/word	25¢/word	$1.12/word
Medical/scientific multimedia presentations	$100	$50	$75	n/a	n/a	n/a	$100/slide	$50/slide	$77/slide
Medical/scientific proofreading	$125	$18	$64	n/a	n/a	$500	$3/page	$2.50/page	$2.75/page
Pharmaceutical writing	$125	$90	$105	n/a	n/a	n/a	n/a	n/a	n/a
NEWSPAPERS									
Arts reviewing	$69	$30	$53	$200	$15	$101	60¢/word	6¢/word	36¢/word
Book reviews	$69	$45	$58	$350	$15	$140	60¢/word	25¢/word	44¢/word
Column, local	n/a	n/a	n/a	$600	$25	$206	$1/word	38¢/word	65¢/word
Column, self-syndicated	n/a	n/a	n/a	n/a	n/a	n/a	$35/insertion	$4/insertion	$16/insertion
Copyediting	$35	$15	$27	n/a	n/a	n/a	n/a	n/a	n/a
Editing/manuscript evaluation	$75	$25	$35	n/a	n/a	n/a	n/a	n/a	n/a
Feature writing	$79	$40	$63	$1,040	$85	$478	$1.60/word	10¢/word	59¢/word
Investigative reporting	n/a	n/a	n/a	n/a	n/a	n/a	$10,000/grant	$250/grant	$2,250/grant

	PER HOUR			PER PROJECT			OTHER		
	HIGH	LOW	AVG	HIGH	LOW	AVG	HIGH	LOW	AVG
Obituary copy	n/a	n/a	n/a	$225	$35	$124	n/a	n/a	n/a
Proofreading	$45	$15	$23	n/a	n/a	n/a	n/a	n/a	n/a
Stringing	n/a	n/a	n/a	$2,400	$40	$525	n/a	n/a	n/a
NONPROFIT									
Grant writing for nonprofits	$150	$19	$70	$3,000	$500	$1,852	n/a	n/a	n/a
Nonprofit annual reports	$100	$30	$64	n/a	n/a	n/a	n/a	n/a	n/a
Nonprofit writing	$150	$20	$77	$17,600	$200	$4,706	n/a	n/a	n/a
Nonprofit editing	$125	$25	$54	n/a	n/a	n/a	n/a	n/a	n/a
Nonprofit fundraising literature	$110	$35	$74	$3,500	$300	$1,597	$1,000/day	$500/day	$767/day
Nonprofit presentations	$100	$50	$73	n/a	n/a	n/a	n/a	n/a	n/a
Nonprofit public relations	$100	$20	$60	n/a	n/a	n/a	n/a	n/a	n/a
POLITICS/GOVERNMENT									
Government agency writing/editing	$100	$20	$57	n/a	n/a	n/a	$1.25/word	25¢/word	75¢/word

	PER HOUR			PER PROJECT			OTHER		
	HIGH	LOW	AVG	HIGH	LOW	AVG	HIGH	LOW	AVG
Government grant writing/editing	$150	$19	$68	n/a	n/a	n/a	n/a	n/a	n/a
Government-sponsored research	$100	$35	$66	n/a	n/a	n/a	n/a	n/a	$600/day
Public relations for political campaigns	$150	$40	$86	n/a	n/a	n/a	n/a	n/a	n/a
Speechwriting for government officials	$200	$30	$96	$4,500	$1,000	$2,750	$200/run min	$110/run min	$155/run min
Speechwriting for political campaigns	$150	$60	$101	n/a	n/a	n/a	$200/run min	$100/run min	$162/run min

RECORDKEEPING 101

Keep Records to Save on Your Taxes

by Joanne E. McFadden

Few people enjoy preparing their tax returns. For the self-employed, which many writers are, this means extra work, namely the Schedule C, Profit or Loss From Business. The extra work, though, results in tax savings, making it worth the time and effort.

I didn't get really serious about my record keeping until a few years ago when I decided to give myself the gift of thorough, stress-free tax preparation. I set up a system that made everything all ready to go at tax time, thus saving me valuable time that I could be writing or researching. I eliminated tax time procrastination and the anxiety of collecting, organizing and adding up my business expenses the night before meeting with my accountant.

In addition to eliminating the stress of filing my tax return, developing a system that made me already prepared at tax time with minimal effort also reduced the amount of taxes I paid because I maintained an extremely thorough accounting of the expenses I could deduct from the amount of my freelance income.

GET MOTIVATED

Being self-employed means that one pays the employer's share as well as the employee's of Social Security and Medicare, which is 7.65 percent twice, for a total of 15.3 percent. Like a regular employer, you get a deduction for the employer's half, points out Internal Revenue Service (IRS) spokesperson Eric Smith. Nevertheless, the better a person keeps track of legitimate, tax-deductible business expenses, the less self-employment *and* federal taxes he pays, legally. This seems to be reason enough to take the time to set up a system that allows you to do just that, without a last-minute scramble before April 15.

Yet, the most common mistake that people make is simply failing to keep adequate records or any records at all, according to Ronald R. Mueller, author of *Home Business Tax*

Savings, Made Easy! who has dedicated a whole career to helping and instructing people with home-based businesses about their taxes. "Paperwork is part of running a business," Mueller said. "People don't recognize the importance of it until they're audited," he said. If a person doesn't have adequate records to prove his expenses at an audit, he could end up having to pay up, with interest.

For me, tax time used to mean facing a hanging file folder full of crumpled up, disorganized receipts that I had to spend hours organizing and tallying. It also meant finding caches of receipts that I had failed to throw in the file folder long after I had filed my tax return, so I paid more taxes than I owed because of my sloppy record-keeping. (If the amount of excluded expenses is significant enough, one can file an amended return, but keeping good records in the first place is far more efficient.)

If this sounds familiar, read on to find out how to keep complete, organized records that will be ready to go at tax time, thus maximizing your income and time, all in alignment with Internal Revenue Service (IRS) regulations.

DO YOUR HOMEWORK

Make some time in your schedule for becoming really familiar with the expenses that you can deduct on your tax return. Employ the same sound research skills that you use for writing an article to finding out about the expenses and what records you are required to keep to document them. In addition to the IRS website, the internet abounds with information for small business owners, and there are also entire books and websites dedicated to just this topic. Familiarize yourself with the eligible expenses; you might even find that there are some you have overlooked.

For the official word and to double-check your research, a good reference is IRS Publication 583, Starting A Business and Keeping Records. It provides an overview and refers the reader to other publications with more detail, said Smith. In addition, it includes some sample record-keeping systems.

SET UP YOUR STRUCTURE

The first critical step in easy record keeping is setting up a system for filing the records of your business expenses. Don't be put off; it's easier and less time consuming than you might think.

Any organizer will tell you it's important to set up a style that fits your personality, which is key to following through with the actual filing of receipts and other supporting documentation of business expenses. This may be hanging file folders, an accordion style file, a day planner, a 3-ring binder, or for the techie-type, a software program on the computer or even an app on a smart phone. (Smith points out that the IRS website has a list of vendors who sell tax preparation software.) If you choose either of the electronic options, be sure to back up files regularly, and know that you also must retain receipts and other documentation that prove those expenses you recorded electronically. It's critical to be honest with yourself and choose the system that you are most likely to use.

USE THE SCHEDULE C FORM

Once you've chosen how to set up your files, decide on the categories for each file. If you're using an electronic system, the program will already have these set up for you. If you're using paper, the Schedule C form, available at www.irs.gov can help with this. Part II of the form lists the different categories of business expenses as they have to be recorded on the tax return. Since each person's expenses are different, make a study of the form to determine which files will be useful to you. For example, if you make business use of your home and take a deduction for that (Line 18), you'll want a file for records related to this expense. If your home office doubles as a guest room making you ineligible to take that deduction, you don't need a tab for that category. If you paid an independent contractor for business-related services, you will want a file for "Contract labor" (Line 11). If you didn't, you don't need this file. (Note that there is a separate line for "Legal and professional services," i.e., attorneys and accountants.)

If it sounds complicated to know what expense goes where, consult the "Instructions for Schedule C" booklet available online that provides details about these expenses as well as other publications to consult for further clarification.

Here are some of the categories that most all writers will have.

- **Vehicle expenses (Line 9).** There is a standard deduction for mileage (the amount changes every year and sometimes even in the middle of the year, so check the IRS website for the most up-to-date figure). This means that you need to document the business-related miles that you drive, and not just the date and mileage, but where you traveled and for what purpose. The simplest way to do this is to keep a mileage log right in your car to write down the date, place you traveled, the business purpose, and number of miles, the four requirements to satisfy an allowable business expense. Mueller, who has a free downloadable Vehicle Use Log on his website, said that mileage is an expense that people often forget to record. He suggests putting the mileage log right on the driver's seat so that you have to move it when you sit down, or to put it on the dashboard where you'll see it. If you do not want to use the standard deduction for mileage, there are additional records that you need to keep about your gas purchases and vehicle maintenance expenses.
- **Depreciation (Line 13).** This can look confusing, but it simply refers to equipment that you put into service in a given year whose life will extend beyond that year. (For writers, this most likely includes their computers and printers.) Reading the

Schedule C Instruction booklet can give you a better idea of what is included in this category and the receipts and records that you need to keep on file for this expense. Since the IRS requires paper (or scanned) receipts for expenses in excess of $75, it is important to keep these. If the receipt is printed on electrostatic paper, make a copy or scan it, Mueller said, because the print will fade over time.

- **Supplies (Line 22).** This is what it sounds like–paper clips, toner cartridges, paper, USB drives, file folders, etc.

- **Travel, meals and entertainment (Line 24).** The IRS asks that the travel costs (like airfare to a writer's conference and hotel expenses) be separated from meals and entertainment (for example, the bill for when you took a source to lunch for an interview, or the meals you incurred while attending the writers' conference). The IRS has very specific rules about which expenses are deductible and which are not, which it spells out in the Schedule C Instruction booklet. Mueller said that in order to claim entertainment expenses, there are five pieces of information that must be recorded: where, when, how much, the name of the person you entertained and the business objective.

> **INFO BOX**
>
> Some recordkeeping resources:
>
> At www.irs.gov:
>
> Publication 583, Starting A Business and Keeping Records
>
> Publication 463, Travel, Entertainment, Gift and Car Expenses
>
> Instructions for Schedule C
>
> For the latest changes to the Schedule C, visit www.irs.gov/schedulec

- **Utilities (Line 25).** This can include your telephone if you have a separate line.

- **Other.** This is for expenses that don't fit into other categories, such as postage, photocopying fees, books and your *Writer's Digest* subscription.

- **Income.** This is where you can keep check stubs, invoices, and other records of payments you receive. When you're paid $600 or more in a year, you should receive a 1099-MISC, but for amounts under that, you might not receive this documentation at the end of the year.

THE SECRET: DO IT NOW, NEVER LATER

Once you've taken the time to set up your filing system, whether it be folders, a notebook, or whatever works best for you, you need to get into the habit of filing receipts there. "Records are your friends," said Smith. "The best records are those that you keep at the time that you're doing whatever it is. A lot of people know to keep a log book to write things down when they pay the expense. It helps them to really keep track of the expenses that they're legitimately entitled to," he said.

Your filing system won't serve you if you don't utilize it. The trick is to do it right away, whether it be recording that trip downtown to do an interview or printing a receipt for something ordered online and tucking it into the right file. If you wait to record a trip, for example, with our lives as busy as they are, you're likely to forget by the end of the week. If you receive an e-mail receipt, if you don't print it out and file it right away, you might forget about it come tax time and lose that deduction. I keep my notebook right on the bookshelf in the kitchen so that it's easily accessible for me to use.

Setting up a time daily to record business expenses and file any receipts you gather while you're out is a good idea. Go through your pocketbook or wallet and pull out any receipts you've acquired and file them. The longer you wait, the bigger the chance that those receipts will be lost or misplaced. Train yourself to get in the habit of recording and filing frequently. When tax time comes, all the receipts you need will be neatly filed away.

A trick that Mueller uses is to write in his day planner in pencil. At the end of each day, he goes through and erases what he didn't get done and writes in what he did do. Then he takes a moment to ask himself if he spent money on anything that might be deductible, and he writes those items in. If items are over $75, he files the receipts for those. "It's a discipline," Mueller said, noting that it only takes three to four minutes a day—the time you would take to brush your teeth—to keep good records.

Maintaining thorough records of your writing expenses can help you to keep more of the income you earn.

SCHEDULE C EXPENSE DOCUMENTATION:

Why (business purpose):

What (description, including itemized accounting of cost):

When (date):

Where (location):

Who (names of those for whom the expense was incurred; e.g., meals and entertainment):

JOANNE E. MCFADDEN has been a freelance writer for 21 years, although she admits it took her almost two decades to get so serious and organized about her bookkeeping. She's worked for three daily newspapers and has published articles in many more publications.

MAKING THE MOST OF THE MONEY YOU EARN

by Sage Cohen

Writers who manage money well can establish a prosperous writing life that meets their short-term needs and long-term goals. This article will introduce the key financial systems, strategies, attitudes and practices that will help you cultivate a writing life that makes the most of your resources and sustains you over time.

DIVIDING BUSINESS AND PERSONAL EXPENSES

If you are reporting your writing business to the IRS, it is important that you keep the money that flows from this source entirely separate from your personal finances. Here's what you'll need to accomplish this:

- **BUSINESS CHECKING ACCOUNT:** Only two types of money go into this account: money you have been paid for your writing and/or "capital investments" you make by depositing your own money to invest in the business. And only two types of payments are made from this account: business-related expenses (such as: subscriptions, marketing and advertisement, professional development, fax or phone service, postage, computer software and supplies), and "capital draws" which you make to pay yourself.
- **BUSINESS SAVINGS ACCOUNT OR MONEY MARKET ACCOUNT:** This account is the holding pen where your quarterly tax payments will accumulate and earn interest. Money put aside for your retirement account(s) can also be held here.
- **BUSINESS CREDIT CARD:** It's a good idea to have a credit card for your business as a means of emergency preparedness. Pay off the card responsibly every month and this will help you establish a good business credit record, which can be useful down the line should you need a loan for any reason.

When establishing your business banking and credit, shop around for the best deals, such as highest interest rates, lowest (or no) monthly service fees, and free checking. Mint.com is a good source for researching your options.

EXPENSE TRACKING AND RECONCILING

Once your bank accounts are set up, it's time to start tracking and categorizing what you earn and spend. This will ensure that you can accurately report your income and itemize your deductions when tax time rolls around every quarter. Whether you intend to prepare your taxes yourself or have an accountant help you, immaculate financial records will be the key to speed and success in filing your taxes.

For the most effective and consistent expense tracking, I highly recommend that you use a computer program such as QuickBooks. While it may seem simpler to do accounting by hand, I assure you that it isn't. Even a luddite such as I, who can't comprehend the most basic principles of accounting, can use QuickBooks with great aplomb to plug in the proper categories for income and expenses, easily reconcile bank statements, and with a few clicks prepare all of the requisite reports that make it easy to prepare taxes.

PAYING BILLS ONLINE

While it's certainly not imperative, you might want to check out your bank's online bill pay option if you're not using this already. Once you've set up the payee list, you can make payments in a few seconds every month or set up auto payments for expenses that are recurring. Having a digital history of bills paid can also come in handy with your accounting.

MANAGING TAXES

Self-employed people need to pay quarterly taxes. A quick, online search will reveal a variety of tax calculators and other online tools that can help you estimate what your payments should be. Programs such as TurboTax are popular and useful tools for automating and guiding you step-by-step through tax preparation. An accountant can also be helpful in understanding your unique tax picture, identifying and saving the right amount for taxes each quarter, and even determining SEP IRA contribution amounts (described later in this article). The more complex your finances (or antediluvian your accounting skills), the more likely that you'll benefit from this kind of personalized expertise.

Once you have forecasted your taxes either with the help of a specialized, tax-planning program or an accountant, you can establish a plan toward saving the right amount for quarterly payments. For example, once I figured out what my tax bracket was and the approximate percentage of income that needed to be set aside as taxes, I would immediately transfer a percentage of every deposit to my savings account, where it would sit and grow a little interest until quarterly tax time came around. When I could afford to do so, I would also set aside the appropriate percentage of SEP IRA contribution from each deposit so that I'd be ready at end-of-year to deposit as much as I possibly could for retirement.

THE PRINCIPLE TO COMMIT TO IS THIS: Get that tax-earmarked cash out of your hot little hands (i.e., checking account) as soon as you can, and create whatever deterrents you need to leave the money in savings so you'll have it when you need it.

INTELLIGENT INVESTING FOR YOUR CAREER

Your writing business will require not only the investment of your time but also the investment of money. When deciding what to spend and how, consider your values and your budget in these three, key areas:

EDUCATION	MARKETING AND PROMOTION	KEEPING THE WHEELS TURNING
Subscriptions to publications in your field	URL registration and hosting for blogs and websites	Technology and application purchase, servicing and back-up
Memberships to organizations in your field	Contact database subscription (such as Constant Contact) for communicating with your audiences	Office supplies and furniture
Books: on topics you want to learn, or in genres you are cultivating	Business cards and stationery	Insurances for you and/or your business
Conferences and seminars	Print promotions (such as direct mail), giveaways and schwag	Travel, gas, parking
Classes and workshops	Online or print ad placement costs	Phone, fax and e-mail

This is not an absolute formula for spending, by any means—just a snapshot of the types of expenses you may be considering and negotiating over time. My general rule would be: start small and modest with the one or two most urgent and/or inexpensive items in each list, and grow slowly over time as your income grows.

The good news is that these legitimate business expenses may all be deducted from your income—making your net income and tax burden less. Please keep in mind that the IRS allows losses as long as you make a profit for at least three of the first five years you are in business. Otherwise, the IRS will consider your writing a non-deductible hobby.

PREPARATION AND PROTECTION FOR THE FUTURE

As a self-employed writer, in many ways your future is in your hands. Following are some of the health and financial investments that I'd recommend you consider as you build and nurture The Enterprise of You. Please understand that these are a layperson's suggestions. I am by no means an accountant, tax advisor or financial planning guru. I am simply a person who has educated herself on these topics for the sake of her own writing business, made the choices I am recommending and benefited from them. I'd like you to benefit from them, too.

SEP IRAS

Individual Retirement Accounts (IRAs) are investment accounts designed to help individuals save for retirement. But I do recommend that you educate yourself about the Simplified Employee Pension Individual Retirement Account (SEP IRA) and consider opening one if you don't have one already.

A SEP IRA is a special type of IRA that is particularly beneficial to self-employed people. Whereas a Roth IRA has a contribution cap of $5,000 or $6,000, depending on your age, the contribution limit for self-employed people in 2011 is approximately 20% of adjusted earned income, with a maximum contribution of $49,000. Contributions for a SEP IRA are generally 100% tax deductible and investments grow tax deferred. Let's say your adjusted earned income this year is $50,000. This means you'd be able to contribute $10,000 to your retirement account. I encourage you to do some research online or ask your accountant if a SEP IRA makes sense for you.

CREATING A 9-MONTH SAVINGS BUFFER

When you're living month-to-month, you are extremely vulnerable to fluctuation in the economy, client budget changes, life emergencies and every other wrench that could turn a good working groove into a frightening financial rut. The best way to prepare for the unexpected is to start (or continue) developing a savings buffer. The experts these days are suggesting that we accumulate nine months of living expenses to help us navigate transition in a way that we feel empowered rather than scared and desperate to take the next thing that comes along.

When I paid off one of my credit cards in full, I added that monthly payment to the monthly savings transfer.

I started creating my savings buffer by opening the highest-interest money market account I could find and setting up a modest, monthly automatic transfer from my checking account. Then, when I paid off my car after five years of monthly payments, I added my car payment amount to the monthly transfer. (I'd been paying that amount for five years, so I was pretty sure I could continue to pay it to myself.) When I paid off one of my credit cards in full, I added that monthly payment to the monthly savings transfer. Within a year, I had a hefty sum going to savings every month before I had time to think about it, all based on expenses I was accustomed to paying, with money that had never been anticipated in the monthly cash flow.

What can you do today—and tomorrow—to put your money to work for your life, and start being as creative with your savings as you are with language?

DISABILITY INSURANCE

If writing is your livelihood, what happens if you become unable to write? I have writing friends who have become incapacitated and unable to work due to injuries to their brains, backs, hands and eyes. Disability insurance is one way to protect against such emergencies and ensure that you have an income in the unlikely event that you're not physically able to earn one yourself.

Depending on your health, age and budget, monthly disability insurance payments may or may not be within your means or priorities. But you won't know until you learn more about your coverage options. I encourage you to investigate this possibility with several highly rated insurance companies to get the lay of the land for your unique, personal profile and then make an informed decision.

HEALTH INSURANCE

Self-employed writers face tough decisions about health insurance. If you are lucky, there is someone in your family with great health coverage that is also available to you. Without the benefit of group health insurance, chances are that self-insuring costs are high and coverage is low. Just as in disability insurance, age and health status are significant variables in costs and availability of coverage. (Once again, I am no expert on this topic; only a novice who has had to figure things out for myself along the way, sharing the little I know with you.)

Ideally, of course, you'll have reasonably-priced health insurance that helps make preventive care and health maintenance more accessible and protects you in case of a major medical emergency. The following are a few possibilities to check out that could reduce costs and improve access to health coverage:

- Join a group that aggregates its members for group coverage, such as a Chamber of Commerce or AARP. Ask an insurance agent in your area if there are any other group coverage options available to you.

- Consider a high-deductible health plan paired with a Health Savings Account (HSA). Because the deductible is so high, these plans are generally thought to be most useful for a major medical emergency. But an HSA paired with such a plan allows you to put aside a chunk of pre-tax change every year that can be spent on medical expenses or remain in the account where it can be invested and grow. 2011 HSA investment limits, for example, are: $3,050 for individual coverage and $6,150 for family coverage.

Establishing effective financial systems for your writing business will take some time and energy at the front end. I suggest that you pace yourself by taking an achievable step or two each week until you have a baseline of financial management that works for you. Then, you can start moving toward some of your bigger, longer-term goals. Once it's established, your solid financial foundation will pay you in dividends of greater efficiency, insight and peace of mind for the rest of your writing career.

SAGE COHEN is the author of *The Productive Writer* and *Writing the Life Poetic,* both from Writer's Digest Books. She's been nominated for a Pushcart Prize, won first prize in the Ghost Road Press Poetry contest and published dozens of poems, essays and articles on the writing life. Sage holds an MFA in creative writing from New York University and a BA from Brown University. Since 1997, she has been a freelance writer serving clients including Intuit, Blue Shield, Adobe, and Kaiser Permanente..

PHOTO © Nyla Alisia

SHOULD YOUR WRITING BUSINESS BE AN LLC?

Business Structures Explained

by Carol Topp, CPA

A new member to my writers group told us her writing business was structured as a corporation. As a certified public accountant, I found that a little odd. I didn't know Connie well, but she had told us she had just written her first book, a self-published memoir. *Why would a brand new author want corporate status for her business?* I wondered. It seemed overly complex to me, so I asked her why she had formed a corporation. "I don't know," she said, "it's what my lawyer and CPA set up." Now I was really concerned. She'd had two professionals set her up in a complex business structure when she hadn't yet sold one copy of her book!

What was going on?

SOLE PROPRIETORSHIP

Most authors prefer the simplest business structure possible—what the IRS calls a sole proprietorship, meaning a business with one owner.

Sole proprietors may go by many names including:

- freelancer
- independent contractor
- self-employed writer
- independent publisher
- self-published or traditionally published author

During a consultation with a new author, I explained the advantages of sole proprietorship. She asked me, "Why would I want to be a sole proprietor? Why not just be a freelancer?" I explained that "sole proprietor" is a tax-related term to describe her profession as a freelance writer.

Sole proprietorships are easy and quick to start. You are in business as soon as you say that you are! Or at least when you are paid for your writing. I became a professional writer when I received $50 for writing a magazine article. A business had been born. Sole proprietorships have minimal government filings and licenses, if any. Usually a writer can use his or her own name as the business name, so business name filing is needed. Best of all, sole proprietorships have the simplest tax structure. Sole proprietors use a two-page form (Schedule C Business Income or Loss) and attach it to their Form 1040 tax return.

I would have thought that Connie's writing business would be structured as a sole proprietorship. Why then was she saying that her writing business was a corporation? I asked her a few more questions.

LIMITED LIABILITY STATUS

"Oh, they set up an LLC," she explained. Now I understood. Connie was talking about limited liability company (LLC) status. She had mistakenly thought that the "C" in LLC meant "corporation," but it means "company." They are quite different. LLC status is a legal standing granted by your state (not the IRS), and it offers limited liability to protect your personal assets from any business liabilities.

It's easy to get confused as Connie did; some advertising adds to the confusion. I've seen one ad that says "Get incorporated today" while showing a smiling woman holding a business card with "Your Business, LLC" circled in red. The ad confused incorporation with LLC status. Incorporating involves forming your business as a corporation for tax purposes; LLC status is a legal standing that limits liability.

LLCs are not one of the three business structures that the IRS recognizes for tax purposes. As a matter of fact, the IRS calls LLCs "disregarded entities." (We all wish the IRS would disregard us a little more!) Certainly, the IRS knows that LLCs exist, but for tax purposes, the LLC status is disregarded, and the business owner must choose one of three structures: sole proprietorship, partnership or corporation.

What LLC status will do for you

So why had Connie's lawyer and CPA set up her sole proprietorship with LLC status? Probably because they wanted to protect her personal assets from any business debts.

LLC status offers limited liability protection. When you read "liability," think "lawsuit" or, more specifically, the money you might owe if sued. LLC status cannot stop a lawsuit, but your liabilities may be limited to your business assets. As a writer, your business assets might include your laptop computer and the cash in your business checking account. The advantage of protecting your personal assets is the main reason why authors and other small business owners obtain LLC status for their businesses.

An example of how LLC status can help involved a ghostwriter who was sued for breach of contract. He was a sole proprietor with LLC status for his business. If he had lost, the lawsuit damages would have been limited to his business assets and could not have touched his personal assets, such as his house or savings. Fortunately, he won his case.

What LLC status won't do for you

Limited Liability Company status will not reduce your taxes. Your business files the same tax forms it did before having LLC status. "If an expense is business related, it's tax deductible, no matter what business structure you use," says tax attorney Julian Block, author of *Easy Tax Guide for Writers, Photographers and Other Freelancers*.

My tax client Russ showed me a handout from a seminar that claimed one of the benefits of LLC status was a health insurance tax deduction, leading Russ to believe he needed LLC status to receive this tax break. This health insurance deduction is available to all sole proprietorships, whether they have LLC status or not. The seminar handout had inadvertently confused him.

LLC STATUS IS NOT BULLETPROOF

For years the bulletproof vest of limited liability was only available to corporations. In the 1980s, LLC status became popular and sole proprietors signed up in droves. Finally, they could receive limited liability protection without the complexities of corporate status. It all seemed too good to be true, and perhaps it was.

Lately, limited liability status has been challenged in court, and several business owners found that their personal assets were at risk. The bulletproof vest has some cracks. "If an author were driving a car while on business and injured someone, he or she could still be sued," explains attorney Julian Block. "It's not a magic bullet."

To avoid piercing your limited liability, you must keep your business separate from your personal life. Mixing assets may lead a court to determine that your LLC status is weak and therefore hold you personally liable. "It isn't enough for business people merely to carry a liability shield; they must also take reasonable measures to this shield," cautions New Hampshire attorney John Cunningham.

There are several ways to protect your shield of limited liability:

- Don't commit fraud. Even LLC status can't protect you if you're a crook!
- Set up a separate checking account for your business.
- Avoid treating business assets as your own.
- Avoid personal guarantees on business loans.
- Purchase professional liability insurance.
- Sign contracts in the name of your LLC.
- Consider placing your home or investments into a trust to further protect your assets.

Disadvantages to LLC status

To obtain LLC status from your state, you file paperwork with an accompanying fee. Often, the paperwork is fairly straightforward, especially for single-member LLCs. Some individuals file for LLC status without assistance, but I recommend you seek professional advice to understand the pros and cons of LLC status for your business. If your LLC has multiple members or is a complex arrangement, you should hire a business attorney to assist you in establishing your LLC.

When should you consider LLC status for your writing business?

Consider LLC status when you wish to protect your personal assets. In Connie's case, her lawyer and CPA were possibly being overly cautious because she had no business income or assets yet.

I operated my accounting business as a sole proprietorship for its first six years. After that, I was attracting more clients and generating more income. I already had professional liability insurance, but I decided it was time to add limited liability status to my sole proprietorship. I applied to be a single member LLC in my state by filing the paperwork and paying a $125 fee. My business name is now Carol Topp, CPA, LLC (are you impressed?) but I still file the same tax forms I did before obtaining LLC status. I hope my limited liability status is never challenged in court, but I have it (and insurance) just in case I am ever sued.

PARTNERSHIPS ARE LIKE MARRIAGE

A second business structure is a partnership with two or more other people. Occasionally, a writer may co-author a book, but these are usually collaborations, not formal business partnerships

I usually discourage co-authors from forming a business partnership, warning them that a partnership is like being married but not being in love. You may be responsible for debts the other person can take on. Partnerships have complex tax situations necessitating professional expertise, and they may require a lawyer to draft the partnership agreement.

"Forming a business partnership really isn't necessary, and that is especially true when it is a one-shot deal," explains Dr. Dennis Hensley, coauthor of more than six titles. Quite frequently a publisher will hire the coauthors and make all the business arrangements. "When I was teamed with Stanley Field to write *The Freelancer: A Writer's Guide to Success*, we signed an agreement defining our writing responsibilities, how we would share earnings, who would serve as lead writer for the project, and how we would communicate during the writing of the manuscript. The publisher was putting us together because we had separate areas of expertise that were needed for the book the publisher wanted to release."

Alternatively, you may come up with a book idea of your own. Dauna and Marcie, long-time friends, decided to write a book together, but they did not form a business partnership. Both women maintained separate sole proprietorships, agreeing on how to split expenses and share the royalties. This kept each of their businesses separate and made the book project easier to operate.

"Before jumping into a business partnership with your life partner, friend, family member or an entrepreneur you know, sit down and talk over expectations with each other,'" advises James Chartrand of Men With Pens. "Create an agreement for sharing work and profits. Decide who does what and when, and how to split up the money—or else you'll be splitting up, period."

WRITER, INC.

The third and most complex business structure is a corporation. There are two types of corporations, S corporations and C corporations. An S corporation has a limited number of shareholders and may have only one shareholder, the owner, while C corporations can have an unlimited number of shareholders and are typically run by a board of directors. If a writer forms a corporation, it is typically an S corporation.

S corporation status may be a desirable business structure for authors who form a publishing company. Felice Gerwitz self-published her books as a sole proprietor for many years. She started publishing other authors and found that forming an S corporation could save on taxes, particularly self-employment tax. "Self-employment taxes as a sole proprietor were killing me," says Gerwitz. "Fortunately, my CPA advised me to form an S corporation, and I saw my self-employment tax drop."

As an S corporation, Gerwitz takes some of her profit as wages and some as ordinary income, which is not subject to self-employment tax. An S corporation has more complex tax preparation than a sole proprietorship, so you should seek professional accounting advice for your record keeping and tax preparation.

CONCLUSION

A writer has three business structures from which to choose: sole proprietorship, partnership or corporate status (S or C). In addition, a writer may obtain limited liability company status to limit his or her liability. Each business structure has advantages and increasing complexity. For most writers, the sole proprietorship with LLC status will serve their needs well.

BUSINESS STRUCTURES

Word pictures can explain the different business structures an author might choose.

Picture a sole proprietorship as a single-family house. Single-family homes are very common, as is the sole proprietorship form of business (78 percent of all small businesses are sole proprietorships).

A partnership is like a duplex with two families living in one house. Living that close together can bring benefits but can also create friction, just like a business partnership.

A corporation is like an apartment building with many tenants in one building. In the same way, a corporation can have many owners called shareholders. Apartment buildings are expensive to start and can be difficult to maintain, just like a corporation.

A limited liability company (LLC) is not any of these. It is a legal status granted by your state, not a business structure in the eyes of the IRS. It is similar to a fence surrounding a building, providing protection. Picture the single family home with a fence protecting it. That would be a sole proprietorship with LLC status. A partnership or corporation can also have LLC protection, just as duplexes and apartment buildings may also have fences.

CAROL TOPP, CPA is a Certified Public Accountant and author of *Business Tips and Taxes for Writers* (Media Angels). She has authored 10 books, both as an indie publisher and author for a small press. Learn more at CarolToppCPA.com and TaxesForWriters.com.

30-DAY PLATFORM CHALLENGE

Build Your Writer Platform in a Month

....

by Robert Lee Brewer

Whether writers are looking to find success through traditional publication or the self-publishing route, they'll find a strong writer platform will help them in their efforts. A platform is not marketing; it's the actual and quantifiable reach writers have to their target audience.

Here is a 30-day platform challenge I've developed to help writers get started in their own platform-building activities without getting overwhelmed. By accomplishing one task for one day, writers can feel a sense of accomplishment and still handle their normal daily activities. By the end of the month, writers should have a handle on what they need to do to keep growing their platform into the future.

DAY 1: DEFINE YOURSELF

For Day 1, define yourself. Don't worry about where you'd like to be in the future. Instead, take a look at who you are today, what you've already accomplished, what you're currently doing, etc.

EXAMPLE DEFINE YOURSELF WORKSHEET

Here is a chart I'm using (with my own answers). Your worksheet can ask even more questions. The more specific you can be the better for this exercise.

Name (as used in byline): Robert Lee Brewer

Position(s): Senior Content Editor - Writer's Digest Writing Community; Author; Freelance Writer; Blogger; Event Speaker; Den Leader - Cub Scouts; Curator of Insta-poetry Series

Skill(s): Editing, creative writing (poetry and fiction), technical writing, copywriting, database management, SEO, blogging, newsletter writing, problem solving, idea generation, public speaking, willingness to try new things, community building.

Social media platforms: Facebook, LinkedIn, Google+, Twitter, Tumblr, Blogger.

URLs: www.writersmarket.com; www.writersdigest.com/editor-blogs/poetic-asides; http://robertleebrewer.blogspot.com/; www.robertleebrewer.com

Accomplishments: Named 2010 Poet Laureate of Blogosphere; spoken at several events, including Writer's Digest Conference, AWP, Austin International Poetry Festival, Houston Poetry Fest, and more; author of Solving the World's Problems (Press 53); published and sold out of two limited edition poetry chapbooks, **ENTER** and **ESCAPE**; edited several editions of **Writer's Market** and **Poet's Market**; former GMVC conference champion in the 800-meter run and MVP of WCHS cross country and track teams; undergraduate award-winner in several writing disciplines at University of Cincinnati, including Journalism, Fiction, and Technical Writing; BA in English Literature from University of Cincinnati with certificates in writing for Creative Writing-Fiction and Professional and Technical Writing.

Interests: Writing (all genres), family (being a good husband and father), faith, fitness (especially running and disc golf), fantasy football, reading.

In one sentence, who am I? Robert Lee Brewer is a married Methodist father of five children (four sons and one daughter) who works as an editor but plays as a writer, specializing in poetry and blogging.

As long as you're being specific and honest, there are no wrong answers when it comes to defining yourself. However, you may realize that you have more to offer than you think. Or you may see an opportunity that you didn't realize even existed.

DAY 2: SET YOUR GOALS

For today's platform-building task, set your goals. Include short-term goals and long-term goals. In fact, make a list of goals you can accomplish by the end of this year; then, make a list of goals you'd like to accomplish before you die.

EXAMPLE GOALS

Here are some of examples from my short-term and long-term goal lists:

SHORT-TERM GOALS:

- Promote new book, Solving the World's Problems.
- In April, complete April PAD Challenge on Poetic Asides blog.

- Get 2015 Writer's Market to printer ahead of schedule.
- Get 2015 Poet's Market to printer ahead of schedule.
- Lead workshop at Poetry Hickory event in April.
- Etc.

LONG-TERM GOALS:

- Publish book on platform development for small businesses.
- Raise 5 happy and healthy children into 5 happy, healthy, caring, and self-sufficient adults.
- Continue to learn how to be a better husband and human being.
- Become a bestselling novelist.
- Win Poet Laureate of the Universe honors.
- Etc.

Some writers may ask what defining yourself and creating goals has to do with platform development. I maintain that these are two of the most basic and important steps in the platform-building process, because they define who you are and where you want to be.

A successful platform strategy should communicate who you are and help you get where you'd like to be (or provide you with a completely new opportunity). If you can't communicate who you are to strangers, then they won't realize how you might be able to help them or why you're important to them. If you don't have any goals, then you don't have any direction or purpose for your platform.

A successful platform strategy should communicate who you are and help you get where you'd like to be (or provide you with a completely new opportunity).

By defining who you are and what you want to accomplish, you're taking a huge step in establishing a successful writing and publishing career.

DAY 3: JOIN FACEBOOK

For today's task, create a profile on Facebook. Simple as that. If you don't have one, it's as easy as going to www.facebook.com and signing up. It takes maybe 5 or 10 minutes. If that.

10 FACEBOOK TIPS FOR WRITERS

Many readers probably already have a Facebook profile, and that's fine. If you have already created a profile (or are doing so today), here are some tips for handling your profile:

- Complete your profile. The most checked page on most profiles is the About page. The more you share the better.
- Make everything public. Like it or not, writers are public figures. If you try to hide, it will limit the potential platform.
- Think about your audience in everything you do. When your social media profiles are public, anyone can view what you post. Keep this in mind at all times.
- Include a profile pic of yourself. Avoid setting your avatar as anything but a headshot of yourself. Many people don't like befriending a family pet or cartoon image.
- Update your status regularly. If you can update your status once per day, that's perfect. At the very least, update your status weekly. If your profile is a ghost town, people will treat it like one.
- Communicate with friends on Facebook. Facebook is a social networking site, but networking happens when you communicate. So communicate.
- Be selective about friends. Find people who share your interests. Accept friends who share your interests. Other folks may be fake or inappropriate connections trying to build their "friend" totals.
- Be selective about adding apps. If you're not sure, it's probably best to avoid. Many users have wasted days, weeks, and even months playing silly games on Facebook.
- Join relevant groups. The emphasis should be placed on relevancy. For instance, I'm a poet, so I join poetry groups.
- Follow relevant fan pages. As with groups, the emphasis is placed on relevancy. In my case, I'm a fan of several poetry publications.

In addition to the tips above, be sure to always use your name as it appears in your byline. If you're not consistent in how you list your name in your byline, it's time to pick a name and stick with it. For instance, my byline name is Robert Lee Brewer—not Robbie Brewer, Bob Brewer, or even just Robert Brewer.

There are times when I absolutely can't throw the "Lee" in there, but the rest of the time it is Robert Lee Brewer. And the reasoning behind this is that it makes it easier for people who know me elsewhere to find and follow me on Facebook (or whichever social media site). Name recognition is super important when you're building your writer platform.

DAY 4: JOIN TWITTER

For today's task, create a Twitter account. That's right. Go to www.twitter.com and sign up—if you're not already. This task will definitely take less than 5 minutes.

As with Facebook, I would not be surprised to learn that most readers already have a Twitter account. Here are three important things to keep in mind:

- **Make your profile bio relevant.** You might want to use a version of the sentence you wrote for Day 1's task. Look at my profile (twitter.com/robertleebrewer) if you need an example.
- **Use an image of yourself.** One thing about social media (and online networking) is that people love to connect with other people. So use an image of yourself—not of your pet, a cute comic strip, a new age image, flowers, robots, etc.
- **Make your Twitter handle your byline—if possible.** For instance, I am known as @RobertLeeBrewer on Twitter, because I use Robert Lee Brewer as my byline on articles, in interviews, at speaking events, on books, etc. Be as consistent with your byline as humanly possible.

Once you're in Twitter, try finding some worthwhile tweeps to follow. Also, be sure to make a tweet or two. As with Facebook, people will only interact with your profile if it looks like you're actually there and using your account.

SOME BASIC TWITTER TERMINOLOGY

Twitter has a language all its own. Here are some of the basics:

- **Tweet.** This is what folks call the 140-character messages that can be sent on the site. Anyone who follows you can access your tweets.
- **RT.** RT stands for re-tweet. This is what happens when someone shares your tweet, usually character for character. It's usually good form to show attribution for the author of the original tweet.
- **DM.** DM stands for direct message. This is a good way to communicate with someone on Twitter privately. I've actually had a few opportunities come my way through DMs on Twitter.
- **#.** The #-sign stands for hashtag. Hashtags are used to organize group conversations. For instance, Writer's Digest uses the #wdc to coordinate messages for their Writer's Digest Conferences. Anyone can start a hashtag, and they're sometimes used to add humor or emphasis to a tweet.
- **FF.** FF stands for follow Friday—a day typically set asides to highlight follow-worthy tweeps (or folks who use Twitter). There's also a WW that stands for writer Wednesday.

DAY 5: START A BLOG

For today's task, create a blog. You can use Blogger (www.blogger.com), WordPress (www.wordpress.com), or Tumblr (www.tumblr.com). In fact, you can use another blogging platform if you wish. To complete today's challenge, do the following:

- **Create a blog.** That is, sign up (if you don't already have a blog), pick a design (these can usually be altered later if needed), and complete your profile.
- **Write a post for today.** If you're not sure what to cover, you can just introduce yourself and share a brief explanation of how your blog got started. Don't make it too complicated.

If you already have a blog, excellent! You don't need to create a new one, but you might want to check out some ways to optimize what you have.

OPTIMIZE YOUR BLOG

Here are some tips for making your blog rock:

- Use images in your posts. Images are eye candy for readers, help with search engine optimization, and can even improve clicks when shared on social media sites, such as Facebook and Google+.
- Use headers in posts. Creating and bolding little headlines in your posts will go a long way toward making your posts easier to read and scan. Plus, they'll just look more professional.
- Write short. Short sentences (fewer than 10 words). Short paragraphs (fewer than five sentences). Concision is precision in online composition.
- Allow comments. Most bloggers receive very few (or absolutely zero) comments in the beginning, but it pays to allow comments, because this gives your audience a way to interact with you. For my personal blog, I allow anyone to comment on new posts, but those that are more than a week old require my approval.

DAY 6: READ AND COMMENT ON A POST

For today's task, read at least one blog post and comment on it (linking back to your blog). And the comment should not be something along the lines of, "Hey, cool post. Come check out my blog." Instead, you need to find a blog post that really speaks to you and then make a thoughtful comment.

Here are a few possible ways to respond:

- **Share your own experience.** If you've experienced something similar to what's covered in the post, share your own story. You don't have to write a book or anything, but maybe a paragraph or two.
- **Add another perspective.** Maybe the post was great, but there's another angle that should be considered. Don't be afraid to point that angle out.
- **Ask a question.** A great post usually will prompt new thoughts and ideas—and questions. Ask them.

As far as linking back to your blog, you could include your blog's URL in the comment, but also, most blogs have a field in their comments that allow you to share your URL. Usually, your name will link to that URL, which should either be your blog or your author website (if it offers regularly updated content).

It might seem like a lot of work to check out other blogs and comment on them, but this is an incredible way to make real connections with super users. These connections can lead to guest post and interview opportunities. In fact, they could even lead to speaking opportunities too.

DAY 7: ADD SHARE BUTTONS TO YOUR BLOG

For today's challenge, add share buttons to your blog and/or website.

The easiest way to do this is to go to www.addthis.com and click on the Get AddThis button. It's big, bright, and orange. You can't miss it.

Here's the thing about social sharing buttons: They make it very easy for people visiting your site to share your content with their social networks... The more your content is shared, the wider your writer platform.

Basically, the site will give you button options, and you select the one you like best. The AddThis site will then provide you with HTML code that you can place into your site and/or blog posts. Plus, it provides analytics for bloggers who like to see how much the buttons are boosting traffic.

If you want customized buttons, you could enlist the help of a programmer friend or try playing with the code yourself. I recently learned that some really cool buttons on one friend's blog were created by her husband (yes, she married a programmer, though I don't think she had her blog in mind when she did so).

Plus, most blogging platforms are constantly adding new tools. By the time you read this article, there are sure to be plenty of fun new buttons, apps, and widgets available.

Here's the thing about social sharing buttons: They make it very easy for people visiting your site to share your content with their social networks via Facebook, Twitter, LinkedIn, Google+, Pinterest, and other sites. The more your content is shared the wider your writer platform.

DAY 8: JOIN LINKEDIN

For today's challenge, create a LinkedIn profile. Go to www.linkedin.com and set it up in a matter of minutes. After creating profiles for Facebook and Twitter, this task should be easy.

LINKEDIN TIPS FOR WRITERS

In many ways, LinkedIn looks the same as the other social networks, but it does have its own quirks. Here are a few tips for writers:

- Use your own head shot. You've heard this advice before. People want to connect with people, not family pets and/or inanimate objects.
- Complete your profile. The more complete your profile the better. It makes you look more human.
- Give thoughtful recommendations to receive them. Find people likely to give you recommendations and recommend them first. This will prompt them to return the favor.
- Search for connections you already have. This is applicable to all social networks. Find people you know to help you connect with those you don't.
- Make meaningful connections with others. Remember: It's not about how many connections you make; it's about how many meaningful connections you make.
- Make your profile easy to find. You can do this by using your byline name. (For instance, I use linkedin.com/in/robertleebrewer.)
- Tailor your profile to your visitor. Don't fill out your profile thinking only about yourself; instead, think about what your target audience might want to learn about you.

LinkedIn is often considered a more "professional" site than the other social networks like Facebook, Google+, and Twitter. For one thing, users are prompted to share their work experience and request recommendations from past employers and current co-workers.

However, this site still offers plenty of social networking opportunities for people who can hook up with the right people and groups.

DAY 9: RESPOND TO AT LEAST THREE TWEETS

For today's task, respond to at least three tweets from other tweeps on Twitter.

Since Day 4's assignment was to sign up for Twitter, you should have a Twitter account—and you're hopefully following some other Twitter users. Just respond to at least three tweets today.

As far as your responses, it's not rocket science. You can respond with a "great article" or "cool quote." A great way to spread the wealth on Twitter is to RT (retweet) the original tweet with a little note. This accomplishes two things:

- One, it lets the tweep know that you appreciated their tweet (and helps build a bond with that person); and
- Two, it brings attention to that person for their cool tweet.

Plus, it helps show that you know how to pick great resources on Twitter, which automatically improves your credibility as a resource on Twitter.

DAY 10: DO A GOOGLE SEARCH ON YOURSELF

For today's task, do a search on your name.

First, see what results appear when you search your name on Google (google.com). Then, try searching on Bing (bing.com). Finally, give Yahoo (yahoo.com) a try.

By searching your name, you'll receive insights into what others will find (and are already finding) when they do a search specifically for you. Of course, you'll want to make sure your blog and/or website is number one in the search results. If it isn't, we'll be covering SEO (or search engine optimization) topics later in this challenge.

OTHER SEARCH ENGINES

For those who want extra credit, here are some other search engines to try searching (for yourself):

- DuckDuckGo.com
- Ask.com
- Dogpile.com
- Yippy.com
- YouTube.com

(Note: It's worth checking out which images are related to your name as well. You may be surprised to find which images are connected to you.)

DAY 11: FIND A HELPFUL ARTICLE AND LINK TO IT

For today's task, find a helpful article (or blog post) and share it with your social network—and by social network, I mean that you should share it on Facebook, Twitter, and LinkedIn at a minimum. If you participate on message boards or on other social networks, share in those places as well.

Before linking to an article on fantasy baseball or celebrity news, however, make sure your article (or blog post) aligns with your author platform goals. You should have an idea of who you are and who you want to be as a writer, and your helpful article (or blog post) should line up with those values.

> Before linking to an article on fantasy baseball or celebrity news, however, make sure your article (or blog post) aligns with your author platform goals.

Of course, you may not want to share articles for writers if your platform is based on parenting tips or vampires or whatever. In such cases, you'll want to check out other resources online. Don't be afraid to use a search engine.

For Twitter, you may wish to use a URL shortener to help you keep under the 140-character limit. Here are five popular URL shorteners:

- bit.ly. This is my favorite.
- goo.gl. Google's URL shortener.
- owl.ly. Hootsuite's URL shortener.
- deck.ly. TweetDeck's URL shortener.
- su.pr. StumbleUpon's URL shortener.

By the way, here's an extra Twitter tip. Leave enough room in your tweets to allow space for people to attribute your Twitter handle if they decide to RT you. For instance, I always leave at least 20 characters to allow people space to tweet "RT @robertleebrewer" when retweeting me.

DAY 12: WRITE A BLOG POST AND INCLUDE CALL TO ACTION

For today's task, write a new blog post for your blog. In the blog post, include a call to action at the end of the post.

What's a call to action?

I include calls to action at the end of all my posts. Sometimes, they are links to products and services offered by my employer (F+W Media) or some other entity. Often, I include links to other posts and ways to follow me on other sites. Even the share buttons are a call to action of sorts.

Why include a call to action?

A call to action is good for giving readers direction and a way to engage more with you. Links to previous posts provide readers with more helpful or interesting information. Links to your social media profiles give readers a way to connect with you on those sites. These calls to action are beneficial to you and your readers when they are relevant.

What if I'm just getting started?

Even if you are completely new to everything, you should have an earlier blog post from last week, a Twitter account, a Facebook account, and a LinkedIn account. Link to these at the end of your blog post today. It's a proper starting place.

And that's all you need to do today. Write a new blog post with a call to action at the end. (By the way, if you're at a loss and need something to blog about, you can always comment on that article you shared yesterday.)

DAY 13: LINK TO POST ON SOCIAL MEDIA PROFILES

For today's challenge, link your blog post from yesterday to your social networks.

At a minimum, these social networks should include Facebook, Twitter, and LinkedIn. However, if you frequent message boards related to your blog post or other social networks (like Google+, Pinterest, etc.), then link your blog post there as well.

I understand many of you may have already completed today's challenge. If so, hooray! It's important to link your blog to your social media accounts and vice versa. When they work together, they grow together.

Is it appropriate to link to my blog post multiple times?

All writers develop their own strategies for linking to their articles and blog posts, but here's my rule. I will usually link to each blog post on every one of my social networks at least once. Since I have a regular profile and a fan page on Facebook, I link to each of those profiles once—and I only link to posts once each on Google+ and LinkedIn. But Twitter is a special case.

The way Twitter works, tweets usually only have a few minutes of visibility for tweeps with an active stream. Even tweeps with at least 100 follows may only have a 30-minute to hour window of opportunity to see your tweet. So for really popular and timely blog posts, I will tweet them more often than once on Twitter.

The way Twitter works, tweets usually only have a few minutes of visibility of tweeps with an active stream.

That said, I'm always aware of how I'm linking and don't want to become that annoying spammer that I typically avoid following in my own social networking efforts.

LINKING TIPS

Some tips on linking to your post:

- Use a URL shortener. These are discussed above.
- Apply title + link formula. For instance, I might Tweet this post as: Platform Challenge: Day 13: (link). It's simple and to the point. Plus, it's really effective if you have a great blog post title.
- Frame the link with context. Using this post as an example, I might Tweet: Take advantage of social media by linking to your blog posts: (link). Pretty simple, and it's an easy way to link to the same post without making your Twitter feed look loaded with the same content.
- Quote from post + link formula. Another tactic is to take a funny or thought-provoking quote from the post and combine that with a link. Example Tweet: "I will usually link to each blog post on every one of my social networks at least once." (link). Again, easy stuff.

DAY 14: JOIN GOOGLE+

For today's task, create a Google+ (plus.google.com) profile.

Many of you may already have G+ profiles, but this social networking site is still rather new compared to Facebook and Twitter. Plus, Google+ status updates often show up in search results on Google's search engine.

I've heard people describe Google+ as a mix between Facebook and Twitter, and I don't think that's too far off the mark. Personally, I think it's still growing, which can be a good and bad thing.

The good news is that you could still be one of the first G+-users on the block; bad news is that you have to wait (and hope) for other people to migrate over to the block. Of course, Google has a huge reach online, so there's no reason to doubt that people will migrate...eventually.

> One tool I've really learned to appreciate on Google+ is the Hangouts feature, which makes it easy to record video chats with other people, including experts in your field on Google+ and then share permanently on YouTube.

One tool I've really learned to appreciate on Google+ is the Hangouts feature, which makes it easy to record video chats with other people, including experts in your field on Google+ and then share permanently on YouTube. Since I feel video is the future of online, I think this is really cool.

As with Facebook and LinkedIn, keep these tips in mind:

- Complete your profile completely. Use your name. Provide easy to find contact information. Describe who you are.
- Use an image of yourself. Not a cartoon. Not an animal. Not a piece of art. Remember that people like to connect with other people.
- Post new content regularly. Let people know you are using your account. That means connecting with other G+'ers as well.

DAY 15: MAKE THREE NEW CONNECTIONS

For today's task, make an attempt to connect with at least three new people on one of your social networks.

Doesn't matter if it's Facebook, Twitter, LinkedIn, or Google+. The important thing is that you find three new people who appear to share your interests and that you try to friend, follow, or connect to them.

As a person who has limited wiggle room for approving new friends on Facebook, I'd like to share what approach tends to work the best with me for approving new friend requests. Basically, send your request and include a brief message introducing yourself and why you want to connect with me.

That's right. The best way to win me over is to basically introduce yourself. Something along the lines of, "Hello. My name is Robert Lee Brewer, and I write poetry. I read a poem of yours in *XYZ Literary Journal* that I totally loved and have sent you a friend request. I hope you'll accept it." Easy as that.

Notice that I did not mention anything about checking out my blog or reading my poems. How would you like it if someone introduced themselves and then told you to buy their stuff? It sounds a bit telemarketer-ish to me.

While it's important to cultivate the relationships you already have, avoid getting stuck in a rut when it comes to making connections. Always be on the lookout for new connections who can offer new opportunities and spark new ideas. Your writing and your career will benefit.

DAY 16: ADD E-MAIL FEED TO BLOG

For today's challenge, add an e-mail feed to your blog.

There are many ways to increase traffic to your blog, but one that has paid huge dividends for me is adding Feedblitz to my blog. As the subscribers to my e-mail feed have increased, my blog traffic has increased as well. In fact, after great content, I'd say that adding share buttons (mentioned above) and an e-mail feed are the top two ways to build traffic.

Though I have an account on Tumblr, I'm just not sure if it offers some kind of e-mail/RSS feed service.

> In fact, after great content, I'd say that adding share buttons and an e-mail feed are the top two ways to build traffic.

The reason I think e-mail feeds are so useful is that they pop into my inbox whenever a new post is up, which means I can check it very easily on my phone when I'm waiting somewhere. In fact, this is how I keep up with several of my favorite blogs. It's just one more way to make your blog content accessible to readers in a variety of formats.

If I remember, this task didn't take me long to add, but I've been grateful for finally getting around to adding it ever since.

DAY 17: TAKE PART IN A TWITTER CONVERSATION

For today's task, take part in a Twitter conversation.

Depending upon the time of month or day of week, there are bound to be any number of conversations happening around a hashtag (mentioned above). For instance, various conferences and expos have hashtag conversations that build around their panels and presentations.

Poets will often meet using the #poetparty hashtag. Other writers use #amwriting to communicate about their writing goals. Click on the hashtag to see what others are saying, and then, jump in to join the conversation and make new connection on Twitter.

DAY 18: THINK ABOUT SEO

For today's task, I want you to slow down and think a little about SEO (which is tech-speak for search engine optimization, which is itself an intelligent way of saying "what gets your website to display at or near the top of a search on Google, Bing, Yahoo, etc.").

So this task is actually multi-pronged:

- Make a list of keywords that you want your website or blog to be known for. For instance, I want my blog to be known for terms like "Robert Lee Brewer," "Writing Tips," "Parenting Tips," "Platform Tips," "Living Tips," etc. Think big here and don't limit yourself to what you think you can actually achieve in the short term.
- Compare your website or blog's current content to your keywords. Are you lining up your actual content with how you want your audience to view you and your online presence? If not, it's time to think about how you can start offering content that lines up with your goals. If so, then move on to the next step, which is...
- Evaluate your current approach to making your content super SEO-friendly. If you need some guidance, check out my SEO Tips for Writers below. There are very simple things you can do with your titles, subheads, and images to really improve SEO. Heck, I get a certain bit of traffic every single day just from my own SEO approach to content—sometimes on surprising posts.
- Research keywords for your next post. When deciding on a title for your post and subheads within the content, try researching keywords. You can do this using Google's free keyword tool (googlekeywordtool.com). When possible, you want to use keywords that are searched a lot but that have low competition. These are the low-hanging fruit that can help you build strong SEO for your website or blog.

A note on SEO: It's easy to fall in love with finding keywords and changing your content to be keyword-loaded and blah-blah-blah. But resist making your website or blog a place that is keyword-loaded and blah-blah-blah. Because readers don't stick around for too much keyword-loaded blah-blah-blah. It's kind of blah. And bleck. Instead, use SEO and keyword research as a way to optimize great content and to take advantage of opportunities as they arise.

SEO TIPS FOR WRITERS

Here are a few SEO tips for writers:

- Use keywords naturally. That is, make sure your keywords match the content of the post. If they don't match up, people will abandon your page fast, which will hurt your search rankings.
- Use keywords appropriately. Include your keywords in the blog post title, opening paragraph, file name for images, headers, etc. Anywhere early and relevant should include your keyword to help place emphasis on that search term, especially if it's relevant to the content.
- Deliver quality content. Of course, search rankings are helped when people click on your content and spend time reading your content. So provide quality content, and people will visit your site frequently and help search engines list you higher in their rankings.
- Update content regularly. Sites that are updated more with relevant content rank higher in search engines. Simple as that.
- Link often to relevant content. Link to your own posts; link to content on other sites. Just make sure the links are relevant and of high interest to your audience.
- Use images. Images help from a design perspective, but they also help with SEO, especially when you use your main keywords in the image file name.
- Link to your content on social media sites. These outside links will help increase your ranking on search engines.
- Guest post on other sites/blogs. Guest posts on other blogs are a great way to provide traffic from other relevant sites that increase the search engine rankings on your site.

DAY 19: WRITE A BLOG POST

For today's task, write a new blog post.

Include a call to action (for instance, encourage readers to sign up for your e-mail feed and to share the post with others using your share buttons) and link to it on your social networks. Also, don't forget to incorporate SEO.

....

I think it's imperative that you post at least once a week.

....

One of the top rules of finding success with online tools is applying consistency. While it's definitely a great thing if you share a blog post more than once a week, I think it's imperative that you post at least once a week.

The main reason? It builds trust with your readers that you'll have something to share regularly and gives them a reason to visit regularly.

So today's task is not about making things complicated; it's just about keeping it real.

DAY 20: CREATE EDITORIAL CALENDAR

For today's task, I want you to create an editorial calendar for your blog (or website). Before you start to panic, read on.

First, here's how I define an editorial calendar: A list of content with dates attached to when the content goes live. For instance, I created an editorial calendar specifically for my Platform Challenge and "Platform Challenge: Day 20" was scheduled to go live on day 20.

It's really simple. In fact, I keep track of my editorial calendar with a paper notebook, which gives me plenty of space for crossing things out, jotting down ideas, and attaching Post-It notes.

EDITORIAL CALENDAR IDEAS

Here are tips for different blogging frequencies:

- Post once per week. If you post once a week, pick a day of the week for that post to happen each week. Then, write down the date for each post. Beside each date, write down ideas for that post ahead of time. There will be times when the ideas are humming and you get ahead on your schedule, but there may also be times when the ideas are slow. So don't wait, write down ideas as they come.
- Post more than once per week. Try identifying which days you'll usually post (for some, that may be daily). Then, for each of those days, think of a theme for that day. For instance, my 2012 schedule offered Life Changing Moments on Wednesdays and Poetic Saturdays on Saturdays.

You can always change plans and move posts to different days, but the editorial calendar is an effective way to set very clear goals with deadlines for accomplishing them. Having that kind of structure will improve your content—even if your blog is personal, fictional, poetic, etc. Believe me, I used to be a skeptic before diving in, and the results on my personal blog speak for themselves.

One more benefit of editorial calendars

There are times when I feel less than inspired. There are times when life throws me several elbows as if trying to prevent me from blogging. That's when I am the most thankful for maintaining an editorial calendar, because I don't have to think of a new idea on the spot; it's already there in my editorial calendar.

Plus, as I said earlier, you can always change plans. I can alter the plan to accommodate changes in my schedule. So I don't want to hear that an editorial calendar limits spontaneity or inspiration; if anything, having an editorial calendar enhances it.

One last thing on today's assignment

Don't stress yourself out that you have to create a complete editorial calendar for the year or even the month. I just want you to take some time out today to think about it, sketch some ideas, and get the ball rolling. I'm 100% confident that you'll be glad you did.

DAY 21: SIGN UP FOR SOCIAL MEDIA TOOL

For today's task, try joining one of the social media management tools, such as Tweetdeck, Hootsuite, or Seesmic.

Social media management tools are popular among social media users for one reason: They help save time and effort in managing multiple social media platforms. For instance, they make following specific threads in Twitter a snap.

I know many social media super users who swear by these tools, but I actually have tried them and decided to put in the extra effort to log in to my separate social media accounts manually each day.

Here's my reasoning: I like to feel connected to my profile and understand how it looks and feels on a day-to-day basis. Often, the design and feel of social media sites will change without notice, and I like to know what it feels like at ground zero.

DAY 22: PITCH GUEST BLOG POST

For today's task, pitch a guest blog post to another blogger.

Writing guest posts is an incredible way to improve your exposure and expertise on a subject, while also making a deeper connection with the blogger who is hosting your guest post. It's a win for everyone involved.

In a recent interview with super blogger Jeff Goins, he revealed that most of his blog traffic came as a result of his guest posting on other blogs. Some of these blogs were directly related to his content, but he said many were in completely different fields.

GUEST POST PITCHING TIPS

After you know where you want to guest blog, here are some tips for pitching your guest blog post:

- Let the blogger know you're familiar with the blog. You should do this in one sentence (two sentences max) and be specific. For instance, a MNINB reader could say, "I've been reading your Not Bob blog for months, but I really love this Platform Challenge." Simple as that. It lets me know you're not a spammer, but it doesn't take me a long time to figure out what you're trying to say.
- Propose an idea or two. Each idea should have its own paragraph. This makes it easy for the blogger to know where one idea ends and the next one begins. In a pitch, you don't have to lay out all the details, but you do want to be specific. Try to limit the pitch to 2-4 sentences.
- Share a little about yourself. Emphasis on "a little." If you have previous publications or accomplishments that line up with the blog, share those. If you have expertise that lines up with the post you're pitching, share those. Plus, include any details about your online platform that might show you can help bring traffic to the post. But include all this information in 1-4 sentences.
- Include your information. When you close the pitch, include your name, e-mail, blog (or website) URL, and other contact information you feel comfortable sharing. There's nothing more awkward for me than to have a great pitch that doesn't include the person's name. Or a way to learn more about the person.

What do I do after the pitch is accepted?

First off, congratulations! This is a great opportunity to show off your writing skills. Here's how to take advantage of your guest post assignment:

- **Write an exceptional post.** Don't hold back your best stuff for your blog. Write a post that will make people want to find more of your writing.
- **Turn in your post on deadline.** If there's a deadline, hit it. If there's not a deadline, try to turn around the well-written post in a timely manner.
- **Promote the guest post.** Once your guest post has gone live, promote it like crazy by linking to your post on your blog, social networks, message boards, and wherever else makes sense for you. By sending your own connections to this guest post, you're establishing your own expertise—not only through your post but also your connections.

DAY 23: CREATE A TIME MANAGEMENT PLAN

For today's task, create a time management plan.

You may be wondering why I didn't start out the challenge with a time management plan, and here's the reason: I don't think some people would've had any idea how long it takes them to write a blog post, share a link on Twitter and Facebook, respond to social media messages, etc. Now, many of you probably have a basic idea—even if you're still getting the hang of your new-fangled social media tools.

Soooo... the next step is to create a time management plan that enables you to be "active" socially and connect with other writers and potential readers while also spending a majority of your time writing and publishing.

> I use social media as a break, which I consider more productive than watching TV or playing Angry Birds.

As with any plan, you can make this as simple or complicated as you wish. For instance, my plan is to do 15 minutes or less of social media after completing each decent-sized task on my daily task list. I use social media time as a break, which I consider more productive than watching TV or playing Angry Birds.

I put my writing first and carve out time in the mornings and evenings to work on poetry and fiction. Plus, I consider my blogging efforts part of my writing too. So there you go.

My plan is simple and flexible, but if you want to get hardcore, break down your time into 15-minute increments. Then, test out your time management plan to see if it works for you. If not, then make minor changes to the plan until it has you feeling somewhat comfortable with the ratio of time you spend writing and time you spend building your platform.

Remember: A platform is a life-long investment in your career. It's not a sprint, so you have to pace yourself. Also, it's not something that happens overnight, so you can't wait until you need a platform to start building one. Begin today and build over time—so that it's there when you need it.

DAY 24: TAKE PART IN A FACEBOOK CONVERSATION

For today's task, take part in a conversation on Facebook.

You should've already participated in a Twitter conversation, so this should be somewhat similar—except you don't have to play with hashtags and 140-character restrictions. In fact, you just need to find a group conversation or status update that speaks to you and chime in with your thoughts.

Don't try to sell or push anything when you join a conversation. If you say interesting things, people will check out your profile, which if filled out will lead them to more information about you (including your website, blog, any books, etc.).

Goal one of social media is making connections. If you have everything else optimized, sales and opportunities will take care of themselves.

DAY 25: CONTACT AN EXPERT FOR AN INTERVIEW POST

For today's task, find an expert in your field and ask if that expert would like to be interviewed.

If you can secure the interview, this will make for a great blog post. Or it may help you secure a freelance assignment with a publication in your field. Or both, and possibly more.

How to Ask for an Interview

Believe it or not, asking for an interview with an expert is easy. I do it all the time, and these are the steps I take.

- **Find an expert on a topic.** This is sometimes the hardest part: figuring out who I want to interview. But I never kill myself trying to think of the perfect person, and here's why: I can always ask for more interviews. Sometimes, it's just more productive to get the ball rolling than come up with excuses to not get started.
- **Locate an e-mail for the expert.** This can often be difficult, but a lot of experts have websites that share either e-mail addresses or have online contact forms. Many experts can also be reached via social media sites, such as Facebook, Twitter, LinkedIn, Google+, etc. Or they can be contacted through company websites. And so on.
- **Send an e-mail asking for an e-mail interview.** Of course, you can do this via an online contact form too. If the expert says no, that's fine. Respond with a "Thank you for considering and maybe we can make it work sometime in the future." If the expert says yes, then it's time to send along the questions.

How to Handle an E-mail Interview

Once you've secured your expert, it's time to compose and send the questions. Here are some of my tips.

- **Always start off by asking questions about the expert.** This might seem obvious to some, but you'd be surprised how many people start off asking "big questions" right out of the gate. Always start off by giving the expert a chance to talk about what he or she is doing, has recently done, etc.

- **Limit questions to 10 or fewer.** The reason for this is that you don't want to overwhelm your expert. In fact, I usually ask around eight questions in my e-mail interviews. If I need to, I'll send along some follow-up questions, though I try to limit those as well. I want the expert to have an enjoyable experience, not a horrible experience. After all, I want the expert to be a connection going forward.
- **Try not to get too personal.** If experts want to get personal in their answers, that's great. But try to avoid getting too personal in the questions you ask, because you may offend your expert or make them feel uncomfortable. Remember: You're interviewing the expert, not leading an interrogation.
- **Request additional information.** By additional information, I mean that you should request a headshot and a preferred bio—along with any links. To make the interview worth the expert›s time, you should afford them an opportunity to promote themselves and their projects in their bios.

Once the Interview Goes Live...

Link to it on your social networks and let your expert know it is up (and include the specific link to the interview). If you're not already searching for your next expert to interview, be sure to get on it.

DAY 26: WRITE A BLOG POST AND LINK TO SOCIAL PROFILES

For today's task, write a new blog post.

In your blog post, include a call to action and link it on your social networks. Also, don't forget SEO.

Remember: One of the top rules of finding success with online tools is applying consistency. While it's definitely a great thing if you share a blog post more than once a week, I think it's imperative that you post at least once a week.

The main reason? It builds trust with your readers that you'll have something to share regularly and gives them a reason to visit regularly.

....

Remember: One of the top rules of finding success with online tools is applying consistency.

....

If this sounds repetitive, good; it means my message on consistency is starting to take root.

DAY 27: JOIN ANOTHER SOCIAL MEDIA SITE

For today's task, join one new social media site. I will leave it up to you to decide which new social media site it will be.

Maybe you'll join Pinterest. Maybe you'll choose Goodreads. Heck, you might go with RedRoom or some social media site that's not even on my radar at the time of this article. Everything is constantly evolving, which is why it's good to always try new things.

To everyone who doesn't want another site to join...

I understand your frustration and exhaustion. During a normal month, I'd never suggest someone sign up for so many social media sites in such a short period of time, but this isn't a normal month. We're in the midst of a challenge!

And no, I don't expect you to spend a lot of time on every social media site you join. That's not always the point when you first sign up. No, you sign up to poke around and see if the site interests you at all. See if you have any natural connections. Try mingling a little bit.

If the site doesn't appeal to you, feel free to let it be for a while. Let me share a story with you.

How I Came to Rock Facebook and Twitter

My Facebook and Twitter accounts both boast more than 5,000 followers (or friends/subscribers) today. But both accounts were originally created and abandoned, because they just weren't right for me at the time that I signed up.

For Facebook, I just didn't understand why I would abandon a perfectly good MySpace account to play around on a site that didn't feature the same level of music and personal blogging that MySpace did. But then, MySpace turned into Spam-opolis, and the rest is history.

....

For Facebook, I just didn't understand why I would abandon a perfectly good MySpace account to play around on a site that didn't feature the same level of music and personal blogging that MySpace did.

....

For Twitter, I just didn't get the whole tweet concept, because Facebook already had status updates. Why tweet when I could update my status on Facebook?

But I've gained a lot professionally and personally from Facebook and Twitter—even though they weren't the right sites for me initially. In fact, Google+ is sort of in that area for me right now. I don't use it near enough, but I started an account, because it just feels like a place that will explode sooner or later. It's not like Facebook is going to be around forever.

The Importance of Experimentation

Or as I prefer to think of it: The importance of play. You should constantly try new things, whether in your writing, your social media networks, or the places you eat food. Not only does it make life more exciting and provide you with new experiences and perspective, but it also helps make you a more well-rounded human being.

So don't complain about joining a new social media site. Instead, embrace the excuse to try something new, especially when there are only three more tasks left this month (and I promise no more new sites after today).

DAY 28: READ POST AND COMMENT ON IT

For today's task, read and comment on a blog post, making sure that your comment links back to your blog or website.

If you remember, this was the same task required way back on Day 6. How far we've come, though it's still a good idea to stay connected and engaged with other bloggers. I know I find that sometimes I start to insulate myself in my own little blogging communities and worlds—when it's good to get out and read what others are doing. In fact, that's what helped inspire my Monday Advice for Writers posts—it gives me motivation to read what others are writing (on writing, of course).

DAY 29: MAKE A TASK LIST

For today's task, make a task list of things you are going to do on each day next month. That's right, I want you to break down 31 days with 31 tasks for each day—similar to what we've done this month.

You see, I don't want you to quit challenging yourself once this challenge is over. Of course, you get to decide what the tasks will be. So if you aren't into new social media sites, don't put them on your list. Instead, focus on blog posts, commenting on other sites, linking to articles, contacting experts, or whatever it is that you are going to do next month to keep momentum building toward an incredible author platform.

Keep it going, keep it rolling, and your efforts will continue to gain momentum and speed. I promise.

Somewhere near the end of the month, you should have a day set aside with one task: Make a task list of things to do on each day of the next month. And so on and so forth. Keep it going, keep it rolling, and your efforts will continue to gain momentum and speed. I promise.

DAY 30: ENGAGE THE WORLD

For today's task, engage the world.

By this, I mean that you should comment on status updates, ask questions, share answers, start debates, continue debates, and listen—that's right, don't be that person who dominates a conversation and makes it completely one-sided.

Engage the world by entering the conversation. Engage the world by having the courage to take risks and share things of consequence. Engage the world by having the courage to make mistakes and fail and learn from those mistakes and failures.

The only people who never fail are those who never try, and those people never succeed at anything except avoiding failure and success. Don't be that person. Engage the world and let the world engage you.

ROBERT LEE BREWER is Senior Content Editor for the Writer's Digest Writing Community. This challenge was originally on his personal blog (http://robertleebrewer.blogspot.com) My Name Is Not Bob. Named Poet Laureate of the Blogosphere in 2010, his debut full-length poetry collection, *Solving the World's Problems*, was recently published by Press 53. For more information, engage Brewer via e-mail at robertleebrewer@gmail.com.

IT TAKES A VILLAGE

Book Marketing Begins at Home

by Mary Shafer

Self-published authors and other indie publishers quickly learn they must work for every sale. Most effective is a grassroots campaign beginning with a thorough marketing plan that includes starting local, building regional buzz, then moving out to larger national and global audiences. No one does it alone—it truly takes the efforts of an extended metaphorical village to successfully launch and sustain a book.

When my first book was published in 1993, I was woefully unprepared to effectively promote it. With no author experience, I fell back on my marketing background and treated my book as I would one of my clients' projects. I began promoting locally, took advantage of every opportunity to build wider buzz by following up on each success, then moved out to a wider audience. I leveraged all my personal and professional networks and gladly allowed the enthusiasm of family, friends, neighbors and colleagues to propel my book to respectable sales. I knew from the start it would take a village to make my book a success.

Though there are more robust promotional tools today, the basis of this success remains the same: Every author and indie publisher needs to enlist the power of their respective "villages" through a five-step book promotion formula:

1. Plan
2. Start local
3. Build buzz
4. Widen reach
5. Be consistent

PLAN

Planning any kind of marketing provides guidelines to keep you on budget, from going off on unproductive tangents and spending too many of your resources for too little return. Things change so rapidly these days that it makes sense to plan the book's launch and first year of marketing, then a year at a time after that. You'll learn as you go, but there are many great books and online resources to help you understand the key components of a sound book marketing plan.

Ideally, you'll begin this plan before you even start writing your book, since there are things you can build into your book to make it more marketable. But whenever you start, there's always something you can do as soon as your plan is written.

START LOCAL

"My advice for newly self-published authors or those published with indie presses is to start locally in person, while embracing the promotional power of Facebook and Twitter," says Barbara Techel, award-winning author and publisher of Joyful Paw Prints Press, LLC (joyfulpaws.com).

"Starting local is so important to building a brand and confidence, then enhancing that with social media avenues. In fact, combining the two right out of the gate is the ideal thing to do." She began talking to local teachers and librarians about her first children's book, *Frankie the Walk 'N Roll Dog*, before it came out. This created awareness and anticipation. When her books were printed, she contacted those same people to schedule the presentations, where she built visibility, credibility, and book sales.

> You can include a brief introduction to your release, suggesting local story angles or tie-ins to topic-related current events. Anything you can do to make editors' and journalists' jobs easier increases your possibilities of coverage.

Create news releases and e-mail them to your local newspapers, magazines and any online local news outlets such as AOL Patch®. You should have a website about you and your book, so post high resolution photos of yourself and your book's cover there, where they can be downloaded at news reporters' convenience, to illustrate any features they may write based on your release. You can include a brief introduction to your release, suggesting local story angles or tie-ins to topic-related current events. Anything you can do to make editors' and journalists' jobs easier increases your possibilities of coverage.

"The first tool I developed was a press kit, which served as an introduction to me and my book," recalls Erika Liodice, self-published author and publisher of Dreamspire Press (erikaliodice.com). "It contained a press release about the launch of my book, *Empty Arms;* my author bio; a professional headshot; early reviews from book bloggers; and media interviews with me. I sent them to local newspapers, magazines, and bookstores, along with a personal letter.

"A few days later, I received my first invitation to do a book signing at the local bookshop, which not only connected me with readers, but scored me valuable shelf space. The event garnered free advertising in area newspapers—space that would've cost me a fortune—and convinced the region's premier lifestyle magazine to review my book."

BUILD BUZZ

Once you've established recognition for your author "brand" and your book, it's time to widen your horizons to include state and national markets. Online, follow other authors in your genre, says Techel. Learn where your readers congregate—whether that's Facebook, Twitter, discussion forums or related blogs. Those places are where you want to hang out, too, and actively participate. Interaction with your audience is key to building credibility, trust and relationships.

"One of the best and easiest ways to build an author brand or platform is through blogging," says Amy Shojai, award-winning author of 26 pet books, who features pet-centric topics on her "Bling, Bitches and Blood" blog (AmyShojai.com). "Blogs draw a following, offer new writers a venue to experiment and find their voice, and provide discipline for getting ass-ets in the chair and WRITING on a schedule." This works even for fiction, and is quite effective if you develop a targeted following.

Learn where your readers congregate—whether that's Facebook, Twitter, discussion forums or related blogs. Those places are where you want to hang out, too, and actively participate.

Research other blogs about your book's topic, find other author blogs in your genre and start hanging out there. "Lurk" quietly for a week or two to get a feel for the conversation, then jump right in! Just remember the first rule of social media: *Give before you get.* On average, out of ten comments you make on anyone else's blog or on other social outlets, nine should give pertinent, valuable information others there can use and enjoy. The tenth comment can be about your book, but use a soft approach. No one likes a blatant self-promoter, and that approach will backfire badly. Promotional comments should contain a link back to your website or blog.

> ### LOCATE RELATED BLOGS
>
> Use these online tools to find blogs related to your book and writing:
>
> - Google Blogs - http://www.google.com/blogsearch
> - Best of the Web - http://search.botw.org/
> - Your Version - http://www.yourversion.com/
> - Technorati - http://technorati.com/
> - Alltop - http://alltop.com/

"Pair your blog with another venue such as Facebook or Twitter (or if very visual, Pinterest)," Shojai advises. "That way, you can share your blog posts on these other venues, and your 'friends, likes, fans' and 'followers' can more easily find you throughout the Internet. Choose social network options you enjoy using. It's all about networking, connecting and building relationships, and *not, not, NOT* about selling your book. Get folks to engage and get to know you first. You become a friend, then they're more interested in checking out what that friend is doing: "Wow, my friend wrote a book? I've got to read that, and tell all MY friends!"

WIDEN YOUR HORIZONS

Techel remembers, "As I built confidence, requested and received wonderful testimonials, I decided to expand my outreach to other states. Not really wanting to travel, I wholeheartedly embraced the free audio and video conferencing technology of Skype. I knew I could do in front of my computer's webcam the same classroom presentation I did locally in person. It allowed me to reach out to schools across the United States and Canada.

"Skype and Facebook have been essential to building my author platform and for creating buzz about my appearances. I've met teachers, librarians and others via Facebook that I would not have otherwise met, and they've helped spread the word about my work."

Liodice says, "As *Empty Arms* gained visibility, I began receiving invitations to exhibit at book festivals and speak at events. Whenever I have the chance to speak publicly about my book, I come prepared with a few key items to maximize the experience for potential buyers:

- a ten-second elevator speech that gets people interested in reading my book
- pocket-size brochures that remind them what it's about and where they can buy it
- folded business cards that look like my book, so people remember me long after our conversation has ended.

BE CONSISTENT

Though you're only planning a year at a time, it's critical to have an "in it for the long haul" attitude and to continue developing strategies to promote your book in creative and outstanding ways. One tactic is to find ways to build credibility and visibility for authors as experts in their chosen subjects.

As a nano-publisher of topical nonfiction on business, finance, and cultural subjects, longtime author Foster Winans of Winans Kuenstler Publishing, LLC (WKPublishing.com) encourages authors to write guest columns and other content for relevant websites, trade and general interest outlets. He says this should ideally begin long before the book is published. That way, when people search the Web for the author or the book, results return more than just an Amazon listing.

....

Though you're only planning a year at a time, it's critical to have an 'in it for the long haul' attitude and to continue developing strategies to promote your book in creative and outstanding ways.

....

"Authoring a book makes one an expert," Winans explains. "In the area of personal finance and investing, I have ghostwritten more than three dozen guest columns and blog posts that have been effective in getting our authors visibility. Most effective so far has been a relationship I developed with Forbes.com. Sites like this and others are hungry for free content from experts. Forbes builds their database of material, and the experts get to hitch their wagons to a trusted brand name. The bigger bang, however, is in tearsheets. Authors can reprint their columns with the Forbes logo and use them as handouts to burnish their credibility."

The key to this tactic is creating material that relates to current events and hot news topics, so it's a good idea to establish Google Alerts to anticipate when related topics are beginning to trend.

> **QUICK TIP**
>
> Each author's topic will determine a different group of potential outlets for contributed material. A general outlet is Quora.com, where people with knowledge in just about any field can answer questions about most any topic.
>
> Free subscription services Help A Reporter Out (HARO.com) and Reporter Connection (ReporterConnection.com) provide daily leads to journalists looking for expert interview subjects.

Then just remember to keep up the effort on an ongoing basis. You don't have to go for broke with every campaign. Ultimately, small efforts done consistently will always be more effective than splashy events done in an unplanned, "shotgun" manner.

"It's important to remember this all takes time, so be patient and commit yourself for the long haul," Techel adds. "Be consistent, build slowly and be authentic — that's what will attract your audience and keep it with you for a long time to come."

MARY SHAFER (maryshafer.com) is an award-winning author, and an independent publisher who served as president of the MidAtlantic Book Publishers Association from 2010-2012. As an unkown author, she promoted her debut regional nonfiction title that wasn't even expected to earn out (make back the author advance), into three printings that sold 15,000 copies and generated royalty checks for five years before it was allowed to go out of print.

HOW TO USE PUBLIC RELATIONS TO PROMOTE YOUR BOOK AND CAREER

by Lorena Beniquez

The beauty of executing your own public relations campaign as a writer is you already possess the crucial skill to be a successful publicist: writing. I know what you are thinking. "I've just poured my heart and soul into writing a book and now you want me to write more?!"

Yes, because your words may not reach a wide enough audience, if you don't use words further to promote yourself. Whether you want to reach a local or national audience, a public relations plan can get you exposure as an author and for your work.

The first thing to ignore when approaching publicity is that little voice in your head that asks, "Why would anyone care about my book?" That voice is just tired from already writing a book and would much rather go play a video game. Ignore it and become your own publicist.

Coffee House Press Publicist Kelsey Shanesy offers, "Being a good publicist is really being a good journalist." Like a journalist, ask, "Who, what, when, where, why and how. These questions will serve as guideposts for your public relations strategy.

Before answering those questions, examine what "public relations" means. It is part of your marketing strategy like advertising. However, unlike advertising you do not pay for placement. Public relations is anything that gets your name out to the public via traditional media, social media or even word of mouth. It can be an article in your local newspaper, a tweet about your upcoming stint at an open mic night or your Aunt Angie telling her bridge club about your book signing (never, never underestimate the power of Aunt Angie). If things go really well, it could be the Associated Press disseminating your story nationwide.

Now that writers have been employing social media, some think they are covered when it comes to publicity. Unless all your friends are editors or talk show producers, you need to go beyond social media. While it is crucial, there are other elements that are just as crucial.

HOW?

Let's start with the last question of "How?". How will you reach out to your public? Pitch letters and press releases will do some of that work for you. Luckily, you just happen to be a writer so these will be a no-brainer.

The "pitch" is really just a public relations term for "query". The same rules apply for both. Like a query letter, it has to be attention grabbing. Shanesy advises that it should be a two to three paragraph e-mail.

The first sentence of your pitch will include your angle. This is what captures the gate-keeper's attention. Again, very much like a query letter.

Take a look at the day's headlines, study what's trending, and monitor what stories are getting play on national shows. One of the easiest ways to grab exposure is to develop an angle tied to a national story. For example, if a story breaks on how donuts are the new health food craze and you just wrote "The Hole Truth about Donuts" offer yourself to media outlets to comment on the craze.

Of course, your angle may have no current event tie-in and that is just fine. Anything about you or your book can help spur an angle. The setting of the book, the subject matter and your background as a writer (and human) are just some things to consider. Have you written a sci-fi graphic novel and happen to be a rocket scientist? The angles are endless with the most obvious being, "Rocket scientist gains lift-off with first book." Have fun with the angles and use your creativity.

....

Take a look at the day's headlines, study what's trending, and monitor what stories are getting play on national shows. One of the easiest ways to grab exposure is to develop an angle tied to a national story.

....

Another tool to employ is the press release. It is a more formal way of communicating. It is best used when you have really big news and need to reach multiple outlets at once. Do an Internet search to learn how a press release is properly constructed by looking at ones that are already out there. Many times, a pitch will also accompany the press release. Include the press release in the body of your e-mail rather than attaching it.

WHO?

Who do you pitch? Just like selecting the proper publisher or editor to approach, know the outlet you are pitching and make sure their target market is your target market. Study the target to see what has been covered in the past and what they are focusing on now. Also, get a feel for their work timelines. Talk show producers prepare for segments about a month in advance, while monthly and regional magazine editors need to be pitched up to six months in advance. Outlets with shorter lead times include wire services, daily newspapers, radio, television news and blogs. Following is partial list of outlets to consider pitching.

Locally: Newsletters, television news, local news websites, daily newspapers, free weeklies, college newspapers and regional magazines.

Nationally: Yahoo News, wire services, metropolitan newspapers, national newspapers (i.e. USA Today), daily talk shows, magazines (just peruse your *Writer's Market*), radio syndicates, trade publications, journals, news websites and blogs.

When pitching to television, keep this in mind. Some assignment desk editors and television producers shy away from covering books and authors because they aren't always visually enticing. They think a writer writing or a book just sitting there isn't spirited enough for video. However, if you give them something exciting to shoot, they will be more willing to offer coverage.

Say you just penned a children's book about a lunatic Siamese cat and you are inviting local news crew to interview you. Give them the option of interviewing you beside a lunatic Siamese cat. This gives them a visual other than a talking head (and maybe that lunatic cat will go viral which would be PR gold).

....

When pitching to television, keep this in mind. Some assignment desk editors and television producers shy away from covering books and authors because they aren't always visually enticing. ... However, if you give them something exciting to shoot, they will be more willing to offer coverage.

....

After sending out your pitch, follow-up via email. Shanesy says that it is best not to call when doing so. "It is rare when I actually talk to editors on the phone. If I have heard there is interest, or I know it is a great fit, then I will follow up on the phone," she says.

WHAT?

What are you pitching? It could be you as an author, your book or a million other reasons. Whenever there is a new development in your writing life, ask yourself if it is something that merits pitching. Got an assignment as a contributor to a book? Crow about it on Linked-In!

Did you just win a book award? Time for a press release. Did your research uncover Jimmy Hoffa's final resting place? You better hold a press conference.

Here are some reasons to crank up the publicity machine: book signing, new writing assignment, book reviews, spoken word readings, speaking engagements, blog updates, new website, securing a publisher, awards, conference participation and volunteer work. Also, always publicize any media coverage you have already received on social sites and websites.

WHEN?

When should you launch your public relations assault? Don't wait to begin your publicity until after you have penned your tome. If you are just now reading this, and have already completed said tome, do not fret. You can still publicize away!

Novelist Dennis R. Miller's day job is in public relations which he has done for over forty years. He says that when he puts aside three hours to write, he uses one of those hours to do his public relations outreach. Shanesy agrees. "Put yourself on a schedule so you post at least two things a day," she advises.

When also asks, "When were you last covered by the media outlet?" If you were just on *The View* last week, they probably will not be asking you back for a while. The same is true with your arts editor at the local newspaper. The media has a lot of ground to cover and must keep content fresh.

WHERE?

Where is your target market? Does your target market prefer newspapers over online news? Do they prefer to pin rather than tweet? Are they sitting in the salon next to you? This will help you better select the public you are pitching and the messages that go out through social media. You will very likely have multiple target markets so make sure you identify all of them and know where they live.

WHY?

Why did you write your book? Why do you write? Every writer has a backstory and many times it is just as compelling as the writer's work. This backstory may lend itself to your PR. Say you wrote a book on autism because your child is autistic. Include your "why" when pitching. It gives the gatekeepers a more rounded picture of who you are and also lends gravitas to the book. You aren't just selling your book's story. You are selling the story of you.

Now that we know the who, what, where, why and how of public relations, you will need to invest some time into getting your public relations campaign rolling. It will take work but it won't be too taxing since you have already jumpstarted the campaign with your writing platforms.

Writing platforms are more than gateways to your words. They also act as your personal publicist. "Early on in my blog [bikesnobnyc.blogspot.com], I was lucky that journalists and publications would contact me," says Eben Weiss (pen name BikeSnobNYC) who authored two cycling books and is a columnist for *Bicycle* magazine. Prior to his blog, Weiss had never written professionally and credits his blog for getting him noticed. "It is an extension of my PR in that people are reading it and the nature of the internet is to promote things that are interesting."

Now it is the time tell everyone why you and your work are interesting and go beyond the internet to do it. Sure, you are going to have to write more. But if you do your job well as a publicist, you will be writing more than just press releases.

LORENA BENIQUEZ has employed her skills as a celebrity publicist, reporter, filmmaker, and freelance writer. As a publicist, Beniquez has worked with Ray Romano, CBS Newworks, Showtime, and Sundance Channel to name a few. She is currently scripting a documentary film commissioned by the Lucille Ball Desi Arnaz Center for Comedy, which Beniquez also directed.

SPEAK MORE, SELL MORE

....

by Dianna Graveman

Book signings are a great way to network, but most indie authors average fewer than two sales per signing, not counting purchases from family members and friends. Speaking events are a much more effective sales tool. Special interest groups and target audiences are more likely to buy your book than are random shoppers.

Let's face it: Indie authors who have not been traditionally published face harsh competition. It can be tough to convince the buying public you have something worthy to offer when you don't have a publishing house behind you.

The trick is to think like a businessperson. Successful authors know that book promotion is not just a hobby. Don't treat it like one. Find your target audience and invite them to learn from you. Offer them value, and make them want your product.

GET THE GIG

Start local. Offer a workshop to area writing groups. Pitch to clubs who may have a special interest in your book's topic or theme. Both historical fiction and nonfiction can land you a gig at your county or state historical society. Contact the event coordinator at your library district or a nearby community college and offer to speak. Investigate the adult and continuing education programs at area school districts; many hire published authors to teach, with no college degree required.

If your book is of interest to seniors, contact the recreation director at a retirement center or try OASIS, a national organization with community chapters that host programs for adults over 50. Not all of these groups will allow you to sell books at the event, but all will provide word-of-mouth publicity and, in some cases, media exposure.

"If you are just starting out, your best bet is to network within the area you have expertise," said fiction writer J. A. Konrath, an outspoken champion of self-publishing who has also published traditionally. "Give free books to schools, businesses, and conferences—anywhere they hire speakers—and be able to pitch your speech in a compelling, succinct way."

Konrath also suggests e-book authors use CreateSpace or Lightning Source to make print copies for speaking events. Make sure your business card has a link to the site where your e-book is sold.

> Check the events section of your local paper for area business groups who may want to hear about indie publishing or book marketing topics.

Book clubs are an obvious audience for published authors. Readerscircle.org lists the location and description of book clubs around the world, searchable by country and zip code. An added bonus is that authors can request that their books be featured at the site and offer to do a half-hour phone chat with interested book clubs.

Check the events section of your local paper for area business groups who may want to hear about indie publishing or book marketing topics. Look for relevant support groups, if you've written a nonfiction book involving a health or social issue.

Award-winning sportswriter and journalist Mike Eisenbath self-published a memoir in 2009 and quickly realized his most effective speaking engagements would be opportunities to talk to people directly interested in his book's topic: clinical depression.

"My memoir had a somewhat focused subject, since it was about clinical depression and how to combat that with spiritual faith," Eisenbath said. "So people who have suffered from the disease or who have had a loved one with the disease were the logical audience. It meant most of the engagements I had were small. And I had to accept that as okay, especially given the intimate and sensitive nature of the topic."

FIND YOUR AUDIENCE ON THE WEB

Special interest groups are searchable by location and topic at Meetup.com. You likely won't be paid to speak to the group, but you will gain word-of-mouth publicity, and you'll walk away with a pocketful of business cards to add to your e-mail list.

Speakerfile is also a great place for authors and topic experts to promote. Set up a profile complete with book covers, slides, links to media interviews, lists of affiliations and accomplishments—even video or photos from previous speaking engagements. Set your rates and availability as a speaker. When you pitch your talk to an organization or group, include a link to your Speakerfile and showcase your talent.

Togather.com is a site exclusively for authors who want to speak, but with a twist: speakers can require a minimum number of attendees for an event, which is canceled if enough registrations aren't received. After the event, fans can leave feedback.

Don't forget to add "Speaker" to your bio on all of your existing online profiles, including Linkedin, Facebook, Twitter, and Goodreads. Make sure your author website announces you are a speaker, too.

PROMOTE YOUR EVENT

Congratulations, you've booked an event! Now it's time to promote.

- Create a Facebook event and invite your contacts.
- Send a press release to your local paper or news site. If Patch.com publishes in your area, pitch yourself as the subject of an article. Create a login so you can post the event on the site yourself.
- Prepare a simple poster or flyer to announce your event and post it on community bulletin boards around town.
- Add an events page to your website or blog. Post upcoming events as well as past events (to show a following) and a list of potential speaking topics for future engagements.
- Radio and television shows can be a tough sell, but blog talk radio hosts are *always* looking for interviewees. Google "blog talk radio" plus "writers," or search for a program with a theme related to your book. Get scheduled as a guest, then promote your upcoming event on the show. Don't forget to promote the interview, too, and post a link to the recorded show on your website.

Add an events page to your website or blog. Post upcoming events as well as past events (to show a following) and a list of potential speaking topics for future engagements.

- Set up a page at Eventbrite.com, then use the site to send custom e-mail invitations and list the event on search engines and in the Eventbrite directory. If you choose to host your own event, you can sell tickets and track your attendance.
- List your event at Zvents.com, and it will be distributed across the site's media network.

- Blog and tweet about your event. Announce it on Linkedin. Set up a Goodreads giveaway in advance of the event to drum up interest.

PREPARE FOR YOUR EVENT

Arlynn Greenbaum, President of Authors Unlimited, is a lecture agent and former Director of Marketing for Little, Brown and Company. Her clients include literary heavyweights Jodi Picoult, Jeffrey Eugenides, and Taylor Branch.

Greenbaum cautions new authors who hope to promote their books through speaking events to get coaching if they're not experienced speakers. "Writing is introverted, and speaking is extroverted," she said. "Not all writers are good speakers. People don't want to just hear you read; they want to listen to you talk about the creative process. If you're going to do it, be good at it."

One way to get coaching and build confidence is through Toastmasters International. You can search for a chapter near you at www.toastmasters.org. The site also hosts several free articles on topics related to public speaking.

Offer a few copies of your book as door prizes. Invite audience members to throw their business cards into a hat for the drawing, with the understanding you have permission to add those contacts to your e-mail list.

Several weeks before your event, send your host a .jpeg file of your book cover, a synopsis of your book, a brief bio, and a headshot of you for posting on the organization's website.

Ask your event organizer if you can sell books at the event, and request an estimate of the expected number of guests. If you can't sell your books, you may still choose to accept the invitation in exchange for publicity. If you do plan to sell, bring a friend to handle your sales so that you can spend all of your time interacting with your audience.

Consider offering a small percentage of your sales from the event to the host organization or a related charity, and ask the event planner to announce that agreement to your audience. You'll make up the lost percentage in sales and good will.

Prepare a thank you note, along with an offer to send a summary of your talk afterward for inclusion in the organization's newsletter.

Remember to pack plenty of bookmarks or business cards. Offer a few copies of your book as door prizes. Invite audience members to throw their business cards into a hat for the drawing, with the understanding you have permission to add those contacts to your e-mail list.

DON'T HARD SELL—ENTERTAIN!

Of course you want to sell books—but don't make sales the obvious point of your talk.

"Give content, not a sales pitch," said travel and history writer Sean McLachlan. "Give them an interesting lecture on Jesse James, and then happen to mention he's a supporting character in your novel."

McLachlan, a former archeologist who has traveled to more than 30 countries in his quest for adventure and the perfect story, enjoys using personal anecdotes to entertain his audience.

"Everyone is interested in hearing about rock climbing in Ethiopia or visiting Babylon in Iraq," he said. "If people think you're an interesting person, they're more likely to give your books a try."

DIANNA GRAVEMAN is a former corporate training designer, teacher, staff editor, and MFA faculty member whose portfolio includes over 160 publishing credits, 22 awards, and coauthorship of four regional histories. Graveman owns 2 Rivers Communications & Design, which provides writing, editing, and marketing services for businesses, and co-owns Treehouse Publishing Group, which provides author services. Learn more at www.2riverscommunications.com and www.treehousepublishinggroup.com..

AUTHOR'S GUIDE TO CREATING AN E-MAIL NEWSLETTER

by Dana Sitar

If you've ever Googled "building a platform," you've likely been told it's time to start a newsletter. "It's all about the list," everyone says, and you're starting to believe it. But you don't want to be another among the slew of salesmen who invade your readers' inboxes every day, and you're not sure where to even begin or how you might benefit.

You may have already read dozens of articles telling you an e-mail list is your best possible marketing tool, and you're eager to add another weapon to your bookselling arsenal. The fantastic power of "The List", however, is not in its potential to garner book sales, but in its ability to help you build genuine relationships with your readers—which leads to not only sales, but to a dedicated, loyal fanbase who will stick with you and your books for years to come.

THE BENEFITS TO THE AUTHOR

A reader signing up for your list gives you something simple but of great value: permission. Through your newsletter, you earn permission to contact readers directly through e-mail, and they may even come to expect and look forward to your correspondence. Creating and meeting that expectation helps you foster goodwill, and the opportunity to touch base with a reader one-on-one will help each of them connect with and remember you.

THE BENEFITS TO THE READER

Many of the tips for writing e-mail newsletters warn you that your readers are overwhelmed with e-mail, that you have to fight to get their attention, that you have to take care not to annoy them with your correspondence—but what if your readers enjoy what you have to say?

While keeping up with an overflowing inbox can be overwhelming, if your newsletter is helpful and entertaining, people will make time to read it. If you focus on fostering relationships, rather than on selling your books or pushing your blog, they'll look forward to the opportunity to connect with you—you're that interesting, and they respect your work!

HOW TO GET STARTED

Follow these simple steps to get started on an e-mail newsletter that will engage your readers and help you build a loyal fanbase for your books.

Step 1: Start with stating your goals.

Before you set anything up, state your goals and determine how your newsletter can support them. Are you trying to sell your book? Build your blog readership? Draw more people to your events? Connect with your loyal community?

Knowing your end goals will help you determine the best format and content for your newsletter, the best way to encourage readers to sign up, and the optimal schedule. Consider a clear action step or two for subscribers: Should they go to your blog after reading each e-mail, share a tweet with a particular message, or hop over to Amazon to pick up your latest book? Once you know where you want to guide readers, your correspondence can be driven by that end goal.

> Knowing your end goals will help you determine the best format and content for your newsletter, the best way to encourage readers to sign up, and the optimal schedule.

Step 2: Pick a direction.

Once you know your goals, you can determine the best type of newsletter to help you achieve them. Here are some common directions your author newsletter could take:

- Occasional news—This type of newsletter is best-suited for authors with an already-established fan base. If your goal is to keep readers abreast of your latest releases and upcoming events, you can focus on sharing these updates through your e-mail list.
- How-to or Informational articles—While time-intensive, this type of newsletter is a great way to offer additional value that attracts new readers. You can write unique articles for each edition of your newsletter, exploring topics of interest to readers in your genre.

- Resources—This round-up style newsletter is another way to offer additional value, but with less of a writing commitment than full articles. You can write a less extensive update that includes categorized links to articles and resources for readers in your genre.
- Blog digest or full posts—If you also write an author blog, your newsletter is a natural traffic-driver. You can send an e-mail when you publish a new blog post that teases the post, or e-mail the full post for readers who prefer to read it in their inbox.

Along with determining the overall direction, decide early on what topics you'll cover. Similar to creating an author blog, knowing the theme of your newsletter from the beginning will ensure consistency in your messages to readers.

Will you stick to personal messages, or include helpful information? If helpful information or resources, will they be on broad topics loosely related to your other work, or will they have a narrower focus for specific readers?

Step 3: Set your schedule.

Once you know the direction you'll take, promise readers a schedule and content. Telling them what to expect and when to expect it will encourage readers to look forward to your correspondence.

....

Before you send your first newsletter, determine your frequency and your theme. Prep your messages ahead just as you would for your blog or a magazine column.

....

Of course, if you make that promise, follow through to foster goodwill and confidence. Forecasting a schedule and straying from it could confuse readers and potentially cause them to unsubscribe. If you don't expect to stick to a particular schedule—especially if you're sharing only occasional news—don't try to promise one.

Before you send your first newsletter, determine your frequency and your theme. Prep your messages ahead just as you would for your blog or a magazine column. Commit to planning a topic, headline, and outline for several editions of the newsletter. This will help you ensure these messages match the tone and quality of your other writing, rather than taking on the hurried, careless tone of e-mail correspondence.

Step 4: Choose a service.

Dozens of services exist to help you manage your e-mail list and send professional-looking newsletters to your readers with little technical know-how on your part. Look around the web before settling for your provider or paying for services you don't need.

Subscribe to the newsletters of your favorite authors and bloggers to get a reader's perspective on the services they use. How do the newsletters look in your inbox? Is subscribing—and unsubscribing—easy or too complicated? Then look at these services from an editorial perspective. Do they offer sufficient support for the size of your audience? Will managing your e-mails and your list be simple enough for your level of technical expertise? Do they offer strong customer service and tutorials to help when it's not?

Step 5: Create an incentive to join.

Unless you have a strong fan base, you may not convince readers to subscribe for the updates alone. Offer an additional incentive to encourage and reward them for sharing their e-mail address. This incentive often takes the form of a free gift to subscribers: a short ebook, a manifesto, a report for your niche, a short story.

You can also create an educational series (a simple e-course) exclusive to subscribers, a series of blog posts only they can access, or offer exclusive discounts on your products and services.

Step 6: Promote the sign-up to your readers.

A flashing pop-up at your website will certainly get readers' attention, but don't miss opportunities for subtler and less-offensive ways to encourage readers to subscribe. A link or embedded sign-up form in your website's sidebar gets attention without disturbing the readers' experience so much.

Also, don't forget to include a link to sign up in your byline for articles at blogs and newsletters, share it with your Twitter followers and Facebook fans, and bring an old-fashioned piece of paper to book signings and events for attendees to add their e-mail address before they leave.

Step 7: Send your e-mails and engage with readers.

Once you start sending e-mails to your list, remember to maintain a focus on reader engagement. This list is an opportunity for readers to touch base and get to know you better, and a great way for you to connect personally. Write personal messages that prompt readers to follow up with you. Pose direct questions, and encourage them to "hit reply" to answer them. This is a great chance to learn from your most dedicated fans exactly what they want from you!

Adding a P.S. to the end of your e-mail is one of the best ways to encourage readers to take action—put your link there, or ask a question you'd like them to answer. After the headline, the P.S. is the second most-read part of an e-mail; you'll be astounded by how much engagement and clicks will increase from this simple addition!

THE MOST IMPORTANT PART

Overall, the most important thing to remember about your e-mail list is that this correspondence is all about the reader. Readers offer you incredible value and faith by signing up, so be sure to return the favor by consistently offering the engagement and value they're expecting.

DANA SITAR is a freelance journalist and indie author. She's been a freelancing (editor and writer) since 2004 with two self-published short story collections out and an information e-book for writers. She's written for The Daily Cardinal, The Onion, Baystages, SF Weekly, Laughspin, and Maximum Ink; as well as dozens of writing and career blogs, including The Creative Penn, Musings from the Slushpile, and Brazen Life. Learn more at http://danasitar.com.

BLOGGING BASICS

Get the Most Out of Your Blog

by Robert Lee Brewer

In these days of publishing and media change, writers have to build platforms and learn how to connect to audiences if they want to improve their chances of publication and over-all success. There are many methods of audience connection available to writers, but one of the most important is through blogging.

Since I've spent several years successfully blogging—both personally and profession-ally—I figure I've got a few nuggets of wisdom to pass on to writers who are curious about blogging or who already are.

Here's my quick list of tips:

1. **START BLOGGING TODAY.** If you don't have a blog, use Blogger, WordPress, or some other blogging software to start your blog today. It's free, and you can start off with your very personal "Here I am, world" post.

2. **START SMALL.** Blogs are essentially very simple, but they can get very complicated (for people who like complications). However, I advise bloggers start small and evolve over time.

3. **USE YOUR NAME IN YOUR URL.** This will make it easier for search engines to find you when your audience eventually starts seeking you out by name. For instance, my url is http://robertleebrewer.blogspot.com. If you try Googling "Robert Lee Brewer," you'll notice that My Name Is Not Bob is one of the top 5 search results (behind my other blog: Poetic Asides).

4. **UNLESS YOU HAVE A REASON, USE YOUR NAME AS THE TITLE OF YOUR BLOG.** Again, this helps with search engine results. My Poetic Asides blog includes my name in the title, and it ranks higher than My Name Is Not Bob. However, I felt the play on my name was worth the trade off.

5. **FIGURE OUT YOUR BLOGGING GOALS.** You should return to this step every couple months, because it's natural for your blogging goals to evolve over time. Initially, your blogging goals may be to make a post a week about what you have written, submitted, etc. Over time, you may incorporate guests posts, contests, tips, etc.

6. **BE YOURSELF.** I'm a big supporter of the idea that your image should match your identity. It gets too confusing trying to maintain a million personas. Know who you are and be that on your blog, whether that means you're sincere, funny, sarcastic, etc.

7. **POST AT LEAST ONCE A WEEK.** This is for starters. Eventually, you may find it better to post once a day or multiple times per day. But remember: Start small and evolve over time.

8. **POST RELEVANT CONTENT.** This means that you post things that your readers might actually care to know.

9. **USEFUL AND HELPFUL POSTS WILL ATTRACT MORE VISITORS.** Talking about yourself is all fine and great. I do it myself. But if you share truly helpful advice, your readers will share it with others, and visitors will find you on search engines.

10. **TITLE YOUR POSTS IN A WAY THAT GETS YOU FOUND IN SEARCH ENGINES.** The more specific you can get the better. For instance, the title "Blogging Tips" will most likely get lost in search results. However, the title "Blogging Tips for Writers" specifies which audience I'm targeting and increases the chances of being found on the first page of search results.

11. **LINK TO POSTS IN OTHER MEDIA.** If you have an e-mail newsletter, link to your blog posts in your newsletter. If you have social media accounts, link to your blog posts there. If you have a helpful post, link to it in relevant forums and on message boards.

12. **WRITE WELL, BUT BE CONCISE.** At the end of the day, you're writing blog posts, not literary manifestos. Don't spend a week writing each post. Try to keep it to an hour or two tops and then post. Make sure your spelling and grammar are good, but don't stress yourself out too much.

13. **FIND LIKE-MINDED BLOGGERS.** Comment on their blogs regularly and link to them from yours. Eventually, they may do the same. Keep in mind that blogging is a form of social media, so the more you communicate with your peers the more you'll get out of the process.

14. **RESPOND TO COMMENTS ON YOUR BLOG.** Even if it's just a simple "Thanks," respond to your readers if they comment on your blog. After all, you want your readers to be engaged with your blog, and you want them to know that you care they took time to comment.

15. **EXPERIMENT.** Start small, but don't get complacent. Every so often, try something new. For instance, the biggest draw to my Poetic Asides blog are the poetry prompts

and challenges I issue to poets. Initially, that was an experiment—one that worked very well. I've tried other experiments that haven't panned out, and that's fine. It's all part of a process.

SEO TIPS FOR WRITERS

Most writers may already know what SEO is. If not, SEO stands for *search engine optimization*. Basically, a site or blog that practices good SEO habits should improve its rankings in search engines, such as Google and Bing. Most huge corporations have realized the importance of SEO and spend enormous sums of time, energy and money on perfecting their SEO practices. However, writers can improve their SEO without going to those same extremes.

In this section, I will use the terms of *site pages* and *blog posts* interchangeably. In both cases, you should be practicing the same SEO strategies (when it makes sense).

Here are my top tips on ways to improve your SEO starting today:

1. **USE APPROPRIATE KEYWORDS.** Make sure that your page displays your main keyword(s) in the page title, content, URL, title tags, page header, image names and tags (if you're including images). All of this is easy to do, but if you feel overwhelmed, just remember to use your keyword(s) in your page title and content (especially in the first and last 50 words of your page).

2. **USE KEYWORDS NATURALLY.** Don't kill your content and make yourself look like a spammer to search engines by overloading your page with your keyword(s). You don't get SEO points for quantity but for quality. Plus, one of the main ways to improve your page rankings is when you...

3. **DELIVER QUALITY CONTENT.** The best way to improve your SEO is by providing content that readers want to share with others by linking to your pages. Some of the top results in search engines can be years old, because the content is so good that people keep coming back. So, incorporate your keywords in a smart way, but make sure it works organically with your content.

4. **UPDATE CONTENT REGULARLY.** If your site looks dead to visitors, then it'll appear that way to search engines too. So update your content regularly. This should be very easy for writers who have blogs. For writers who have sites, incorporate your blog into your site. This will make it easier for visitors to your blog to discover more about you on your site (through your site navigation tools).

5. **LINK BACK TO YOUR OWN CONTENT.** If I have a post on Blogging Tips for Writers, for instance, I'll link back to it if I have a Platform Building post, because the two complement each other. This also helps clicks on my blog, which helps SEO. The one caveat is that you don't go crazy with your linking and that you make sure your links are relevant. Otherwise, you'll kill your traffic, which is not good for your page rankings.

6. **LINK TO OTHERS YOU CONSIDER HELPFUL.** Back in 2000, I remember being ordered by my boss at the time (who didn't last too much longer afterward) to ignore any competitive or complementary websites—no matter how helpful their content—because they were our competitors. You can try basing your online strategy on these principles, but I'm nearly 100 percent confident you'll fail. It's helpful for other sites and your own to link to other great resources. I shine a light on others to help them out (if I find their content truly helpful) in the hopes that they'll do the same if ever they find my content truly helpful for their audience.

7. **GET SPECIFIC WITH YOUR HEADLINES.** If you interview someone on your blog, don't title your post with an interesting quotation. While that strategy may help get readers in the print world, it doesn't help with SEO at all. Instead, title your post as "Interview With (insert name here)." If you have a way to identify the person further, include that in the title too. For instance, when I interview poets on my Poetic Asides blog, I'll title those posts like this: Interview With Poet Erika Meitner. Erika's name is a keyword, but so are the terms *poet* and *interview*.

8. **USE IMAGES.** Many expert sources state that the use of images can improve SEO, because it shows search engines that the person creating the page is spending a little extra time and effort on the page than a common spammer. However, I'd caution anyone using images to make sure those images are somehow complementary to the content. Don't just throw up a lot of images that have no relevance to anything. At the same time...

9. **OPTIMIZE IMAGES THROUGH STRATEGIC LABELING.** Writers can do this by making sure the image file is labeled using your keyword(s) for the post. Using the Erika Meitner example above (which does include images), I would label the file "Erika Meitner headshot.jpg"—or whatever the image file type happens to be. Writers can also improve image SEO through the use of captions and ALT tagging. Of course, at the same time, writers should always ask themselves if it's worth going through all that trouble for each image or not. Each writer has to answer that question for him (or her) self.

10. **USE YOUR SOCIAL MEDIA PLATFORM TO SPREAD THE WORD.** Whenever you do something new on your site or blog, you should share that information on your other social media sites, such as Twitter, Facebook, LinkedIn, online forums, etc. This lets your social media connections know that something new is on your site/blog. If it's relevant and/or valuable, they'll let others know. And that's a great way to build your SEO.

Programmers and marketers could get even more involved in the dynamics of SEO optimization, but I think these tips will help most writers out immediately and effectively while still allowing plenty of time and energy for the actual work of writing.

BLOG DESIGN TIPS FOR WRITERS

Design is an important element to any blog's success. But how can you improve your blog's design if you're not a designer? I'm just an editor with an English Lit degree and no formal training in design. However, I've worked in media for more than a decade now and can share some very fundamental and easy tricks to improve the design of your blog.

Here are my seven blog design tips for writers:

1. **USE LISTS.** Whether they're numbered or bullet points, use lists when possible. Lists break up the text and make it easy for readers to follow what you're blogging.
2. **BOLD MAIN POINTS IN LISTS.** Again, this helps break up the text while also highlighting the important points of your post.
3. **USE HEADINGS.** If your posts are longer than 300 words and you don't use lists, then please break up the text by using basic headings.
4. **USE A READABLE FONT.** Avoid using fonts that are too large or too small. Avoid using cursive or weird fonts. Times New Roman or Arial works, but if you want to get "creative," use something similar to those.
5. **LEFT ALIGN.** English-speaking readers are trained to read left to right. If you want to make your blog easier to read, avoid centering or right aligning your text (unless you're purposefully calling out the text).
6. **USE SMALL PARAGRAPHS.** A good rule of thumb is to try and avoid paragraphs that drone on longer than five sentences. I usually try to keep paragraphs to around three sentences myself.
7. **ADD RELEVANT IMAGES.** Personally, I shy away from using too many images. My reason is that I only like to use them if they're relevant. However, images are very powerful on blogs, so please use them—just make sure they're relevant to your blog post.

If you're already doing everything on my list, keep it up! If you're not, then you might want to re-think your design strategy on your blog. Simply adding a header here and a list there can easily improve the design of a blog post.

GUEST POSTING TIPS FOR WRITERS

Recently, I've broken into guest posting as both a guest poster and as a host of guest posts (over at my Poetic Asides blog). So far, I'm pretty pleased with both sides of the guest posting process. As a writer, it gives me access to an engaged audience I may not usually reach. As a blogger, it provides me with fresh and valuable content I don't have to create. Guest blogging is a rare win-win scenario.

That said, writers could benefit from a few tips on the process of guest posting:

1. **PITCH GUEST POSTS LIKE ONE WOULD PITCH ARTICLES TO A MAGAZINE.** Include what your hook is for the post, what you plan to cover, and a little about who you are.

Remember: Your post should somehow benefit the audience of the blog you'd like to guest post.

2. **OFFER PROMOTIONAL COPY OF BOOK (OR OTHER GIVEAWAYS) AS PART OF YOUR GUEST POST.** Having a random giveaway for people who comment on a blog post can help spur conversation and interest in your guest post, which is a great way to get the most mileage out of your guest appearance.

3. **CATER POSTS TO AUDIENCE.** As the editor of *Writer's Market* and *Poet's Market*, I have great range in the topics I can cover. However, if I'm writing a guest post for a fiction blog, I'll write about things of interest to a novelist—not a poet.

4. **MAKE PERSONAL, BUT PROVIDE NUGGET.** Guest posts are a great opportunity for you to really show your stuff to a new audience. You could write a very helpful and impersonal post, but that won't connect with readers the same way as if you write a very helpful and personal post that makes them want to learn more about you (and your blog, your book, your Twitter account, etc.). Speaking of which...

5. **SHARE LINKS TO YOUR WEBSITE, BLOG, SOCIAL NETWORKS, ETC.** After all, you need to make it easy for readers who enjoyed your guest post to learn more about you and your projects. Start the conversation in your guest post and keep it going on your own sites, profiles, etc. And related to that...

6. **PROMOTE YOUR GUEST POST THROUGH YOUR NORMAL CHANNELS ONCE THE POST GOES LIVE.** Your normal audience will want to know where you've been and what you've been doing. Plus, guest posts lend a little extra "street cred" to your projects. But don't stop there...

7. **CHECK FOR COMMENTS ON YOUR GUEST POST AND RESPOND IN A TIMELY MANNER.** Sometimes the comments are the most interesting part of a guest post (no offense). This is where readers can ask more in-depth or related questions, and it's also where you can show your expertise on the subject by being as helpful as possible. And guiding all seven of these tips is this one:

8. **PUT SOME EFFORT INTO YOUR GUEST POST.** Part of the benefit to guest posting is the opportunity to connect with a new audience. Make sure you bring your A-game, because you need to make a good impression if you want this exposure to actually help grow your audience. Don't stress yourself out, but put a little thought into what you submit.

ONE ADDITIONAL TIP: Have fun with it. Passion is what really drives the popularity of blogs. Share your passion and enthusiasm, and readers are sure to be impressed.

SOCIAL MEDIA PRIMER FOR WRITERS

How to Use Social Media the Right Way

by Robert Lee Brewer

Beyond the actual writing, the most important thing writers can do for their writing careers is to build a writer platform. This writer platform can consist of any number of quantifiable information about your reach to your target audience, and one hot spot is social media.

Here's the thing: I think it's more important to chase quality connections than quantity connections on social media. More on that below.

So social media is one way to quantify your reach to your target audience. If you write poetry, your target audience is people who read poetry (often other folks who write poetry). If you write cookbooks, your target audience is people who like to cook.

And in both cases, you can drill down into more specifics. Maybe the target audience for the poetry book is actually people who read sonnets. For the cookbook, maybe it's directed at people who like to cook desserts.

4 SOCIAL MEDIA TIPS FOR WRITERS

Anyway, social media is one way to connect with your target audience and influencers (like agents, editors, book reviewers, other writers) who connect to your target audience. Sites like Facebook, Twitter, LinkedIn, YouTube, Pinterest, Goodreads, Red Room, and so many more–they're all sites dedicated to helping people (and in some cases specifically writers) make connections.

Here are my 4 social media tips for writers:

1. **Start small.** The worst thing writers can do with social media is jump on every social media site ever created immediately, post a bunch of stuff, and then quit because they're overwhelmed on the time commitment and underwhelmed by the lack of

response. Instead, pick one site, complete all the information about yourself, and start browsing around in that one neighborhood for a while.

2. **Look for connections.** Notice that I did not advise looking for leads or followers or whatever. Don't approach strangers online like a used car salesman. Be a potential friend and/or source of information. One meaningful connection is worth more than 5,000 disengaged "followers." Seriously.

3. **Communicate.** There are two ways to make a mistake here. One, never post or share anything on your social media account. Potential new connections will skip over your ghost town profile assuming your account is no longer active. Plus, you're missing an opportunity to really connect with others. The other mistake is to post a million (hopefully an exaggeration) things a day and never communicate with your connections. It's social media, after all; be social.

....

One meaningful connection is worth more than 5,000 disengaged 'followers.'

....

4. **Give more than you take.** So don't post a million things a day, but be sure to share calls for submissions, helpful information (for your target audience), fun quotes, great updates from your connections (which will endear you to them further). Share updates from your end of the world, but don't treat your social media accounts as a place to sell things nonstop. Remember: Don't be a used car salesman.

One final tip: Focus. Part of effective platform building is knowing your target audience and reaching them. So with every post, every status update, every Tweet, every connection, etc., keep focused on how you are bringing value to your target audience.

POPULAR SOCIAL NETWORKING SITES

The social media landscape is constantly shifting, but here are some that are currently popular:

- Bebo (http://bebo.com)
- Digg (http://digg.com)
- Facebook (http://facebook.com)
- Flickr (http://flickr.com)
- Google+ (http://plus.google.com)
- Habbo (http://habbo.com)
- Hi5 (http://hi5.com)
- Instagram (http://instagram.com)

- LinkedIn (http://linkedin.com)
- MeetUp (http://meetup.com)
- Ning (http://ning.com)
- Orkut (http://orkut.com)
- Pinterest (http://pinterest.com)
- Reddit (http://reddit.com)
- StumbleUpon (http://stumbleupon.com)
- Twitter (http://twitter.com)
- Yelp (http://yelp.com)
- YouTube (http://youtube.com)
- Zorpia (htttp://zorpia.com)

9 THINGS TO DO ON ANY SOCIAL MEDIA SITE

Not all social media sites are created the same. However, there are some things writers can do on any site to improve the quantity and quality of the connections they make online.

1. Use your real name. If the point of social media is to increase your visibility, then don't make the mistake of cloaking your identity behind some weird handle or nickname. Use your real name—or that is, use your real byline as it appears (or would appear) when published.
2. Use your headshot for an avatar. Again, avoid concealing your identity as a cartoon image or picture of a celebrity or pet. The rules of online networking are the same as face-to-face networking. Imagine how silly it would be to see someone holding up a picture of a pet cat while talking to you in person.
3. Complete your profile. Each site has different ways to complete this information. You don't have to include religious or political views, but you do want to make your site personal while still communicating your interest and experience in poetry. One tip: Give people a way to contact you that doesn't involve using the social networking site. For instance, an e-mail address.
4. Link to websites. If you have a blog and/or author website, link to these in your profile on all social media sites. After all, you want to make it as easy as possible for people to learn more about you. If applicable, link to your previously published books at points of purchase too.
5. Make everything public. As a poet, you are a public figure. Embrace that state of mind and make everything you do public on social media. This means you may have to sacrifice some privacy, but there are pre-Facebook ways of communicating private matters with friends and family.
6. Update regularly. Whether it's a status update or a tweet, regular updates accomplish two things: One, they keep you in the conversation; and two, they let people

you know (and people you don't know) see that you're actively using your account. Activity promotes more connections and conversations, which is what writers want on social media sites.

> Give people a way to contact you that doesn't involve using the social networking site. For instance, an e-mail address.

7. Join and participate in relevant groups. One key to this tip is relevancy. There are lots of random groups out there, but the ones that will benefit you the most are ones relevant to your interests and goals. Another key is participation. Participate in your group when possible.
8. Be selective. Piggybacking on the previous tip, be selective about who you friend, who you follow, which groups you join, etc. Don't let people bully you into following them either. Only connect with and follow people or groups you think might bring you value—if not immediately, then eventually.
9. Evolve. When I started social media, MySpace was the top hangout. Eventually, I moved on to Facebook and Twitter (at the urging of other connections). Who knows which sites I'll prefer in 5 months, let alone 5 years, from now. Evolve as the landscape evolves. In fact, even my usage of specific sites has had to evolve as user behavior changes and the sites themselves change.

FINAL THOUGHT

If you have a blog, be sure to use it to feed your social media site profiles. Each new post should be a status update or tweet. This will serve the dual purpose of bringing traffic to your blog and providing value to your social media connections.

AUTHOR PLATFORM 2.0

by Jane Friedman

You've been through the drill already. You know about establishing your own website, being active on social media, plus networking up and down the food chain. You've heard all the advice about building your online and offline presence—and perhaps you've landed a book deal because of your strong platform.

But platform building is a career-long activity. It doesn't stop once your website goes live, or after you land a book deal. In fact, your continued career growth depends on extending your reach and uncovering new opportunities. So what's next?

I'll break it down into three categories:

- Optimize your online presence.
- Make your relationships matter.
- Diversify your content.

OPTIMIZE YOUR ONLINE PRESENCE

First things first. You need your own domain (e.g., JaneFriedman.com is the domain I own), and you should be self-hosted. If you're still working off Blogger or Wordpress.com, then you won't be able to implement all of my advice due to the limitations of having your site owned or hosted by someone else.

Once you truly own your site, hire a professional website designer to customize the look and feel to best convey your personality or brand. If you don't yet have a grasp on what your "personality" is, then hold off on a site revamp until you do. Or you might start simple, by getting a professionally designed header that's unique to your site.

Website and blog must-haves

Here's a checklist of things you should implement aside from a customized design.

- Readers should be able to subscribe to your blog posts via e-mail or RSS. You should be able to track the number of people who are signing up, and see when they are signing up.
- Customize the e-mails sent to anyone who subscribes to your blog posts. This can be done if you use Feedburner (free service) or MailChimp (free up to 2,000 names). Each e-mail that your readers receive should have the same look and feel as your website or whatever branding you typically use. You should also be able to see how many people open these e-mails and what they click on.
- If you do not actively blog, start an e-mail newsletter and post the sign-up form on your site. This way you can stay in touch with people who express interest in your news and updates. Again, MailChimp is a free e-mail newsletter delivery service for up to 2,000 names. You should also have e-newsletter sign-up forms with you at speaking engagements.
- Install Google Analytics, which offers valuable data on who visits your site, when they visit, what content they look at, how long they stay, etc.
- Add social sharing buttons to your site and each post, so people can easily share your content on Facebook, Google, etc. This functionality might have to be manually added if you have a self-hosted site.

Review your metrics

As I hope you noticed, many of the above items relate to metrics and measurement. Advance platform building requires that you study your numbers. Especially think about the following:

- How do people find your site? For example, if you're dumping a lot of energy into Twitter to drive traffic to your blog posts, but very few people visit your site from Twitter, that means your strategy is not working, and you might need to course correct.
- What content is the most popular on your site? This is like a neon sign, telling you what your readers want. Whatever it is, consider how you can build on it, repurpose it, or expand it.
- What causes a spike in traffic, followers, or subscribers? When you achieve spikes, you've done something right. How can you repeat the success?
- What's extending your reach? Most days, you're probably talking to the same crowd you were yesterday. But every so often, you'll be opened up to a new audience—and from that you can find new and loyal readers. Identify activities that have a broad ripple effect, and make you heard beyond your existing circles. (In Google Analytics, this would mean tracking how new visitors find you.)

Advanced social media monitoring and involvement

Just about everyone by now has a Facebook profile or page, a LinkedIn profile, a Twitter account, etc. But static profiles can only do so much for you. Social media becomes more valuable when you decide how to interact and how to facilitate valuable discussion among your followers. Here are a few areas to consider.

- Implement an advanced commenting system. Sometimes the most valuable part of a blog is having a comments section where people can contribute and interact with each other. But this usually means actively filtering the good comments from the bad. Using a robust system like Disqus or Livefyre (and paying for access to their filtering tools) can help you develop a quality discussion area that rewards the most thoughtful contributors.

- Add a forum or discussion board. Very popular bloggers, who may have hundreds of comments on a post, will often add a forum or discussion board so their community can interact in an extended way. If your site is Wordpress-based, plug-ins can help you add a forum to your site in one step. Or you can consider using a private Facebook group or Ning (ning.com) as the base for your community.

- Use HootSuite to be strategic with your social media updates. HootSuite is a free, Web-based software that helps you schedule updates primarily for Twitter, but also for other sites. It also helps you analyze the effectiveness of your tweets (e.g, how many people clicked on a link you tweeted?).

- Use Paper.li (free service) to automatically curate the best daily tweets, updates, and posts on whatever subject you're an expert on—based on the people or organizations you follow and trust. Sometimes curating is one of the best services you can provide for your community—not only do you provide valuable content, you help people understand *who else* provides valuable content!

A final word about social media: Everyone knows about the usual suspects (Facebook, Twitter, Google Plus). Make sure you're not missing a more niche, devoted community on your topic. For example, All About Romance (www.likesbooks.com) is a very popular site for readers and authors of romance.

MAKE YOUR RELATIONSHIPS MATTER

A key component to platform is the relationships you have and grow. Often when you see a successful author, it's only the *visible* aspects of their online presence or content that are apparent. What you can't see is all of the relationship-building and behind-the-scenes conversations that contribute to a more impactful and amplified reach.

Am I saying you have to know big-name people to have a successful platform? No! Do you need to build relationships with successful or authoritative people (or organizations/businesses) in your community? Yes. Here's how to amplify your efforts.

Make a list of who's interacting with you the most

Regardless of where it's happening (on your site or on social media), take note of who is reading, commenting on, or sharing your content. These are people who are already paying attention, like what you're doing, and are receptive to further interaction.

If you're ignoring these people, then you're missing an opportunity to develop a more valuable relationship (which will likely lead to new ones), as well as reward and empower those you're already engaged with.

What does "rewarding" and "empowering" look like? You might drop a personal note, offer an e-book or product for free, or involve them somehow in your online content. You might have a special newsletter for them. Do what makes sense—there are many ways to employ this principle. Christina Katz, who teaches classes to writers, creates "Dream Teams" of writers who are selected from previous students. It's a great idea that rewards both Christina and the students she coaches.

Make a list of your mentors and how you can help them

You should have a list (or wish list!) of mentors. If not, develop one. We all have people who are doing something we dream of, or operate a few steps beyond where we're currently at.

> Do not approach this as something you're going to "get something" out of, or it will backfire.

If you're not already closely following your mentors on their most active channels of communication (blog, Twitter, Facebook, etc), then start. Begin commenting, sharing, and being a visible fan of what they do. Consider other ways you can develop the relationship, e.g., interview them on your blog or review their book. But most of all, brainstorm how you can serve them.

If you engage mentors in an intelligent way (not in a needy "look at me" sort of way), then you may develop a more meaningful relationship when they reach out to acknowledge your efforts. But be careful: Do not approach this as something you're going to "get something" out of, or it will backfire.

Do watch for opportunities that mentors will inevitably offer (e.g., "I'm looking for someone to help moderate my community. Who wants to help?") I once helped an author arrange a book event when he stopped in Cincinnati, and that helped solidify a relationship that had only been virtual up until that point.

Finally, don't forget a time-honored way to cozy up to mentors: offer a guest post for their blog. Just make sure that what you contribute is of the highest quality possible—more high quality than what you'd demand for your own site. If you bring a mentor considerable traffic, you'll earn their attention and esteem.

Look for partnerships with peers

Who is attempting to reach the same audience as you? Don't see them as competitors. Instead, align with them to do bigger and better things. You can see examples of partnership everywhere in the writing community, such as:

- Writer Unboxed website (where I participate)
- Jungle Red Writers blog
- The Kill Zone blog

We all have different strengths. Banding together is an excellent way to extend your platform in ways you can't manage on your own. When presented with opportunities to collaborate, say yes whenever you'll be exposed to a new audience or diversify your online presence.

Stay alert to your influencers and who you influence

There are many ways to identify important people in your community, but if you're not sure where to start, try the following.

- Blog rolls. Find just one blog that you know is influential. See who they're linking to and recommending. Identify sites that seem to be on everyone's "best of" list—or try searching for "best blogs" + your niche.
- Klout. This social media tool attempts to measure people's authority online by assigning a score. It will summarize who you influence, and who you are influenced by.
- If you use the Disqus commenting system, it will identify the most active commenters on your site.

DIVERSIFY YOUR CONTENT

Writers can easily fall into the trap of thinking only about new *written* content. It's a shame, because by repurposing existing content into new mediums, you can open yourself up to entirely new audiences.

For example, I have a friend who has a long solo commute by car, plus he walks his dogs while listening to his iPod. Nearly all of his media consumption is podcast driven. He rarely reads because his lifestyle doesn't support it. That means that if he can't get his content in audio form, he won't buy it.

Envision a day in the life of your readers. Are they likely to be using mobile devices? Tablets? (Guess what: Google Analytics tells you the percentage of mobile and tablet visits to your site!) Do your readers like to watch videos on YouTube? Do they buy e-books? Are they on Twitter?

If you adapt your content to different mediums, you will uncover a new audience who didn't know you existed. While not all content is fit for adaptation, brainstorm a list of all the content you currently own rights to, and think of ways it could be repurposed or redistributed.

> If you adapt your content to different mediums, you will uncover a new audience who didn't know you existed.

A popular repurposing project for longtime bloggers is to compile and edit a compilation of best blog posts, and make it available as an e-book (free or paid). Some bloggers will even do that with a handful of blog posts that can serve as a beginner or introductory guide to a specific topic. Fiction writers: How about a sampler of your work in e-book or PDF form? Poets: How about a podcast of you reading some of your favorite poems?

Some forms or mediums you might want to explore:

- Creating podcasts and distributing through your own site (or via iTunes)
- Creating videocasts and distributing through YouTube or Vimeo (did you know that YouTube is now the No. 2 search engine?)
- Creating tips or lessons in e-mail newsletter form
- Creating PDFs (free or paid), and using Scribd to help distribute
- Creating online tutorials or offering critiques through tools such as Google Hangouts, Google Docs, and/or Screencast.com
- Creating slide presentations and distributing through SlideShare

The only limit is your imagination!

HOUSEKEEPING

On a final note, I'd like to share a few housekeeping tips that can help boost your image and authority online. While they may seem trivial, they go a long way in making a good impression and spreading the word about what you do.

- Get professional headshots that accurately convey your brand or personality—what people know you and love you for.
- For your social media profiles, completely fill out *all* fields and maximize the functionality. This is important for search and discoverability. For instance, on LinkedIn, add keywords that cover all of your skill sets, pipe in your Twitter account and blog posts, and give complete descriptions of all positions you've held. On Google Plus, list all the sites that you're a contributor for. On Facebook, allow people to subscribe to your public updates even if they aren't your friends.

- Gather updated testimonials and blurbs, and use them on your site and/or your social media profiles if appropriate.

However you decide to tackle the next stage of your platform development, ensure consistency. Whether it's your website, e-newsletter, Facebook profile, business cards, or letterhead, be consistent in the look and feel of your materials and in the message you send. Unless you are appealing to different audiences with different needs, broadcast a unified message no matter where and how people find you. Believe me—it doesn't get boring. Instead, it helps people remember who you are and what you stand for.

JANE FRIEDMAN is a former publishing and media exec who now teaches full-time at the University of Cincinnati. She has spoken on writing, publishing, and the future of media at more than 200 events since 2001, including South by Southwest, BookExpo America, and the Association of Writers and Writing Programs. Find out more at http://janefriedman.com.

KALLYPSO MASTERS

Indie Is the Only Way

....

by Robert Lee Brewer

In my very first exchange with author Kallypso Masters, she let me know her feelings on indie publishing: "I purposely chose to be indie," she says. "The only time I ever submitted anything to a publisher was in May 2009 when I submitted a novella to Samhain for an anthology they were doing. They said it wasn't right for the anthology, but they'd like to see something else—but I just never submitted anything else.

"My day job (a part-time editor at a small liberal-arts college) took over for the next two years until I just had to quit because of the stress. Last day was April 15, 2011. In early May, I created a Facebook page for Kallypso Masters (a name I actually had created for Twitter in 2009), and I started writing *Masters at Arms* (the intro to my series and my marketing piece that I now give away free).

"By then, the indie revolution was a year at least under way and I had friends who were showing you could actually make a living writing (unlike all the friends who had been writing for publishers for 20 years and still working their day jobs). My husband gave me a year to make a success of it. In January 2012, I grossed more than $12,000 in sales. Didn't even take a year!"

And so begins the story of Kallypso Masters, indie publishing phenom. She even apologizes about her enthusiasm. "Sorry," she says. "I am passionate about indie publishing! I'm always trying to encourage others to at least put some of their books in the self-publishing market. There's so much fear about it, which I just don't understand."

How did you get started writing?

I've been writing as a hobby since high school, but seriously began studying the craft a decade later. I joined a national romances writers association and its local chapter, found critique partners, attended a six-week Romance-writing class at a community college, and I wrote.

I didn't submit anything I'd written (rightly so), but just kept writing and improving. In 1996, I went back to college in my late 30s and earned a degree in journalism in 2001, but always with an eye to someday being a full-time Romance novel writer.

What drew you to self-publishing?

I quit my stressful day job at the age of 53 in April 2011 on the spur of the moment and needed to find a new way to make a living—fast. My husband gave me one year to pursue my lifelong dream of becoming a full-time romance writer and we would borrow from our retirement savings during that year. He pretty much figured he'd kissed that money goodbye, so was quite surprised when I replenished our savings and then some the following year.

Timing is everything and this was about a year after the self-publishing revolution began so the media was talking about the successes of Bella Andre and other "Amazon million" writers. At my May 2011 writers group meeting, member Donna McDonald spoke. She'd just started self-publishing in March and already showed some success within her first two months. Having hung around romance writers for decades, most of whom still had their day jobs, I knew making a living within a year would be unheard of if I pursued a traditional publishing contract.

I knew I wouldn't be going the vanity press route, but would actually put out books worthy of any publishing contract. Still, I hemmed and hawed, sought advice from published authors (mostly traditional) for a week or two. I was advised over and over to go the traditional route first and build a name for myself before self-publishing.

While making a living was what appealed to me most initially, I learned quickly that having control of my story, my career, and my brand would only happen if I self-published.

But this was the closest I'd ever come to my lifelong dream of being a romance writer, so I asked the chapter president if she knew of any freelance editors. She'd just picked up the cards of two at a Romantic Times Booklovers Convention in April and one happened to be in my price range. (She's since learned she was pricing herself way too low!).

While making a living was what appealed to me most initially, I learned quickly that having control of my story, my career, and my brand would only happen if I self-published. I kept being advised by the traditionally published, "Oh, you can't do that." Why not? "Well, it's just not the way it's done." For instance, I wanted to put out prequels to the first few romances in my series as a single free or 99-cent volume to introduce my writing and my characters in what we now call a loss leader. I was told New York publishers wouldn't put out such prequels until an author had several successful titles published in a series. Apparently they have no idea how frustrating it is to the reader to find out that book four actually should have been book one.

Maybe it's the *Star Wars* mindset (where the last three should have been the first three in the movie series) or something, but it's just not the way readers want to dive into a series. I have been thanked many times for putting out the prequel first and then the romances. Readers are finding that the indie voices are so much more authentic and less formulaic. One wrote to say, "I love your books. I never know where the black moment will be. I just turn the page and BAM!"

> I also have total control of all business and marketing aspects. Sometimes that's a pain and cuts down on my writing time, but one thing both the traditional and indie authors said over and over was that publishers do not market for you anymore. If I was going to have to do that anyway, I might as well be the one who receives the royalties, not a publisher who did very little to earn them.

Having control of the story, especially when you write character-driven stories and have some very persistent characters insisting their story happened THIS way, not THAT way, is one of my favorite things about being a self-published author. A colleague said her publisher wouldn't let her have a hero and heroine who were 25 years apart (like one of my couples), so she had to change their ages to fit the publisher's guidelines, not what the characters were telling her in their story. Another said her erotic-romance e-publisher wouldn't let her have a heroine who had a one-night-stand in her backstory. I've heard many nightmares about New York publishing SNAFUs, too (e.g., such as putting the books in a series out in the wrong order), so I am thankful I chose to maintain complete control over my creative products.

I also have total control of all business and marketing aspects. Sometimes that's a pain and cuts down on my writing time, but one thing both the traditional and indie authors said over and over was that publishers do not market for you anymore. If I was going to have to do that anyway, I might as well be the one who receives the royalties, not a publisher who did very little to earn them.

Of course, I didn't have the money my first seven months to pay an artist, so I asked a friend of mine to do them. (Another no-no, I was told by traditionals. I was supposed to hire a professional to do my cover or use a cover stock mock-up because these are delicate things that must be done just so.) I think my cover artist does a great job—and she only designs covers for me, so they are unique. Fewer than seven months after she designed the first cover, she was paid for the first three covers.

Did you ever try going the traditional route?

Once. In March 2009 I discovered the Erotic Romance subgenre after attending my first writers conference in probably a decade. What attracted me to this genre was hearing about so many authors who were making a living in a short time (rare among the Romance-genre writers I knew). I went home and penned one in about a month and submitted it to Samhain, an e-publisher, in a call for submissions for an anthology. I received a "good" rejection saying it wasn't right for that anthology, but that they would like to see something else.

While waiting for that rejection, I drafted *Nobody's Angel*. But life intruded and the next two years my job consumed all of my energy. I didn't write another word of fiction until about a month after I quit the tech writing/editing job and was able to tap back into my creativity. I pulled out *Nobody's Angel* and began revising it. Then I wrote *Masters at Arms* to serve as a 58,000-word introduction to that series and my loss leader. Writing that book was a godsend because I can't plot, so writing the backstory in real time telling how these three men met and bonded on the battlefield helped me flesh out these characters much better in their Romances to follow.

What projects are you currently working on?

In addition to having my first four titles translated and published in Spanish, I am finishing up book five in the Rescue Me series, *Somebody's Angel*. It will be released in 2013 and continues the story of the couple who couldn't quite get to Happily Ever After in their earlier book, *Nobody's Angel*.

My series is very much a saga with installments, rather than stand-alone novels where all the problems resolved at the end of each novel. I prefer the realistic, gritty approach to writing Romance.

Any new projects on the horizon?

After at least the first three Spanish editions are out, I want to hire a translator to start working on the German ones. Germany is where I have my best sales in a primarily non-English-speaking country, and I've heard that my genre sells well there.

For the heck of it, I also recently sent the Samhain-rejected novella to one of my five professional editors asking her to look it over as a beta reader (not an editor) and tell me if it could be turned into a stand-alone novel or novella with minimal work on my part. I don't want to spend too much time away from writing my signature series, but thought perhaps I could give readers something a bit different in between Rescue Me books to keep them happy.

I also am trying to get my books in front of a more mainstream audience and am considering working on a Romantic Suspense I penned in 2008-2009 before I discovered Erotic Romance. I hope to lure in some "vanilla" readers who then will give my kinkier titles a try, since none of my books are primarily about the sex. I probably have the only "erotic" Romance where the couple doesn't have sex until the Epilogue in one book.

Within my Rescue Me series, though, I also want to explore writing a historical Western (erotic with bondage elements, of course) and perhaps even have some novellas around the holidays to help readers catch up on earlier characters as they continue to work through their issues without having them disrupt another couple's primary plot in their book. Of course, my characters are closely connected and will continue to come back into each other's books in more than cameo appearances.

In your view, what is the hardest part of self-publishing a book?

It takes so long to get everything done the way I want it done. That's partly because I'm a perfectionist, but also because of the learning curve. I have to find and hire the professionals who are going to work for me, whether it's with translations or audio (if I go that route) or designing and imprinting promotional items for my swag store.

With print-on-demand books, unless they ask their bookstore to order and sell the titles, they just don't make it onto the shelves.

While Amazon and Kobo are making it easier to get my books into a global market, even getting them into local bookstores here in the States is a monumental challenge. That's not a huge problem, because I make a living on e-books, not print ones, but readers e-mail or message me all the time saying they can't find my books in their bookstores.

With print-on-demand books, unless they ask their bookstore to order and sell the titles, they just don't make it onto the shelves. I usually leave signed copies behind when I do signings, but I only do a handful of bookstore signings each year, so that isn't going to make a dent in the paperback market. Having my books in stores and libraries would be a great way of finding a more mainstream audience, though.

How do you go about getting the word out about your books?

I write books that people can't help but want to talk about with friends (and have a Facebook discussion group with 2,000 fans who do that daily), so word of mouth is my biggest and best strategy. Before I had legions of fans pouncing on any friend or stranger they thought would be interested in my books, though, I was discovered by several Romance book bloggers who took notice of me and my postings and excerpts on Facebook and my blog in the summer of 2011. They started to tell their followers and also engaged with me on social media, which attracted their followers to me.

I started my Kallypso Masters Facebook account in May 2011 with 200 primarily author friends. I sent very few friend requests beyond those. When my first book came out two months later, I had 625 Facebook friends, almost all of whom I had gotten from word of mouth and book bloggers. That book sold 248 copies in the 20 days. We can't rely on book reviews in newspapers and print magazines anymore if we want to attract an e-book reading audience.

Sending complimentary review copies and ARCs to online book bloggers is a great way to get your books in front of your intended audience. I'm in the process of building a Spanish-reading audience by pursuing bloggers in that language and hope to repeat my success there.

Once I established a following of avid fans and sales went to grossing five figures a month for a few months, I hired a virtual assistant. Among other things, she set up a "street team" for me filled with some of my most avid fans who talk about my books anywhere and everywhere. I once took a poll of my discussion-group fans asking how they discovered me. After a free read, I learned most found me as a result of a recommendation. No doubt, many of them heard about me from a member of my street team or other avid fans. I've even had my erotic romances touted in bible studies!

Sending complimentary review copies and ARCs to online book bloggers is a great way to get your books in front of your intended audience.

In exchange for lots of promotional materials (swag) for street-team members to hand out, I engage with the team (mine are Kallypso's Street Brats) in a private Facebook group. I give them advanced peeks at book covers, previews on news, and I send them prizes and perks to show them my appreciation. Some sign up just for the freebies, but if you make it possible for fans to get free swag in other ways and you ask them to fill out a commitment form to join the team, you can attract those who truly want to "pimp" out your books.

Do you earn income from products or services that aren't books?

In May 2013, I opened my Kally Swag Store where I sell merchandise I've had designed and imprinted relating to my books—t-shirts, aprons, evil sticks (an impact toy used in one of my books that are hand-made for me to resell), key chains and other accessories, and, of course, my signed books.

I also had my first Rescue Me Series sightseeing tour that same month in Southern California. While that was a beta experiment, it was so successful I hope to spend a whole weekend with readers there in October 2014.

How do you balance your writing time with everything else that goes with self-publishing?

Not very well. During my first seven months as a full-time writer, I published three titles totaling about 315,000 words. It took me nine months (eight months actively writing it) to get the next title out (although it was a hefty 172,000 words). Now I'm looking at 11-12 months for book five.

As I said earlier, I have to do marketing the same as any author, so I can't blame self-publishing on that time drain. (I didn't have a lot to market that first 7 months—I was still writing the books and trying to get to that magical third book which is where sales pick up for most authors.) After the fourth book came out, I also spent a couple of months editing the first four books for paperback versions (rather than working on book five).

Now I am working on Spanish translations. I still love having control of my creative content and it would take a lot of convincing and perks for me to trust my books to a third party or publisher, but it does mean that I will probably have to settle for publishing one full-length new book a year. I know that's so New York publishing, but that's the way it is.

Now I am working on Spanish translations.

To help keep up with marketing and to engage with readers, I am never without my iPhone or laptop. I didn't even own a smartphone or a phone with texting until right before attending my first reader convention. It has helped me keep up with Facebook and Twitter and e-mails. I also spend a lot of time on my mini-laptop to write (and do more social media). I also adore meeting my fans.

I know I won't be able to have that kind of personal connection with them forever, but I am so appreciative of the readers who have taken me from an unknown author to one who occasionally makes a splash in publishing. Sometimes I just post an event page on Facebook telling readers where I'll be and when and they RSVP to hang out with me and talk about my books and characters. I've also started combining vacation with research and other travel activities (such as meeting readers!). I am probably suffering from undiagnosed ADD, but need to go from one thing to the next fairly often to keep from getting bored or bogged down.

But I don't just juggle writing and business/marketing. I also want to enjoy my life and my family. My first grandchild was born a week after the last book came out. I often share my personal life with readers on social media, too, whether it's my Gramma time or my worry about a sibling in stage four cancer. Showing readers you are a real person with a family and a life, not a writing automaton, makes them much more patient with you in between books.

If you could pass on only one piece of advice to other writers looking to self-publish, what would it be?

Hire professional editors and form an editorial team. Some publish without hiring even one professional editor, but I've learned no one editor can do it all. I round out my team finding those who are the best at the various aspects of editing—content, plot, character development, grammar and punctuation, consistency, and line edits.

I was fortunate in the beginning to have talented professionals volunteering as beta readers for me. Now they get paid well for their services. Writer friends are great as critique partners, but they are not editors. Editing will make or break your work, so hire or recruit the best team you can afford.

JEFF GOINS

Outlast the Lucky, Outwork the Lazy

....

by Robert Lee Brewer

For two years now, Jeff Goins has been atop the WriteToDone.com best writing blogs list. He has a legion of adoring fans and avid supporters. So he must be great at promoting himself online, right?

"You know," says Goins, "I really don't think that way. I use social media to help people, and I believe that makes people want to help my writing spread and succeed."

In fact, Goins, the author of *Wrecked: When a Broken World Slams Into Your Comfortable Life* (Moody Publishers), cites his best writing experience as a moment of helping his family.

"Telling my wife she didn't have to go back to work after having our son," explains Goins. "We were fortunate enough to make some side income through my book, e-book, and online course, that she could now be a full-time mom—something she'd wanted to do for a while. I'm more proud of that than any other writing accomplishment to date."

But maybe it was just payback to a person who helped him realize what he wanted to do with his life.

Let's start at the beginning. Was there a moment you realized you wanted to become a writer?

I always wanted to be a writer but would never admit it to myself. A few years ago, I attended a conference that was all about launching a dream. It was full of people who were ready to take the next step with their passion, but I was there to find mine.

But then the speaker said this, "Some of you have said you don't know what your dream is." I nodded along, resting in the fact that I wasn't the only one. "But I don't believe that's true; I believe you know what your dream is. You're just afraid to admit."

My heart sank.

I went home that night and told my wife I didn't know what my dream was, and she said, "Sure you do. It's to be a writer." And she was right. So I began to want to figure out how to be a writer.

Of course, it's one thing to want something and another to do it. It would be awhile before I'd actually start calling myself a writer—and that's when everything began to change.

I found you through your blog (goinswriter.com), which has built a following over the past few years. Could you explain the main thing you think your blog is doing that works?

Great question. It feels slightly weird to talk about my "success" because I still very much feel like I'm in process, on my way to where I want to be. That said, I know I've learned some things that could help others. So here are the three things I think I've done fairly well with my blog:

- **I only publish my very best content.** This is less common with bloggers than it should be; most are throwing a brain dump onto the screen and calling it "art." I really try to write articles for my blog that I would be proud of. As a result, I've built a resource of evergreen content.
- **I try to help people and be generous.** This means although I write for myself (passion must be primary), what I write—and how I write it—is intended to help others. I also try to give more than I take and ask permission every step of the way. As a result, my audience seems to really trust me, which I don't take lightly.
- **I guest post widely.** My blog is only two years old. The first year I wrote something like 100 posts for other blogs (in addition to the 300+ articles I wrote for my own blog), and many of those blogs were outside of my niche. Guest posting, I believe, is the single best way to expand your reach as a blogger. I still credit it as the main cause for my blog's growth.

Your writing presence seems to meld together two main goals—writing and making a difference. How do you personally manage to write while making a difference in the world?

I believe writers are difference-makers. It took me a long time to understand this, because I believed that words were cheap. They're not. They're invaluable. Words hold the power to give life or bring death; they can raise a person's spirit or destroy it.

Understanding that what we say has impact—and realizing we actually have a message to share—is the first step to making an impact in your family, your community, and your world.

Your recent book, Wrecked, tackles misfortune and spins it into a positive. Could you share how inconvenience has opened opportunities in your life?

I don't grow when I'm on the couch with a blanket on my lap (which happens to be the posture I'm currently in). I become a better me when I'm out there in the mess of the world, trying to make sense of things.

For example, getting my evening interrupted by a homeless man in Spain was the incident that gave me clarity about how I should be spending the rest of my life. And because it felt like a disruption to the "plan," I almost missed it.

Every major growth opportunity in my life has come disguised as an inconvenience. The more I talk with people about this idea, the more it seems to be a universal truth.

Earlier books you released were specifically for writers, including The Writer's Manifesto and You Are a Writer: Start Acting Like One. Your manifesto, in particular, encourages writers to write for the sake of writing, which is how many of us get started. Could you elaborate on this a little?

We all think we want the stage, the audience, the fanfare. But the reality is life is pretty lonely in the hotel room after the big show in the auditorium. We only have to read a few biographies of famous people to understand this.

Writers mistakenly believe fame is the answer to their problems—why they can't get published, why they're not a pro yet, etc.—but it's not. What holds us back is a lack of passion, a lack of effort due to indifference.

What sustains a writer to help her get through the ups and downs of the creative life isn't the handful of mountaintop experiences she might get. It's the love of the craft. That's the only way you can stick with writing long enough to succeed.

So write what you would enjoy even if nobody ever reads it (because sometimes, nobody ever does). The irony is this is how we create our best work.

Now I just wrote over 150 words, which is more than one-sixth the size of that manifesto (which is available for free on my website).

I believe both e-books were self-published. Could you share a little about your process with self-publishing?

The days of submitting to gatekeepers are over. I had those messages in me and wanted to get them out into the world. I didn't want to get anyone's permission and felt the urgency; they needed to be shared now.

The beauty of self-publishing is that's actually possible, easy, and cheap now. We truly live in the age of No Excuse. If you have a message or story the world needs to hear but hasn't, it's nobody's fault but your own.

You speak frequently on writing, marketing, and making a difference. What do you consider the top two or three things to deliver a good presentation?

One, make personal connections. If people wanted a monologue, they could listen to your podcast on iTunes. Be rough, spontaneous, and human.

Two, tell stories. People relate to what you've done more than to what you know. Show your scars, tell your truth.

Three, practice. Yes, be spontaneous and occasionally off-the-cuff, but don't be sloppy. People are giving you their trust; don't abuse it.

You're the Communications Director for Adventures in Missions, an international nonprofit organization. Could you first describe Adventures in Missions?

Adventures (adventures.org) is a mission organization that sends churches, individuals, and groups on mission trips around the world. We have an emphasis on prayer and personal development, while ministering first to the poorest areas in the world.

Then, could you share a little about what's involved in your role as Communications Director?

I oversee all the content that our organization puts out. This means I lead a team of writers, helping them grow in their craft and making sure all our content is consistent with our organization's voice. I also help our executive director with various writing and communication projects.

If you could pass on only one piece of advice for other writers just getting started on their journey, what would it be?

Don't quit. Outlast those who are lucky and outwork those who are lazy.

NAKIA R. LAUSHAUL

A New Beginning

by Rekaya Gibson

When nighttime falls, author Nakia R. Laushaul, born and raised in Los Angeles, California, lights a candle in a dark room and sits down at her clean desk to start writing. A beam of light shines from underneath the computer keyboard as The Temptations play on a Pandora channel, setting the mood for her next novel, *Locked in Purgatory*.

She is a poet, an award-winning novelist, and an entrepreneur. She wrote and published her first collection of poetry and essays titled, *The Truth As I See It: In Poetry & Prose* which Serendipity Bound Books released in 2010. In April 2011, she also released her debut fiction novel, *Running from Solace*.

"When I decided to write, it changed my life," she explains. However, to get there, she had to overcome her fear. Then, she had to deal with the hurdles which came with becoming an independent author. Still, she knew if she worked hard, she could dispel the myths and achieve some positive outcomes.

When she did, she encouraged others with her advice. With a demanding full-time career, it didn't leave much time to write. Furthermore, she discovered that her job was making her physically ill, so she had to make a tough decision. She prepared to leave her place of employment to embrace this journey of destiny from which she's never turned back.

OVERCOMING FEAR

Though Laushaul knew she wanted to write at the tender age of nine, she didn't start writing until her 20s. She had always loved reading, writing assignments, and telling stories as a young person. She used to win oratorical contests and write speeches. While living in California, she read a book by a popular novelist.

"If she can write that, then I can write this," she says about *Running for Solace*, the work she'd conceptualized 12 years ago in her head. The story was embedded in her conscience. Fear of rejection hindered her from transcribing her thoughts to paper. "I was scared to finish it. I was scared that people wouldn't think it was good." Once she overcame her doubt, she wrote an impressive 60,000 words in one month to complete the book.

Then, she began writing poetry in December 2008. She had never felt the desire to, even though she enjoyed reading and listening to it. She didn't even know that she could; it just came to her. Her first poem was entitled, *I am a Tree*, and then she wrote more. The process of writing poetry taught her how to create better imagery in a few words.

Not long after, she wanted her verse published. She set off to organize all her work and spent time learning about the writing and publishing industries. Her path became clear and doors opened up for her.

SELF-PUBLISHING

Laushaul decided to self-publish her book after attending the Black Writers Reunion & Conference (BWRC) in Las Vegas. She didn't like the idea of submitting her work, and then getting rejection letters.

When she started the process, she loved the control and the freedom of making decisions about every aspect of her manuscripts. In addition, Laushaul could listen to her readers and incorporate feedback.

"I didn't want to have to beg for permission to sit at the table. I felt as though I had been asking for permission my entire life," she commented. She met people at BWRC who had self-published; she knew that she could do it too. The conference experience gave her the foundation, confidence, and inspiration to give it a go.

When she started the process, she loved the control and the freedom of making decisions about every aspect of her manuscripts. In addition, Laushaul could listen to her readers and incorporate their feedback. She couldn't imagine relinquishing that control even if a publisher offered her a book deal.

She feels as though there is still a stigma about indie authors. Some people think that the book quality is subpar. She admits that she thought that herself. She spends a lot of time, money, and energy investing in her books, whereas, others do not take the time to cultivate their work.

One of the biggest obstacles about being self-published is getting others to see her as their equal. She thinks readers are getting there though, especially since the onset of e-books. It has opened up gates for exposing more authors.

The other challenge she faces, is having wide distribution so that people will recognize her name. She also wants readers to find her books on the shelves at bookstores. She prefers that her readers have instant gratification opposed to waiting for the orders to arrive to the store.

Her goal is to see her book sitting in the front of the store when she walks in as well as in the general fiction section. This is why she has not oversaturated the market with her work; she wants to take her time. She cannot wait to see her books everywhere she travels.

....

One of the biggest obstacles about being self-published is getting others to see her as their equal.

....

When asked if she would consider publishing other authors, she states that she thinks about this all the time. However, "I would have to screen folks. I want someone who is serious and marketable. The person would have to be ready for this journey. It's a daily grind. Maybe in 2014," she says, adding she would have the same criteria as other publishers.

OUTCOMES

Laushaul works hard to spread the word about her books and she has received awards for her accomplishments. She attends various literary events to meet as many readers as she can and she uses tons of social media. As a result, she has more than 130 reviews on Amazon for her book, *Running from Solace*. In addition, she became the 2012 Next Generation Indie Book Award Finalist and received the 2011 USA Book News Best Books Award.

All of these honors were unexpected. She remarks, "I did not expect anyone to find my books the way that they did."

She wrote the story and kept it simple, telling the story the way it was registered in her thought process for the previous 10 years. What does someone need to do to write an award-winning novel? "Tell the story, keep it simple, and add simple language so that people can understand it."

She wanted readers to identify with the characters, whether feelings of love or hate were being expressed. Furthermore, she heard from readers that they found her characters relatable. They tell her how they had been helped by reading her material. She appreciates their feedback and connecting with them, especially book clubs.

She cannot think of a better way to reach 10 to 15 people at one time. They read her work, look for her online, and e-mail her. She hosts discussions with them via Skype, or conference calls. She stays engaged through social media.

WRITING ADVICE

The best advice she has for independent authors is to "grow thick skin… when given advice, take it and sleep on it." Ponder it over before getting angry or mad.

Laushaul recollects receiving positive feedback from a bestselling author. She didn't tell her what she liked about it, but rather shared what she hated. She remembers crying about it, but later she went back over the work.

Her recommendations to aspiring authors are to do their own research and spend time learning as much as they can about the craft of writing and publishing. She would like authors to realize that not everyone will like their work, so she encourages them not to give up on their dreams.

MAKING HARD DECISIONS

Laushaul quit her job to spend more time writing. She could no longer put it off; the work-related stress was making her sick. Moments before giving notice, Laushaul videotaped how she was feeling from her car. She appeared nervous and confessed to being scared.

She walked out on faith, even though she was making good money at a great company. She was still unhappy and her passion to write consumed her. She also wanted to help others with writing and publishing. She knew she couldn't do it with a full-time job.

She shared a recording of the aftermath; she felt relieved. She knew that she had done the right thing. She also realized that it was never about the job. "It was about overall life balance and peace."

Now, she is overjoyed about what she is doing. She never wants to work for anyone else the rest of her life.

PREPARATION

Laushaul did not make an elaborate plan nor did she have writing and typesetting assignments lined up before giving a two-week notice. Opportunities just started flowing her way. When her book sales picked up, she began paying off credit cards and she stopped shopping. She reduced her bills to a manageable range. She plans to reach out to publishing companies to see if they will outsource work to her. Customers think she does great work.

Not everyone can leave the way she did, but for those who are planning to do it, she recommends considering an entire skill set before abruptly quitting a job; discover all possible business options. She turned all her skills into a business. For example, she planned all the company events while on the job.

Those talents can be implemented into event planning. In addition, during this process, she realized her ideas have value, so she became a consultant as well.

LOOKING FORWARD

Recently, Laushaul finished her third book and is now working on her fourth and fifth book at the same time. She plans to expand her business while continuing to evolve, herself. She would like to apply her skills into becoming a story editor for motion pictures, so she is conducting research on how to break into the industry. In the meantime, Laushaul will spend time performing spoken word poetry.

REKAYA GIBSON is the author of three novels, a children's picture book, and a bilingual coloring book. She's written articles for Cabo Living Magazine, Dessert Saints Magazine, Relocating in Las Vegas Magazine, and more. Now, she writes cookbook reviews for Cuisine Noir Magazine and articles for her blog, The Food Temptress/Enchantress. In October 2012, she launched her own publishing company, Gibson Girl Publishing Company LLC.

TAMIKA NEWHOUSE

Living the Dream

....

by Rekaya Gibson

Independent author, Tamika Newhouse created Delphine Publications at just 21 years old. She doesn't have a formula or a secret to successfully writing and publishing award-winning novels.

"I just remain consistent," she says. This consistency shows through her efforts of engaging readers, in building a business, and in mentoring aspiring writers. Her love for what she does spills over into her writing and self-promotion as well. Inspiring others and impacting lives affirms her destiny to write for a living, making even the challenges well worth it.

Newhouse has been writing since she could hold a pencil, and at the age of 12, she wrote a full-length novel entitled, *Nothing to Lose*. It was then she realized she wanted to become a publisher. She also wrote many poems, songs, and love letters until her journey took an unexpected turn.

She became pregnant at the age of 16, so she put her writing on hold like many other writers have to do within this industry. After her mom passed away, Newhouse resumed her love affair with writing to cope with her loss. As a result, she penned another book, *The Ultimate No-No*, in just three weeks. She was just 20 years old.

ENGAGING READERS

While attempting to learn everything possible about the publishing industry, she founded *African Americans on the Move Book Club*, an online book club and Internet radio show for avid readers across the nation. She created it as a way to meet people after moving to a new city.

Though she was a wife and a stay-at-home mother with two children, she had no friends and was lonely. In order to create an outlet while she dreamt of seeing her book in print, she organized a 'built-in' audience for her future books, and she didn't even realize it.

She posted books on MySpace and hosted discussions. Soon, African-American authors were querying to have their books be selected for her page. She read many self-published books—many she had never heard of before. She agreed and began spreading the word about their novels. In addition, she conducted book reviews, hosted literary awards, and interviewed authors on a weekly radio show.

As of 2011, there were more than 1,200 book club members, and the club opened to the public. She continues to reach more readers through social media as well as her Blog-TalkRadio. She plans to invest more money into AAMBC to get more exposure. She wants it to become the reader 'go-to' website for books.

BUILDING A BUSINESS

Newhouse was inspired to launch Delphine Publications. "I started the company to publish my book and to honor my mother's name." Some of her initial start-up costs consisted of obtaining a business license, post office box, and a checking account. The 21-year-old entered the literary community by storm.

She set out to target an African-American audience. She attended black writers' events and festivals. She connected with readers at book clubs, through literary magazines, and on radio shows. Nine months after her debut novel of *The Ultimate No-No*, she won Self-Published Author of the Year at the 2009 African American Literary Awards. Furthermore, it sold so many copies that Kensington Publishing Corporation approached her and offered her a deal to have it reproduced it in mass-market paperback. She did not use an agent to negotiate the contract; she represented herself in one of her proudest moments to date.

> She set out to target an African-American audience. She attended black writer's events and festivals. She connected with readers at book clubs, through literary magazines, and on radio shows.

Early in her career, she learned that lots of time and energy goes into self-publishing. Newhouse felt green on how to market her book, where to travel, and who to use for editing. She gained her knowledge by reading articles and books. In addition, she observed and spoke to others who were in the industry.

Now, she urges individuals not to cut corners when publishing their works. Furthermore, she does not recommend vanity presses. She encourages those she coaches to invest in their books and have their manuscripts professionally edited and typeset. She says to spend extra time creating a book cover image that stands out, and avoid using unusual fonts that are difficult to read.

Most importantly, she emphasizes doing research about every aspect of publishing. This includes areas such as marketing, design, and legal. Traditional publishers handle these areas for their authors, whereas, self-published authors either handle these responsibilities themselves or outsource them.

Currently, she has 11 authors on the Delphine roster in urban fiction, and she has an office in Atlanta, Georgia. When asked what makes her company different from the rest, she responds, "I keep it family oriented. I let authors know the foundation it was built on—to expose different literary voices." She coaches and teaches each novelist. "I talk to them and respond to their e-mails." Her goal is to make each author under the Delphine brand successful.

When she emerged on the scene, no one knew who she was, so she sold books one by one. Bookstores did not want to sell them because she was self-published. The popularity in e-books increased her sells and helped create a buzz about her as well as her authors. In turn, paperback sales increased, but nowhere close to e-books totals. "Delphine sells about 10,000 e-books and about 200-300 paperbacks per quarter."

She uses paperback books for promos and touring purposes. She is not looking to have novels placed into bookstores, which isn't a big deal since the company has sold more than 80,000 copies worldwide.

'I tell authors that they are not salesmen. They are traveling to create a brand and to spread the word about what they are doing. That is writing books.'

ENCOURAGING WRITERS

Newhouse encourages people, especially new authors, to organize book signings and meet as many people as they can. "They need to get out there and learn Marketing 101," she says.

Literary events are worth attending, depending on the person's career. Some are good for networking, connecting with book clubs, and speaking opportunities. "Have an agenda and an objective for going to these events."

Newhouse stresses the importance of branding and being unique. "I tell authors that they are not salesmen. They are traveling to create a brand and to spread the word about what they are doing. That is writing books."

In addition, writers need to have an online presence such as a blog, a frequently updated website, and accounts on all social media handles. They must remember that marketing and promoting is their responsibility whether if they decide to self-publish or not.

The industry is hard. At times, she contemplates quitting, but at the same time, people motivate her to keep going. "My hard work inspires others; their energy keeps me motivated. I get inspired by people telling me I inspire them; however, they don't see the behind the scenes at all—the things it took to get here."

While the praises keep her grounded, the negative comments sting and sometimes she wants to walk away. "If I turn around and quit, I feel responsible for others, because they tell me that I am the reason they keep moving forward. If I stop, what's going to happen to them? I feel sometimes it's my responsibility to make sure they succeed." She wants to be an example to others.

WRITING

With her busy schedule, when does she find time to write? "I pinpoint a timeframe to write every day. For example, I write and complete a book in six to eight weeks, writing 2,000-5,000 words a day until it is finished," she says.

She loves the creative process, but she cringes when it comes to the editing part. Many authors would concur. Traditionally published authors would celebrate the flexibility in their writing and editing schedules, but they tend to have concrete deadlines to stay on their label's production schedule. Furthermore, from start to finish, the publisher may take a year or more in making the author's book available. Indie publishers can have their works available in short as a month or two.

WHAT'S NEXT?

Newhouse has seven published books to share with the world. "I have setup an 18-city tour," she says. "I am attending women's expos and networking events, but I'm not going to any literary events for the next few years. I'll be branching out to other industries such as blogging, fashion, and entertainment."

She likes to switch it up each year, but she stays consistent. Newhouse spends time updating her blog, *Passionate Spot,* and heavily promoting herself online. In addition, she is preparing her new authors for their debut novels; some are even planning to release their sophomore fiction work.

Every year, she has a company launch party with a celebrity host in order to promote current and future titles. She will continue to inspire and coach authors one on one to create their brand within Delphine Publications.

Newhouse is one of the hardest working author/publishers in the independent book industry. She knew she wanted to self-publish, and she made it happen, even during times when she didn't realize the progression of her efforts. It is not for everyone.

Indie publishing comes with huge responsibilities and obstacles. Individuals have to consider the advantages and disadvantages for becoming an indie publisher or going the traditional route. The popularity of e-books may persuade some to take that leap, but they still have the daunting task of self-promoting and marketing their novels. This does not always equate to instant success. Not everyone is willing to invest in the research and work involved because of the amount of effort it takes.

In Newhouse's case, her passion and dream got the ball rolling, then, her commitment and consistency knocked the dreams out of the park. When are you going to step up to the plate?

HEATHER BELL

Self-Publishing Is Pointless Without Fans

....

by Robert Lee Brewer

Heather Bell is sort of a nomad poet in the sense that she's been published extensively in literary journals, but she's self-published two of her poetry collections, including her most recent (*Expletive Deleted*). Her first collection (*How to Make People Love You*) was also self-published, and then, she has two other collections *Nothing Unrequited Here* (Verve Bath Press) and *Facts of Combat* (Achilles Chapbooks).

Heather's work has been published in many publications, including *Rattle, Grasslimb, Barnwood, Poets/Artists,* and *Third Wednesday.* She was nominated for the 2009, 2010, and 2011 Pushcart Prize from *Rattle* and also won the New Letters 2009 Poetry Prize (judged by Kim Addonizio). More details can be found on her blog: http://hrbell.wordpress.com.

Here's a poem from her collection *Expletive Deleted*:

Interview

It has been two years, how am I to
explain the lack of work? Each morning:
the rhinoceros pajamas, the roots growing
from the ceiling, occasionally

the hallucinations. I dip my body slowly
into a suit coat and flatten my
hair. How to explain

that I spent the last two years as a mad
woman? Everyone suggests that I refer to
that time as a "personal matter," instead

of strange, or drowned,

or tailed by men with hound faces.

I slip my resume across the table
like a love note.

My shoes shriek when I get up because
the floor is made of people who watched
this and it made them shocked and sad
that I can still be so untruthful.

What are you currently up to?

I'm currently a stay-at-home mom to a wonderful 18-month-old daughter, Anna, and pregnant with my second. I try to write when I can, but we live in a 100-year-old house that we're doing a complete remodel on, so it can be quite hard to find the time. I did finish my fifth book and am in the process of searching for a home for it.

Your collection *Expletive Deleted* was self-published. What has that experience been like?

My first book, *How To Make People Love You*, was also self-published, so I knew the process at this point. Self-publishing is interesting and I have gotten a lot of writers asking me about it, thinking it's an easy way to success. I generally tell them to publish in journals and magazines first, as self-publishing is pointless without fans of your work (aka customers).

The best way for me to do it (and this is very different for other people) is to buy about 200 copies (my first book went through three reprints, so I thankfully knew my magic number). It will take me a year or more to sell them all, mostly through advertising through social media and word of mouth.

I prefer to use POD publishers in the same way you would make copies of a book you constructed at Kinko's: cut out the middle man (the POD publisher) and just do the work yourself, because at the end of the day, a self-publishing online marketplace really isn't helping you sell your work (I suppose there are exceptions to the rule, but I personally don't troll them looking for books, so I assume others also don't). The only thing you can do is be confident in your work, continue to publish in magazines and journals and let your writing speak for itself.

This isn't a knock at traditional publishing, because I have also gone that route and loved it, but self-publishing can be a good thing depending on how much you believe in your writing and how much other people want to see it.

I know recently you've been submitting work and many of your poems have found homes in literary publications. Do you have a submission process or routine?

My routine is to currently be looking for new magazines that jazz my socks off, through friends and fellow writers. That's really where I start. From there, you obviously have to know what you're submitting to (like using common sense, don't send a sci-fi poem to a magazine that only publishes horror, things like that). Know who are the "big guys" in the business and if you're ready to go there. And prepare yourself to make a three-piece suit out of all the rejections! Ha!

Just have a thick skin and press on.

When you're in love with someone, there are occasional winters where a wolf breaks into your garage and eats all of your emergency stored food.

This voice in your poems is often very immediate and confessional. Do you attempt to draw a line between truth and fiction in your poetry?

This is an interesting question because I get asked it often, specifically about my Klimt poem. The question usually is "is it true?"

Here's a fun writing exercise, go and find a poem that is really boring (feel free to start at any "big" magazine … haha … kidding, kind of!). Then, take their theme and make it into something that a person will walk away from and think about it all day and wonder, "Is it true?"

Here's my issue: I'm tired of love poems where people kiss and make up. When you're in love with someone, there are occasional winters where a wolf breaks into your garage and eats all of your emergency stored food. Can you write a poem about what is on the edges of subjects and then connect it TO your subject?

And no, "Love" is not true, just in case anyone is now wondering. I was actually doing a "Klimt-esque" sort of oil painting and I admit I am a terrible painter, so it looked like the top figure was pushing down on the female. It got me thinking about the original, and how people make assumptions about poems, paintings, every kind of art. If Klimt DID beat his wife, does HIS history make you look at every one of his paintings differently or does it matter?

If I write a therapy poem but I have never been in therapy, does it matter? Or maybe I'm writing now from a mental health clinic. The poem still sits as it does, truthful or not, the point is to make it stay rooted in your brain even when you walk away.

Do you have any pet peeves when reading poetry? Are there things you try to avoid in your own poems?

Boring poems, ha!

I think poets are kind of egomaniacs and we have a tendency to think all our poems are really super amazing and glorious. The trick is to write something and then come back to it as the reader, not the writer. How many poems have I read about the winter's beauty? How many do I remember lines from (not many!).

Modern poetry isn't read by most people simply because it's either flat or so abstract that you need the writer to explain what the heck is going on (at the point in which you are explaining, you have failed, sorry). Anne Carson is actually one of my favorite writers and she can get pretty abstract and yet, still make sense. You have to know what you're doing.

When I write my own poems, I am trying to connect with another human being. Is poetry boring to any person off the street? Yes. Does that person watch back-to-back episodes of *Jersey Shore* at home at night? Maybe. Does that mean we discount that person as someone who can never "get" our poetry? You know what's the true challenge? Writing the *Jersey Shore* of intellectual poems and getting that person to reflect, think about it, and want more.

> Modern poetry isn't read by most people simply because it's either flat or so abstract that you need the writer to explain what the heck is going on (at the point in which you are explaining, you have failed, sorry).

You aren't writing anything dumbed down, you're actually making someone dig deeper, but at the same time be entertained. This is such an issue with me with modern poetry, how it can really ignore a huge population of people and act like some people just aren't smart enough to understand. It's YOUR job to write a poem that makes people think, not the person's job to have to get a Master's Degree in Greek literature in order to understand whatever is in your poetry!

Best poetry experience to date. What is it and why?

Winning the New Letters Poetry Award in 2009! I was in the process of moving from Arizona to New York and we had broken down in a corn field in Indiana (sounds more romantic than it was–ha ha!). I have always thought I was hitting my head against a brick wall and winning made me feel like I had some relevance.

It shouldn't be about awards, but I'm a weak-hearted and scared writer just like anyone else, so it really blew me away. I don't think I ever thanked them enough or truly told them what it meant to me, but maybe someone from New Letters will read this!

Who (or what) are you currently reading?

I'm mostly reading *Green Eggs and Ham* these days. Ha! I actually have a backlog of books that haven't been touched, because I just can't find the time (I still have no ceiling in my dining room, if that's any excuse).

Because I now feel like a terrible person, I will list my all-time favorites: *The Beauty of the Husband*, by Anne Carson; *No One Belongs Here More Than You*, by Miranda July; and anything by Paul Celan, Amy Hempel, Alice Walker, and Sherman Alexie.

If you could share only one piece of advice for other poets, what would it be?

That you can do it. That the world needs you to be there and bright and amazing. I know a lot of writers who blow away anyone being published now, but are too afraid to publish or keep saying they just don't have the time. You do have the time. Because you watched TV today (could have submitted), you brushed your hair (could have submitted), you ate a sandwich (could have submitted) and you spent all afternoon researching new utensils on Amazon (could have submitted).

No excuses, guys. I'm tired of boring poetry, so you need to rise up like crazy apocalyptic looters with backpacks of poems and take over the literary magazines.

CHUCK WENDIG

Hybrid Author Taking Risks

....

by Robert Lee Brewer

Chuck Wendig first came on my radar as a blogger, specifically his Terribleminds blog (terribleminds.com). On the blog, there's a quick about me message: "Chuck Wendig is a novelist, screenwriter, and game designer. This is his blog. He talks a lot about writing. And food. And the madness of toddlers. He uses lots of naughty language. NSFW. Probably NSFL. Be advised."

And that's a great introduction to Wendig, who has carved out a special niche as a blogger, but he's also earned his chops as an author. His novels include *Blackbirds, Mockingbird,* and *Double Dead.* He also writes books on writing, including *250 Things You Should Know About Writing.*

....

He talks a lot about writing. And food. And the madness of toddlers.

....

Outside of being a successful writer, Wendig is hard to define. "As I am what is referred to in the publishing canon as a 'hybrid author,'" Wendig explains, "I walk both self- and traditional-publishing paths.

"In fact, the majority of my work is traditionally published (at this time I have published or am contracted for 16 novels across a variety of small and large publishers)."

How did you get started writing?

I was born and the words came soon after.

More correctly, I wrote stories since I was a wee tiny human, and then one day I saw an opportunity for freelancing in the game industry. I wrote a very pretentious essay about the internal and external loci of fear and got hired for one game-writing job on the basis of that. I was hired again a few more times based on writers who had screwed up their work or who had dropped out.

Many moons later, I wrote my first novel and my first screenplay and now, here I am.

What drew you to self-publishing?

Freedom and control.

What projects are you currently working on?

I'm editing the third book in my Miriam Black series (a cantankerous girl can touch you and see how you're going to die; mayhem ensues), The Cormorant. And I'm writing a new hush-hush can't-talk-about-it book. So shhhh.

Any new projects on the horizon?

My teen detective series, the Atlanta Burns books (which began as a self-published novella and then moved to a Kickstarted sequel) has been picked up by Skyscape (formerly Amazon Children's Publishing). That includes the novella, Shotgun Gravy, and the novel, Bait Dog, along with a follow-up novel, currently titled Frack You.

In your view, what is the hardest part of self-publishing a book?

The lack of hard data across self-publishing. A lot of anecdotal information (aka "artisanal data") out there that creates a lot of noise and a bevy of false expectations.

....

Just the same, it's not like all 20,000 Twitter followers buy my books, you know? Social media for me isn't just about marketing. It's also not about shouting out to my audience, but rather, being among them as a person and a creator, not just a content machine.

....

You have a very active online presence. Do you find online essential to getting the word out about your books?

I don't know that it's essential, but it's very useful. I get 250,000 views at my website, terribleminds.com, per month. I have over 20,000 Twitter followers. So, it's certainly how I amplify my signal and get the word out about my books.

Just the same, it's not like all 20,000 Twitter followers buy my books, you know? Social media for me isn't just about marketing. It's also not about shouting out to my audience but rather, being among them as a person and a creator, not just a content machine.

Do you earn income from products or services that aren't books?

Nope. I am a full-time professional writer. (High-fives self, because it's totally awesome.)

If you could pass on only one piece of advice to other writers looking to self-publish, what would it be?

Take risks and embrace the freedom that self-publishing offers. I see a lot of samey-samey when it comes to indie publishing—if you're going to do the same thing traditional publishing is doing, whether in terms of genre or format, that's not thinking big enough, I suspect.

Take those risks and write what you want to write; embrace your own creative desires above the elusive and often imaginary desires of the so-called "marketplace."

ANDREW E. KAUFMAN

Putting His Readers First

by *Robert Lee Brewer*

Some writers get started in the trade earlier than others. For instance, journalist-turned-author Andrew E. Kaufman says, "I think I was actually born a writer—I suppose a lot of us probably say that, but I almost feel as though it was encoded into my DNA."

Living in Southern California, along with his Labrador Retrievers, two horses, and a very bossy Jack Russell Terrier who thinks she owns the place, Kaufman was named one of the highest-grossing independent authors in the country when his total number of books sold pushed well past the six-figure mark. His recent release, *The Lion, the Lamb, the Hunted: A Psychological Thriller* was on Amazon's Top 100 for more than 100 days. It became their seventh bestselling title out of more than one million e-books available nationwide and number one in its genre.

Kaufman's first novel, *While the Savage Sleeps*, made the Top 100 as well and was number one in its genre, passing up two of Stephen King's current releases at the time. Both books are bestsellers in the UK and Germany, and both books were simultaneously number one in their genres in the U.S.

Kaufman's success resulted in signing an international dual publishing deal with Thomas & Mercer and 47North. His newest work, *Darkness & Shadows*, an intense psychosexual thriller, is due out in 2013. He is represented by Scott Miller, Executive Vice President of Trident Media Group in New York.

His recent success may have helped him secure a great book deal, but it began with a love of the written word. "For as far back as I can remember," Kaufman says, "I've had this insuppressible passion for the written word. I got my first book when I was three, entitled, Nobody Listens to Andrew. For reasons I wasn't quite aware of yet (and also maybe because I shared the protagonist's name), it became my all-time favorite. I used to make my grandmother read it to me constantly. While I'm sure she grew tired of it after about the tenth round, I never did because the message resonated so strongly.

"Because of that, I don't think there was ever any question whether I would write for a living—the hard part was figuring out how to do it."

After receiving his journalism and political science degrees at San Diego State University, Kaufman began his writing career as an Emmy-nominated writer/producer, working at the CBS affiliate in San Diego, and then in Los Angeles. For more than 10 years, he produced special series and covered many nationally known cases, including the O.J. Simpson Trial.

"I suppose in time—and in my own way," Kaufman says, "I finally figured out how to get people to listen to me. By the way, I still have a copy of, *Nobody Listens to Andrew* displayed prominently in my office where I write. I like to look back and remember where it all began."

Did you ever try going the traditional route?

That was actually the next phase. After working in San Diego, I moved on to the number two market in Los Angeles. It was the big time…and it was also where I finally realized I was in the wrong business.

Cranking out minute-and-a half segments and only bare facts was starting to feel old—even more, it felt like a drain on my creative process. I remember writing about real-life events and thinking, *this story would be a hell of a lot more exciting if…*. As you can imagine, at that point, I knew I was in trouble, and as fate would have it, I eventually got laid off.

Being pushed from my comfort zone was good because it forced me to make decisions about the direction I wanted my career to go. I knew I still wanted to be a writer—that never came into question—but the real dilemma was figuring out how to make a living at it. I moved back home to San Diego and decided it was finally time to begin writing the novel I'd been thinking about since I was a kid. At that point, I really didn't know whether I could actually do it, but I figured it was worth a shot.

Being pushed from my comfort zone was good because it forced me to make decisions about the direction I wanted my career to go.

Of course, having a completed manuscript didn't necessarily make me an author—and while I was completely cognizant of this, what I didn't know was that getting it published would seem nearly impossible.

But I was about to find out.

I don't know how many rejections I actually racked up, because I stopped counting after about a hundred. I would send my query letters out to agents, and very quickly (sometimes within seconds) the boilerplate boomerangs came flying back—and that was from the ones who actually bothered responding. It was very discouraging. I knew I had writing skills, but even more than that, deep in my gut, I believed in my manuscript.

What drew you to self-publishing?

That was actually the next chapter (so to speak), and at times, it felt like it might have been the last. After exhausting every avenue and being unable to find agent representation—let alone a publisher—the road ahead was starting to look very narrow and very short. Then the Kindle Publishing Platform came along, and I saw it as my last hope. At that point, nobody knew how huge it would become—certainly, I didn't—and my intent at the time was only to get my work "out there" and, best-case scenario, maybe find a few readers. So, I uploaded my novel and with a shaky finger, hit the "Publish" button.

Unfortunately, after that I faced a different kind of rejection.

I think I sold a total of four books my first month—one of them I bought, and my editor was kind enough to buy another. The second month wasn't much better and produced similar results. Still, I refused to give up. I wrote the manuscript while battling cancer, losing my mother to it, and after becoming unemployed. Comparatively speaking, conquering this battle felt like a ride on the gravy train.

So I got busy studying everything I could about marketing, speaking to every author who would talk to me, and spending six-plus hours a night learning the fine art of promotion.

And finally, it paid off.

A few months later, *While the Savage Sleeps* started gaining traction, and I began working even harder. Before I knew it, the book was climbing the bestsellers lists, eventually becoming #1 in its genre (even passing up two of Stephen King's current releases at the time).

....

I love telling that story, especially to unpublished writers, because I've completely been where they are now—but I want them to know they can totally do this regardless of how impossible it might seem. I want them to know what I've learned: do not give up.

....

A year after finding my audience, I released my next book, *The Lion, the Lamb, the Hunted*: a *psychological thriller*, and the results were even better. It took off like a rocket and spent more than 100 days on Amazon's Top 100, becoming their seventh bestselling novel out of over one-million available worldwide. My number of books sold had pushed into the six-figure mark, and soon the agents were actually contacting me.

As you might imagine, it was one of those surreal moments in life, and even now it's difficult to quantify with words—all I really could do was smile. Even though these were the people who rejected me, it was an amazing and wonderful feeling. I never felt like, *I showed you*; it was more like *I showed me*. I love telling that story, especially to unpublished writers, because I've completely been where they are now—but I want them to know they can totally do this regardless of how impossible it might seem. I want them to know what I've learned: do not give up.

So to make a very long story short, oddly enough, I ended up landing exactly where my target had been from the start, despite taking a circuitous route to get there. I ended up finding my dream agent, and then signing a dual publishing deal with Thomas & Mercer and 47North.

You're repped by Scott Miller of Trident Media Group. How did you both connect, and what's that relationship like?
He was actually one of the agents who contacted me, and I liked him right from the get-go. Trident is one of the biggest agencies in the world, and Scott is one of the best. Besides being authentic and dedicated, he's a straight shooter and very smart.

....

When you sign with an agent, you trust him with your career— that's a really big deal.

....

Even more important, he's just a really nice guy who I can relate to. That's so important in this business. When you sign with an agent, you trust him with your career— that's a really big deal.

What projects are you currently working on?
Right now we're wrapping up production on *Darkness & Shadows*, which is due out on October 22. I just got the proofs back for the interior and cover, and I'm so damned excited about this one I can hardly stand it.

I'm also currently working on my next book for Thomas & Mercer, which will be out in October of 2014. It's another psychological thriller, a standalone, and it's the book I've been dying to write my whole life but was never sure whether I had the skill to accomplish. With three books under my belt, I finally felt confident enough to take that leap.

To my surprise, I finished the first draft in just under six weeks, which has never happened for me. I'm a notoriously slow writer, but somehow, the words seemed to flow from my fingertips to the keyboard, so I guess the time was in fact right.

Any new projects on the horizon?

I'm not really sure where I'm headed next, but oddly enough that feels great. It's a wonderful thing to reach a point in my career where I can actually say that and not feel worried.

I know I'll keep writing books, and hopefully, I'll keep getting better at it.

Your novel Darkness & Shadows comes out October 2013. Could you give a brief synopsis of that book?

I'd love to: The only woman Patrick Bannister ever loved has died ... again.

Struggling professionally and reeling from the psychological wounds left by a horribly abusive mother, Patrick is driven over the edge by a news report. A wealthy socialite couple has been murdered, and while the wife's name isn't familiar, her face certainly is. It's his first and only love, Marybeth, the woman who he lost to a horrific fire years ago.

Is he losing his mind?

Patrick's obsession to find the truth sends him scouring records and documents that lead to a shocking discovery: there's no evidence Marybeth ever lived or, for that matter, ever died. Was the love of Patrick's life just a product of his abused psyche?

The truth may kill him.

His quest for answers takes him on a twisted mental odyssey that forces him to question his own reality. He might not be able to trust his memories and perceptions of the past, but the answers may still lie in the darkest recesses of his mind.

But Patrick will soon find out that by stoking the flames from that long ago fire, he's blazing a path straight into danger. And this time, not only is he about to get burned—he could also end up losing his life.

> Though I've managed to find my readers, there's no guarantee I'll keep them, so each time I release a new book, it feels as though I'm starting all over again, because I find so much has changed.

In your view, what is the hardest part of self-publishing a book?

Without a doubt, finding and keeping an audience.

When I started out, things weren't nearly as difficult as they are now, and nobody could have guessed the pool would get so deep and so wide. That said, it's not showing any signs of slowing down, and the competition is only becoming more fierce. Though I've managed to find my readers, there's no guarantee I'll keep them, so each time I release a new book, it feels as though I'm starting all over again, because I find so much has changed.

I used to obsess over this until I realized that all I can do is keep writing the best books I'm capable of and hope the rest takes care of itself.

How do you go about getting the word out about your books?

I actually get e-mail messages regularly from authors asking me this question, and they go something like this: "What's your secret?"

I have to laugh sometimes, because I honestly don't know what to tell them and because there really is no secret. I've tried to figure out what led to my success, and each time I seem to come back to the same thing: it's all about the readers—I treat them like gold (because they are that important to me) and write the best books I can for them.

....

You have to love interacting with your audience and enjoy investing time in them. I realize how simplistic that sounds, but that's how I market my books.

....

I communicate with my audience on the various social media sites, but even more, I listen to what they tell me. Most importantly, I never forget for a second that they are the ones who helped get me where I am today. I always tell people that I built my readership one person at a time, and that's completely true.

And really, it's that simple. There's no formula. I still know many of my readers' names and even some of their dogs' names. In today's publishing climate, marketing means so much more than advertising. You have to love interacting with your audience and enjoy investing time in them. I realize how simplistic this sounds, but that's how I market my books.

Do you earn income from products or services that aren't books?

I'm fortunate (and thrilled) to be able to say that writing is my full-time job!

How do you balance your writing time with everything else that goes with self-publishing?

I do my best to stay up on the latest news but spend a majority of the time writing 8 to 12 hours a day, seven days a week. Quite honestly, my books are the number one priority, and everything else has to take a back seat.

Being with a publisher means there are deadlines to meet, and I take those very seriously. So I do the best I can to keep up with the ever-changing industry trends but try not to be hard on myself when I can't keep up on them.

If you could pass on only one piece of advice to other writers looking to self-publish, what would it be?

Don't shoot yourself in the foot before you ever get out of the gate by making the same mistake so many others have. Do not release your work before it's ready just because you can. You only get one chance to make a first impression, so make it your best. Your readers deserve that, but even more, you deserve that for yourself.

Hire an editor, and spend the time necessary to craft a great story and polish your writing—if you do this, I guarantee the readers will reward you for it.

SELF-PUBLISHING COMPANIES

///

Finding a self-publishing company willing to work with you on your book project is relatively easy. However, some self-publishing companies are better fits for your specific project than others. For instance, some companies may specialize in e-publishing but not do much in print. Others may have a long history in print but not cover every platform you want in digital publishing.

On top of that, some self-publishing companies offer an array of extra services, including assistance with editing, proofing, design, promotion, and more. Depending on the goals for your self-published book, you may or may not want to spend a lot of money on these extras. Since pricing can add quick if you do go with these extras, shop around before settling on the first company you find.

You may find that extra expenses for book design are more affordable by using a freelance designer. Also, editing-related expenses may be better serviced by a freelance editor. Check pricing and experience before spending a lot of money you may never recoup.

If you're unsure of what reasonable freelance rates are for a service, check out the "How Much Should I Charge?" pay rate chart. It lists various services with their most common pay scales, including highs, lows, and averages.

KEEP IN MIND

Self-publishing requires a lot of research and iniative. After all, self-publishers wear more hats than anyone else in publishing: author, publisher, marketer, publicist, accountant, designer, editor, and more. While writers can see that success is possible by reading the interviews in this book, it should also be noted that it's a competitive business. As such, avoid letting any service provider "sweep you off your feet" and/or put "stars in your eyes" when it comes to self-publishing. Rather, stay grounded and price conscious.

Writers can have a very successful self-publishing experience, but the whole point behind self-publishing is that they're now in control of the business side of publishing, in addition to the writing. As a business owner, do your due diligence and research which options are best for your book project.

ABBOTT PRESS

F+W Media, Inc., 10151 Carver Road, Suite #200, Blue Ash OH 45242. (866)697-5310. **Website:** www.abbottpress.com.

ADDITIONAL INFORMATION "Abbott Press offers publishing services that will help your book stand out in the marketplace. Throughout the entire publishing process you have the freedom to determine when and how your book is published. No matter if your goal is to publish for family and friends or advance an already successful writing career, we can help you achieve your goals."

ARBOR BOOKS

244 Madison Ave., #254, New York NY 10016. (877)822-2500. **E-mail:** info@arborbooks.com. **Website:** www.arborbooks.com. **Contact:** Marketing Director: Olga Vladimirov.

ADDITIONAL INFORMATION "Arbor Books is a full-service ghostwriting and book-packaging company with a full-time staff of 15 writers, designers, and publicists, as well as 85 subcontractors, including the world's top printers, distributors, and other publishing experts and services. Arbor Books ghostwrites and publishes fiction and nonfiction including business books, novels, children's books, memoirs, and every other literary form and genre. Arbor Books services include ghostwriting, editing, rewriting, proofreading, research, typesetting, cover design, registrations (copyright, Library of Congress, ISBN, Books In Print), getting reviews and endorsements, printing, e-books, audio books, POD (print on demand) books, book marketing, kits, press releases, booking TV and radio programs, book and author publicity, speaking tours and book signings, negotiating with producers and agents, and more. Cost: Submit quote request online or contact by phone. See website for additional information

ARDITH PUBLISHING

8345 NW 66th St., #7689, Miami FL 33166. (877)288-0114. **Fax:** (305)351-0685. **E-mail:** info@ardithpublishing.com. **Website:** www.ardithpublishing.com.

ADDITIONAL INFORMATION "Ardith is a self-publishing service company that provides book editing, design, marketing, publicity, distribution, and printing services to both the United States and Canada." Services in their self-publishing package ($399) include paperback or hardcover formatting; predesigned page and cover layouts; and registration with major online booksellers, national distributors, and Books in Print; book printing and shipping costs are not included. Non-package services available at individual cost include manuscript evaluation, copyediting, content editing, ghostwriting, research/fact checking, proofreading, indexing, book and cover layout and design, e-book conversion, marketing campaigns, and book distribution. Cost: Provides online book printing calculator; contact for final price estimate. See website for breakdown of all pricing and additional information.

ARTISAN BOOKWORKS

Sequim WA 98382. (425)954-5277. **E-mail:** contact@artisanbookworks.com. **Website:** www.artisanbookworks.com. **Contact:** Kelly Lenihan, owner/designer. Estab. 2008. KSL Designs - Web Design & Consulting was established in 2008. To meet market demands, the company expanded its offerings and was renamed Artisan Bookwords in 2012.

ADDITIONAL INFORMATION "Finding the right company to provide publishing services can be a daunting task. Whether you are writing a book, promoting your work, or searching for online publishing services to self-publish your book, Artisan Bookworks provides an array of services, enabling you to customize your publishing experience. At Artisan Bookworks, we offer a variety of fee-based editorial, graphic design, and book-formatting services tailored to meet your needs, whether you simply need your book formatted for Kindle or everything from copyediting to final cover design. We also provide custom WordPress and website design, and Facebook and Twitter customization."

ASTA PUBLICATIONS

P.O. Box 1735, Stockbridge GA 30281. (678)814-1320. **Fax:** (678)814-1370. **E-mail:** info@astapublications.com. **Website:** www.astapublications.com.

ADDITIONAL INFORMATION "Our mission is to continue building Asta Publications into company that is respected by our authors, our clients, and our peers, while maintaining our firm resolve to effectively deliver a superior product."

KATHY BOLTZ PH.D.

Phoenix AZ 85044. (480)235-8517 (cell). **E-mail:** kathy.boltz@cox.net. **Website:** www.kathybphd.com. **Contact:** Kathy Boltz.

ADDITIONAL INFORMATION Kathy Boltz is an expert at medical writing and consulting who has been freelancing for a year. She has excellent written and oral communication skills in English and is experienced at editing manuscripts by ESL authors. Kathy is familiar with ICH, CONSORT, GPP2, and AMA Manual of Style. She is proficient with Microsoft Word, PowerPoint, Excel, Adobe Acrobat, EndNote, RefManager, and SigmaPlot. Her Ph.D. is in Plant Biology, emphasis on biochemistry and enzymology, Arizona State Univ. See a list of her skills on her website. "Selected areas of expertise: Biochemistry, glycobiology, biophysics, biotechnology, bacterial infection, antibiotics, cell biology, cancer biology, host-pathogen interactions, influenza, immunology, infectious disease, microarrays, nutrition, food science, food chemistry, peptides, structural biochemistry, analytic and synthetic chemistry, bioengineering, enzymology, molecular biology."

BOOKLOCKER.COM, INC.

P.O. Box 2399, Bangor ME 04402-2399. **Website:** www.booklocker.com.

ADDITIONAL INFORMATION "Booklocker is a print-on-demand and e-book publishing services and distribution company. We help authors who want to self-publish get their book into the market quickly usually within a month using print-on-demand and e-book technology. Using print-on-demand technology, we offer a package where authors can produce their manuscripts as print books, and have those print books sold directly to a customer via the Internet, including through sites like Amazon.com, as well as offered to bookstores who would then resell the books to customers. Our e-books are in PDF and/or EPUB format and our system lets customers instantly download the e-book after they purchase it." BookLocker does all sales, fulfillment, and customer service tasks associated with selling a book. The author retains all rights to the book and can terminate with 24-hours notice via email.

BOOKMOBILE

5120 Cedar Lake Rd., Minneapolis MN 55416. (763)398-0030. **Fax:** (763)398-0198. **E-mail:** rholscher@bookmobile.com. **Website:** www.bookmobile.com. **Contact:** Rachel Holscher, Manager of Design & Publishing Services. Estab. 1996.

ADDITIONAL INFORMATION Offers print-on-demand and e-book services as well as hard cover and softcover printing. Services include content editing and copyediting, cover and interior design, page lay-

out, print management, and distribution. Cost: Submit quote requests online. See website for additional information.

BOOKPROS

8716 N. Mopac Expressway, Ste. 200, Austin TX 78759. (512)623-7270. **Fax:** (512)236-5138. **E-mail:** info@bookpros.com. **Website:** www.bookpros.com. "BookPros is an independent publishing firm offering

ADDITIONAL INFORMATION "BookPros is an independent publishing firm offering editing, cover and interior design, publishing, printing, distribution, and publicity services to authors. BookPros has three imprints with various distribution options through collaborations with Ingram, Baker & Taylor, Midpoint Trade Books, and National Book Network. Printing options include hardcover and paperback. Cost: Each proposal is custom-created but BookPros has an online form for a free book analysis and consultation. See website for additional information."

BRAVADO PUBLISHING

1196 Echo Dr., Roseburg OR 97470. (541)673-0636. **E-mail:** kristen@bravadopublishing.com. **Website:** www.bravadopublishing.com. **Contact:** Kristen James, Editor.

ADDITIONAL INFORMATION "Speciality in custom layout and personal service. We publish novels, nonfiction, poetry, cookbooks, color children's books, art books, family history, anthologies, hardcover for b&w interior books, or any other type of project you would like to see in published book form. Offering many sizes and binding types." Services include editing/critiquing, proofreading, industry book formatting, cover design, barcode, ISBN, and distribution. Cost:$600- $1000. Contact for price quote on custom publishing package (including color children's book); editing is .02/word; proofreading is .50/page. See website for additional information.

BROWN BOOKS PUBLISHING GROUP

16200 N. Dallas Parkway, Suite 170, Dallas TX 75248. **E-mail:** publishing@brownbooks.com. **Website:** www.brownbooks.com. Ian Birnbaum, editor. **Contact:** Kathryn Grant, acquisitions editor. "Brown Books Publishing Group provides a wide variety of professional book publishing services that will put your book on the road to book publishing success. Our publishing services offer various combinations of publishing, marketing and editorial features. Perhaps most importantly, you retain all the rights to your book and you are in control of its production."

ADDITIONAL INFORMATION Brown Books Publishing Group is a full-service independent publisher committed to producing high quality, award-winning books of all genres for authors who choose to retain the rights to their intellectual property. Milli Brown formed Brown Books Publishing Group based on one central concept, "building successful relationships with authors in order to develop Manhattan quality books for those who wish to retain the rights to their intellectual property and keep the profits from their books' sales. Brown Books Publishing Group ushered in a New Era in Publishing, helping authors navigate the often complicated world of publishing and offering expert guidance in manuscript development, creative design, fulfillment, distribution, marketing and public relations. At Brown Books, authors gain the best of both worlds by taking advantage of over fifteen years of publishing expertise while retaining complete control over their projects."

CCB PUBLISHING

E-mail: info@ccbpublishing.com. **Website:** www.ccbpublishing.com.

ADDITIONAL INFORMATION Print-on-demand book and e-book publisher. Distribution channels include Ingram Books, Baker & Taylor, and the Espresso Book Machine® (EBM), an ATM-style on-site book printer. Contact or see website for additional information.

CHANGEMAKERS PUBLISHING AND WRITING

750 La Playa, #952, San Francisco CA 94121. (415)571-8282. **Website:** www.changemakerspublishingand-writing.com. **Contact:** Gini Graham Scott, Ph.D., J.D. Estab. 1968.

ADDITIONAL INFORMATION "I consult with and write books, articles, and scripts for clients, working from rough drafts, notes, interviews, tapes of workshops/seminars, and other materials. I also help clients publish and promote their books or find mainstream publishers, agents, and film producers. I have published over 50 books of my own, have written 15 original scripts, several under option, and have written, produced, and sometimes directed over 40 short films, including book and script trailers, which can be seen at www.youtube.com/changemakersprod. I also conduct workshops, seminars, teleseminars, and We-binars on writing, publishing, and promoting one's books and articles."

COLORPAGE

formerly Tri-State Litho, 71 Ten Broeck Ave., Kingston NY 12401. (800)836-7581. **Fax:** (845)331.1571. **Website:** www.colorpageonline.com.

ADDITIONAL INFORMATION Print-on-demand publisher. "We can create unique publications in short-runs, at affordable prices. Use our instant, online book price wizard for your next project." Cost, additional information, and free publishing guide available.

CONTENT KINGPIN

29 via Regalo, San Clemente CA 92673. (949)813-0182. **E-mail:** amy@sourcedmediabooks.com. **Website:** www.contentkingpin.com. **Contact:** Amy Cook, publisher. Estab. 2009. Content Kingpin creates and manages premium-quality content for businesses, brands, and authors. "Prices are affordable to help individuals and small businesses build their platforms, engage their audiences, and identify with their consumers right along with Fortune 500 companies."

ADDITIONAL INFORMATION Services include book publishing, website design and hosting, press releases, publicity tours, blog tours, marketing materials, social media management, ghostwriting, list building, newsletters, contests and giveaways, audiobooks, videography, photography, illustration, business and legal services, affiliate marketing, and market research.

CREATESPACE

Amazon.com Inc., 100 Enterprise Way, Suite A200, Scotts Valley CA 95066. **E-mail:** info@createspace.com. **Website:** www.createspace.com. **Contact:** David Keys, Exec. Customer Relations. Estab. 2007.

ADDITIONAL INFORMATION "BookSurge and CreateSpace are uniting under the CreateSpace platform and brand to offer you more publishing options than ever before. In addition to the same personal customer care, professional publishing services, and top-notch print quality authors currently receive at BookSurge, you can also take advantage of these great options and benefits through CreateSpace: Flexible royalty model allows you to set your own list price and royalty. Save with everyday, low wholesale book pricing, regardless of order quantity! Choose the do-it-yourself publishing option with no setup fees if you have print-ready PDF files or take advantage of professional book design, editing, and marketing services if you're looking for more assistance. Network with thousands of other authors and industry professionals in the free online CreateSpace Community. Gather feedback on your work using the free Preview tool."

DADIVAN BOOKS

3104 E. Camelback Road #160, Phoenix AZ 85016. (347)291-1779. **Fax:** (928)268-9181. **E-mail:** dadivanbooks@gmail.com. **Website:** www.dadivanbooks.com. **Contact:** Bootsie Martinez, editor. Estab. 1989. "We are professional writers, editors, and publishers with over a century of combined experience in the publishing world."

ADDITIONAL INFORMATION Dadivan Books also offers complete self-publishing from soup-to-nuts, including economical subsidy publishing services. "We specialize in helping authors achieve their individual dreams, whether that dream is improving a manuscript through proofreading or editing, preparing a manuscript in e-publishing formats, preparing a manuscript in paperback layout, designing the perfect cover, or fulfilling another editorial need, including ghostwriting and book doctoring. All services are available a la carte or as part of an economical package."

E-BOOK TIME, LLC

6598 Pumpkin Rd., Montgomery AL 36108. (877) 613-2665. **E-mail:** publishing@e-booktime.com. **Website:** www.e-booktime.com. Estab. 2004.

ADDITIONAL INFORMATION "Whether it's Christian publishing, poetry publishing, or some other genre, we can make your dream of getting your book published a reality. Don't worry about formatting your manuscript. We will take care of everything needed to format your manuscript into a published book you can be proud of. Important points to consider: Paperback $395. Hardcover and paperback $695. Sold by BarnesandNoble.com, Amazon.com and others. Five free copies. You keep all rights. Discounted book price for authors. Printed manuscripts accepted. Ready in 4-6 weeks. Excellent royalty rates. ISBN assigned to print books. Copyright registration service. Copyedit service available."

EPIGRAPH PUBLISHING SERVICE

27 Lamoree Rd., Rhinebeck NY 12572. (845)876-4861. **E-mail:** Bookcohen@aol.com. **Website:** www.epigraph.com.

ADDITIONAL INFORMATION "Epigraph Publishing Service offers a full range of services for authors, organizations, and other publishing companies. Our services are available on an ala carte basis or as part of a publishing plan." Package services include book interior and cover design, ISBN, Library of Congress, and barcode. Individual services available at additional cost include copyediting, proofreading, line editing, developmental editing, ghostwriting, indexing, and marketing and publicity services; see website for pricing. Cost: Full custom design and book distribution packages start at $899. Contact or see website for additional information.

GLOBAL AUTHORS PUBLICATIONS

E-mail: gapbook@yahoo.com. **Website:** www.globalauthorspublications.com. **Contact:** Kathleen Walls.

ADDITIONAL INFORMATION "GAP offers the best of both worlds. Now you can have the convenience and low cost of print-on-demand and the returnability and pricing of your own self-publishing company." Books must be at least 48 pages and not more than 700 pages. Cost: $2,000 (payable in 2 installments) with an annual $150 fee to cover recordkeeping. Cost includes one copy of book, copyediting, formatting, photographic cover design, ISBN, registration in *Books in Print*, a Library of Congress number, membership in an authors' forum, and book link on the GAP website. Contact or see website for additional information.

GOOSE RIVER PRESS

3400 Friendship Rd., Waldoboro ME 04572. (207)832-6665. **E-mail:** gooseriverpress@roadrunner.com. **Website:** www.gooseriverpress.com.

ADDITIONAL INFORMATION Traditional royalty publisher who also offers a self-publishing option. "Self-publishing services are offered to those books that do not meet our high standards for publication or those who simply choose to publish themselves. We offer copy editing and typesetting services for those who need help preparing camera-ready copy, complete book production (we can print as few as 50 copies), and promotion. We work with Ingram, Baker & Taylor, Barnes & Noble, Amazon.com, and more. For those who wish to self-publish under another press name, Goose River Press can provide fee-based editing and printing services at competitive rates." Send SASE for complete information or send us e-mail.

IBJ BOOK PUBLISHING

IBJ Media, 41 East Washington St., Ste. 200, Indianapolis IN 46204. (317)634-6200. **Fax:** (317)263-5402. **E-mail:** info@ibjbp.com. **Website:** www.ibjbookpublishing.com.

ADDITIONAL INFORMATION "We are a full-service resource for authors who want to self-publish the highest quality book in a professional, cost effective and timely manner." Optional services available include book coaching, copyediting, proofreading, ebook conversion, print on demand services, an online booksotre, placement on amazon and marketing collateral. Cost: Contact for a quick estimate.

INSIDEOUT PRESS

P.O. Box 2666, Country Club Hills IL 60478. (708)957-6047. **E-mail:** kim@insideoutpress.com. **Website:** www.insideoutpress.com. **Contact:** Kim Olver, president. Estab. 2009.

ADDITIONAL INFORMATION "We are a full-service self-publishing company, providing cover design, personalized back cover, interior page layout, image insertion, ISBN assignment, eBook formatting, Amazon and Barnes & Noble set-up, Amazon search inside program, personalized InsideOutPress Bookstore page, promotional materials, social media set-up, book signing kit, index service, Library of Congress control number, US copyright registration, author website set-up, media kit set-up, and printer estimates."

LAREDO PUBLISHING

465 Westview Ave., Englewood NJ 07631. (201)408-4048. **Fax:** (201)408-5011. **Website:** www.laredopublishing.com. Estab. 1991.

ADDITIONAL INFORMATION Co-edition publisher. "We are a seasoned publishing company, providing editorial, production, translation, and creative services to help our clients develop content-driven products." Cost: General Publications: Economy ($299), Executive ($1.499), and Ambassador ($2,199). Star ($499), Gold ($899), and Platinum ($2,899) children's book packages. See website for additional information.

LB PRESS

750 Putnam Dr., Reno NV 89530. **Website:** lbpresspublishing.com. **Contact:** Cindie Geddes, co-owner. Estab. 2009. LB Press, a subsidiary of Lucky Bat Books, is a full-service fee-based publishing company, offering one-on-one project management and personalized care for writers wanting full control of their work.

ADDITIONAL INFORMATION "We work with writers to find just the right combination of services to help make each project a success. We do not upsell; our fees are all listed on our site; we take no percentages and we encumber no rights. You wrote it; you own it."

LLUMINA PRESS

7101 W. Commercial Blvd., Suite 4E, Tamarac FL 33319. (954) 726-0902. **Fax:** (954) 726-0903. **Website:** www.llumina.com. **Contact:** Deborah Greenspan.

ADDITIONAL INFORMATION "*Llumina Press* was created by writers for writers. We know how to help you because we've been there. We know how it feels to get a rejection letter, and how it feels to finally get that book published. We've been through writer's block, torn our collective hair out trying to find exactly the right words, and suffered over whether to leave our finest phrases in or take them out. We are experienced writers and editors, and after eleven years of publishing, we've got a handle on that too."

OMEGA PUBLICATIONS

15826 Cherry Cove, Palm Springs CA 92262. (858) 222-4550. **E-mail:** info@omegapublications.net. **Website:** www.omegapublications.net. Gayle Farmer, editor. **Contact:** Jeff Farmer, publisher.

ADDITIONAL INFORMATION "Set-up fees: $1,050 Basic Paperback Package; $1,450 Paperback plus E-book Package. Standard products/services: POD Publishing, Editing, Page Layout, Cover Design. Additional services: eBook Setup, Hardcover and Paperback editions, Kindle Editions, Full distribution, Author market material, author Websites, PressKits, Copywriting. Details: When it comes to producing books, speed is not the only consideration and POD printers are as different as night and day. Attention to detail is job one at Omega Publications. From editing your manuscript to designing your book cover we work to make your book the best it can be. Our printer pays close attention to craftsmanship when producing your book. Ten quality control checks on each book, sharp cover graphics and crisp text. You will find the quality of your book is superior to many of the books on bookstands today."

ROSEDOG BOOKS

Dorrance Publishing Co., Inc., 701 Smithfield St., Ste. 301, Pittsburgh PA 15222. (866)380-0923. **E-mail:**

rosedog@rosedogbooks.com. **Website:** www.rose-dog.com.

ADDITIONAL INFORMATION Print-on-demand publisher of print and digital books. Package services include author support, book production (cover, page design, and printing), industry registrations (ISBN, copyright, and Library of Congress), and merchandising; editing, illustration, and promotion services available at additional cost. Cost: RoseDog Basic, $980; RoseDog Basic with Promotion, $1,980. Offers free publishing guide. See website for additional information.

SCHIEL & DENVER BOOK PUBLISHERS

10685-B Hazelhurst Dr., Ste. 8575, Houston TX 77043. (888)629-4449. **E-mail:** enquiries@schieldenver.com. **Website:** www.schieldenver.com. Estab. 2008.

ADDITIONAL INFORMATION "Schiel & Denver is a book publishing services infrastructure provider, with a strong international dimension. We specialize in providing a comprehensive range of ISBN book publishing, book production, editorial, book marketing, and global book distribution solutions for authors and creative people, with the support of a professional book publishing team. The company publishes in a broad range of writing genres, and publishes children's books under our Heirloom imprint." Services include professional editing and transcription, book design and artwork, printing, copyright and registration, marketing and publicity, bookselling, and author website design. Cost: Offers a range of packages starting at $599; package descriptions and rates provided online. Offers free publishing guide and online publishing tutorials. Also operates an office in the United Kingdom. Contact or see website for additional information.

SYNTAX AND STYLE

North Andover MA 01845. **E-mail:** mary@syntaxandstyle.com. **Website:** www.syntaxandstyle.com. **Contact:** Mary McAvoy, owner/founder. Estab. 2006. Syntax and Style will customize a web platform for an author. Web platform consists of website, blog, Facebook fan page, LinkedIn profile, Twitter account.

ADDITIONAL INFORMATION Syntax and Style will also guide an author through the process of self-publishing.

WELLSPRING BOOKS

Divison of Sourced Media Books, 29 via Regalo, San Clemente CA 92673. (949)813-0182. **E-mail:** amy@sourcedmediabooks.com. **Website:** www.wellspring-book.com. **Contact:** Amy Cook, publisher. Estab. 2009. Wellspring Books is the self-publishing division of Sourced Media Books, a traditional publishing company based in California.

ADDITIONAL INFORMATION Offering a full spectrum of services, from developmental editing to final press production, Wellspring Books offers traditional publishing quality at self-publishing prices. Some of these services include coaching, copy editing, typesetting, proofreading, cover design, ISBN registration, Library of Congress registration, working with digital and/or offset presses, and distribution (national, online, or both). Website design and marketing services are also available upon request.

WHITEHALL PRINTING COMPANY

4244 Corporate Square, Naples FL 34104. (800)321-9290. **Fax:** (239)643-6439. **E-mail:** info@whitehall-printing.com. **Website:** www.whitehallprinting.com. Estab. 1959.

ADDITIONAL INFORMATION Book printer. Softcover book manufacturing from 100 to 25,000 copies. Design, editing and fulfillment. Contact or see website for additional information.

WINDWARD RESOURCES, LLC

P.O. Box 214, Shoreham VT 05770. **E-mail:** windwardesq@gmail.com. **Contact:** Ann Dumaresq, director/managing editor. Estab. 2009. Windward specializes in guiding the nonfiction author by means of providing full service editing, book design, and self-publishing assistance.

ADDITIONAL INFORMATION "Staffed by former St. Martin's Press and Macmillan professionals, one of our current projects is to edit and design Dr. James Martin's 462-page book, for which the working title is *The War and Peace of the Nuclear Age*."

EDITORIAL SERVICES

///

Finding the right editor for your project can make the difference between success and failure. One knock against self-publishing that still persists is that self-published books are of lesser quality. By using freelance editors, you can work to overcome that specific hurdle in the self-publishing process.

However, there are a variety of editing services available with different pricing structures. It's important to remember that sometimes you get what you pay for, and it's possible to pay (or overpay) for services you don't really need. The "How Much Should I Charge?" pay rate chart should help with determining an appropriate fee with your freelance editor.

Beyond determining a fair rate, self-publishers need to know what type of editorial assistance they need. For instance, do you just need someone to read through the manuscript for bad spelling and grammar? Do you need fact checking assistance? Could you use help with the structure and pacing?

Each service may have a different fee and a different amount of time required to complete the work. In determining freelance rates, you'll need to know the hourly rate and time requirement to assign a fair fee that will result in quality work. Setting unfair expectations is bad for the freelancer, but it also puts your project at risk, because you're counting on the freelancers to give their best.

KEEP IN MIND

Starting locally will allow you to research each company carefully and learn about their past performance and make it easier to have face-to-face discussions about the manuscript. Realize that any face-to-face time and time on the phone may be considered "billable hours" by your freelancer. Be sure to agree on all such fees and get it in writing before starting work.

It will help ensure a more professional working relationship and provide both sides with more security.

Going local is not a requirement. In fact, you may find that going with another editor outside of your area is more affordable or provides you with a freelancer who has better qualifications. Always ask for previous experience and consider checking references, especially if you're investing a lot of money in the editorial process. After all, you want to make sure your money will be money well spent.

ACTION EDITORS

P.O. Box 53036, CO Ryan Reeh, Washington DC 20009. **E-mail:** jenniferkuhneditor@gmail.com. **Website:** http://actioneditors.wordpress.com. **Contact:** Jennifer Kuhn, MPS, editor. Estab. 2011.

ADDITIONAL INFORMATION "Action Editors is a team of 3 writing and editing professionals, each holding a Master's degree in Publishing from GWU. Together we have backgrounds in and over 25 years of combined experience in public relations, scholarly publishing, newsroom, nonprofit, teaching, and freelance work." Editing Services: substantive editing, basic copy editing, proofreading. Writing Services: press releases, career documents, web copy, e-mail marketing copy & more. Project Management Services: peer review management, transfer of copyright management, permissions management.

A+EDITHER

Las Vegas NV. **E-mail:** susangarcia@aplusedither.com. **Website:** http://aplusedither.com. **Contact:** Susan Garcia, editor.

ADDITIONAL INFORMATION Years in field: 5. Years as a freelancer: 1. "Primary Services I Provide: Editing (nonfiction preferred): I bring a unique editing perspective to material on leadership and management, human resources, or self-help topics. As a former senior leader and instructor at a military academy, I not only "walked the talk" but also taught curriculum on conflict management, organizational behavior, team-building, communication skills, personality assessments (e.g., Myers-Briggs Type Indicator, DiSC), motivational theory, etc. Editing (technical): As a full-time technical editor, I ensured subject matter experts clearly conveyed their ideas and research to a wider audience. My focus is always to improve the clarity of the language without "dumbing down" the content. I not only improve the narratives of technical documents but also enhance accompanying tables, graphs, figures, and maps. Always seeking to improve my skills, I am currently enrolled in the Technical Communication certification at the University of California, San Diego. Copyediting/Proofreading: Naturally meticulous and detail oriented, I have an affinity for editing each line of your writing. I will find and resolve the grammar, syntax, punctuation, and formatting issues, being careful not to change your stylistic voice or intended meaning. I am certified in the Professional Sequence in Editing program, University

of California, Berkeley." See previous experience at www.the-efa.org/members/data/resumes/garcias.pdf.

TIINA ALEMAN

P. O. Box 6635, Jersey City NJ 07306. (551)580-0428. **E-mail:** tiinaaleman@gmail.com. **Contact:** Tiina Aleman.

ADDITIONAL INFORMATION Editor specializing in copy editing and translation editing. Worked in desktop publishing as production editor; worked in type shops as a copy editor and proofreader. Translates from the Estonian into English. Received her editorial certification. Skills: Manuscript editing, copyediting, line editing, translation editing, copywriting, proofreading, typography, desktop publishing, prepress, production management, project management, web development, production and site management. Proficient in the following software applications: InDesign, Photoshop, Illustrator; Adobe Professional and Distiller; QuarkXpress, FrontPage; Word; Fetch; BarCode Producer; DropStuff; Suitcase; ScanWizard; Entourage; Outlook; Skype. She is looking for any editorial projects that can be done off-site. See more at www.the-efa.org/members/data/resumes/iannottita.txt.

ALEUROMANCY

Anna Genoese Freelance Editorial Services. **E-mail:** anna@annagenoese.com. **Website:** www.annagenoese.com. **Contact:** Anna Genoese.

ADDITIONAL INFORMATION Services offered include developmental editing, polishing, copyediting, and proofreading.

ALL MY BEST BUSINESS AND NONFICTION COPYEDITING

5852 Oak Meadow Dr., Yorba Linda CA 92886. (714)777-1238. **E-mail:** lynette@allmybest.net. **Website:** www.allmybest.net. **Contact:** Lynette M. Smith.

ADDITIONAL INFORMATION "Contact Lynette Smith, owner of ALL MY BEST Business and Nonfiction Copyediting, to benefit from her 30 years' experience in proofreading and copyediting, up to and including the level of minor rewrites. Lynette can help you, whether you're a nonfiction author, publisher, printing firm, small business, corporation, consultant, speaker, marketer, teacher, or graduate student. She is most familiar with APA (American Psychological Association) and AP (Associated Press) style formats, is competent in Chicago Manual of Style, and can adapt to your house style or personal writing style as needed. Visit website for more information, including testimonials and free writing tips. When you're ready for assistance (or you would like a free, no-obligation sample edit and quote on a manuscript of at least 35,000 words), send e-mail."

ALWAYS WRITE PROOFREADING & EDITING

Ingram TX. (936)825-1900. **E-mail:** writingspecialist@alwayswrite.us. **E-mail:** writingspecialist@alwayswrite.us. **Website:** www.alwayswrite.us. **Contact:** Dawn S. Herring, Owner/Writing Specialist.

ADDITIONAL INFORMATION Dawn Herring has been in the field for 20 years, with 5 years as a freelancer. She provides affordable and professional proofreading, editing, and revising services. Dawn has both a BA and an MA in English, with a specialization in linguistics/grammar. She has over 20 years combined professional experience in the following: proofreading and editing scholarly articles, theses and dissertations, website content, creative works, newsletters, resumes, technical reports, and numerous types of business documents; teaching college writing and grammar courses; tutoring writing and grammar; and developing and presenting seminars on her skills. See her resume at http://www.the-efa.org/members/data/resumes/herringds.pdf.

AMPERSAND EDITORIAL SERVICES

(415)987-6759. **E-mail:** lisa@ampedit.com. **Website:** www.ampedit.com. **Contact:** Lisa Gluskin Stonestreet.

ADDITIONAL INFORMATION Offers freelance writing, editing, and consulting to clients in business, technology, and the arts. Editorial services include proofreading, copyediting, line editing, developmental editing, and editorial review. Inquire for costs and additional information.

LYNNE ANDERSON

3191 West Mark Ave., Salt Lake City UT 84119. (801)840-5905; (801)809-8890. **E-mail:** lynneflcw@gmail.com. **Contact:** Lynne Anderson, editor/proofreader/writer.

ADDITIONAL INFORMATION Lynne Taloa Anderson is a fiction editor, book reviewer, and freelance writer. She works with authors on original, novel-length manuscripts from acceptance to publication. Her 4 years of freelance editing includes developmental, content, and line editing. List of titles edited and proofread available upon request. For more info,

see www.the-efa.org/members/data/resumes/andersonly.pdf.

JENNY ANDERSON EDITING

Saint Paul MN. (612)234-1536. **E-mail:** jenny@jennyandersonediting.com. **Website:** http://jennyandersonediting.com. **Contact:** Jenny Anderson.

ADDITIONAL INFORMATION "Jenny Anderson is an accomplished editor and proofreader with a reputation for top-rate editing skills and outstanding attention to detail. Areas of expertise include: Substantive/developmental editing, copyediting, and proofreading; Document design; Content management; Technical communication. She provides editing and proofreading services for a variety of writing projects, including: Technical writing; Training materials; Marketing collateral; Website content; Resumes; Academic papers and reports; Special writing projects, including manuscripts, articles, and books."

JEAN ANDREWS

172 Mar St., St. Pete Beach FL 33706. (727)367-8349. **E-mail:** egret27@tampabay.rr.com. **Contact:** Jean Andrews.

ADDITIONAL INFORMATION Jean Andrews has been in the field for 30 years. As a freelancer for 20 years, Jean has extensive copyediting/proofreading (online and print) experience on student textbooks and teacher's editions for Houghton Mifflin Harcourt: grades K–12 language arts/reading, science, math, and social studies programs and related test and instructional materials; reviewed other copyeditors' work; occasional writing and substantive editing; additional extensive writing/editing experience for daily newspaper; weekly/monthly industry magazines/newsletters; university publications for both general and specialized audiences; corporate and organizational marketing/advertising/public relations materials. He holds a B.A. in English/Art/Publications; B.S. in Natural Resource Studies/Zoology; M.A. in Library and Information Science. Can read basic Spanish. See more at www.the-efa.org/members/data/resumes/andrewsj.pdf.

SUSAN L. ANDREWS

260 Riverside Dr., New York NY 10025. (212)666-7724. **E-mail:** slandrew2@aol.com. **Contact:** Susan L. Andrews.

ADDITIONAL INFORMATION "Editorial skills include line editing and copyediting (online included), rewriting (when requested), translations of technical language into more consumer-friendly language, editing murky prose for clarity and precision, proofreading, and production editing. Subject matter edited for book and journal publishers has varied from health and nutrition to history, psychology, social sciences, and cultural studies. Also worked four years in an inhouse copyeditor for an educatonal publishing company (k-12). Proofreading has also included fiction." See previous experience at www.the-efa.org/members/data/resumes/andrewssl.pdf.

APPAINK COPYWRITING

E-mail: lauren@appaink.com. **Website:** www.appaink.com. **Contact:** Laura Appa.

ADDITIONAL INFORMATION Ten years in the field as freelancer. Copywriter and marketing professional with a background in newspaper reporting and magazine feature writing. Specializes in smart copy that grabs attention, communicates effectively, and persuades. Provides all types of marketing collateral: brochures, press releases, trade publication articles, web content, direct mail, advertisements, copy editing, and sustainable services marketing. Degree in journalism from University of Texas at Austin; Certificate in Sustainable Business from Bainbridge Graduate Institute. Responds to email within 24 hours.

CYNTHIA AQUILA

Brooklyn NY. (646)705-3218. **E-mail:** cynaq@earthlink.net. **Contact:** Cynthia Aquila.

ADDITIONAL INFORMATION Cynthia Aquila is a professional writer and editor with 14 years in the field of editorial, publication management and corporate communications experience. Her areas of expertise include developing editorial strategy for print and online, and creating and editing content for print, web and other business communications. "Excellent communicator and collaborator with proven ability to present complex subjects clearly and creatively, sound editorial judgment, a keen attention to detail, and a commitment to client service." Cynthia received an American Express Corporate Affairs and Communications Awards for Excellence. She is available to provide freelance professional writing and editorial services to businesses and not-for-profit organizations. See previous experience information at www.the-efa.org/members/data/resumes/aquilac.pdf.

CARL ARNOLD

156 Prospect Park, West Brooklyn NY 11215. (718)788-5944 (phone & fax); (347)254-0527 (cell). **E-mail:** carlarnold@mac.com. **Website:** http://www.edit1to1.com/. **Contact:** Carl Arnold.

ADDITIONAL INFORMATION For 25 years Carl Arnold has worked in areas of publishing (mostly book manuscripts and large education projects for Scholastic and McGraw-Hill), advertising, finance and law, and has also worked one-to-one with people writing dissertations as well as essays for college and graduate school applications, helping them with English. He has varying ability with Greek, French, German, Turkish, Hebrew and Arabic. See more at http://www.the-efa.org/members/data/resumes/arnoldc.pdf.

ARTIS LINGUA COMMUNICATIONS

P.O. Box 3646, Wichita Falls TX 76301. (940)257-2118. **E-mail:** artislingua@gmail.com. **Contact:** Ysabel de la Rosa.

ADDITIONAL INFORMATION 25+ years in business communications, including publishing, advertising, and public relations. "I provide editorial and design services in English and Spanish. My experience includes working with books, magazines, feature articles, profile articles, and poetry. I do a great deal of work in translation and translation management in Latin American and Castilian Spanish and Portuguese (both Brazilian and Portuguese). I have a team of translators, designers and editors who work with me on large projects. Please contact me for rates and terms information. I will gladly furnish references and work samples on request." Native language is English. Fluent in Spanish. Skilled in translation management of complex communications in multiple languages. Winner of 170+ awards for editorial, advertising, and public relations work. Education: B.A., *Summa Cum Laude*, Southwestern University. See previous experience at hwww.the-efa.org/members/data/resumes/campbelly.pdf.

AUTHOR SUPPORT CO-OP

P.O. Box 256, Eugene OR 97440-0256. (541)484-0731. **E-mail:** ASC@efn.org. **Website:** AuthorSupportCoop.com. **Contact:** Patricia Robinett, owner. Estab. 2005.

ADDITIONAL INFORMATION Additional Information: Designs your covers and interiors, pamphlets, manuals, newsletters. Formats POD paperbacks, PDFs, e-books, and Kindles. Editing with kind, patient, personal attention. Prices vary according to complexity. Accepts PayPal.

A WORD AFFAIR LLC

(201)404-0217. **E-mail:** trishpeters@msn.com; ppeters@awordaffair.com. **Website:** www.awordaffair.com. **Contact:** Patricia C. Peters. Estab. 2004.

ADDITIONAL INFORMATION A Word Affair LLC is a professional editorial services company established by Patricia Peters in 2004. The editorial services include manuscript critique, conceptual editing, line editing, copyediting, proofreading, and analysis of the submission package. Whether you are a publisher, literary agent, published or unpublished writer, A Word Affair's mission is to make your project shine. An editing professional for 15 years, Patricia has worked with various genres, editing projects for Random House, Simon & Schuster, McGraw-Hill, Bamboo Books, CDS Books, Gale, and private clients. Her projects include crime fiction, romance novels, young adult fiction, children's fiction, biography, memoir, health, spirituality, business books, essays, reference books, earth sciences, and social sciences. Patricia has been a guest editor and panelist at the Pacific Northwest Writers Association Conference and the Colorado Gold Conference. She holds a Ph.D. in English Literature from Drew University in Madison, New Jersey, and has taught courses in freshman composition, creative writing, and American literature.

LAUREN P. BAKER, PHD, ELS - BIOMEDICAL EDITING SERVICES

1606 10th Avenue West, Seattle WA 98119. (206)769-5689. **E-mail:** laurenb_wa@yahoo.com. **Website:** www.laurenbakerediting.com. **Contact:** Lauren Baker.

ADDITIONAL INFORMATION Lauren Baker provides professional editing, rewriting, and fact-checking of biomedical publications materials; copyediting and proofreading, formatting, and reference checking of basic and clinical research articles and other documents, many written by non-native English speakers. "Hardcopy and online editing. Deadline oriented." Lauren was a Senior Fellow, Department of Pharmacology; University of Washington, Seattle, WA. For more information, see www.the-efa.org/members/data/resumes/bakerl.pdf.

BALAGOT COMMUNICATIONS, INC.

Chicago IL. **E-mail:** ChicagoWriter@outlook.com. **Contact:** Maija Rothenberg. "Years in field: 27. Years as freelancer: 27. Award-winning business and healthcare writer, editor, and collaborator with 27 years' ex-

perience developing books, articles, newsletters, and marketing communications. My goal is to make ideas fly off the page into the reader's mind through graceful, insightful writing, laser-sharp editing, and compulsive fact checking. Former president of Independent Writers of Chicago. Former instructor in the University of Chicago Publishing Program."

NICOLE BALANT EDITING

Newcastle ME. (207)319-9522. **E-mail:** NicoleBalant@roadrunner.com. **Contact:** Nicole Balant, copyeditor/proofreader.

ADDITIONAL INFORMATION Years in field: 33. Years as a freelancer: 26. "Versatile and experienced copy editor and proofreader of humanities, social and hard sciences, business, and fiction; trained in-house at Greenwood Publishing Group and as a graphic designer; MS technical writing (Rensselaer Polytechnic); BA psychology and English (Bryn Mawr College). Nonfiction projects for academic presses, college textbook publishers, and business references; fiction projects include a suspense novel that debuted at Number 1 on the New York Times bestseller list."

JENNIFER BALLINGER EDITORIAL SERVICES

Huntington IN. **E-mail:** editor@jpballinger.com. **Website:** www.jpballinger.com. **Contact:** Jennifer Ballinger.

ADDITIONAL INFORMATION Jennifer Ballinger has worked in the publishing world for more than 13 years (in both full-time and freelance capacities) on a wide range of projects, including: Encyclopedia articles covering the arts, humanities, linguistics, and basic and applied sciences; highly specialized scientific research; textbooks for university and graduate-level students; books and articles written by nonnative English speakers; and fiction and nonfiction for general readers. Through the course of her career, she has performed developmental editing, substantive or content editing, copyediting, and proofreading for many different audiences. For more information, please visit www.jpballinger.com. Jennifer is a graduate of Middlebury College, Middlebury, Vermont with a B.A. in English Literature with High Honors, *Magna Cum Laude.*

KATHLEEN A. BARRY

San Diego CA. (858)433-6885. **E-mail:** katieabarry@gmail.com. **Website:** www.linkedin.com/in/katiebarry. **Contact:** Katie Barry, writer/editor. Estab. 2012.

ADDITIONAL INFORMATION Writing and editing for businesses, with a focus on marketing communications.

IRIS BASS

167 West Park St., Lee MA 01238. (413)243-2862. **E-mail:** ibbooks@verizon.net. **Contact:** Iris Bass. Estab. 2001.

ADDITIONAL INFORMATION Iris Bass turned to freelance as a copy editor and proofreader after 30 years in the field. "Her unique background in text design and attention to detail are put to use chiefly in nonfiction, particularly in the genres of cookbooks and culinary histories, craft books, 19th-century biography/history, as well as projects that contain complex typographic elements, such as self-help titles. She meets deadlines conscientiously. If you have a monstrous project that you shudder to hand to your usual stable of freelancers, give her a call! Iris is skilled in Americanizing British and Australian texts, and converting from American units to metric or vice versa. Electronically, she works primarily in Word (Windows XP) and is adept at Track Edit; she is also comfortable copyediting hard copy. Some of her book publishing clients have been: Harry N. Abrams, Andrews & McMeel, Avalon Publishing, and Bloomsbury USA. Education: Hunter College, NYC. Graduated *cum laude* 1975. B.A. in Math, Minor in Art; High School of Art & Design, NYC. Graduated 1971, with Regents Scholarship. See previous experience at www.the-efa.org/members/data/resumes/bassi.txt.

GREG BATES

Monroe ME. (207)525-0900. **E-mail:** gbates2@gmail.com. **Website:** http://scribblejuice.com. **Contact:** Greg Bates.

ADDITIONAL INFORMATION Greg Bates edits nonfiction books, dissertations, and research papers, with a specialty in editing ESL—English as a second language. He has edited a wide range of nonfiction academic and popular books over 30 years. Greg's core message as an editor: "make sure the writer's work has integrity, is believable, is persuasive, and addresses the reasonable objections of an open-minded reader." Education: Masters in Education, Harvard University.

BECKER EDITORIAL SERVICES

Pittsburgh PA. **E-mail:** contact@beckereditorial.com. **Website:** www.beckereditorial.com. **Contact:** Stacey Becker. Estab. 2005.

ADDITIONAL INFORMATION Stacey Becker has been copyediting and proofreading since 1997. Works on a wide variety of materials, specializing in academic and research-oriented materials such as journal articles, book chapters, grant proposals, personal statements, classroom materials, and dissertations (particularly in neuroscience, autism research, and marketing psychology). Working with ESL authors is a particular specialty and a pleasure of mine. I have extensive experience in ESL editing, working with authors who are non-native English speakers from many countries, including India, Italy, Germany, and Switzerland." See website for more information.

BENNETT VALLEE COMMUNICATIONS

769 N. Walton Lakeshore Dr., Inlet Beach FL 32413. (850)217-7542. **E-mail:** editor@susanvallee.com. **Website:** http://susanvallee.com. **Contact:** Susan Vallee, owner.

ADDITIONAL INFORMATION Years in field: 16. Years as a freelancer: 12. "Member info: I'm an award-winning writer and editor with 16 years experience. I'd like to assist you on your project. I currently create two community magazines for resorts in Northwest Florida. My company oversees the graphic design, ad sales, story production, photography, printing and distribution. This enables my clients to sit back and relax while I do all the hard work and they enjoy the exposure and ad revenue. I also write for online clients, have created my own site, www.kidfriendlyflorida.com, and have been published in Florida Travel + Life, www.babble.com, Birmingham Magazine and more." See previous experience at www.the-efa.org/members/data/resumes/vallees.pdf.

DEBORAH BERLYNE

717 Marshall Ave., Rockville MD 20851. (301)340-0075. **E-mail:** djberlyne@gmail.com. **Website:** www.dberlynewriter.com. **Contact:** Deborah Berlyne.

ADDITIONAL INFORMATION Years as freelancer: 14. "Debby Berlyne, Ph.D., offers more than 25 years of experience as a medical writer and editor, with a specialty in medical and health-related subjects. She writes and edits reports, articles, journal manuscripts, and meeting proceedings for numerous federal agencies, as well as several non-profit and private sector organizations, including pharmaceutical companies. The medical topics with which she has experience include bioterrorism, cardiology, clinical medicine, epidemiology, health disparities, health services research, hematology, infectious diseases, kidney disease, mental health, nutrition, oncology, organ transplantation, pediatrics, psychiatry, reproductive medicine, substance abuse, and women's health. Dr. Berlyne has written technical reports and manuscripts intended for scientific audiences and translated technical documents into plain language for lay audiences and legislators, including the U.S. Congress." She is fluent in French. For more information see http://www.the-efa.org/members/data/resumes/berlyned.pdf.

FRAN BERMAN

12 Locust Ave., Exeter NH 03833. (603)772-3995. **E-mail:** f.berman@comcast.net. **Contact:** Fran Berman. **ADDITIONAL INFORMATION** Fran Berman has been a freelance editor for 18 years. She copy edits and proofreads copy for feature articles, academic journal articles, reference publications, websites, newsletters, press releases, and annual reports; fact checks citations and journal content. Ensures consistency of style, spelling, punctuation. Has an undergraduate degree in English and an MBA with a concentration in finance and marketing. Has worked on a *pro bono* basis for nonprofits, producing annual reports, newsletters, and press releases. Clients have included Sloan Management Review, Cambridge University Press, Reader's Guide to Periodical Literature, the New York Philharmonic, Jewish Federation of New Hampshire, nonfiction authors, and *Consumer Guide*." See previous experience at http://www.the-efa.org/members/data/resumes/bermanf.pdf.

JENNIFER BISHOP

Bethesda MD. (240)340-1149. **E-mail:** jbishop@gmail.com. **Contact:** Jennifer Bishop, editor/writer. **ADDITIONAL INFORMATION** Years in field: 10. Years as a freelancer: 3. "Jennifer Bishop is a skilled editor, writer, designer, and publications manager with more than 11 years' experience serving federal agencies and science advisory groups. She has written conference proceedings and meeting minutes; developed annual reports, brochures, fact sheets, posters, and websites; and has edited technical reports, regulatory documents, and journal articles. She has worked on publications for the National Institutes of Health, Centers for Disease Control and Prevention, Department of Education, Interagency Committee on Disability Research, Nuclear Regulatory Commission, National Institute of Standards and Technology, American Library Association, and the National

Academy of Sciences, among others. She has a B.F.A from Cornell University and is pursuing an M.S. in technical communication at Northeastern University."

BJORNER & ASSOCIATES

1110 Springfield Pike #8, Cincinnati OH 45215. **E-mail:** bjorner@earthlink.net. **Website:** www.bjorner.info.
ADDITIONAL INFORMATION Bjørner & Associates provides contracted services to publishers, authors, researchers and librarians to assist them in distributing high quality work in print and online. Susanne Bjørner will write, edit, and proofread for publication of: Web sites, journals, magazines, newsletters, books. She has experience with academic (college and university; K-12), library, business, and technical markets. Her prior career as a librarian and information professional assures excellent fact-checking skills in a wide range of subjects. Languages: American English native; knowledge of Danish and Spanish.

CYNTHIA BLAIR

Stony Brook NY. (631)689-6119; (631)880-0432 (cell). **E-mail:** cynthiawriter@gmail.com. **Contact:** Cynthia Blair.
ADDITIONAL INFORMATION Cynthia Blair has 17 years in field and is an experienced, versatile writer and editor who is thorough, works quickly, and never misses a deadline. She is the author of more than 50 books and is widely-published in newspapers, magazines, and trade publications "in a wide range of non-fiction topics, especially business (MBA from the M.I.T. Sloan School of Management)." Specialties: business; health, diet, and nutrition; travel; fiction. "My specialty [in nonfiction] is taking other people's thoughts and ideas, either written or oral, and turning them into a coherent, well-written piece. I am particularly adept at "translating" complicated or obscure information about every possible topic into prose that can be easily understood."

BLOOM INK

3497 Bennington Court, Bloomfield Hills MI 48301. (248)642-1816. **E-mail:** info@bloomwriting.com. **Website:** bloomwriting.com. **Contact:** Barbara Bloom, founder and principal. Estab. 2008. "Barbara Bloom of Bloom Ink is a detail-oriented, committed writer and editor. Barbara brings more than 20 years of successful publishing and communication experience to her work. She has worked for Simon & Schuster Trade and Wayne State University Press and managed the publishing program at the Norton Simon Museum. As a freelance editor and writing coach, she promotes clear writing across a range of genres and styles. Barbara works with clients to put their best narrative forward, whatever the form: fiction or nonfiction manuscripts (trade, academic, children's, self-publishing) or B2B and B2C communications (white papers, marketing materials, and more)."

ADDITIONAL INFORMATION Offers copyediting, developmental editing, proofreading, e-books, self-publishing, abridging, book proposals, query letters, ghostwriting, and coaching services.

BLOSSOM EDITING

E-mail: carol@blossomediting.com. **Website:** www.blossomediting.com. **Contact:** Carol Hansson.

ADDITIONAL INFORMATION "With over 13 years of experience in both copyediting and proofreading, you will receive a clean copy in a short amount of time." Example projects include: novels, resumes, cover letters, essays, and articles. Resume and references available upon request. Simple editing (including spelling and grammar): For all documents under and including 40 pages*: $5 a page. Substantive editing (including spelling, grammar, point-of-view and continuity errors): For all documents under and including 40 pages: $7 a page. Also specializes in web editing and writing. See more pricing and information on website.

BLUE HORIZON COMMUNICATIONS

Rehoboth Beach DE. (302)227-1749. **E-mail:** books@bluehorizoncommunications.com. **Website:** www.bluehorizoncommunications.com. **Contact:** Laurel Marshfield.

ADDITIONAL INFORMATION Laurel has 25 years' experience working with physicians, lawyers, educators, holistic practitioners (healers, intuitives), healthcare professionals, and business people shaping their prose. "I worked as a freelance writer and editor, as well as in house (or on staff)—as senior staff writer at a medical center; copy director at a public relations firm specializing in marketing professionals and their professions, or businesses; and communications consultant at two global insurance companies. My bylined work, and articles I ghosted, appeared in countless trade magazines for diverse professional fields–-from medicine, to land conservation, to law—and in such general interest magazines and newspapers as *The Philadelphia Inquirer, Philadelphia Daily News, The Pennsylvania Gazette, Philadelphia Magazine*, and Main Line Today Magazine. I provide a complete editorial service for authors—from book development through manuscript completion and final polish, to publication options, to author and business website development and copywriting, to promotional or marketing consultation. Please see the page on my site titled "Four Author Profiles" for a detailed look at my work with four very different authors: a business book author, a novelist, a biographer, and a memoirist. Please also see the website www.FeelBetterNow-CI.com for an example of my website planning and copywriting for an author client. I would be happy to discuss your book project by phone during a free initial consultation call. And am always willing to share my expertise with authors or prospective authors and offer recommendations. Please fill out the Contact Us form on my site to arrange a free initial consultation call: www.BlueHorizonCommunications.com/contact.html. If you live in the U.S. or Canada, I would be glad to call you at a mutually convenient time."

BOOK EDITOR: LAURIE ROSIN, THE

P.O. Box 7688, Sarasota FL 34278. (941) 921-0906. **E-mail:** laurie@thebookeditor.com. **E-mail:** laurie@thebookeditor.com. **Website:** www.thebookeditor.com. Estab. 1979.

ADDITIONAL INFORMATION : Laurie Rosin has more than 30 years editing and consulting experience in all genres. Over 50 million copies in print. Writing Fellow, National Endowment for the Humanities. Offers comprehensive chapter-by-chapter critiques and line editing; also offers one-on-one Master Class. Fee determined by word count.

BOOKMARK EDITING

Austin TX. (512)318-8259. **E-mail:** kellly@bookmarkediting.com. **Contact:** Kelly Besecke.

ADDITIONAL INFORMATION Years as freelancer: 3. "I am a developmental editor and copyeditor for scholars, students, nonfiction authors, and organizations. I draw on fifteen years of experience with academic writing and publishing to ensure focused arguments, clear explanations, and an organized and reader-friendly presentation of ideas. My greatest strengths as an editor are organizing ideas, explaining complex ideas clearly, and helping writers develop their thinking about works in progress. My copyediting services emphasize clarity, flow, and grammatical correctness. My developmental editing services can involve coaching and consulting with authors from the beginning to the end of their writing projects or simply helping them take a draft to the next level. I listen hard and read carefully to fully understand authors' intentions so I can help them think through and develop their ideas and communicate them well." See previous experience at www.the-efa.org/members/data/resumes/beseckek.pdf.

BOOKMARKER EDITORIAL SERVICES

20 Lower Via Casitas, Unit #3, Greenbrae CA 94904. (415)785-4985; (732)513-1276 (cell). **Fax:** (415)785-4836. **E-mail:** cnixon@bookmarker-es.com. **E-mail:** bookmarker_es@yahoo.com. **Website:** www.bookmarker-es.com. **Contact:** Cindy B. Nixon. Estab. 1996.
ADDITIONAL INFORMATION Years in field: 21 Years as freelancer: 17. "Bookmarker Editorial Services can meet any and all of your editorial needs, whether basic or detailed proofreading; light or heavy copyediting; minor or major copy revisions; full-service writing projects from scratch; and everything in between—like fact-checking, ghostwriting, line editing, project management, and desktop publishing. Bookmarker serves large and small clients as well as simple and complex projects. "Clients can feel completely confident knowing that publications will be thoroughly consistent, accurate, and error-free, so that they'll look and read their best. Owner and operator Cindy B. Nixon has been specializing in promotional copywriting, fiction/nonfiction copyediting, and general proofreading since earning her master's in English from Rutgers University in 1991."

BOOKMARK SERVICES

P.O. Box 793, 227 Prospect St., Housatonic MA 02136-0793. (413)274-6573; (413)717-1243. **E-mail:** victoria@bookmarkservices.net. **Website:** bookmarkservices.net. **Contact:** Victoria Wright, owner. Estab. 1995. Special rates for seniors and students. MasterCard, VISA, and PayPal accepted.
ADDITIONAL INFORMATION Victoria and her merry band of experts offer assistance for your written words: manuscript evaluation, developmental editing, copyediting, proofreading, ghostwriting, fact-checking, research, APA formatting, audio transcription, layout, cover design, query letters, book proposals, self-publishing. "We are happy to work with writers of every level of skill and experience, in virtually every area of focus: fiction, nonfiction, young adult, memoirs, business, technical, and academic."

BOOKWORM, INC.

E-mail: cindy@bookworminc.com; info@bookworminc.com. **Website:** www.bookworminc.com. **Contact:** Cindy Corliss. Estab. 2004.
ADDITIONAL INFORMATION Years in field: 9. "I created Bookworm, Inc. to provide professional editorial services. I have extensive experience writing, copyediting, technical editing, and developmental editing of print courses, online courses (e-learning), and technical manuals. In addition, I create advertising content. Throughout my life, I've been an avid reader. So much reading has given me a discerning eye for detail and an ear for what "sounds" right. Trust me to create fluid, attention-grabbing publications for you. Please visit my website or contact me for additional information."

MARIA M. BOYER

Palmyra PA. (717)202-5034. **E-mail:** mariamboyer@gmail.com. **Website:** www.mariamboyer.webs.com. **Contact:** Maria M. Boyer.
ADDITIONAL INFORMATION Maria M. Boyer has been a professional copyeditor and proofreader since 1997. She's been in the field for 27 years. Holds a B.A. in English Communications and Business Management. Specializing in *The Chicago Manual of Style*, as well as APA style; Proficient with the Track Changes features of Microsoft Word, as well as with Adobe Acrobat Professional 9 software. See previous experience and client remarks at her website.

BRIGHT IDEAS

Richland WA. (509)521-8461. **E-mail:** info@georganneoconnor.com. **Contact:** Georganne O'Connor.
ADDITIONAL INFORMATION Years in field: 30. Years as a freelancer: 26. "Highly skilled nonfiction writer, researcher, and editor. Proven track record in book development and line editing, particularly related to natural history, world history, memoir, and travel. Published book, magazine, and news writer experienced at communicating complex concepts and sharing technical information with scientific and academic communities. Excel at writing that contributes to enhanced understanding of technical subjects for audiences from school-age to adults. Lover of words, sentences, and stories of all kinds. Experienced at developing, packaging, and selling ideas." See previous experience at www.the-efa.org/members/data/resumes/oconnorg.txt.

JUDY K. BRODY

306 Breezewood Dr., Bay Village OH 44140. (440)617-9741; (440)653-7103. **Fax:** (440)617-9741. **E-mail:** jkb7810@aol.com. **Contact:** Judy K. Brody.

ADDITIONAL INFORMATION Judy Brody has spent 25 years in the field; 12 years as a freelancer. "Text and photo permissions editor with a concentration in college textbooks; Photo researcher and Archivist."

MARLENE BROEMER, PH. D.

6827 SW Montauk Circle, Lake Oswego OR 97035. (503)372-6325; (503)902-2380. **E-mail:** marlenemp@yahoo.com. **Contact:** Marlene Broemer, Ph. D.

ADDITIONAL INFORMATION Marlene Broemer has 25 years in the field. "My personal experience as a writer includes both fiction and poetry, but I have worked most of my life with practical texts—grant applications, business proposals, essays, journal articles for academic and business publications, documentation for government agencies, including groups such as the United Nations and the European Union. One specialty I have is working with writers for whom English is a 2nd or 3rd language. Depending on my familiarity with the native language I may be able to help the writer to better conceptualize materials in English. My languages are: French, Russian, Swedish, and Finnish." Education and degrees: Univ. of Helsinki, Ph.D. Comparative Literature; San Francisco State University., M.A., Comparative Literature; Michigan State Univ., B.A. English &Education. See previous experience at www.the-efa.org/members/data/resumes/broemerm.pdf.

KIM BROOKS

(773)654-1968 (home); (312)953-0076 (cell). **E-mail:** kabrooks@mac.com. **Contact:** Kim Brooks.

ADDITIONAL INFORMATION Years in field: 6. Years as freelancer: 6. "A published author and experienced editor with a Masters degree in creative writing from the Iowa Writers' Workshop at the University of Iowa, Kim approaches all projects with enthusiasm, creativity, and a well-honed editorial eye. Her own work has appeared in such publications as Salon.com, Babble.com, Glimmer Train, One Story, and Epoch. From years of practicing her craft, Kim understands both the hard work and imagination that goes into good writing. She has eight years experience teaching creative writing and composition on the college level, and is comfortable working with clients on everything from concept and narrative to line editing."

VALERIE BROOKS

The Write Edit, Santa Fe New Mexico 87507. **Fax:** (505)988-1473. **E-mail:** Valerie@TheWriteEdit.com. **Website:** http://thewriteedit.com. **Contact:** Valerie Brooks, M.A..

ADDITIONAL INFORMATION Valerie Brooks has worked in the field for 10 years as an editor and proofreader, specializing in fiction and nonfiction manuscripts. She follows Chicago and AP style. Her "areas of expertise include health and wellness, performing arts, animals, spiritual, memoir, spas, and travel. She earned a M.A. in Writing and Publishing from Rosemont College, PA and a B.A. in Journalism from Hofstra University, NY. For more information, see www.the-efa.org/members/data/resumes/brooksv.txt.

JANICE K. BRYANT

200 Pinehurst Ave., Apt. 2C, New York NY 10033. (212)795-2808; (646)512-2791. **E-mail:** janicekbryant@gmail.com. **Contact:** Janice K. Bryant.

ADDITIONAL INFORMATION "I've copyedited and proofread magazines, elementary and high school textbooks, trade publications, websites and more. I'm accustomed to working in a high-pressure, deadline environment. In fact, I find it invigorating. I have a good ear and a good eye. Since leaving Essence Communications in December 2008, I have been writing small features for *Heart & Soul* magazine, marketing materials for a nonprofit, promotional sell sheets for a major book publisher, and online articles for African-American cultural websites. I also know American history and stay on top of the news, which comes in handy with editing and copyediting. I've seen writers make major blunders simply because they don't know current events." Janice holds an M.A. in Journalism; B.A. in English Education. She has been in the field for 15 years. See her resume at www.the-efa.org/members/data/resumes/bryantjk.pdf.

BUCKLEY/SWARTZ

(781)584-4800; (617)921-8421. **Fax:** (781)584-4801. **E-mail:** rbuckley@buckley-swartz.com. **Website:** www.buckley-swartz.com. **Contact:** Rita Bona Buckley. Buckley/Swartz is a medical and healthcare communications firm providing writing and editing services to authors of books and articles, professional societies, journal publishers, university and independent publishing houses, pharmaceutical companies, nonprofit organizations, consumer health websites, and clients in academic medicine.

ADDITIONAL INFORMATION "Years in field: 20. Years as freelancer: 20. Writing and Editing Services: Owner/writer Rita Buckley specializes in the delivery of publication-ready manuscripts that typically involve some combination of research, writing, editing, and proofreading services. These include: conference and symposium coverage and reporting; book proposals and manuscripts; book chapters; original research articles; web content; patient recruitment materials; grants; journal supplements; consumer health writing; and manuscripts for publication in peer-reviewed journals." See previous experience at www.the-efa.org/members/data/resumes/buckleyrb.pdf.

SHEILA BUFF

500 Milan Hill Road, Milan NY 12571. (845)758-3035. **E-mail:** sheilabuff@frontiernet.net. **Website:** www.sheilabuff.com. **Contact:** Sheila Buff.

ADDITIONAL INFORMATION Sheila Buff brings 20 years of successful experience in publishing to her clients. Her editorial skills can help you with book proposals, manuscript reviews, editorial input, article editing and review. Her recent book projects have been with HarperOne, Rodale, William Morrow, Hyperion, Kaplan, Globe Pequot, Avon Books, and G.P. Putnam's Sons. "In addition to my medical book work, I am the author of numerous titles on birdwatching, natural history, gardening and the outdoors." See publication list at http://www.the-efa.org/members/data/resumes/buffs.pdf.

STACY BURNS

Denver CO. (310)938-2602. **E-mail:** stacylburns@gmail.com. **Contact:** Stacy Burns.

ADDITIONAL INFORMATION "I hold an MFA in Creative Writing and have five years of editing experience and three years of experience teaching college-level composition and creative writing courses. I have worked in all stages of the written communication process—from brainstorming, research, and outlining to writing, proofreading, fact checking, and line editing, to designing layout, typesetting, and publishing. The publications I have worked on range from literary journals to church newsletters to international computer specification standards." See previous experience at http://www.the-efa.org/members/data/resumes/burnss.pdf.

ROBERT M. CAMMAROTA

215 West 92d St., 12E, New York NY 10025. (212)724-3775. **E-mail:** robert.cammarota@gmail.com. **Contact:** Robert M. Cammarota.

ADDITIONAL INFORMATION "With more than 30 years' professional experience as a freelance writer, editor, and researcher, I have edited an array of publications, including financial reports, scholarly articles, museum catalogues, encyclopedia entries, college textbooks, corporate and community newsletters, fiction, and nonfiction. As a long-term consultant to a number of global financial institutions, including Bankers Trust / Deutsche Bank, Financial Security Assurance, and JPMorgan Chase, I have managed a broad range of print and electronic publications, working directly with heads of corporate communications and members of their teams. In addition to my freelance work, I worked in-house as a full-time member of Invesco's corporate communications team, where I edited all communications from this Fortune 500 asset manager (formerly AMVESCAP), including quarterly and annual reports, marketing brochures, and letters from the chairman."

CATHY CAPUTO

San Francisco CA. **E-mail:** cathycaputo@gmail.com. **Website:** www.cathycaputo.com. **Contact:** Cathy Caputo.

ADDITIONAL INFORMATION Years in field: 5+. Years as freelancer: 4. Cathy Caputo is a "freelance editor and proofreader specializing in non-fiction books and professional and promotional materials for individuals and businesses. Past clients include publishers, accountants, psychologists, and artists. Graduate of the University of San Francisco School of Law (J.D., magna cum laude)."

CAROL'S CORRECTIONS

P.O. Box 381, Cedar Bluffs NE 68015-0381. **E-mail:** carolweber@windstream.net. **Website:** www.carolscorrections.weebly.com. **Contact:** Carol Weber. Estab. 2012.

ADDITIONAL INFORMATION "Please note that I will not do erotica, the occult or horror. Period. All services require a 50% deposit before I begin, with the second half due upon receipt of the edited work. What I offer: A Sample Edit - You'll want to ensure you're going to like my editing style; I will want to ensure your manuscript is ready for editing, and that I'll be a good fit for your manuscript. I'll be happy to edit, for free, five to ten pages of your manuscript. Carol's Corrections - Everywhere you look, there is a different phrase for the same service. My work is content editing, or line editing, depending on whose definition you use. Carol's Catches - This is intended to be the final look-through a book before you call it done, and declare it ready for the public."

KATHY CARTER

Peoria IL. (309)685-6389. **E-mail:** kathy@carteredit. com. **Website:** www.carteredit.com. **Contact:** Kathy Carter.

ADDITIONAL INFORMATION Kathy Carter has edited books since 1982 andstarted her own editing business in 2006. She is a "reliable freelanceeditor specializing in nonfiction books. Meticulous editing with special emphasis on structure and organization." Services include developmental, structural, substantive, and copy editing. Clients include Beacon Press, Unitarian Universalist Association, Glencoe/McGraw-Hill, and numerous individual authors. Kathy can be contacted through her website.

CAVANAUGH EDITORIAL SERVICES

400 Mayberry Road, Schwenksville PA 19473. (484)552-0671. **E-mail:** lori@cavanaugheditorial. com. **Website:** www.cavanaugheditorial.com. **Contact:** Lori Cavanaugh. Estab. 1998.

ADDITIONAL INFORMATION "Cavanaugh Editorial Services is a professional freelance copyediting and proofreading company with extensive experience in the publishing industry." Services include manuscript copyediting, proofreading, typesetting code, electronic/online editing, electronic proofreading, and jacket copywriting. Cost: $20-25/hour or $3-6/page for copyediting; $15-20/hour or $2-4/ page for proofreading; also considers quoting a flat fee after reviewing a project. See website for additional information.

CDT EDITORIAL, LLC

Wykoff NJ. (201)652-1105; (201)248-8320. **Fax:** (201)652-5145. **E-mail:** cdtedit@yahoo.com; cdtedit@gmail.com. **Contact:** Carolyn Tillona, editor.

ADDITIONAL INFORMATION Years in field: 30. Years as a freelancer: 7. Senior medical editor providing services for promotional, pharmaceutical marketing, managed care, continuing medical education (CME), clinical research, and academic publications. Services include substantive and copy editing, proofreading, quality control, fact checking, literature searching, obtaining reprint permissions, participating in medical/legal/regulatory review meetings, and editorial project management. Editorial experience includes journal articles and supplements, managed care materials, PowerPoint presentations, Web-based offerings, speaker training and meeting materials, iPad apps, proposals, and related content, across multiple therapeutic categories. Available to work on-site.

C.F. EDITORIAL SERVICES

624 E. 18th St. N., Newton IA 50208. (641)417-9378. **E-mail:** cfedits@hotmail.com. **Contact:** Cynthia Freeman, copyeditor.

ADDITIONAL INFORMATION "Copyeditor/developmental editor with 19 years experience, specializing in peer reviewed scientific publishing, ESL or native English, in subjects ranging from physics and materials engineering to tire science and technology. Editing for organization, subordination, and redundancy, as well as grammar and syntax, punctuation, form and use of symbols, nomenclature, and clarity of expression. CMS and ACS style, and meticulous use of house styles." For more information, see www. the-efa.org/members/data/resumes/freemanc.pdf.

AMY CHAMBERLAIN

Philadelphia PA. **E-mail:** chamberlainedit@aol.com. **Contact:** Amy Chamberlain, copy editor/proofreader.

ADDITIONAL INFORMATION "I have been working as a copyeditor and proofreader, full-time and in a freelance capacity, for nine years. I take on nonfiction trade projects: cookbooks, coffee table books, and general-interest books about everything from Japanese robot toys to equality in academe. I work on college textbooks about language development and educational assessment for major textbook publishers. I proofread monthly shelter and lifestyles magazine, marking changes in Acrobat. My broad liberal arts education with a concentration in Latin exposed me to many subjects that I still pursue, privately and professionally: architecture, art, Buddhism, cooking and food ways, ethnobotany/economic botany, ethics, gardening, nature, organic farming, philosophy, plant biology, religion, sustainability, taxonomy, and yoga. I am meticulous, logical, flexible, prompt, and easy to communicate with."

CHANGEMAKERS PUBLISHING AND WRITING

750 La Playa, #952, San Francisco CA 94121. (415)571-8282. **Website:** www.changemakerspublishingandwriting.com. **Contact:** Gini Graham Scott, Ph.D., J.D. Estab. 1968.

ADDITIONAL INFORMATION "I consult with and write books, articles, and scripts for clients, working from rough drafts, notes, interviews, tapes of workshops/seminars, and other materials. I also help clients publish and promote their books or find mainstream publishers, agents, and film producers. I have published over 50 books of my own, have written 15 original scripts, several under option, and have written, produced, and sometimes directed over 40 short films, including book and script trailers, which can be seen at www.youtube.com/changemakersprod. I also conduct workshops, seminars, teleseminars, and Webinars on writing, publishing, and promoting one's books and articles."

CHRISTINA CHENG

Austin TX. **E-mail:** christina.atx@gmail.com. **Contact:** Christina Cheng.

ADDITIONAL INFORMATION Christina Cheng has been in this field for 4 years. "My editing experience runs the gamut from light proofreading or copy editing to developmental editing. I have edited novels, news copy, marketing collateral, Web copy, and academic papers and essays. Although I am adept at working with almost all genres, I am particularly interested in food writing and cookbooks. I am a published author and ghostwriter and also have extensive experience writing copy for print, Web, and marketing collateral that creates targeted, result-oriented content. What I care about most is helping my clients get their message across in a compelling way that preserves and showcases their unique voice as clearly and concisely as possible. For me, no project is too big or too small. While I have a soft spot for the serial comma and the Chicago Manual of Style, written by my alma mater, I am also proficient in AP and MLA styles. Regardless of one's preferred style guide, consistency and clarity are key above all else." Languages: Basic written and conversational Spanish and conversational Mandarin Chinese. Christina earned a M.A. in Journalism (professional track in writing) from the Univ. of Texas at Austin and a B.A. in Sociology from the Univ. of Chicago." See previous experience at www.the-efa.org/members/data/resumes/chengc.pdf.

ANNE L. CHERNEY

133 Woodridge Dr., Douglasville GA 31034. (330)283-8409. **E-mail:** anne.thebairdgroup@gmail.com. **Contact:** Anne L. Cherney, editor/writer/project manager.

ADDITIONAL INFORMATION Extremely versatile project manager, editor and writer with experience in a wide range of topic areas including: gradeappropriate student computer fundamentals; carpentry; basic, intermediate, and advanced Microsoft Office skills; English, history and the hospitality and tourism industry. See resume: www.the-efa.org/members/data/resumes/cherneyab.pdf.

DANIELLE JANE CHOUHAN

9 Highland Park, Malden MA 02148. (617)818-7123. **E-mail:** dchouhan@pagetoportal.com. **Contact:** Danielle Jane Chouhan, editor.

ADDITIONAL INFORMATION Years in field: 8; years as freelancer: 5. "I offer editorial services and production project management for a variety of projects—big and small. I am a full-time, freelance editorial specialist with experience in K-12 as well as the college and higher-education markets." Danielle offers project management, copyediting, and proofreading, and prefers—but am not limited to—online mark-up and softproofing. Experience includes: school curriculum textbooks, scholarly journals, software instructional textbooks, corporate materials, and online database/encyclopedia content. Education: Napier University: Edinburgh, Scotland, UKMaster's Diploma in Publishing with Business; Brandeis University: Waltham, MABA in Sociology; Humanities Interdisciplinary Minor; La Sorbonne: (Université de Paris VII): Paris, France. Completed Spring Semester Abroad through the New York University program in France. See resume: www.the-efa.org/members/data/resumes/chouhand.pdf.

CHRYSALIS EDITORIAL

6439 Barnaby St., NW, Washington DC 20015. (202)363-2522. **Website:** www.chrysaliseditorial.com. **Contact:** Herta B. Feely, owner.

ADDITIONAL INFORMATION "My passion resides in the written word! I've been an editor and writer for the past 20 years, though I wrote my first short story ("Bombs Away!") when I was 12.Seven years ago, after working as the executive editor for a literary agency, I established Chrysalis Editorial to focus on serving writers in a variety of capacities. My manuscript critiques have helped countless writers hone and revise their work into publishable shape. I also copy edit, provide agent and publishing advice, and act as a writing coach to numerous clients, many of whom have gone on to obtain agents and publish their work. I have a BA in Latin American History from UC Berkeley and attended graduate school there in the field of journalism. I also have a Master of Arts in Writing from Johns Hopkins University. I've attended several writing workshops, including Bread Loaf, Squaw Valley Community of Writers, and the Iowa Summer Writing Workshops, where I worked and studied with some terrific authors: Wayne Johnson, Ursula Hegi, Mary Morris, Howard Norman, Percival Everett, Ann Hood, Margaret Meyers, and Claire Messud."

MELANIE CLARK COMMUNICATIONS

P.O. Box 22213, Nashville TN 37202. (888)519-3976. **E-mail:** info@melanieclarkcommunications.com. **Website:** www.mcommunications.websitebuilderpro.com. **Contact:** Melanie Clark. Estab. 2012.

ADDITIONAL INFORMATION "Founded in early 2012, Melanie Clark Communications is an award-winning marketing and communications agency that focuses on content marketing strategies to help organizations grow and prosper. The company was built on the premise that it is possible for all types (and sizes) of organizations to develop and implement highly effective marketing solutions that engage the community and boost awareness of the brand. MCC has a proven record of success in helping its clients with their marketing strategies, both on and offline. We work with our clients as an extension of their own marketing department. We do not recommend courses of action that we cannot measure, or that we do not fully believe can boost your prosperity. We can act as consultants, advising you on different opportunities that you can implement in-house, or we can work with you to develop the right content and ensure that it reaches your target market and achieves your objectives." Services: Ad and website content optimization, audio branding, business marketing consulting, copy and ghost writing, editing and proofreading, event coordination, social media marketing, translating, video advertising.

CLEAR COPY EDITORIAL SERVICES

Boise ID. (208)426-0772. **E-mail:** editors@clearcopy. com. **Website:** www.clearcopy.com. **Contact:** Harvey McCloud.

ADDITIONAL INFORMATION "Our business is writing, editing, and proofreading text documents, both technical and nontechnical." Services include, writing, substantive editing/rewriting, copyediting, proofreading, and research. Cost: $40-50/hour depending on the service. Contact for a quote or additional information.

CLOSE READER EDITING

(361)442-1503. **E-mail:** closereaderedit@aol.com. **Contact:** Stephen Delaney.

ADDITIONAL INFORMATION Stephen Delaney is an editor and proofreader of fiction and non-fiction with 8 years in the field, 6 as a freelancer. Specialties: short stories, novels, poetry, science fiction, fantasy, memoir, and creative non-fiction. See more info at www.the-efa.org/members/data/resumes/delaneys. pdf.

COACH BONNIE

P.O. Box 6075, Evanston IL 60204. (847)962-4770. **E-mail:** bonfire770@gmail.com. **Website:** www.coach-bonnie.com. **Contact:** Bonnie Kustner. Estab. 1999. Offers one-on-one coaching services for the writer, the writer-to-be, the writer who thinks he can, the writer who is stuck, and the writer who is soaring. "Coaching brings consistency, accountability, and sometimes (but only when needed) a major kick in the butt."

ADDITIONAL INFORMATION "Terrific for the writer who isn't sure how to get started, fabulous for the writer who got started but then got stuck, and pure genius for the writer who needs to finish, edit, proof, polish, and publish their extraordinary oeuvre."

COFFEE HOUSE FICTION EDITING SERVICES

P.O. Box 399, Forest Hills MD 21050. **E-mail:** info@ coffeehousefiction.com. **Website:** www.coffeehousefiction.com. Estab. 2007.

ADDITIONAL INFORMATION "To advance our objective of elevating excellent fiction, we've been supplying editing services to promising authors for over two years. We can focus on grammar, punctuation, and basic elements of style, readability, and sentence structure. We can also provide you with content editing, a more involved holistic reading of the fiction, and work with you on overall style, theme, complexity, and structure of a story. While fiction is a passion, we've worked with a number of authors of nonfiction; and we happily and meticulously edit documents of all types." Cost: generally runs 1.25¢ per word. Other editorial services and assistance are available upon request. Accepts submissions and inquiries by e-mail only.

BRUCE COLE

726 Tyner Way, Incline Village NV 89451. (775)831-7747. **E-mail:** rbacole@hotmail.com. **Contact:** Bruce Cole.

ADDITIONAL INFORMATION Bruce Cole has spent 32 years in thie field as freelancer. He was first published in 1980. His articles and reviews have appeared in *Worldview Magazine, The Willamette Valley Observer, The Catholic Sentinel, The Portland Oregonian, The Downtowner, The North Lake Tahoe Bonanza, and Tahoe World.* His extensive proof-reading experience was acquired at The Liturgical Press, Yale University Press, and some magazines and newspapers. He has expertise in history and biography, theology and philosophy, current events, literature, health and insurance issues. Available for articles, book reviews, and editorials; proofing and editing of manuscripts of all sizes. He is affiliated with Editorial Freelancers Association, Organization of American Historians, Society for the History of the Early American Republic. See resume: www.the-efa.org/members/data/resumes/coleb.pdf.

COMMA SENSE EDITING

252 Bayview Ave., East Patchogue NY 11772. **E-mail:** lvediting@gmail.com. **Website:** www.commasense.net. **Contact:** Lourdes Venard, president. Estab. 2010. CommaSense Editing was founded by Lourdes Venard, an editor with more than 20 years experience.

ADDITIONAL INFORMATION "We offer developmental editing, copyediting, proofreading, translations (from Spanish to English), and basic interior formatting for e-books. We work mostly with individual authors, whether they plan to self-publish or are seeking an agent/publishing house. CommaSense specializes in crime fiction, science fiction, YA, Hispanic-themed books, and memoirs."

DAVID COMPTON

E-mail: compton@authoredit.com. **Website:** www.authoredit.com.

ADDITIONAL INFORMATION "I'm a New York Times best selling author and editor and 'book doctor' who can fix your manuscript." Services offered: manuscript evaluation, structural editing, copy editing for novels and nonfiction, marketing.

CONTEXT EDITORIAL SERVICES, INC.

56 Dufferin St., P.O. Box 847, Lunenburg NS B0J 2C0 Canada. (902)634-3280. **E-mail:** nsixsmith@contextedit.com. **Website:** www.contextedit.com. **Contact:** Nancy E. Sixsmith.

ADDITIONAL INFORMATION "Specializing in copyediting, proofreading, and research/fact-checking of digital and hard-copy materials across a wide range of topics and disciplines, I offer almost two decades of wide-ranging experience in research, editing, and proofreading of computer books, scientific/technical articles, reference books, textbooks, academic bulletins, web pages, articles, marketing/business materials, and other documents." Holds advanced degree in Library and Information Science.

COPY HOSPITAL

(617)935-1446. **E-mail:** hanna@copyhospital.com. **Website:** www.copyhospital.com. **Contact:** Hannah Schonthal.

ADDITIONAL INFORMATION "Copy Hospital is a professional editorial service for individuals and institutions in medicine, biotechnology, and allied health. Whether your goal is to publish a journal article, educate patients, market a product, or improve your academic performance, our skilled medical editors and English-language experts help you get your message across the right way. Clients include major publishers and industry leaders. Reasonable rates, arrangeable per project, per hour, per page, or per word. For client list and additional information, please visit www.copyhospital.com."

THE COPYMANCER

Brooklyn NY. (720)334-8749. **E-mail:** rose@copymancer.com. **Website:** www.copymancer.com. **Contact:** Rose Jasper Fox, editor.

ADDITIONAL INFORMATION Years in field: 17. Years as a freelancer: 11. "I edit short and long fiction, primarily focusing on genre fiction. I specialize in helping new authors get their first novels ready for querying agents or self-publishing." Types of work: Copy editing, proofreading, line editing, project editing, substantive editing, critique, research. Types of material: Books, manuscripts, short stories, novels. Subjects covered: Fiction (science fiction, fantasy, horror, romance, erotica, pornography) related to mythology, folklore, history, geography and travel, language and linguistics, spelling and grammar, writing and journalism, mathematics, science, medicine, sexuality, sex and gender, politics and activism, technology, crafts, food and cooking, dance, and music.

COPYWRITE TECHNICAL WRITING & EDITORIAL SERVICES

Worcester MA. (508)798-2885. **E-mail:** copywrit@charter.net. **Contact:** Deena Madnick.

ADDITIONAL INFORMATION 21 Years in the field, and a freelancer for more than 11 years, Deena Madnick has written "technical manuals and edited technical, business, literary, academic, scholarly manuscripts and Web site content." Deena's writing experience includes: "software user manuals for the financial, investment and banking industries and editing a 160-page standard operating procedures manual for the manufacture of thermal plastics; doctoral dissertations on software user interface research, Buddhism, a settlement house, and educational philosophy; a World War II-POW memoir; a major textbook in English language arts series; and employee handbooks for third-party medical payer firms." See previous experience at www.the-efa.org/members/data/resumes/madnickd.pdf.

JUDY CORCORAVN

325 West 52nd St., 2G, New York NY 10019. (212)315-2449. **E-mail:** judycorc@aol.com. **Website:** www.JudyCorcoran.com. **Contact:** Judy Corcoran.

ADDITIONAL INFORMATION "Judy Corcoran is a highly respected writer, copywriter, copyeditor and proofreader. She has worked at magazines such as *Real Simple, Good Housekeeping, Better Homes and Gardens* and *Golf Digest*, writing advertorials, marketing materials and merchandising proposals. She authored *The Concise Guide to Magazine Marketing: Tips, Tools and Best Practices* and the co-author of *Joint Custody with a Jerk: Raising a Child with an Uncooperative Ex* and *Volleyball: Playing with Your Head at Any Height.* Judy offers professional service, a quick turn-around time, and crisp, accurate copy at an affordable price." She has been in the field for 25 years, 15 as a freelancer. See more information at www.the-efa.org/members/data/resumes/corcoranj.pdf.

CREATIVE PURSUITS EDITORIAL

Apopka FL. **E-mail:** creativepursuitsed@mac.com. **Website:** http://creativepursuitseditorial.com. **Contact:** Thom Winckelmann.

ADDITIONAL INFORMATION "CPE provides substantive editing, copyediting, project management, research, writing/ghostwriting, and writing consultation for non-fiction projects. Areas of special interest include history, the humanities, politico-military issues, international affairs, biographies, human trafficking, and Holocaust/genocide studies, as well as topics related to travel, coffee, cuisine, and equestrian pursuits."

CRESCENT EDITORIAL SERVICES

Beverley MA. **Website:** http://crescenteditorial.wordpress.com.

ADDITIONAL INFORMATION "We are a versatile group of Boston-area editors and tutors, who feel at home editing anything from scientific articles to poetry, with many stops in between. Our editors have MFAs, and experience editing and tutoring at scientific journals, craft publishers, and schools (from middle school to universities) around the greater Boston area."

JENI CROCKETT-HOLME

Charlottesville VA. **E-mail:** jrc6va@yahoo.com. **Contact:** Jeni Crockett-Holme.

ADDITIONAL INFORMATION "Jeni Crockett-Holme is a project manager and editor. She did her graduate work in gerontology at the Medical College of Virginia and specializes in content related to health, human services, and technology. She has more than 15 years of experience editing daily news, professional journals, corporate communications, and scholarly manuscripts."

CROSS-BORDER EDITORIAL SERVICES

San Diego CA. (858)243-0781. **E-mail:** gaddis@cbes.biz. **Contact:** David Gaddis Smith, editor/writer/researcher.

ADDITIONAL INFORMATION Year in field: 30. Years as a freelancer: 3. "David Gaddis Smith is a writer, editor, researcher and Spanish-to-English translator with extensive knowledge about Mexico, border, Middle East, and other international issues. Long the foreign editor of the San Diego Union-Tribune, he now edits for the Al-Monitor website and writes and edits for MexicoPerspective.com and other organizations involved with Mexico and border issues."

CAROLE CUDNIK

101 Rockywood Way, Niceville FL 32578. (850)974-3392. **Website:** www.carolecudnik.com. **Contact:** Carole A. Cudnik, editorial services provider. Estab. 2013. Carole Cudnik has more than 20 years experience in writing, proofreading, and editing technical reports and assessments for the U.S. Dept. of Defense and the U.S. Intelligence Community. In her freelance career, she provides copy and content editing, proofreading and research assistance, as well as manuscript and website evaluations.

ADDITIONAL INFORMATION "Whether your project is a future fiction novel, an inspirational guide, a technical publication or an online magazine article, she enjoys providing one-on-one attention to assist you." She is a member of the Editorial Freelancers Association (EFA) and the Christian Proofreaders and Editors Network (Christian PEN). Cudnik has an A.A. in Communications Applications Technology and a BA in History.

MEGHAN CUNNINGHAM

2611 Formosa Ave., Orlando FL 32804. (321)480-2558 (cell); (407)893-5296. **E-mail:** mcunigan@bellsouth. net. **Contact:** Meghan Cunningham.

ADDITIONAL INFORMATION Meghan Cunningham has 14 years in the field. "I have textbooks published with both Cengage and McGraw-Hill; in addition, I have worked on website content for developmental readers for McGraw-Hill. My writing and editing skills are extremely adaptable; I have worked on legal documents, textbook and educational materials, health materials, and classified goverment material. For 10 years, I taught college-level developmental reading and writing. In addition to teaching developmental English, I have taught research-based composition courses and ESL courses. My teaching experience has given me an edge in meeting the demands of today's students and being able to adapt my teaching style to many different types of students." "I have extremely high standards, am a strict grammarian, and am interested in producing only quality work." Provides writing samples and references. See CV at www.the-efa.org/members/data/resumes/cunninghamma.pdf

KAREN CURE

Hastings on Hudson NY. (917)975-1727 (cell). **E-mail:** karencure@gmail.com. **Contact:** Karen Cure.

ADDITIONAL INFORMATION "Years in field: 35. Years as freelancer: 17. Books and magazine articles mix with grant applications, business proposals, and advertising on my lifetime writing and editing project list. I have a nuanced ear for language, and I'm adept at copyediting in Chicago and AMA styles as well as resourceful and experienced at research, proficient at leading and managing complex projects, and enthusiastic as a collaborator. I give 110 percent to channel clients' ideas and thoughts into smart, polished editorial packages. Highlights: Held editorial director-level positions at Fodor's/Random House and Globe Pequot Press. Wrote the best-selling travel guidebook of all time. For an international AIDS program, helped compile and edit dozens of grant proposals ranging in length from 300 to 4,000 pages. Designed, edited, and did layout for the national guidelines for adult and pediatric HIV care and treatment. Have written and edited new business and how to establish a residential program for at-risk youth. Designed and edited a master plan for a landscape architecture firm and researched printing-and-binding options."

BARBARA CURIALLE

838 West End Ave. #BB, New York NY 10025. (212)316-5306. **E-mail:** bacurialle@nyc.rr.com. **Contact:** Barbara Curialle. Years in field: 36. Years as freelancer: 16. Performs edits on screen using Microsoft Word Track Changes function and Acrobat Pro. Extensive developmental editing, line editing, copy editing, project management, and Web research: college textbooks, professional books, and trade nonfiction. Topics include history (U.S. and world), political science, applied music and music history, business, psychology, humanities, sociology, geology, literature, communications, applied art and art history, business, medicine, and engineering. See previous experience at www.the-efa.org/members/data/resumes/curialleb.pdf.

DADIVAN BOOKS

3104 E. Camelback Road #160, Phoenix AZ 85016. (347)291-1779. **Fax:** (928)268-9181. **E-mail:** dadivanbooks@gmail.com. **Website:** www.dadivanbooks. com. **Contact:** Bootsie Martinez, editor. Estab. 1989. "We are professional writers, editors, and publishers with over a century of combined experience in the publishing world."

ADDITIONAL INFORMATION Dadivan Books also offers complete self-publishing from soup-to-nuts, including economical subsidy publishing services. "We specialize in helping authors achieve their individual dreams, whether that dream is improving a manuscript through proofreading or editing, preparing a manuscript in e-publishing formats, preparing a manuscript in paperback layout, designing the perfect cover, or fulfilling another editorial need, including ghostwriting and book doctoring. All services are available a la carte or as part of an economical package."

MARGARET DAISLEY

61 Lexington Ave., 3H, New York NY 10010. (917)847-7445. **E-mail:** mdaisley@msn.com. **Contact:** Margaret Daisley.

ADDITIONAL INFORMATION "Experienced NYC-based senior editor/writer with substantial experience working with all stakeholders within the publishing enterprise—staff and freelance writers, editors, and researchers; creative/graphics and production personnel; and marketing and advertising staff. Almost 10 years as staff editor; six years as freelance editor; occasional writer of freelance articles. Deep expertise in research-based publishing. Currently also working with writers of non-fiction books, editing/managing their projects to completion, including publishing through POD printers for distribution through Amazon, Barnes & Noble, and other international outlets. " See previous experience at www.the-efa.org/members/data/resumes/daisleym.pdf.

DAYBERRY MEDIA LAB

Kungsklippan 20, Stockholm 11225 Sweden. **E-mail:** mh@mirandholmqvist.com. **Website:** www.mirandaholmqvist.net. **Contact:** Miranda Holmqvist, freelance editor. Estab. 2008. Writing services include proofreading, editorial work, copy, editorial advice on manuscript, article and essay. Journalistic research and fact-checking.

ADDITIONAL INFORMATION Data visualization including infographics, charts, digital art and photographic illustration. Ghostwriting within fiction, nonfiction, and memoir.

JILL DEARMAN

(212)841-0177. **E-mail:** Jill@JillDearman.com. **Website:** www.bangthekeys.com. **Contact:** Jill Dearman.

ADDITIONAL INFORMATION Services include coaching and workshops, editing and ghostwriting, and company seminars.

CHERI DELLELO

2758 Piedmont Ave., Montrose CA 91020. (818)275-3314. **E-mail:** cheri@dellelo.com. **Website:** www.dellelo.com.

ADDITIONAL INFORMATION "The Editorial Freelancers Association's Southern California Liaison, Cheri is an editor with 10 years of experience in college textbook and scholarly works publishing. She is available for developmental and line editing, project management, and writing. Cheri has worked in-house for leading academic publishers McGraw-Hill, Reed Elsevier, and Sage and held positions as a developmental editor, sales representative, and acquisitions editor. As a freelancer, she has worked for companies such as Cengage, Jossey-Bass, McGraw-Hill, Routledge, Sage, and Worth, as well as for individual academics needing help with their journal articles. Area of specialty: social sciences (with expertise in psychology)."

DESK OF JESS

P.O. Box 74, Boonville MO 65233. (660)888-0447. **Website:** http://deskofjess.com. **Contact:** Jessica Walker, owner. Estab. 2010.

ADDITIONAL INFORMATION Offers copy editing and proofreading on: case studies, business plans, marketing plans, executive summaries, annual reports, business articles, press releases.

DIGITAL WRITING SERVICES

1600 Keeler Ave., Wichita Falls TX 76301. (940)923-7704. **E-mail:** cliffball@digitalwritingservices.com. **Website:** www.digitalwritingservices.com. **Contact:** Cliff E. Ball, Jr..

ADDITIONAL INFORMATION Proofreader, editor, and writer with 20 years of experience as a freelancer. Digital Writing Services offers affordable copy editing for $1.25 per page to businesses, students, authors and anyone who needs their documents edited for grammar, punctuation, spelling, and clarity. Cliff Ball holds a B.A. in English a certificate in Technical Writing.

ANNE DILLON

P.O. Box 912, Waitsfield VA 05673. (802)496-3656. **E-mail:** clerestory@madriver.com. **Contact:** Anne Dillon.

ADDITIONAL INFORMATION Editor and ghostwriter for all genres. Screenplays a specialty.

JANE DINEEN

172 Main St., Lovell ME 04051. (207)925-1333. **E-mail:** janedineen@gmail.com. **Contact:** Jane Dineen. **ADDITIONAL INFORMATION** "Since 1985, I have been an editor for academic, technical, and corporate publications and computer-based text. I was a technical writer-editor for Bolt Beranek and Newman, and then a self-employed editor and designer of educational and informative multimedia programs. I hold a master's degree in archaeology from Boston University. I edit in American or British English and translate from French." See previous experience at www.the-efa.org/members/data/resumes/dineenj.txt.

DR. TOD EDITING SERVICES

8 American Court, Catonsville MD 21228. (410)744-9349; (410)782-5646. **E-mail:** marytod@me.com; mary@drtodediting.com. **Website:** www.drtodediting.com. **Contact:** Mary Tod. "Whether you are a medical publisher or an academic researcher looking for an experienced copyeditor, I can provide you with just the right dose of medical editing. My background as a medical scientist ensures that I know and understand the scientific lingo, and my excellent language skills and training as a copyeditor allow me to polish scientific writing in a way that conforms to my publishing clients' style guides and formats." **ADDITIONAL INFORMATION** Freelance editor since 1996. Medical journal and book editing. Trade book proofreading, both fiction and nonfiction. Board-certified Editor in Life Sciences. PhD in Physiology. 10 years' experience as medical researcher on faculty of medical school. Experienced editor for ESL authors in medical fields. Author or coauthor of more than 30 scientific articles published in peer-reviewed journals.

HEATHER DUBNICK EDITORIAL SERVICES

39 Dodge St. #356, Beverly MA 01915. (508)932-6955. **E-mail:** hdubnick@gmail.com. **Website:** www.heatherdubnick.com. **Contact:** Heather Dubnick. Estab. 2004. Heather Dubnick Editorial Services offers copyediting, developmental editing, manuscript evaluation, coaching, researching, fact-checking, proofreading, formatting, and indexing. **ADDITIONAL INFORMATION** "I work in Spanish as well as English."

CAROL DWYER

9 Osborne Road, Poughkeepsie NY 12601. (845)452-0751. **E-mail:** cdwyer.writer@gmail.com. **Contact:** Carol Dwyer.
ADDITIONAL INFORMATION "I create original copy, correct errors and clear up confusion in existing copy, and manage editorial projects. In my 25 years in communications—writing, editing, proofreading and project management—I have learned to make words work. I specialize in explaining difficult and complex subjects in easy-to-understand language. I help people close the gap between the words they use to understand their own thoughts and the words they need to make their thoughts clear to others. I use the powerful impact of clear, on-target messages to inform, inspire and motivate people. Proofreading: Check typeset copy against original or previous proof for accuracy and consistency." Clients: General Electric, GE Consumer & Industrial, Daimler Chrysler, Capital Services, Mercedes Benz Credit Corporation, Pitney Bowes. See previous experience at www.the-efa.org/members/data/resumes/dwyerc.pdf.

ECO-WRITE, LLC

Environmental and Life Science Writing and Editing, State College PA (814)238-8070, **E-mail:** jdrohan@nasw.org. **Website:** www.eco-write.com. **Contact:** Joy R. Drohan.
ADDITIONAL INFORMATION Joy Drohan is a freelance science editor and award-winning writer whose clients have been the U.S. Forest Service, Island Press, Carnegie Institution, Grand Canyon Association, Geological Society of America, University of Nevada, Las Vegas, Natural Resource, Agriculture, and Engineering Service (NRAES), Cornell University, NATO. See her rèsumè at www.the-efa.org/members/data/resumes/drohanjr.pdf.

ECWORDSMITH

80 Morristown Road, #231, Bernardsville NJ 07924. (908)256-5150. **E-mail:** eclarke333@aol.com. **Website:** www.ecwordsmith.com. **Contact:** Ellen Clarke, editor/proofreader.
ADDITIONAL INFORMATION "My goal is to connect with people - both private and professional in any industry - who need a second pair of eyes to proofread documents before "going public." If you write marketing materials, white papers, essays, catalogues, manuals - contact me. I also aim to connect with writers looking to perfect their work, whether to send to an

agent or self-publish. I edit e-documents as well as hard copy. Specialties ECWordsmith is a freelance business - I have flexibility in the delivery of your documents, as well as flexibility of time. My clients communicate with me directly. Besides my writing and editing experience, I have a BA in Music, and an AS in Chemistry and Biology. I have an ongoing self-education in Astronomy, Meteorology, and other Earth Sciences."

EDELSACK EDITORIAL SERVICE

Vestal NY. (607)770-4248. **E-mail:** pedelsack@aol.com. **Contact:** Paula Edelsack. Estab. Paula Edelsack has been in the publishing field 31 years, 23 as a freelancer..

EDITING (AND MORE) BY SUE

1 Hill Hollow Road, Lake Hopatcong NJ 07849. (973)362-5382. **E-mail:** sue_toth@editingbysue.com. **Website:** www.editingbysue.com. **Contact:** Sue Toth, president. Estab. 2012. "I am an accomplished editor with more than 25 years of experience in all types of writing, from fiction to news to medical editing, with my specialty being fiction."

ADDITIONAL INFORMATION "I offer everything from developmental editing of your manuscript to proofreading a final copy. I can also help you with e-book formatting, as well as promoting your book and managing your social media plan."

EDITLAW

Seattle WA. (206)409-2604. **E-mail:** legaleditor@comcast.net; sharon_rutberg@editlaw.com. **Contact:** Sharon C. Rutberg.

ADDITIONAL INFORMATION Sharon Rutberg has 28 years in the field; 8 as a freelancer. "As a former attorney, I specialize in editing legal publications, including treatises for practicing lawyers, articles for professional journals, and books by attorney-authors. I also work regularly on a variety of other non-fiction materials, ranging from consultant reports on the pharmaceutical industry to books and catalogues on the visual arts. My goal is to help you create a clear, accurate, elegant presentation of your complex information. I bring to every project a love of order and logic, an eye for detail and visual harmony, and a passion for perfection. Whether you need help developing and organizing your ideas (developmental editing), revising your rough draft (copyediting), polishing your final draft (line editing), or proofreading the end product, I will bring out the best in your publication. I work

on-line in Word using TrackChanges or in hard copy, and am familiar with Chicago and AP styles and the Bluebook. I am also comfortable working with your house style, or I can help you develop one." Selected clients: Bureau of National Affairs (BNA), Books Division, Washington State Bar Association, Carl Anderson, Regulatory Compliance Consultant, Marquand Books (publisher of fine-art books), John Ransom Phillips (individual author), Conaway & Strickler, P.C. Education: Northwestern University School of Law, J.D. *cum laude*, 1988 Swarthmore College, B.A. with honors in art history, 1981."

EDITMORE EDITORIAL SERVICES

501-I South Reino Road #194, Newbury Park CA 91320. **E-mail:** tammy@editmore.com. **Website:** www.editmore.com. **Contact:** Tammy Ditmore, owner/editor. Estab. 2011. Offers copyediting, proofreading, and developmental editing for nonfiction authors.

ADDITIONAL INFORMATION "I have been working with words for more than 3 decades—editing and writing for a wide range of authors and publications. I can help you get the most out of your words whether you are creating a book, article, website, annual report, or grad school assignment. Let me focus on the details so you can concentrate on the ideas."

EDITOR EXTRAORDINAIRE

Calgary AB Canada. **Fax:** (206)352-8418. **E-mail:** editor.extraordinaire@gmail.com. **Website:** editorextraordinaire.books.officelive.com/default.aspx. **Contact:** Audra Gorgiev.

ADDITIONAL INFORMATION Years in field: 15; Years as freelancer: 12. "I am a professional freelance editor (copyediting, line editing, technical editing, and substantive editing) and proofreader offering a wealth of experience editing a wide variety of written material (including textbooks, scientific, medical, and technical journal articles, academic documents, marketing materials, ESL documents, as well as other nonfiction work)." See rèsumè at http://www.the-efa.org/members/data/resumes/gorgieva.pdf.

EDITORIAL ALCHEMY

(941)377-7640. **E-mail:** Carol@EditorialAlchemy.com. **Website:** www.EditorialAlchemy.com. **Contact:** Carol Gaskin, Editor.

ADDITIONAL INFORMATION Services include manuscript critiques, marketing, line editing, development for fiction and nonfiction, writing tutorials, and occasional ghostwriting.

THE EDITORIAL DEPARTMENT

7650 E. Broadway, Suite #308, Tucson AZ 85710. (520)546-9992. **Fax:** (520)722-5539. **Website:** www.editorialdepartment.com. **Contact:** Renni Browne.

ADDITIONAL INFORMATION "The Editorial Department is pleased to provide a wide range of services for fiction manuscripts, appropriate for works at just about any stage of development." Services offered include manuscript evaluation, consultation, and development, marketing, line and copy editing, agent matchmaking, book proposals, and more. Handles fiction and nonfiction.

EDITORIAL INSPIRATIONS

15086 Brown Pleasants Road, Montepelier VA 23192. (804)883-7480. **E-mail:** editor@editorialinspirations.com. **Website:** www.editorialinspirations.com. **Contact:** April Michelle Davis, owner.

ADDITIONAL INFORMATION Editorial Inspirations provides editing, indexing, and proofreading services to both publishers and authors. April Michaelle Davis has been a freelance editor, indexer, and proofreader since 2001. She has a B.A. in English from Messiah College, a M.A. in publishing from The George Washington University, and several field-related certificates, including ones in book publishing and editing from the University of Virginia, along with one in professional editing from EEI Communications. April has worked with authors and publishers in a variety of genres, including training, engineering, carpentry, real estate, law, memoir, self-help, historical, biographical, scholarly, children's literature, and religion. See http://www.the-efa.org/members/data/resumes/davisam.pdf.

THE EDITORIAL NOTE

Wilmette IL. **E-mail:** calcohen75@gmail.com. **Website:** www.editorialnote.net. **Contact:** David H. Cohen.

ADDITIONAL INFORMATION "David Cohen has been a professional writer and editor for over two decades. His work has appeared in the Financial Times of London, Crain's Chicago Business, Time magazine, Chicago Wilderness and other publications. His corporate editorial clients have been in the areas of healthcare and financial services. A long-term conservationist, Cohen was formerly a writer and editor for the Chicago Audubon Society, and has worked in Europe, Asia and Latin America. As a professional educator, Cohen has taught at Chicago-area universities and has developed workplace literacy programs."

EDITORIAL SERVICES OF LOS ANGELES (ESOLA)

Los Angeles CA. **E-mail:** EditorialServicesofLA@gmail.com. **Website:** http://editorialservicesofla.com. **Contact:** Lisa Rojany Buccieri, proprietor.

ADDITIONAL INFORMATION ""Editorial Services of Los Angeles (ESOLA) has been in business for over 20 years and has helped hundreds of writers of both children's and adult books of fiction and nonfiction get published by traditional means and self-publishing. ESOLA offers everything from detailed content/line editing with critique letter, writing and ghostwriting, to eBook editing and pdf typesetting." Other services include book doctoring, copyediting, proofreading, manuscript evaluation, and more. Cost: E-mail for quote; professional membership discounts available. Offers free query letter edit with service. See website for additional information.

THE EDITOR'S MARK

5797 Southwater Dr., Mason OH 45040. (513)754-8670. **Website:** www.theeditorsmark.com. **Contact:** Jill R. Hughes.

ADDITIONAL INFORMATION Jill Hughes has been in the publishing business for more than 10 years. She specializes in substantive editing, copyediting, proofreading, book design, and research. Clients include: Bloomsbury USA/Holtzbrinck, Avalon Publishing Group, Perseus Books Group, Pegasus Books. "One of the most interesting experiences I've had is working on on former ambassador Joseph Wilson's book, *The Politics of Truth* and meeting him in person at Book Expo in Los Angeles. My non-publishing background includes marketing and teaching, which means I have a wide variety of skills to contribute to my work. I've done quite a few projects on military history, literary criticism, and health." Jill earned a B.A. in Marketing, University of Michigan.

EDITS BY BERGER

P.O. Box 146, Grantham PA 17027. **E-mail:** sharon.r.berger@gmail.com. **Contact:** Sharon Berger, editor. Estab. 2009.

ADDITIONAL INFORMATION Editorial services include proofreading, standard copy editing, extensive copy editing, typesetting, and design. Specialized in academic writing. Proficient in Chicago, APA, and AP editing styles; also capable in MLA.

EDITWRITEDESIGN

(704)584-9653. **E-mail:** editwritedesign@yahoo.com. **Website:** www.editwritedesign.com.

ADDITIONAL INFORMATION Editorial services include proofreading and comprehensive editing. Other services include book cover layout, interior formatting, e-book cover design, and RTF to HTML conversion for Kindle. Cost: Contact for quote. See website for additional information.

EDWARDS MEDIA DEVELOPMENT, INC.

180 Brevator St., Albany NY 12206. (518)459-0676; (518)429-8592. **E-mail:** aedwards@nycap.rr.com. **Contact:** Andrea J. Edwards.

ADDITIONAL INFORMATION "I have been involved with educational textbook publishing for 22 years - 7 years as a full-time freelancer and 15 years at Thomson/Cengage. My work has focused on the soft side of publishing with specialties in developmental editing, proofreading, writing, editing, market research, project management, survey compilation, and competitive analysis. I have worked with Pearson/Prentice Hall, McGraw-Hill, Elsevier/Saunders, and Cengage publishers in areas as diverse as criminal justice, early childhood education, hospitality, tourism, allied health, agriculture, cosmetology, automotive, electrical, massage therapy, and the social sciences." See previous experience at www.the-efa.org/members/data/resumes/edwardsaj.pdf.

JOHANNA EHRMANN

Auburndale MA 02466. (617)558-9373. **E-mail:** johanna@herworkplace.com. **Contact:** Johanna Ehrmann.

ADDITIONAL INFORMATION "More than 15 years spent editing and copyediting textbooks have given me a good understanding of what works and what doesn't in a book or series. I bring a laser-sharp focus to each project, and I think about the text on many levels—content, flow, style, and grammar. I also enjoy writing for young people and have written leveled readers—both fiction and nonfiction—and SE and TE copy for literature, math, and social science books. Though most of my experience has been with textbooks, I welcome projects that push me into new areas. Americanizing a cookbook, copyediting mythology reference works, and even proofreading a company history were great fun." Johanna earned a B.A. in psychology from Brandeis Univ. See more information at http://www.the-efa.org/members/data/resumes/ehrmannj.pdf.

EMBREE LITERARY SERVICES

138 W. Alta Green, Port Hueneme CA 93041. (805)985-1113. **E-mail:** maryembree@gmail.com. **Website:** www.maryembree.com. **Contact:** Mary Embree, owner/manager. Estab. 1990. Mary Embree is an author, freelance editor, literary consultant, seminar and workshop presenter, and public speaker. Since 1990, she has helped writers with their book manuscripts from first to final draft, guiding and editing their book projects according to professional book publishing standards. Her services include writing and editing book proposals, query letters to literary agents and book publishers, and preparing manuscripts for presentation.

ADDITIONAL INFORMATION If authors choose to self-publish, she guides them through the entire process, such as registering their copyright and getting ISBNs, barcodes, and Library of Congress Control numbers. Embree and her associates desing and typeset interior pages of the book as well as eye-catching book covers, providing print-ready PDF files.

THE EQUALIZER

(613)329-9942. **E-mail:** bob@communication.ca. **Website:** www.communication.ca/editor. **Contact:** Bob MacKenzie.

ADDITIONAL INFORMATION "WRITE, REVISE, EDIT, PROOFREAD. 40+ years experience. Published author, poet, critic. Marketing professional. Bob MacKenzie, B.A., M.A., B.Ed."

DAVID J. ESTRIN

510 West 110th Street, #12F, New York NY 10025. (212)749-7563. **E-mail:** theeditor@mindspring.com. **Contact:** David J. Estrin. Estab. 1998.

ADDITIONAL INFORMATION Full-time freelance editor and consultant. Manuscript development, project management, copyediting, seminars on writing and publishing, consulting. Disciplines: Anthropology, Business, Criminal Justice, Critical Theory, History, Comparative Literature, Education, Economics, Geography, Law, Philosophy, Political Science, Public Administration, Policy Studies, Psychology, Religion, Sociology, Social Work/Social Welfare, Urban Affairs, and Women's Studies. Recommended editor, Columbia Univ. School of Social Work. Earned a B.A. in Government, Oberlin College. "I have worked in academic publishing for more than 28 years. I was an acquisition editor at Longman for 7 years, during which time I signed and developed dozens of textbooks in the social sciences... and more than 100 scholarly works and textbooks in a variety of disciplines." David Estrin is currently the copy editor of the International Journal of Africana Studies. See previous experience at www.the-efa.org/members/data/resumes/estrindj.pdf.

AMY FASS

New York NY. (212)923-4447. **E-mail:** anom@nyct.net. **E-mail:** anom@nyct.net. **Contact:** Amy Fass.
ADDITIONAL INFORMATION Amy Fass has 25 years in the field, and 15 years as a freelancer. Amy is a medical and science editor with extensive experience in substantive editing, copy editing, proofreading, fact-checking, and abstract writing in a wide range of topics (see list below), in formats including journal articles, slides, conference papers and posters, books, newsletters, interactive online presentations, and educational materials for doctors, nurses, physician assistants, and patients. Well versed in AMA style and CME requirements. English or Spanish, paper or PC. Green business. Medical topics include cardiology (including electrocardiography and echocardiography), infectious disease, diabetes, pulmonology, urology, gastroenterology, vaccinations, osteoporosis, trauma medicine, neurology (including parkinsonism, Alzheimer's disease, multiple sclerosis, and ADHD), cancer, pain medicine, headache, gynecology, stroke, clotting disorders, malnutrition, ophthalmology, and epidemiology. Nonmedical topics include electrical engineering, zoology, astronomy, math, petroleum geology, ecology, nutrition, math, science fiction, finance, politics, and statistics.

FAST EDITING

Silver Spring MD. (240)389-3095. **Fax:** (240)331-6597. **E-mail:** jeanette@fastediting.biz. **Website:** www.fastediting.biz. **Contact:** Jeanette Fast Redmond.
ADDITIONAL INFORMATION "Astute, Versatile, and Efficient Editor with a Decade of Publishing Experience. Strong familiarity with publishers' goals, processes, and budget constraints in a rapidly changing industry. Subject matter knowledge combined with passion for learning. Holistic approach with unrelenting attention to detail. Efficient processes that produce high-quality results in less time. Specialty in Catholic liturgy, social teaching. Jeanette set the standard for editing books issued by the U.S. Conference of Catholic Bishops, the *USCCB Style Guide*. See

previous experience at www.the-efa.org/members/data/resumes/redmondjf.pdf.

GAIL FAY

270 Malabar Rd SW, Box 108, Palm Bay FL 32907. (321)243-8599. **E-mail:** gail@faywordworks.com. **Website:** www.faywordworks.com. **Contact:** Gail Fay, writer/copyeditor.
ADDITIONAL INFORMATION Years in field: 8. Gail Fay is a professional copyeditor, proofreader, writer specializing in the nonfiction educational market. Gail is a former English teacher. She works with the Chicago Manual of Style and Publication Manual of the APA. She copyedits educational, scholarly, reference, and trade titles; works in MS Word using track changes, querying the author and incorporating the author's responses into the final version; creates a detailed style sheet including decisions on punctuation, capitalization, spelling, and style; proofs electronically using Adobe Acrobat Professional. Gail has been the only proofreader of the Scarecrow Press journal *Teacher Librarian* for over 2 years. She is called on for high-profile titles and meticulous proofing. "In 2009 I started writing nonfiction children's books for the school and library market. Titles include "Battles of the Civil War" (Heinemann Library, 2011), "Using Money" and "Economies around the World" (both Heinemann Library, 2012), and "Malcolm X" and "Pocahontas" (both Heinemann Library, 2013). My first nonfiction book for young adults, titled "Sports: The Ultimate Teen Guide" (Scarecrow Press), was released in December 2012." See previous experience at www.the-efa.org/members/data/resumes/fayg.pdf.

ELIZABETH FIALA

4322 279th Ave SE, Fall City WA 98024. (425)785-8200. **E-mail:** eafiala@gmail.com. **Contact:** Elizabeth Fiala.
ADDITIONAL INFORMATION "I have a Bachelor of Arts degree in International Communications from the American University of Paris and am currently pursuing an Editing Certificate from the University of Washington. I started my editorial and writing career by serving as a reporter and copy-editor for various school publications, and then went on to do editorial-related internships in South Africa and the United States. I began my freelance career by editing and translating academic projects for my peers, and have since branched out to working with various businesses, mostly within the greater Seattle area. I

am bilingual in English and French." See previous experience at www.the-efa.org/members/data/resumes/fialae.pdf.

FIRSTLIGHT VENTURES, INC.

3 Mariposa Road, Santa Fe NM 87508. (435)688-2835. **E-mail:** cynthiawrites@msn.com. **Contact:** Cynthia Lane.

ADDITIONAL INFORMATION Cynthia Lane is a writer, ghostwriter and substantive and developmental editor with more than 26 years experience. Her topics include personal and spiritual development, the environment, international development and politics, complementary healthcare/stress management, corporate communications (training manuals, newsletters, professional papers and reports). Ghostwriting projects have included books on the environment, complementary healthcare and personal growth. She has also edited and/or written and published numerous journal and news articles, promotional materials and encyclopedia entries.

MARTIN FISCHER

Oak Park IL. **E-mail:** martinfischer@hotmail.com. **Website:** http://martinfischer.webs.com. **Contact:** Martin Fischer.

ADDITIONAL INFORMATION "Experienced amateur genealogist Martin Fischer is available to conduct freelance family history projects including searching online databases, building family trees, editing memoirs and creating genealogical websites."

KATHLEEN FLORIO

16645 S.E. 18th St., Bellevue WA 98008. (425)746-8525. **E-mail:** klflorio@msn.com. **Contact:** Kathleen Florio.

ADDITIONAL INFORMATION Years in field: 30 Years as freelancer: 25. "I provide editing and writing services to deliver print and online materials that are accurate, clear, and tailored to the target audience. Areas of interest include education (including education technology), arts and culture, nature, environmental issues, business and finance, history, politics, travel, food, music, and gardening. I work with individual authors, publishers, corporations, nonprofits, and universities. Sample clients include the Panasonic Foundation, Microsoft, the Merck Institute for Science Education, and Susquehanna University." See previous experience at http://www.the-efa.org/members/data/resumes/floriok.pdf.

FOOD EDITOR

New York NY. (212)875-1977; (917)575-0771. **E-mail:** Deri@DeriReed.com; DeriReed@nyc.rr.com. **Website:** www.derireed.com. **Contact:** Deri Reed.

ADDITIONAL INFORMATION Deri Reed has 20 years in the field as an experienced food editor, copyeditor, web and recipe editor, and a project manager. Her specialty is cookbooks based on complex diets and menus. Her clients include International Masters Publishers, Rodale, Hachette, Perseus, Andrews McMeel, Sasquatch, Sterling/Hearst Books, Artisan/Workman, Smallwood and Stewart, Barnes & Noble Books, Rebus, Weight Watchers Publishing Group.

FORMANDSUBSTANCE

Asheville NC (828)279-4250. **Website:** http://www.formandsubstance.com. **Contact:** Helen Glenn Court.

ADDITIONAL INFORMATION Helen Glenn Court has been in the field of line editing, substantive editing, copy editing, developmental editing, and proofreading for 20 years; 15 as a freelancer. Her emphasis is on books in the social and library sciences, humanities, and general nonfiction; articles, reports, and books in international affairs and environmental science; academic journals in criminology, political science, and wildlife. Helen states that versatility has always been her strong suit, whether in genre or discipline. "In sum, I am a wordsmith and, as it happens, a book designer." See her previous experience at www.formandsubstance.com/hgc_resume.php.

FOUR EYES EDIT

45-08 40th St., #A22, Sunnyside NY 11104. (646)234-2628 (Margarita); (917)561-5616 (Adela). **E-mail:** foureyesedit@gmail.com. **E-mail:** foureyesedit@gmail.com. **Website:** www.foureyesedit.com. **Contact:** Margarita R. Kurtz; Adela Brito. Estab. 2008.

ADDITIONAL INFORMATION "We are two editing and writing professionals with years of experience in publishing and education. We've honed our editorial and coaching skills through our work at McGraw-Hill, Scholastic, The New Yorker, and Sylvan Learning Center. Adela Brito holds a Bachelor's in English from Florida International University and Margarita Kurtz holds a Bachelor's in Literature from Purchase College State University of New York. Both continue to sharpen their writing skills by taking creative writing courses, with a focus on memoir and fiction, at Gotham Writers' Workshops in New York City, along with other workshops on business writing." Services:

"We can help you edit and write: memoirs, e-books, novels, college essays, academic papers, personal statements, theses, and dissertations (using MLA, APA style format), textbooks and teachers' guides, newsletters, grants, and marketing materials."

PENELOPE FRANKLIN

E-mail: info@creativeliteraryalliance.com; penelope@creativeliteraryalliance.com. **Website:** www.creativeliteraryalliance.com. **Contact:** Penelope Franklin.

ADDITIONAL INFORMATION Penelope Franklin is a versatile editor and writer who has been in the field for over 25 years. She is associated with such major publishers as Reader's Digest Books, Columbia University, the United Nations, Oxford University Press, American Heritage magazine and Current Biography magazine. As a consultant to UNICEF, she assisted writers around the world who used English as a second language. She works with first-time authors and established ones, with an emphasis on developing each client's unique voice. She studied at the Publishing Institute of New York University and is a graduate of Columbia University. Her services include manuscript evaluation; developmental, line and substantive editing; rewriting; ghostwriting and co-authorship; and production of personal histories. She is also a skilled writing coach and does copywriting for advertisements, brochures and other promotional materials.

FREELANCE EDITING SERVICES, INC.

Burlington NC. (336)222-7026. **E-mail:** editquickly@earthlink.net. **Website:** www.editquickly.com. **Contact:** Kim Fields. Estab. 2001.

ADDITIONAL INFORMATION Freelance Editing Services took on its first project in 2001 and became incorporated in 2005. The company's specialty is the editing of educational materials (e.g., teacher resource books, teacher editions, student textbooks, standardized test items) for the PreK-Grade 8 market. Kim Fields is a former elementary and middle school teacher. Her specialty was teaching Language Arts, with an expertise in writing instruction. She also has experience as an in-house editor for an educational publisher specializing in the primary grades. This includes formatting, copyediting, applying styles, determining art layouts, evaluating appropriateness for grade level, and checking for consistency and accuracy. Her rates are negotiable; she can charge by the

page or project. No job is too small or large. See her resume on the website.

FREESTYLE EDITORIAL SERVICES

Ellicott City MD. (410)999-5426. **E-mail:** jlatta@freestyleservices.com. **Website:** www.freestyleservices.com. **Contact:** Joseph Latta, editor.

ADDITIONAL INFORMATION Years in field: 15. Years as a freelancer: 4. "I specialize in developing clear, concise business and marketing content for professional services companies and nonprofits. With nearly 15 years of writing, editing, and management experience in the corporate environment, I have worked closely with organizations to create persuasive sales/grant proposals, white papers, marketing brochures, website content, business books, corporate communications, and other business development materials. I am passionate about helping my clients stand apart from the competition."

HENRY GUSTAVO FUENTES

San Diego CA. **E-mail:** hgfuentes@yahoo.com. **Contact:** Henry G. Fuentes.

ADDITIONAL INFORMATION "Southern California-based editor/writer brings more than three decades of major media experience to copy editing assignments that include corporate and educational communications, newsletters and textbooks, with a focus on turning text into tighter, more readable copy. My background includes 16 years as a copy editor at the Los Angeles Times (1990-2006), including editing of the opinion and editorial pages, and 3 1/2 years as chief copy editor of the op-ed pages at The San Diego Union-Tribune (2006-09), an assignment that included turning often lengthy and poorly written letter to the editor submissions into concise letters with corrected grammar and improved clarity while retaining the writer's message. I've also been a reporter (10 years at a large metro daily), and wrote a television treatment for a nationally broadcast PBS documentary. And, with my newspaper background, I am very deadline-conscious." See previous experience at www.the-efa.org/members/data/resumes/fuenteshg.pdf.

FULL STOP EDITORIAL

Fort Collins CO. (970)266-9157. **Website:** www.fullstopeditorial.com. **Contact:** Lisa Péré.

ADDITIONAL INFORMATION Editing, Writing, Project Management; 12 years' experience. "Full Stop Editorial excels in clarifying your message, on time and on budget. The result: Winning proposals, educated end users, increased readerships, satisfied clients, and greater profitability." Lisa Péré lets you choose the depth of edit you want—surface (copy) edit or deep (developmental) edit. She provides fast, efficient review of existing material. Proficient in French. Affiliated with Editorial Freelancers Association, Northern Colorado Writers, and Business Women's Network of Fort Collins. See www.linkedin.com/in/llperellpere@fullstopeditorial.com. References and clips available upon request. See previous experience at www.the-efa.org/members/data/resumes/perel.pdf.

JERRI CORGIAT GALLAGHER

4631 N. 124th St., Kansas City KS 66109. **Website:** www.jerricorgiat.com. **Contact:** Jerri Corgiat Gallagher, editor. Estab. 2006. Offers copyediting, line editing, and content development.

ADDITIONAL INFORMATION Author of 5 novels as Jerri Corgiat. "Currently working on book six in the series."

DIANE GARDNER

502 Spring Creek Ct., Colorado Springs CO 80919. (719)531-9175. **E-mail:** degardner@pcisys.net. **Contact:** Diane Gardner.

ADDITIONAL INFORMATION Over 10 years of experience in writing, editing, proofreading, and research. Education: B.A., Journalism – CSU, Fresno; M.A., Mass Communications and Journalism – CSU, Fresno. See previous experience at www.the-efa.org/members/data/resumes/gardnerd.pdf.

FRAN GARDNER

2716 SE Main St., Portland OR 97214. (503)267-4303. **E-mail:** fran@hevanet.com. **Contact:** Fran Gardner.

ADDITIONAL INFORMATION "Building on more than three decades of newspaper writing, editing, and copy editing experience, I have a thriving business as a freelance writer and editor." "Knowledge of ancient Greek has been helpful in transliterating New Testament citations and Latin in ensuring the accuracy of scientific names. Also French, Polish, German, Spanish, Turkish. I am familiar with the AP Stylebook, The Chicago Manual of Style, The Food Lover's Companion, Fowler's English Usage, and Garner's Modern American Usage. Interested in food and recipes, gardening (special strength in taxonomy), how-to, photography, popular physics, philosophy, psychology, self-help, spirituality, the uses of technology, other nonfiction, and books for children and young adults."

See more information at www.the-efa.org/members/data/resumes/gardnerf.pdf.

SHAWN-MARIE GARRETT

52 Prospect Ave., Apt. 1, Sea Cliff NY 11579. (917)575-2981. **E-mail:** smgarrett0524@gmail.com. **Contact:** Shawn-Marie Garrett.

ADDITIONAL INFORMATION Shawn-Marie Garrett, D.F.A. is a published editor and author with an arts/humanities doctoral degree from Yale. With over 20 years of writing, editing, and publishing experience at all levels, at every stage in the publication process, Shawn specializes in cultural journalism, professional arts/humanities criticism and scholarship. Shawn is a researcher, educator, editor, and writer, specializing in scholarship, nonfiction, and drama and film. She is "thoroughly trained and experienced in editorial as well as in curatorial, archival, publishing, grant-making, administrative, and theatrical production practices." Over 10 years' experience of Ivy League teaching in the arts and humanities at the graduate and undergraduate levels. See previous experience at www.the-efa.org/members/data/resumes/garrettsm.pdf.

DONNA J. GARZINSKY

Wharton NJ. (973)361-5224. **E-mail:** garwarnj@yahoo.com. **Contact:** Donna J. Garzinsky, editorial.

ADDITIONAL INFORMATION Donna Garzinsky has been in the field for 16 years, and as freelancer 6. She has worked with publishers and curriculum developers, with focus on reading comprehension, leveling, and/or assessment; phonics; grammar/usage/mechanics; writing process; spelling; and for ESL/ELD students. Donna is experienced in using InCopy and Acrobat.

MARY GAWLIK

Cheverly MD. (301)773-0657. **E-mail:** megawlik04@comcast.net. **Contact:** Mary Gawlik.

ADDITIONAL INFORMATION Mary Gawlik has 16 years' experience in copyediting and developmental editing, primarily on computer. She uses Chicago style, APA style, GPO style, AP style. Her focus is on nonfiction, including books, manuals, journals and magazines, reports, monographs, working papers, essays, biographies, grant proposals, dissertations, and online courses. She has attained a wide range of editing experience, including education, disabilities, social sciences, infants and toddlers, health care, business and finance, research, and more. She attended training in editing and book publishing through the University of Virginia certificate program; she also has a Master's in Behavioral Science/Organizational Psychology. Clients describe her as "incredibly thorough; professional; on target; proactive and forward thinking; excellent at maintaining an author's voice and at querying authors in a positive, sensitive manner. Mary "enjoys working on complex, difficult documents; absolutely loves all phases of editing,"

GD PROOFS

San Marco FL 34145. (201)988-2658. **E-mail:** gdproofs@yahoo.com. **Website:** www.gdproofs.vp-web.com. **Contact:** Gabriella Deponte.

ADDITIONAL INFORMATION Gaby Deponte is a versatile copy editor, proofreader, and translator who's been in the field for more than 20 years. She has experience editing and writing in the financial, fiction, and nonfiction areas. Gaby edits book manuscripts as well as brochures, articles, marketing letters, and presentations. Her expertise includes refining the work of non-native speakers. With excellent written and verbal communications skills, she works collegially and respects deadlines. For more information, please visit her website or see her resume at http://www.the-efa.org/members/data/resumes/deponteg.pdf.

LIZ GELLER

Project Management & Editorial Services, 101 East 16th St., # 6E, New York NY 10003. (212)614-3078. **Fax:** (212)375-1216. **E-mail:** elizgeller@earthlink.net. **Contact:** Liz Geller.

ADDITIONAL INFORMATION Liz Geller has done project management and substantive editing of academic scientific material. She has 20+ years experience with McGraw-Hill, WH Freeman, Worth Publishers and more, and 3 years as a freelancer. See her resume at www.the-efa.org/members/data/resumes/gellerl.pd.

GEMSTONE EDITING

550 Belmont St., Apt. 37, Watertown MA 02472. (617)924-9185. **E-mail:** sblake@gemstone-editing.com. **Contact:** Sue A. Blake, editor/proofreader.

ADDITIONAL INFORMATION For 30 years, has edited works by authors in civil, environmental, software engineering; scientific research; strategy consulting; education; arts/architecture. Content has included scholarly articles, periodicals, white papers, Web content, books, textbook chapters, environmental impact statements, software documentation. Sue

has a special talent for technical and scientific texts. Holds a B.A., Religion, Earlham College, and M.Ed., Rehabilitation Counseling, Boston University, has morphed into a strong affinity for the geosciences and protecting our planet. Sue Blake will clarify your writing so that readers can understand what you're saying without rereading. "I suggest edits or query anything that is ambiguous or distracting or that otherwise blocks understanding: incorrect spelling, punctuation, or grammar; wordiness; redundancy; confusing or missing content. (Examples available.)" Speak Portuguese, read French, know some Spanish and German. See previous experience at www.the-efa.org/members/data/resumes/blakesa.pdf.

KRISTEN GEORGI, MAT/MAT, DMH(C)

37 Bellvale Lakes Road, Warwick NY 10990. (845)986-8175; (845)597-4148. **E-mail:** kgeorgi@optonline.net. **Website:** www.kristengeorgi.com. **Contact:** Kristen Georgi.

ADDITIONAL INFORMATION Kristen Georgi has "18 years as a freelance and staff editor and writer; Writer/editor of healthcare industry B-to-B reports; Editor of Current Clinical Practice for primary care physicians; Editor of APCToday.com for nurse practitioners and physician assistants; Editor-in-chief of national newspaper of Chinese medicine; Healthcare journalist for daily newspaper and national consumer magazines; High level decision-making and problem-solving capabilities with exceptional multitasking capacity. Member, American Medical Writers Association." See previous experience at http://www.the-efa.org/members/data/resumes/georgik.pdf.

GHOSTWRITER CENTRAL

Hatteras St., Tarzana CA 91356. (888)743-9939; (818)433-4050; (747)333-8660 (text only). **E-mail:** mikemckla@aol.com. **Website:** www.ghostwords.com. **Contact:** Michael McKown, editor. Estab. 2002.

ADDITIONAL INFORMATION "Every project undertaken by Ghostwriters Central, from a one-page document to a 300-page manuscript, is handled with the utmost care. We always deliver clients' projects with excitement, secure in the knowledge that we have devoted great effort to the cause." Services offered: book mss, scripts, speeches, wedding vows, resume, copywriting, script doctoring, letter writing, editing, and rewriting. See website for fee schedule.

CAROL GIVNER MANUSCRIPT EDITING

E-mail: goldduets@aol.com. **Website:** www.myeditorcarol.com. **Contact:** Carol Givner.

ADDITIONAL INFORMATION Offers editorial services and speech writing, manuscript editing, and consulting.

LYNNE GLASNER

27 West 96th St., New York NY 10025. (917)744-3481. **E-mail:** lyngla@rcn.com. **Contact:** Lynne Glasner.

ADDITIONAL INFORMATION Lynne Glasner has 20 years of experience in the field and 10 years as a freelancer in developmental and line editing, copy editing, fact checking, and proofreading, including trade books (nonfiction and fiction) and textbooks. "Textbook focus: teacher and pupil editions for all populations, including ESL and special needs, in basal reading, math, science, and social studies series, and supplementary printed matter; high school texts; teacher training materials. Trade book focus: politics, contemporary social issues, media issues."

MARYANNE M. GOBBLE

Raleigh NC. (919)452-0857. **E-mail:** maryanne.gobble@gmail.com. **Website:** www.maryannegobble.com. **Contact:** MaryAnne M. Gobble.

ADDITIONAL INFORMATION "I am a writer and editor with over 18 years of experience, 11+ of them freelance. My career has taken me from management consulting to academia to copy writing. I've also been a teacher, university instructor, and trainer; a grants submission coordinator; and most recently, an editorial manager. All of these experiences have given me a unique set of analytical and communication skills. I am an adept collaborator, used to working with contributors who have a broad range of experiences and competencies; I've been called a 'force of nature' in the classroom; and I assimilate information and acclimate myself to new contexts very quickly." See previous experience at: http://maryannegobble.com/wp-content/uploads/2009/10/MaryAnne-Gobble-Resume1.pdf.

GOOD WORDS

216 Snow Road, Durham ME 04222. (207)353-3190; (207)353-2748. **Contact:** Laura S. Uhl.

ADDITIONAL INFORMATION Laura Uhl is a copy editor, developmental editor, and occasional writer who has been in the field as a freelancer for 9 years. She specializes in science education, including Web and print curricula. Laura's current primary clients are: TERC (Cambridge, MA); National Science Teachers Association; WGBH Educational Outreach for NOVA, NOVA science, NOW, Design Squad, FETCH!, and more; University of Nebraska/Lincoln science education projects. Education: Skidmore College, B.S.; University of Arizona, M.Ed., Harvard University, M.Ed.

JENNA GWYN-LEININGER

106 Byron Road, Pittsburgh PA 15237. (412)337-1042. **E-mail:** jennagwyn@gmail.com. **Contact:** Jenna Gwyn Leininger.

ADDITIONAL INFORMATION "I am a freelance editor for a Pittsburgh-based book publishing company. I have three years' experience in the industry editing and writing magazine articles, screenplays, and copyediting upward of nine books. I graduated from the University of Pittsburgh *magna cum laude* with a B.A. in English, and am experienced with MLA, Chicago, and AP styles. I have a keen eye for errors and can handle tight deadlines with accuracy and timeliness." See more information at www.the-efa.org/members/data/resumes/gwynleiningerj.pdf.

MAUREEN HAGGERTY

320 Patrick Place, Chalfont PA 18914. (215)822-2229. **E-mail:** maureenhaggerty@verizon.net. **Contact:** Maureen Haggerty.

ADDITIONAL INFORMATION Maureen is an established freelance writer/editor/proofreader of 20 years who has been in this field for 30 years. "I thrive on the challenges a diversified assignment docket affords. Corporations, associations, research and patient-care facilities, publishers, marcom agencies, and individuals benefit from my creativity, resourcefulness, and ability to see the big picture without losing sight of critical details. Specializing in health- and/or aging-related topics, I most enjoy empowering consumers to make informed decisions. I've edited a national association's award-winning magazine, created patient information materials and print and PowerPoint CME programs, and "translated" scripts written by non-native speakers of English into English as it's spoken in America. I've also edited or proofed novels, memoirs; travel, relationship, and investment guides; and a manuscript introducing a novel management theory. Recent projects have included adding historical context to transform a client's genealogical research into a prized family heirloom and chronicling the first 100 years of a township's history. References and estimates for long- or short-term projects and rush jobs are available on request."

GAIL HARRIS CREATIVE

8 Donovan Lane, Framingham MA 01701. (774)258-0222. **E-mail:** gail@gailharriscreative.com. **Website:** www.gailharriscreative.com/creative. **Contact:** Gail Harris.

ADDITIONAL INFORMATION Gail Harris has 25 years experience as a copywriter, 10 as a freelancer, and has written everything from print ads to direct mail to corporate communications/websites. Her work has been recognized with the prestigious ANDY award, among others. "My areas of expertise are spirituality, self-help and women's issues, but I enjoy working on any project where the client is reaching for clarity, authenticity and getting to the heart of the matter, whether an ad or manuscript. With developmental editing projects, my greatest strengths are working with a manuscript that needs core changes and bringing it up to publication standards, and fostering a respectful working relationship with my client." See her resume at www.the-efa. org/members/data/resumes/harrisg.pdf.

HARTBRIGHT EDITORIAL SERVICES

P.O. Box 870, Sweetwater TN 37874. (423)337-6977. **Fax:** (423)337-6402. **E-mail:** julius@hartbright.com. **Website:** www.hartbright.com. **Contact:** Stephen Tedder Henson.

ADDITIONAL INFORMATION Stephen Tedder Henson "the sober, sound-minded, persnickety, and quick founder and editor in chief of Hartbright Editorial Services, has more than twenty years' experience in publishing as a writer, researcher, and editor. He has been a newspaper correspondent and photographer, a bookstore manager, a copy editor, and an in-house book editor. Henson writes and edits, supervises freelancers and associate editors, and distributes related work to other experts in the publishing field: designers, photographers, typographers, technical writers, and researchers. We welcome both fiction (from short shorts to novels) and nonfiction (from articles and reports to books) by both established and new writers." Editorial services include rewriting, content- and line-editing, manuscript critique/evaluation, proofreading, and copyediting. Inquire for costs and additional information.

JENNIFER READ HAWTHORNE

Vero Beach FL. (772)774-8260 (land); (612)865-4550 (cell). **E-mail:** jennifer@jenniferhawthorne.com. **Contact:** Jennifer Read Hawthorne.

ADDITIONAL INFORMATION "Jennifer Read Hawthorne is an award-winning author/editor specializing in editing books, book proposals, articles, and blog posts. Genres include business, self-help, spirituality, health, memoir, and how-to. Her extensive writing/editing experience includes books; newspaper, magazine and broadcast journalism; poetry; and technical writing. She has also taught business and technical writing at the Master's level and in the corporate world. Jennifer is the author/editor of 7 books (four bestsellers), including the #1 bestsellers *Chicken Soup for the Woman's Soul* and *Chicken Soup for the Mother's Soul*. Her books have sold more than 14 million copies."

HEART & SOUL WRITING CENTER

Donna Peerce, 4204 Hillsboro Road #108, Nashville TN 37215. (615)279-8144. **E-mail:** donna@donnapeercewriter.com. **Website:** www.donnapeercewriter.com. **Contact:** Donna Peerce.

ADDITIONAL INFORMATION Services offered include ghostwriting, developmental editing, book doctoring, book proposals, marketing plans/analyses with agent access, manuscript critiques, screenplays, video, television and radio services, documentaries, and marketing/branding campaigns for businesses.

MARCELLE HEATH

Portland OR. (503)975-2680. **E-mail:** marcelleheath@ymail.com. **Website:** www.marcelleheath.com. **Contact:** Marcelle Heath.

ADDITIONAL INFORMATION Marcelle Heath has worked more than 10 years in the field as a freelance editor and writer. Her clients include writers, publishers, and creative agencies. She is based in Portland, Oregon.

HIGH PLAINS EDITORIAL SERVICES

Rugby ND. (307)760-4421. **E-mail:** hiplainseditor@gmail.com. **Contact:** Catherine Minick.

ADDITIONAL INFORMATION Catherine Minick has spent 21 years in the field, 12 as a freelancer. Editor of primarily medical text for more than two decades: in-house editor for editorial offices of peer-reviewed medical journals and freelance/contract project manager/editor/proofreader for publishers, packagers, and other entities. Managed editorial processes for peer-reviewed medical journal, managed production for journals (freelance), and trained off-site editors and proofreaders. Developed complex style sets (manuals) and efficient workflow processes and checklists. Specialties: Medical/allied health, K-12 and college, and other technical text. Other content areas include psychology, social work, criminal justice, and legal.

HMMOORE EDITING

38A Shadow Church Ln., Valatie NY 12184. (518)758-9257; (518)755-1129. **E-mail:** hmmooreniver@berk.com. **Contact:** Heather M. Moore Niver.

ADDITIONAL INFORMATION "Working since 1996 to ensure concise, consistent text through careful, attentive copy editing, substantive editing, and developmental editing as well as proofreading. Skills: Hard copy, electronic, and online copy editing, coding, and proofreading culinary arts, education, economics, environment, finances, business, medical arts, art, education, economics, environment, and business in textbooks, journal articles, encyclopedias, and technical manuals. Editing manuscripts ranging from adult and young adult fiction, plays, and a cookbook to memoirs and political history texts for style, continuity, and character development. Substantive editing of real estate articles for republication with careful attention to spelling, grammar, punctuation, and consistency. Ensuring proper use of grammar, punctuation, and general readability in financial and investment publications in newsletters, imprints, and booklets; researching, writing, editing, proofreading, and formatting fund descriptions using the Internet, Word, Adobe Acrobat, and Excel. Writing, proofreading, and editing job procedures. Peer mentoring and editorial review of peer proofs." See previous experience at www.the-efa.org/members/data/resumes/niverhm.pdf.

NINA HNATOV

51 Roslyn Dr., Glen Head NY 11545. (516)532-3535. **E-mail:** nina.hnatov@gmail.com. **Contact:** Nina Hnatov.

ADDITIONAL INFORMATION Freelance editor/copyeditor/proofreader; well-versed in a variety of disciplines. "I have many years of varied editorial experience, ranging from educational textbooks and testing materials (Kindergarten-University Press) to books, periodicals, newsletters, magazines, catalogs, art publications, research studies, annual reports and financial materials. Areas of expertise include art history, bioinformation/genetics, business/marketing, calculus, child development, computer architecture, economics, English language arts, fine arts, health care/nursing, history, mathematics, parenting, physics, psychology, science, self-help, social studies and sociology. I live on Long Island, New York, and am available on a per project/ongoing basis. My fees are reasonable and I am certain you will find my work to be meticulous, thorough and conscientious, and always completed on your time schedule." See previous experience at www.the-efa.org/members/data/resumes/hnatovn.pdf.

NANCY L. HOFFMANN

115 W. 23rd Street, #24, New York NY 10011. (212)691-1445. **E-mail:** nhoffmann77@yahoo.com. **Website:** http://tomatodesign.net. **Contact:** Nancy Hoffmann.

ADDITIONAL INFORMATION "I have many years in advertising design (art direction, graphic and web design), plus 5 years as an agency copywriter. I have worked as a freelance copy editor and proofreader, and have an exceptional grasp of the English, as well as French. Over the years I have worked in a wide range of industries, and have a large professional vocabulary, as well. My spelling skills are excellent: I even taught 4th and 5th grades at one point, with an emphasis on spelling and grammar, among other topics." Besides English, Nancy knows French (fluent); Spanish, German (conversant); Arabic (3 years' study in Syria, Turkey, and the US). Nancy has 20 years' experience in the field. See previous experience at www.the-efa.org/members/data/resumes/hoffmannnl.pdf.

KAREN HOHNER EDITING SERVICES

Palo Alto CA. (650)328-0381. **E-mail:** khohner@gmail.com. **Contact:** Karen Hohner.

ADDITIONAL INFORMATION "I have over 20 years' experience editing textbooks at the secondary and college levels, specializing in programs for foreign language instruction. I am fluent in German and French, and have a strong background in Russian. I have also worked on programs for Arabic, Chinese, and Spanish, editing the English portions of those textbooks."

HOLLAND EDITORIAL

Durham NC. (919)360-0743. **E-mail:** rosemary@hollandeditorial.com. **Website:** www.hollandeditorial.com. **Contact:** Rosemary Holland.

ADDITIONAL INFORMATION Years in field: 10. Years as freelancer: 4. "Holland Editorial offers publications management, web content development, writing, editing, proofreading, and Spanish translation services for businesses, non-profits, individuals, arts organizations, educational institutions, and government. Holland Editorial crafts fresh, clear, persuasive content for websites, brochures, publications, annual reports, performing arts programs, grants, manuals, newsletters, business documents, you name it....Rosemary Holland has worked for the non-profit and academic sectors as well as for multi-national corporations, including Sony Music's classical record label in New York and Saatchi & Saatchi Advertising in Sydney."

CAROL HOLMES

New York NY. (917)941-9476. **E-mail:** inastrongcity@aol.com. **Contact:** Carol Holmes.

ADDITIONAL INFORMATION Carol Holmes has been proofreading encyclopedias in the humanities and social sciences since 1976. Her work is in many Scribner and Oxford University Press sets; she also worked for Macmillan. "I'm the one called in when the job has gone wrong, when it's been worked on by too many hands, or when it hasn't been worked on at all. I look for the fix that entails the fewest changes, and I won't copyedit in proof—unless you ask me to." For more information, see www.the-efa.org/members/data/resumes/holmesc.pdf.

PETER HOMANS EDITORIAL SERVICE

390 Riverside Dr., Apt. 1C, New York NY 10025. (212)666-4153. **E-mail:** homansp@aol.com. **Contact:** Peter Brooks Homans. Estab. 2010.

ADDITIONAL INFORMATION Began editing career in 1984. Legal proofreader/copyeditor for Matthew Bender; Copy editor of journals related to law, banking, real estate and accounting for Gorham & Lamont; assistant editor for a books department; freelance copy editor for Garland Publishing, Simon and Schuster, and the United Nations Yearbook; full time copy editor for Chain Drug Review (relating to retailing, business and pharmaceuticals) and Mass Market Retailers. Languages: French, moderate speaking and reading ability; Spanish, moderate. Software skills: Microsoft Word; Adobe InCopy; Finale 2005a. See previous experience at www.the-efa.org/members/data/resumes/homanspb.pdf.

HOOK, ARC, AND TWIST EDITING

Cambridge MA. (617)230-7027. **E-mail:** editor@hookarcandtwist.com. **Website:** www.hookarcandtwist.com. **Contact:** Elizabeth Nordberg Stokes.

ADDITIONAL INFORMATION Elizabeth Stokes has spent 18 years in the field, 10 years as a freelancer. "I offer a variety of editorial options: - Manuscript Critique: a deep analysis of all narrative elements of your story - Manuscript Feedback: a high-level evaluation of what's working and what's not - Developmental Editing: support as you begin writing or planning a major revision - Line Editing: polish for your manuscript in the areas of language and style. I represent both the reader's and the author's interests, providing neutral but clear feedback about where those may differ. My goal is to contribute to your manuscript so that it retains your voice, your intent, and your skill. I am dependable and prompt." Elizabeth has a Journalism and English Lit degree from Boston University.

MARY HORNER

St. Peters MO. **E-mail:** mehorner@charter.net. **Website:** www.writrteachr.blogspot.com. **Contact:** Mary Horner. Estab. 2011. Award-winning journalist with more than 15 years experience in the publishing industry and author of *Strengthen Your Nonfiction Writing* provides editing services that include content, grammar, and style.

ADDITIONAL INFORMATION References available.

EMMY HUNTER

105 Duane St., 29A, New York NY 10007. (212)374-0428. **E-mail:** emmy.hunter@yahoo.com. **Contact:** Emmy Hunter.

ADDITIONAL INFORMATION Emmy Hunter has worked on everything from electronics trade magazines and sociology journals to trade books and business training seminar material. She is skilled at grammar, punctuation, and syntax and brings clarity to documents. She has been a freelancer for the last 14 years. She has an M.A. English Literature, Columbia Univ., 1991; Brooklyn College: M.F.A. Writing (poetry), 1986; University of California at Berkeley: B.A. Comparative Literature, 1981. Fluent in French; some Italian and German. See www.the-efa.org/members/data/resumes/huntere.txt for more information.

IMPROOF PROOFREADING, EDITING & CONSULTING

P.O. Box 165, Katonah NY 10536. (818)400-4442 and (914)401-9005. **E-mail:** dagmar@improofing.com. **Website:** www.improofing.com. **Contact:** Dagmar Bleasdale.

ADDITIONAL INFORMATION 13 Years in the field. 9 years as freelancer. Career editor/copyeditor/proofreader/consultant. Clients include writers (fiction and nonfiction), Honda/Acura and Amgen, publishers, advertising agencies, and business owners.

INDIGO EDITING & PUBLICATIONS

P.O. box 1355, Beaverton OR 97075. (503)629-9216. **E-mail:** info@indigoediting.com. **Website:** www.indigoediting.com. **Contact:** Ali McCart, senior editor. Estab. 2006.

ADDITIONAL INFORMATION "Indigo Editing & Publications is a firm of editors with various specialties. We find strength in working as a team, offering at least two sets of eyes for projects that require multiple editing rounds, and providing you with the highest quality of editing services. Indigo Editing & Publications is based in the Portland, Oregon, area, and services clients across the country." Offers developmental editing, line editing, reader's response, consulting, proposal development. Specialties include: nonfiction in the areas of health and wellness, spirituality, cookbooks, how-to, history, and anthropoloy; fiction, including literary, mystery/thriller, fantasy, science fiction, magical realism, historical, and women's; young adult fiction and nonfiction, children's books, and various non-book items such as catalogs, calendars, newspapers, and more. E-mail for a free sample edit and estimate for your project. We're thrilled to offer **Monthly Workshops** to support the writing community. Each month, we offer two workshops—one to coach your craft, one to boost your writing as a business that combine into three insightful hours for only $50. **March 19**, 10 a.m. to 1 p.m. Next one is April 16. See website for additional information. Each class is limited to 10 students. All classes will be held at the Indigo office, 519 SW 3rd Ave., 5th-floor conference room, Portland, Oregon. Preregistration is required. Future workshops fall generally on third Saturdays. If you have suggestions for workshop topics, please share them with us at workshops@indigoediting.com.

INK INC

1920 McGraw Ave., Apt. 6E, Bronx NY 10462. (917)705-1351. **E-mail:** ink.inc.aek@gmail.com. **Website:** www.leekottner.com/inkinc.html. **Contact:** Ann E. Kottner.

ADDITIONAL INFORMATION "As a freelancer, I've worked on projects as diverse as popular science books, learning materials for children's museums, reports on the status of women in physics and pharmaceutical biopartnering, fiction, documentation for

historical exhibits, and encyclopedia entries, writing, rewriting, copy editing, and proofreading." In addition to 20 years in the field, with more than 15 years of freelance editorial experience, Ann Kottner worked part-time for 10 years at "one of New York City's largest multidisciplinary environmental consulting firms (AKRF, Inc.), 7 of those years as a copy editor and proofreader in their publications department." See more at www.the-efa.org/members/data/resumes/kottnera.pdf.

INKWELL INTERNATIONAL

87779 571 Ave., Laurel NE 68745. **E-mail:** inkwellinternational@gmail.com. **Website:** inkwellinternational.com. **Contact:** Nanette Day, editor and writing consultant. Estab. 2009. Inkwell International provides developmental editing and copyediting in a variety of areas, including but not limited to book manuscripts, journal and research articles, web content (including blog posts, articles, and social media posts), and newsletters. Inkwell International also offers manuscript evaluation services and ghostwriting.

ADDITIONAL INFORMATION As a self-publishing consultant, Inkwell International helps writers navigate through the production process to make the best choices for their individual situations by providing insights on publishing services versus self-publishing, manuscript evalutaions, help connecting authors with reputable service providers, and support in developing marketing plans and building author platforms.

PATRICK B. INMAN

Chapel Hill NC. **E-mail:** patinman@earthlink.ne. **Contact:** Patrick B. Inman.

ADDITIONAL INFORMATION Patrick Inman has been helping others write for over 25 years in business, non-profit organizations, and academia. His 12 years of freelance services include: "developmental editing, comprehensive editing, and line- and copyediting of books, articles, dissertations, papers, and grants in the humanities, social sciences, medicine, and public affairs; proposal writing; coordination of collaborative work; coaching for research, writing, and stress reduction, business writing including analysis and documentation of business processes; co-authorship (when my role requires original writing and research); translation from Spanish and German." Works frequently with foreign scholars: authors from China, Estonia, Ethiopia, Hungary, India, Mexico, Pakistan,

Senegal, South Korea, Spain, Thailand, Tibet, Venezuela, and the Ukraine. "My clients include scholars in archaeology, anthropology, economics, education, history, literature, medicine, political science, psychology, and public health, graduate students in education, history, information and library science, journalism and mass communications, maternal and child health, psychology, and public policy, and non-fiction authors and biographers."

INTEGRATIVE INK

(941)366-0111. **E-mail:** scribe@integrativeink.com. **Website:** www.integrativeink.com.

ADDITIONAL INFORMATION ""Integrative Ink offers a range of publishing pre-production services, including copyediting, interior book design, cover layout/design, e-book creation (Kindle and ePub formats), promotional cover art, and free publishing consultations. We work with all of the major print-on-demand companies for print books, and we also assist authors in publishing ebooks on the most popular ereader devices. " Cost: "Once we receive your manuscript, we will complete a sample edit or format, free of charge, and return it to you with a quote, which will specify job fee, suggested service type, turnaround, and possible start dates. Current prices and design samples are also provided on our website."

INTENSIVE CARE COMMUNICATIONS

Biomedical Editing and Writing, 3626 Fords Lane, Baltimore MD 21215. (410)585-1522. **E-mail:** altus@intensivecarecomm.com. **Website:** www.intensivecarecomm.com. **Contact:** Michael S. Altus.

ADDITIONAL INFORMATION Michael has worked 16 years in the field; 14 years as a freelancer. "Working with the authors, we can determine what is necessary to ready the manuscript, which can include the following: Preparing a writing plan; Searching the literature; Editing and rewriting for clarity; Formatting according to instructions for authors. I am scientifically trained (doctorate in cell biology; postdoctoral experience; publications); editorially skilled (Certified Editor in the Life Sciences, Board of Editors in the Life Sciences), and broadly experienced (successfully completed many assignments in clinical medicine and basic science). I have worked on dozens of manuscripts to greatly shorten time to submission."

BECKY JACOBY

1300 Ivory Court, Wilmington NC 28411. (910)399-3351. **E-mail:** contact@beckyjacoby.com. **Website:** www.beckyjacoby.com. **Contact:** Becky Jacoby.

ADDITIONAL INFORMATION Becky Jacoby has 20 years in the field, and 5 as a freelancer. She is a graduate of Temple University with a B.A. in Journalism, holds an A.A. in Business from Stephens College, is certified in Desktop Publishing and has received advanced training in editing, publishing, health and wellness, instructional design, insurance and parenting education. She is experienced with all levels of corporate, agency, entrepreneurial and nonprofit environments. Becky has written/edited and developed nonfiction books, websites, web content, ebooks, blogs, special reports, magazines, video scripts, newsletters, features, editorials, articles, proposals, presentations, sales materials, training materials, manuals, guides, letters, media releases, and announcements. "I am adept at taking complex information and materials and turning them into engaging, understandable text. Additionally, as an award-winning graphic designer my work includes the ability to synergize visuals with text." See her website.

JD WORDSMITH LLC

Millstone Township NJ. (732)598-7724. **Fax:** (732)308-9498. **E-mail:** jane@jdwordsmith.com. **Website:** www.jdwordsmith.com. **Contact:** Jane DeTullio, editor.

ADDITIONAL INFORMATION Years in field: 12. Years as a freelancer: 3. "I served as Director of the Monmouth University Writing Center for 8 years and as a full-time instructor of composition and literature prior to that. In the role of Director, I trained hundreds of students, professionals and faculty to assist with editing college-level writing, from higher order concerns of organization and development to documentation of source material (APA, MLA, Chicago) and on to grammar and punctuation. Through my faculty experience, I have researched and produced scholarship and am familiar with many discipline-specific writing formats. Under my direction, the Monmouth University Writing Center produced 80 skills sheets, in Acrobat PDF files for web delivery, that pertain to particular writing and research skills. Additionally, we designed and wrote a quarterly newsletter, promoting Writing Center strategies and accomplishments. I am knowledgeable in medical terminology as I am a regular freelance writer for

CentraState Healthcare System in central New Jersey. I also edit dissertations, theses, manuscripts for publication, and business documents. Additionally, I have an excellent track record in assisting students with writing and editing college application essays for undergraduate and graduate school applications."

JEWELL COMMUNICATIONS

Dona Hightower Perkins, 9205 Seven Oaks Ln., Denton TX 76210. (940)891-4240. **E-mail:** donaperkins@verizon.net. **Contact:** Dona Perkins.

ADDITIONAL INFORMATION Dona Perkins has 16 years of experience in editing, copyediting, and proofreading for publishers, small and large businesses, and individual clients. This includes content editing, developmental editing, copyediting, proofreading, and electronic editing; developmental editing and copyediting of college textbooks; editing of course curriculum, guidelines, articles, journals, and dissertations for major universities. "Expert proficiency in standard copyediting and proofreading guidelines. Over ten years of experience with the Chicago Manual of Style, Publication Manual of the American Psychological Association, and American Medical Association Manual of Style." See previous experience at www.the-efa.org/members/data/resumes/perkinsd.txt.

JMW EDITOR

Chicago IL 60625. **E-mail:** jmweditor@yahoo.com. **Website:** www.jmweditor.com. **Contact:** Monica Wanat, editor. Estab. 2009. Offers copyediting services.

ADDITIONAL INFORMATION Sample edits first 5 pages for potential clients.

PHIL JOHNSON

Colleyville TX. (817)498-0509. **E-mail:** phil@valuewriter.com. **Website:** www.valuewriter.com. **Contact:** Phil Johnson.

ADDITIONAL INFORMATION Phil Johnson is a freelance business writer/editor and speechwriter with over 20 years of experience writing for the Forbes and Fortune 500/1,000/2,000, as well as top private companies and institutions of higher education across the country and around the world. Heavily involved in editing; journalism background.

JOLLEY GOOD EDITING

2000 Blue Bonnet Dr., Fort Worth TX 76111-1605. **E-mail:** sandy.jolley@sbcglobal.net. **Website:** www.JolleyGoodEditing.com. **Contact:** Sandy Jolley.

ADDITIONAL INFORMATION Sandy Jolley's book indexing and editing company provides friendly, professional services to publishers of technical, business, educational, self-help, political science, legal, and medical books. See more info at www.the-efa.org/members/data/resumes/jolleysam.pdf.

JONATHAN M.A. JUCKER

1816 16A St. SW, #303, Calgary AB T2T 5S2 Canada. (403)695-8643. **E-mail:** jonjucker@hotmail.com. **Contact:** Jonathan M.A. Jucker.

ADDITIONAL INFORMATION Jonathan Jucker has been a freelance copy editor for 3 years, specializing in the general interest, textbook, and academic fields. He reads French, Spanish, and Portuguese, and speaks French and Spanish fluently, and Portuguese at a basic conversational level. He has a B.A. (Honours), History and English Literature—Trinity College, University of Toronto (2000). For more information see www.the-efa.org/members/data/resumes/juckerjm.pdf.

JUST-IN-TIME EDITORIAL SERVICES

4110 Yorkshire, Detroit MI 48224. (313)318-4809. **E-mail:** roseatsea@hotmail.com. **Contact:** Amy R. Rose, Ph.D.. Estab. 1991.

ADDITIONAL INFORMATION Years as freelancer: 20. "I have over 30 years of experience as an instructional writer, editor, facilitator, and researcher. I have been self-employed since 1991. As an editor, I have done copy- and style-editing and proofreading in a variety of subjects, including books on scientific and technical topics as well as in the humanities. I offer fast, accurate turnaround on your editing project. I am proficient in the use of Word's Track Changes function, but I am also happy to use the traditional blue-pencil editing technique." Amy also designs and develops employee training for a broad range of industries and in various media, including web-based and e-learning courses. Earned a Ph.D., Classical Studies, Univ. of Colorado; B.A., Classical Studies, Univ. of Colorado. See previous experience at www.the-efa.org/members/data/resumes/rosear.pdf.

KARR EDITORIAL, LLC

1148 Lakepointe St., Grosse Pointe Park MI 48230. (313)821-0778. **E-mail:** justin@karreditorial.com; info@karreditorial.com. **Website:** www.karreditorial.com. **Contact:** Justin Karr, president. Estab. 2004.

ADDITIONAL INFORMATION Offers professional copyediting, proofreading, project management

—"comprehensive editing solutions tailored to meet the specifications of your project." See Justin's resume at http://www.karreditorial.com/pdf/Justin_Karr_Resume.pdf.

THERESA L. KAY

398 Nordstrasse, Fairbanks AK 99709. **E-mail:** theresa.ae@gmail.com; treekay@cowboys.uwyo.edu. **Contact:** Theresa L. Kay, communications. Estab. 2002.

ADDITIONAL INFORMATION As a freelance proofreader and copy editor, Theresa Kay's subject specialties include education (theory, practice, all levels kindergarten through college, administration, textbooks), social sciences, anthropology, psychology, sociology, criminology, American studies, cultural studies, history, reference materials and encyclopedias, and fiction. She worked full-time as the senior editorial associate for a nonprofit education journal for five years. She is skilled at copyediting using Word and proofreads on paper or electronically. See more information at www.the-efa.org/members/data/resumes/kaytl.pdf.

CHARLOTTE KELCHNER

3231 N. Hamlin Ave., Chicago IL 60618. (773)267-0036. **E-mail:** Charlotte@KelchnerCommunications.com. **Website:** www.linkedin.com/in/charlottekelchner; http://kelchnercomminications.com. **Contact:** Charlotte Kelchner.

ADDITIONAL INFORMATION Years in field: 15. Years as freelancer: 7. Editor and writer specializing in science and technical materials. "I began my career in publishing at Encyclopaedia Britannica, where I was the Earth Sciences editor. Now a full-time freelancer, I primarily edit or write materials for nonfiction trade books, geoscience journal articles, and textbooks. I hold MS degrees in Marine Science and Earth Science, and I teach geology, oceanography, and geography at the college level. My clients include the Society of Exploration Geophysicists, Esri Press, Encyclopaedia Britannica, McGraw-Hill Ryerson, and Holt McDougal." See previous experience at www.the-efa.org/members/data/resumes/kelchnerc.pdf.

SUSAN E. KENNEDY

Londonderry NH. **E-mail:** skennedy09@yahoo.com. **Contact:** Susan E. Kennedy.

ADDITIONAL INFORMATION Years in field: 6. Years as freelancer: 4. "Thorough line editor, proofreader, and copyeditor who enjoys all types and lengths of fiction and nonfiction manuscripts. I correct grammar and punctuation, improve sentence structure, word flow, and clarity. Experience includes literary and genre novels (adult and YA), memoirs, scholarly texts, short story anthologies, technology how-to, nonprofit (publications such as membership) newsletters, and general interest nonfiction." Susan has worked with a wide range of clients, including college professors, new writers, established authors, and publishers. She has been in the field for 6 years and as a freelancer is particularly interested in fiction and manuscripts on historical topics.

ANNE KETCHEN

446 Brook St., Carlisle MA 01741. (978)369-1661. **E-mail:** anneketchen@comcast.net. **Website:** http://anneketcheneditor.yolasite.com. **Contact:** Anne Ketchen.

ADDITIONAL INFORMATION Years in field: 21 Years. Anne Ketchen is a text and multimedia editor with 15 years of freelance experience. She does instructional editing for training companies, workshop materials, and e-learning. Some subject areas: pharmaceutical sales training, medical/allied health, managed care, CNS disorders, osteoporosis, benign prostatic hyperplasia, contraception, cerebrovascular disease, arthritis, and diabetes. Also copyedits college-level textbooks and course materials. Recent topics: project management, business analysis, digital moviemaking, researching history papers, and English composition. Anne holds a B.A. in English from Univ. of Maine and MS in Occupational Therapy from Columbia University. Her related experience includes 10 years as a Registered Occupational Therapist (working with spinal cord injury patients, muscular dystrophy patients, and children with learning disabilities). She has a Certificate in Native Plant Studies from New England Wild Flower Society and a strong interest in natural history, especially native plants." See previous experience at www.the-efa.org/members/data/resumes/ketchena.pdf.

KLIMLEY COMMUNICATIONS

28 Riverside Ave. #6H, Red Bank NY 07701. (732)530-1639; (917)626-4838 (cell). **Fax:** (732)530-1669. **E-mail:** april@klimley.com. **Website:** www.klimley.com. **Contact:** April Klimley.

ADDITIONAL INFORMATION "Klimley Communications provides freelance marketing/communications and editorial services for corporations and associations. Our firm creates, writes and edits many types of communications—from marketing newsletters to annual reports, speeches, employee benefit brochures, magazines, advertising sections and internet text. We also provide media relations services in Monmouth County and Northern New Jersey, as well as production and writing of advertising sections on topics such as diversity and biotechnology. Our clients are large and small financial institutions, non-profit associations, major public corporations and national business publications. At KC, you will find experienced professionals who can craft your message in a way that gives you the results you want with key audiences. E-mail or phone us for a free half hour phone consultant on your communications challenge. "

JOAN KOCSIS

601 Head of the Bay Road, Buzzards Bay MA 02532. (508)759-2549. **E-mail:** kocsis@verizon.net. **Contact:** Joan Kocsis.

ADDITIONAL INFORMATION Joan Kocsis has more than 30 years in the field, 25+ years as a freelancer. "Reading and language arts assessment for grades 3 to 12 is one current specialty. I also write feature articles on food and cooking. Beyond that, I have many years of editing experience (line and substantive) in el-hi, college, trade, and medicine. I freelance full-time and am serious about meeting deadlines. Talk to me about your project!" See details at www.the-efa.org/members/data/resumes/kocsisj.txt.

HENRY KRAWITZ

Briarwood NY. (718)846-5118. **E-mail:** henrykrawitz@verizon.net. **Contact:** Henry Krawitz.

ADDITIONAL INFORMATION Henry Krawitz has 35 years in the publishing field. "As a generalist, I am able to edit manuscripts in the humanities and social sciences. In addition, I possess special strengths in scholarly/academic material and currently edit manuscripts for major university presses as well as smaller academic publishers. I have developed particular expertise in the interdisciplinary approach and can handle such diverse subjects as national literatures (comparative literature was my undergraduate and graduate major), art and music history, theater, film, and dance. Styling bibliographies and notes for consistency is another skill subset. Having been raised in a European household, my comprehension of French and German is near-native." Henry Krawitz is experienced in both trade and academic/scholarly/reference book publishing with 5 years in the copy-editing

department at Doubleday; 10 years as associate editor at Oxford University Press. "As far as my work habits are concerned, I am a detail-oriented, organized individual. I can follow either a house style, The Chicago Manual of Style, Words into Type, or more specialized style manuals (such as MLA). I pride myself on the quality of my work and try to maintain the highest editorial standards without sacrificing deadlines. My hourly rates vary ($25–30), depending on the complexity of the project." For more information see www.the-efa.org/members/data/resumes/krawitzh.pdf.

TERESE LOEB KREUZER

377 Rector Place, Apt. 10H, New York NY 10280. (212)807-7509. **E-mail:** tereseloeb@mac.com. **Contact:** Terese Loeb Kreuzer.

ADDITIONAL INFORMATION Terese Loeb Kreuzer is a writer, editor, photographer, multimedia producer/director and project manager. She has been freelancing for 26 years. She is the founder and editor of the Travel Arts Syndicate and co-author with Carol Bennett of *HOW TO MOVE TO CANADA: A PRIMER FOR AMERICANS*. She also designed, laid out and edited a newsletter for *The New York Times* Newspaper-in-Education program. Terese has a B.A. with honors from Swarthmore College, where she majored in art history and minored in English and French literature. She is listed in the second and third editions of Marquis's Who's Who in Entertainment. See more information at: www.the-efa.org/members/data/resumes/kreuzertl.pdf.

KRISTEN CORRECTS

4315 N. Vera St., Boise ID 83704. (208)447-0860. **E-mail:** kristen@kristencorrects.com. **Website:** www.kristencorrects.com. **Contact:** Kristen House, owner. Estab. 2012. Kristen Corrects provides professional manuscript editing and business writing services at a competitive price. "Kristen House, a certified editor with an impressive portfolio, offers high-quality editing and writing work at a competitive price."

ADDITIONAL INFORMATION "With astounding qualifications and flawless master of the complexities of the English language, Kristen has the editing skills to bring refinement to any manuscript." Kristen specializes in editing fiction (SFF) manuscripts, website content, and blogs.

KWB HEALTH COMMUNICATIONS

2316 Steeplechase Road, Edmond OK 73034. (405)640-6196. **Fax:** (405)285-2622. **E-mail:** kwb@

kwbhealthcom.com. **Website:** kwbhealthcom.com. **Contact:** Kristina Wasson-Blader.

ADDITIONAL INFORMATION Kristina Wasson-Blader, PhD, has more than 10 years of experience writing and editing scientific and medical communications. These projects include scientific manuscripts, abstracts, poster and slide presentations, review articles, grant proposals, white papers, and monographs. She has worked in the following therapeutic areas: autoimmunity, women's health, endocrinology, diabetes, oncology, medical diagnostics, ophthalmology, microbiology, and parasitology. For more info, see www.the-efa.org/members/data/resumes/wassonbladerk.pdf.

GWEN KWO

Los Angeles CA. (310)465-6868. **E-mail:** gkwo@yahoo.com. **Website:** www.copyeditorgwen.com. **Contact:** Gwen Kwo.

ADDITIONAL INFORMATION Copy Editor Gwen Kwo provides copyediting, proofreading and copywriting services. "Contact me to discuss your project, however small or large. I have worked extensively with health care materials and materials for the food/nutrition, educational games, automotive, film, and real estate industries. Further, I am proficient in Spanish at a high intermediate level, and I hold a certificate in teaching English as a foreign language (TEFL)."

MARCELA LANDRES

Brooklyn NY. (718)208-5810. **E-mail:** marcelalandres@yahoo.com. **Website:** www.marcelalandres.com. **Contact:** Marcela Landres.

ADDITIONAL INFORMATION "Years in field: 17 Years as freelancer: 10. "A former Simon & Schuster editor, Marcela Landres helps writers get published by editing their work and educating them on the business side of publishing. She edits a wide variety of fiction and nonfiction including but not limited to: novels (literary, mainstream, commercial, adult, young adult, chick lit, street lit, women's, romance, historical, mystery, thriller, suspense), short story collections, memoirs, self-help, inspiration, pop culture, and New Age. She does not, however, edit poetry, children's books (specifically, anything for middle grade or younger readers), Spanish works, or fantasy. Her clients range from best-selling and/or award-winning authors such as Dora Levy Mossanen (Harem) and Sergio Troncoso (*The Last Tortilla and Other Stories*) to self-published authors such as Terry B. (*At Mid-night*) and Marcia Smart (*Decorating by Instinct*). While she works with writers of all backgrounds, as one of the few Latina editors in the book business she has extensive experience in Latino/Hispanic and multicultural publishing." For more, go to website, click on Services. Memberships: Women's Media Group, Editorial Freelancers Association, and Las Comadres. A graduate of Barnard College, she has been a Peer Panelist for the National Association of Latino Arts & Culture Fund for the Arts, on the Literature Panel for the New York State Council on the Arts, and was a judge for the Beyond Margins Award for PEN and the Latino Book Awards. Marcela is the author of the e-book *How Editors Think: The Real Reason They Rejected You*, and is the Publisher of Latinidad®, an award-winning e-zine which was chosen as one of the 101 Best Web Sites for Writers by Writer's Digest Magazine. "The media, including *The Wall Street Journal*, *The Chicago Tribune*, and *Writer's Digest*, often quotes her as a publishing expert."

SHERI LANZA

2622 Oakledge Ct., Vienna VA 22181. (703)242-3887. **E-mail:** srl@srlanza.com. **Contact:** Sheri R. Lanza.

ADDITIONAL INFORMATION Years as freelancer: 15. Sheri Lanza works primarily in the information industry, geared to researchers, searchers, librarians, and other information professionals. "I have been a member of AIIP (Association of Independent Information Professionals) for 14 years and have served a term as secretary of the organization and have been a member of various committees. I write articles on topics related to the information industry and have written two books: *International Business Information on the Web* and *Finding Market Research on the Web*. I am editor of *The CyberSkeptic's Guide to Internet Research* (www.cyberskeptic.com/cs), a monthly publication aimed at business, news, technical, medical, legal, and international research information professionals. I work on a freelance and/or contract basis."

LIVIA MARIE LARRABEE

2263 Sunrise Ct., Green Bay WI 54302. (510)717-7365. **E-mail:** lmlarrabee@gmail.com. **Contact:** Livia Marie Larrabee, editor.

ADDITIONAL INFORMATION Years in field: 2. "I am an Assistant Editor at a natural health magazine where I copy edit articles (line editing, proofreading, and everything in between), and I have previously freelanced as an editor of scholarly articles and papers for biomedical research companies. I have a good ear for style and clarity and can capably edit in a wide range of topics. I have experience, as well, in editing marketing collateral, including proofreading for companies such as Pottery Barn. I'm proficient in the Chicago Manual of Style and the AP Stylebook, and can adapt quickly and easily to new style guides. I have a MA in Creative Writing from the University of Glasgow and a BA in Classical Languages from UC Berkeley, and have written a young adult novel. I have edited and provided feedback on fiction, short stories, and screen plays."

JODY LARSON

Safety Harbor FL. (727)726-2986. **Contact:** Jody Larson.

ADDITIONAL INFORMATION "Years in field: 31 Years as freelancer: 23. Author-friendly, well-seasoned editor and nonfiction writing specialist. Developmental work, writing, and copyediting in biology, A/P, botany, genetics, ecology, environment, astronomy, physics, and chemistry. Also indexing and proofreading. Established publishing companies only, please."

BETH LASSER

(248)925-2003; (718)638 8787. **E-mail:** bethlasser@gmail.com. **Contact:** Beth Lasser.

ADDITIONAL INFORMATION "Experienced multimedia editor, content developer and project manager with a multi-focused skill base; strong abilities in and knowledge of structural editing, copyediting, proofreading, and research and writing. Creative problem-solver who is able to adapt to changing and challenging environments. Work happily in a team environment and quickly learn new skills; a capable, independent worker with initiative. Global resident (Australia, the Czech Republic, England and the United States), U.S. citizen; educated abroad; avid traveler with cross-cultural experience and knowledge of American, British and Australian English. Edit and proofread books, instructional guides, academic articles, websites and marketing materials for a variety of clients." M.A., Editing and Communications, Univ. of Melbourne, Melbourne, Australia. Coursework: Structural Editing; Editorial English; Advanced Editing for Digital Media; Technical Writing; Internship (with research component); Print Production and Design. Recognized on the Dean's Honours List for graduating at the top of her class. Beginner Czech, Intermediate Spanish. See previous experience at www.the-efa.org/members/data/resumes/lasserb.pdf.

MARIE LAVINIO

P.O. Box 478, Housatonic MA 01236. (413)281-6975. **Contact:** Marie Lavinio.

ADDITIONAL INFORMATION Self-employed freelancer who works as a copy editor, managing editor, proofreader, and transcriber. "My specialty is book publishing, but I also welcome smaller projects such as newsletters, marketing and public relations projects, and magazine articles. If a project needs to be printed, I work with an experienced and talented art director with whom I have partnered on many projects and in whom I have complete trust. My projects come in on time and with great care to detail and efficiency." Marie earned a B.A. in English from Univ. of Bridgeport, *magna cum laude.* See previous experience at www.the-efa.org/members/data/resumes/laviniom.pdf.

HANA LAYSON

1155 West Farwell Ave., #2, Chicago IL 60626. (773)793-5588. **E-mail:** hana. layson@gmail.com. **Contact:** Hana Layson.

ADDITIONAL INFORMATION "I am a freelance writer and editor with over ten years of experience helping writers express themselves in clear, persuasive prose. I teach writing at the college and graduate levels, coach individuals of all ages through various writing projects, and assist nonprofits in grantwriting and editing. I am interested in editing at all levels from copyediting to developmental editing and for projects of all sizes from newsletters to book manuscripts." Han Layson holds a Ph.D. in English Literature, University of Chicago, Chicago, IL, 2003; B.A. in English Literature, magna cum laude, Kenyon College, Gambier, OH, 1994. See previous experience at www.the-efa.org/members/data/resumes/laysonh.pdf.

LEFT LANE COMMUNICATIONS

123 Nolen Ln., Chapel Hill NC 27516. (919)594-7663. **E-mail:** pat.french@leftlanecomm.com. **Website:** www.leftlanecomm.com. **Contact:** Patricia A. French.

ADDITIONAL INFORMATION Years in field: 20; Years as freelancer: 15. "Pat French, principal of Left Lane Communications, has been providing writing and editing support to biomedical researchers, publishers, and educators since 1989. Extensive experience in academic, industry, and government/nonprofit settings and in multiple therapeutic areas. Products include articles for peer-reviewed journals, posters, abstracts, books and book chapters, slide presentations, and other nonregulatory materials." See http://www.the-efa.org/members/data/resumes/frenchpa.pdf.

LEGAL PRO EDITORS

5619 Knobby Knoll, Houston TX 77092. (832)444-6623. **E-mail:** editors@legalproeditors.com. **Website:** http://legalproeditors.com. **Contact:** Brooke E. Smith. **ADDITIONAL INFORMATION** "I am a Harvard Law graduate with over 20 years litigation experience who became a full-time freelance editor over 5 years ago. I have either done content edit, developmentally edited, or done both on over 80 books. Fiction ranges from mainstream through most genres, including legal suspense, mystery/suspense, historical, science fiction/fantasy, romance/erotica, and young adult. Nonfiction works include motivational, memoir, religious/New Age, how-to, and promotional. While I still do a lot of legal editing (journal articles and treatises) for attorneys, my current focus is books, particularly novels involving attorney characters or legal issues/procedure for which I do developmental as well as content/line editing." See more information at http://www.the-efa.org/members/data/resumes/smithb.txt.

MARCIA LERNER

395 11th St., Brooklyn NY 11215. (718)930-9639. **E-mail:** marcialerner2@gmail.com. **E-mail:** marcialerner2@gmail.com. **Contact:** Marcia Lerner. **ADDITIONAL INFORMATION** "Meticulous, organized editor and writer, specializing in transforming complex information into clear, comprehensible prose. Expertise in business, personal finance, children's literature, and health care; adaptable and flexible." Awards Received: New York Public Library Award, books for the teen ager, for Math Smart II, 1997. Parents Choice Award, gold, for Math Smart Junior, 1996. Award from the Henfield Foundation for fiction writing, 1995. Writing Fellowship teaching post with stipend, The Johns Hopkins University Creative Writing program, 1994. Education: The Johns Hopkins University, MA in fiction writing; Brown University, BA. See professional history at: www.the-efa.org/members/data/resumes/lernerm.pdf.

ANNE LESSER COMMUNICATIONS

West Stockbridge MA 01266. (413)232-8577. **Fax:** (413)232-4001. **E-mail:** anne@annelessercommunications.com. **Website:** www.annelessercommu-nications.com. **Contact:** Anne Lesser. Anne Lesser Communications offers expert editorial and writing services. We're sensitive to the needs of our varied group of clients, managing every detail of a project without losing sight of the whole. And in more than two decades, we've never missed a deadline. Our goal is to make all your communications distinctive, concise, accessible, and consistent. We help you get the word out, and as a result you realize your value in the marketplace. **ADDITIONAL INFORMATION** Anne Lesser has been a freelancer for 22 years. She has been offering comprehensive editorial services, with outstanding attention to detail, high energy, and excellent follow-through. Her editing formats include: "AMA, APA, CMS, MLA, any house style as required. Textbooks, journals, newspaper articles, web content, and more. Produces expert and highly efficient work using macros, two monitors, and an extended keyboard for coding. Subjects include medical, allied health, personal finance, education, psychology, music/art history."

LAURIE LEWIS

New York NY. (212)369-5359. **Fax:** (212)369-4434. **E-mail:** lewislaurie@earthlink.net. **Contact:** Laurie Lewis. **ADDITIONAL INFORMATION** Laurire Lewis has spent 40 years in the field; 23 years as a freelancer doing medical editing and writing. Works on material for diverse audiences, including physicians, nurses, other health care providers, researchers, and the general public. Skilled in translating technical information into a clear, concise, accurate, and engaging presentation. Has worked on printed publications (books, newsletters, etc), corporate communications (press releases, backgrounders), and websites. Author of the book *What to Charge: Pricing Strategies for Freelancers and Consultants*. Samples available by links. Prefers phone contact.

LIGHTWORDS EDITORIAL SERVICES

167 West 71st St., New York NY 10023. (212)799-4365. **E-mail:** phyllisstern2002@yahoo.com. **Website:** lightwords-editorial.blogspot.com. **Contact:** Phyllis Stern. **ADDITIONAL INFORMATION** Phyllis Stern is an "Experienced editor, specializing in books on health, psychology, spirituality, the arts and education, as well as fiction and memoir. Skilled at editing for grammar, usage and clarity of style with attention

to the writer's voice. Strong interest in creative work and books on personal growth and conscious living." Phyllis holds an M.A. in English literature, and has published articles in major magazines. "I have taught creative writing with grants from the New York State Council on the Arts, and am also a practitioner of holistic healing. As a writer myself, I am sensitive to preserving the tone and nuance of the author's style, while helping to polish the work for publication. I help present your work with clarity and vision."

MAUREEN LILLA

77 State Road, Plymouth MA 02360. **E-mail:** mlilla777@aol.com. **Contact:** Maureen Lilla, principle. Estab. 1986. Offers developmental editing for authors, professionals, and business writers; development of query letters and book proposals; writing and ghostwriting; book doctoring; book and book cover design. **ADDITIONAL INFORMATION** Client list available upon request.

MIKE LINDGREN EDITORIAL SERVICES, INC.

210 E. 29th St., 2A, New York NY 10016. (212)481-6488. **E-mail:** mike_lindgren@yahoo.com. **Website:** www.mikelindgren.com. **Contact:** Michael Lindgren. **ADDITIONAL INFORMATION** Michael Lundgren is a writer, reviewer, editor, copyeditor, proofreader, copywriter, critic, musician, poet, painter, activist. He has spent 19 years in the field, 7 as a freelancer. His specialties include: rock music, popular culture, contemporary art, poetry, literature, baseball, critical theory. Michael Lindgren graduated with honors from Dartmouth College with a B.A. in English. He spent ten years in the publishing industry in Boston, Massachusetts, as an editor for Harcourt/Academic Press and Zoland Books, before turning to bookselling and freelance writing. He now spends his time between Manhattan and Pennsylvania. His base rate is $25/hour.

THE LINGUISTIC EDGE

2233 W. Balboa Blvd., #104-108, Newport Beach CA 92663. (714)637-6264. **Website:** www.linguisticedge.com. **Contact:** Dorothy M. Taguchi. **ADDITIONAL INFORMATION** Dorothy M. Taguchi has been in the field 25 years: 5 years as a freelancer. Dorothy's specialties include managing publishing projects, producing and editing educational products and children's books, and polishing the language of children's books, including those translated from in-

ternational acquisitions. Dorothy's other pursuits include writing, editing, and proofreading brochures, catalogs, packaging, Web sites, and television and print advertising. Dorothy created the voice and style of the Hooked on Phonics product line and Sylvan Learning consumer products. Prior to that, she gained experience in technical communications, during her nine years as a technical writer, editor, and manager of a technical writing and editing section at a Fortune 500 aerospace company.

DOUGLAS ORR LOGAN

2 Long Point Road, Branford CT 06405. (203)506-8550. **E-mail:** loganct@gmail.com. **Website:** www.loganeditorial.com. **Contact:** Douglas Orr Logan. **ADDITIONAL INFORMATION** Douglas Logan has been a professional editor since 1979, splitting his time between staff positions and as a freelancer. He has worked as both editor and writer in fiction and nonfiction books, glossy magazines, newsletters, standard websites, and blogs. "Much of my background is in the marine and health fields, but I can work with technical material from a wide variety of industries." His skills include adapting writing quickly to any style or voice, distilling complex scientific and technical language into clear, easily readable form, structural and line editing, and working closely with authors and publishers to achieve creative and commercial goals. Employers and clients have included the New York Times Magazine Group, Miller Publishing, Time-Life Books, Belvoir Publications, A.D.A.M., and others. See more info at www.the-efa.org/members/data/resumes/logando.pdf.

MATTHEW J. LUBIN

Jersey City NJ. **E-mail:** mattlubin@yahoo.com. **Website:** http://mattlubin.weebly.com. **Contact:** Matthew J. Lubin. **ADDITIONAL INFORMATION** "I am a repatriated writer, editor, proofreader, and social media consultant from New Jersey." Matthew Lubin has worked over 3 years in Shenzhen, China and for The New Jersey Law Journal as assistant editor, and as a freelance editor and writer. Most recently Matthew Lubin was professor of academic writing in English at Harbin Institute of Technology Shenzhen Graduate School. "In December 2008, I created the only English-language, China-themed literary journal, Terracotta Typewriter. Since it was created, I have published five quarterly issues on the site." Skills: Windows & Mac O/S:

QuarkXPress; MS Word, Excel, Publisher, and PowerPoint; HTML; Adobe Photoshop; StarOffice 5.2; Final Draft; FTP; Winfax. Foreign Languages: Mandarin Chinese. Get more information at: www.the-efa.org/members/data/resumes/lubinm.pdf.

MAGGIE LYONS

P. O. 291, Callao VA 22435. **E-mail:** maggielyons66@gmail.com. **Website:** http://lyonseditorialservices.yolasite.com. **Contact:** Maggie Lyons.

ADDITIONAL INFORMATION Maggie Lyons' editorial services include academic documents (theses, textbooks, articles, papers), fiction and nonfiction mss, query/cover letters, children's literature, marketing, PR, and fundraising communications, corporate reports, manuals, ESL documents, U.K. English documents, resumes. She has international experience (30+ years) in academic publishing, educational, business, and corporate communications in the U.S.A., Europe, and the U.K. through trade, federal sales, public affairs, legal, manufacturing, and nonprofit organizations, Oxford University, and academic publishing. Recent editing projects include a thesis, academic and legal documents in English by nonnative writers (ESL), marketing materials for a renewable energy company, marketing materials and Web content for a marketing company, and a language. "As an academic editor I have worked with university professors to review and develop mss in a broad variety of disciplines through to textbook and electronic publication. Humanities and sciences include, but are not restricted to, history, literature, religion, music, art, geology, and astronomy." Maggie has a B.A. in French (German and music minors) and M.A. in Public Communications and has spent 30 years in the editing field, 5 as a freelancer.

DONNA LYSAK

3 Lyman St., Cazenovia NY 13035. (845)699-3301. **E-mail:** donna@dexterhaven.com. **E-mail:** donna@dexterhaven.com. **Contact:** Donna A. Lysak.

ADDITIONAL INFORMATION 15 years' experience and BELS certification, publishing professional with extensive experience in STM journal and trade book copy editing. Accepts general copyediting and proofreading projects. Professional memberships: Board of Editors in the Life Sciences (BELS), Council of Science Editors, American Medical Writers Association, Editorial Freelancers Association. Complete history on PDF: www.the-efa.org/members/data/resumes/lysakd.pdf.

JAN MAAS

Washington DC. **E-mail:** janmaas@mindspring.com. **Website:** www.linkedin.com/in/janmaas11231. **Contact:** Jan Maas.

ADDITIONAL INFORMATION Jan Maas has 20 years in the field; 4 as a freelancer. Recent copyediting assignments: Oxford University Press: Oxford Encyclopedia of British Literature (2006); Oxford Encyclopedia of the Modern World (2008) M. E. Sharpe, Inc.: Latino History and Culture in America); The Asian American Experience: History, Culture, and Scholarship; 10 years editor, monthly newspaper, Episcopal Diocese of New York; 5 years writer/reporter, *New York Daily News*. Meticulous copyediting, proofreading, and fact checking; Strong proficiency in MS Word, Excel, Publisher, PowerPoint, WordPerfect; Knowledge of XML, HTML. Professional-level experience in research using databases and Internet Familiarity with German, French, Spanish, Latin, Biblical Greek and Hebrew; Expert competence in reading music notation. See more informaton at www.the-efa.org/members/data/resumes/maasja.pdf.

KIM MACQUEEN

1105 Sarasota Dr., Tallahassee FL 32301. (850)727-3788. **E-mail:** kimmacqueen@gmail.com. **Website:** http://kimmacqueen.com. **Contact:** Kim MacQueen.

ADDITIONAL INFORMATION Years in field: 25. Years as a freelancer: 15. "Kim MacQueen has been a writer and editor for research, legal and general interest newspapers, magazines and books for more than 20 years, specializing in educational publications. Since 2000, she's also made forays into online course development and grant proposal writing and administration." See previous experience at www.the-efa.org/members/data/resumes/macqueenk.pdf.

MALLORY EDITING

Saint Petersburg FL. **E-mail:** malloryediting@gmail.com. **Contact:** Jeannine Mallory.

ADDITIONAL INFORMATION 15 years in the field. 15 years as a freelancer.

MALONE EDITORIAL SERVICES

(903)326-4945. **E-mail:** maloneeditorial@hotmail.com. **Website:** www.maloneeditorial.com. **Contact:** Susan Mary Malone.

ADDITIONAL INFORMATION "The vast majority of freelance editors working today are copy editors. Which is fine and dandy-in its place. But a good copyedit isn't the first step in the process of bringing a manuscript to publication. Nor is it the second or third steps. Rather, a hard going over for grammar, punctuation, spelling, etc., makes up the last step before going to print. Long before that, manuscripts need in-depth, comprehensive, substantive editing. The kind that deals with the nuts and bolts of organization and structure, of plotting and pacing, of characterization, of voice and tone, along with all of the stylistic elements and overall substance that go into creating a great read. Whether fiction or nonfiction, every book (or short story or article) needs the type of thorough going over that only a developmental editor can provide." Offers developmental editing for fiction and nonfiction.

ROBIN MALTZ

9 Orchard St., Northampton MA 01060. (347)276-3211. **E-mail:** robin.maltz@gmail.com. **Contact:** Robin Maltz.

ADDITIONAL INFORMATION Robin Maltz is a nonfiction editor, writer, and indexer, with more than 20 years experience in book, magazine, academic, and business publishing. She has a client-centered approach with proven ability to meet deadlines, produce excellent results, and exceed expectations. Her skills include substantive editing, copy editing, article writing, brochures, reports, and web copy, back-of-book indexing, proofreading, research, fact checking, copyright permissions. Her interests are in self-published books, small presses, journal articles, academic books in all fields, marketing materials, business and legal reports. See more information at www.the-efa. org/members/data/resumes/maltzr.pdf.

MANSBRIDGE EDITING & TRANSCRIPTION

149 Cedar Ridge Circle, St. Augustine FL 32080. (904)461-9564. **Contact:** Beth Anne Mansbridge. Estab. 1998.

ADDITIONAL INFORMATION Years in field and as freelancer: 15. Beth has been a real estate agent, medical transcriptionist, legal secretary, and a secretary at the French Trade Commision in the Sultanate of Oman. She edits fiction and nonfiction "works of many genres, query and proposal letters, promotional materials, and websites. Beth strives for excellence and is pleased to say that her clients often win literary awards and contests." References available to prospective clients.

THE MANUSCRIPT COACH

David Bischoff, 1430 Willamette St. #317, Eugene OR 97401. (888)785-2415. **E-mail:** david.bischoff@gmail. com. **Website:** www.davidbischoff.com. **Contact:** David Bischoff.

ADDITIONAL INFORMATION Services offered include manuscript evaluation, coaching, and critiques, editing, ghostwriting, and marketing, and rewrites.

MANUSCRIPT CRITIQUE

Michael Garrett, Creative Inspirations, Inc., P.O. Box 100031, Irondale AL 35210. **E-mail:** mike@manuscriptcritique.com; mgteach352@gmail.com. **Website:** www.manuscriptcritique.com. **Contact:** Michael Garrett.

ADDITIONAL INFORMATION " I'm an internationally respected editor and author. As credited in Mr. King's non-fiction book *On Writing: A Memoir of the Craft*, I served as Stephen King's first editor. Twenty years of professional book editing experience with New York publishers. Your best choice among all book editors for mystery, suspense, romance, thriller, horror, mainstream, and nonfiction." Services offered include ms critique and editing, and comprehensive structural advice.

MANUSCRIPT EDITING

(469)789-3030. **E-mail:** editor@manuscript-editing. com; bookeditors@manuscriptediting.com. **Website:** http://manuscriptediting.com. **Contact:** Lynda Lotman.

ADDITIONAL INFORMATION "I will realistically assess your writing skills, and I'll tell you honestly if I feel that you need a light copy edit, a heavier developmental edit, or could benefit from more formalized writing instruction (or multiple options in between)." Additional services include editing, ghostwriting, query letters, synopses, content development, critique/analysis, fact-checking and research, technical writing, indexing, tape transcription, graphic design, self-publishing assistance, and book marketing. Cost: "Cost, time frame, and other questions can only be answered after submission."

STEVEN J. MARCUS

Newton MA. (617)964-1580. **E-mail:** smarcus@nasw. org. **Contact:** Steven J. Marcus.

ADDITIONAL INFORMATION Harvard educated, Steven J. Marcus has been in this field 30 years; 12 as a freelancer. As an experienced editor, Steven is "especially adept at transforming the writing of 'expert authors' into engaging and useful communications for general audiences. I'm also a very capable editor of professional writers." His assignments involve science, technology, or medicine, but also edits copy from other fields, such as economics and cultural affairs. His clients include: The National Academies, Howard Hughes Medical Institute, Mayo Clinic, Dana Foundation, Commonwealth Fund, Abt Associates, Argus Research Company, Environmental Defense, Union of Concerned Scientists, United Hospital Fund, National Science Foundation, Massachusetts Health Quality Partners, W.K. Kellogg Foundation, NOVA, Brookings Institution, Science magazine, Spectrum magazine, Sloan Management Review, University Business magazine, BioMedNet, Vanderbilt University, University of Georgia, University of Miami, Harvard University, University of Texas, Idaho National Energy and Environmental Laboratory. See previous experience at www.the-efa.org/members/data/resumes/marcussj.txt.

MARKETING MEYVN CONSULTING

312 Ronalds St., Iowa City IA 52245. (319)354-5692; (319)621-4671. **E-mail:** wasson.julia@gmail.com. **Contact:** Julia Wasson.

ADDITIONAL INFORMATION "Energetic and creative writer with special expertise in marketing communications that give businesses personality and interest. Also skilled at ghostwriting for executives, writing press releases and other public relations pieces, creating scripts for marketing or instructional videos,writing advertising copy. Careful and thorough copy editor with an eye for detail. Experienced educator with extensive background in writing for educational publishing, including the test preparation and testing industry." See previous experience at www.the-efa.org/members/data/resumes/wassonj.pdf.

MARK MY WORDS

7424 South 15th Dr., Phoenix AZ 85041. (480)248-7093. **Fax:** (888)366-0272. **E-mail:** markmywords@telecommutepros.com. **Contact:** Susan Walker.

ADDITIONAL INFORMATION "Mark My Words is a company comprised of freelancers who provide a variety of services including copyediting, proofreading, graphic design, translation, writing, educational publishing services, indexing, and much more. We connect clients with the freelancers who meet their needs best. Contact us for more information about working with us OR utilizing our services." See more info at www.the-efa.org/members/data/resumes/walkers.pdf.

JILL MASON

Winooski VT. (802)655-8915. **E-mail:** jill@masonedit.com. **Website:** www.masonedit.com.

ADDITIONAL INFORMATION Jill Mason edits books—nonfiction and fiction, scholarly and trade—as well as journals, magazines, business materials, theses and dissertations. "I do all levels of editing—copyediting, substantive editing, and developmental editing—as well as proofreading and indexing. I am familiar with the Chicago Manual of Style and the APA Publication Manual. I typically work in Word using its Track Changes feature but am also used to working with hard copy. I'm accustomed to working with authors whose first language is not English, and I have at least some familiarity with French, Spanish, German, and Italian. I try always to retain the author's voice, no matter what I'm editing and what shape it's in." Education: B.A. in psychology, University of Vermont; Workshop for Experienced Manuscript Editors, University of Chicago; Grantwriting for Nonprofit Organizations Workshop

STACIE L. MCCLINTOCK

Northeast Writing & Editorial Services, 145 Newbury St., Floor 3, Portland ME 04101. (207)939-8268. **E-mail:** stacie@northeastediting.com. **Website:** www.northeastediting.com. **Contact:** Stacie L. McClintock.

ADDITIONAL INFORMATION "Writer, managing and developmental editor and experienced proofreader and copyeditor offers over nine years of comprehensive experience, along with a B.A. in English and an extensive list of satisfied clients." With nearly a decade of experience as a full-time freelance editor and proofreader, I have a diverse background in the academic publishing world, including work with ESL students." See Stacie's resume at www.the-efa.org/members/data/resumes/mcclintocksl.pdf.

DANIEL MCCOURT

65 Cottage St., Apt. 2B, Port Chester NY 10573. (914)393-1136; (914)937-0065. **E-mail:** danmccourt@optonline.net; dan@takehimdowntown.com. **Contact:** Daniel McCourt.

ADDITIONAL INFORMATION Daniel McCourt is experienced in Freelance Copy Editing, Proofreading, Inputting Corrections and Electronic Production. Some magazines he's worked on include *Saltwater Sportsman, Science Illustrated, Yachting, The Nation, Hallmark,* and *Good Housekeeping.* "I have primarily checked copy and proofread around book closings, but I have also helped working in InDesign, and in Quark." Daniel is also a freelance baseball writer. See previous experience at www.the-efa.org/members/data/resumes/mccourtd.pdf.

MCLAMB COMMUNICATIONS

630-203 St. Joseph Street, Carolina Beach NC 28428. (910)520-9035. **E-mail:** mclambcommunications@charter.net. **E-mail:** mclambcommunications@gmail.com. **Contact:** Teresa McLamb, owner.

ADDITIONAL INFORMATION Years in field: 40 Years as freelancer: 35. Professional History: Owner, McLamb Communications - public relations, special events, freelance writing and editing, business communications. Event Coordinator for GE. Reporter/Photographer. Education: MA - English, UNC Wilmington; BA - Journalism, UNC Chapel Hill NC. Licensed Real Estate Broker. Selected Professional Honors/Affiliations: Editorial Freelancers Association, Greater Wilmington Communicators Roundtable, Brunswick County TDA, Brunswick County Chamber Board, Chair 2001. CASE Grand Award - Radio Programs CASE Award of Excellence - Radio Programs Outstanding Leadership Award, Wilmington Leadership Institute Communication Excellence Award, GE Corporate Communications. See previous experience PDF at: http://www.the-efa.org/members/data/resumes/mclambt.pdf.

MCL EDITING, ETC.

P.O. Box 11627, Chicago IL 60611. (312)573-1586 (home/bus.); (312)810-7898 (cell). **E-mail:** mclwriter@msn.com; maryc@mcleditingetc.com. **Website:** www.mcleditingetc.com. **Contact:** Mary C. Lewis. Estab. 1977.

ADDITIONAL INFORMATION "MCL Editing, Etc. is an editorial services firm. The owner, Mary C. Lewis, has over 20 years' experience in: writing, editing, critiques, revising, fact-checking, proofreading. With this expertise I help firms, organizations and individuals transform ideas into well-crafted, polished writing. From word choices to structure to final product, I stand for excellence. I stand by every job I undertake."

MIDDLEOFTHENIGHT EDITORIAL SERVICES

31 Lorraine St., Roslindale MA 02131. (617)553-2999; (617)413-7204 (cell). **E-mail:** middleofthenight@comcast.net. **Contact:** Ellen Kaplan-Maxfield.

ADDITIONAL INFORMATION Complete editorial services, including back-of-the-book scholarly indexing (specializing in psychology and philosophy works); developmental editing, substantive editing, and copyediting; and InDesign book design, typesetting and layout, creating print and ebooks ready for publication. Years in field: 10; Years as freelancer: 30. Specializing in back-of-the-book indexing of scholarly manuscripts with expertise in psychology and philosophy. Familiarity with SKY indexing software and embedded indexing in MS Word. "Working on deadline, skillful and sensitive editing as well as perfectionist proofreading of book manuscripts (list of published titles available upon request; see work references. Familiarity with Track Changes in Word and with typemarking." See previous experience at http://www.the-efa.org/members/data/resumes/kaplanmaxfielde.pdf.

FELICE MIKELBERG

8 Cherry Tree Ln., Middletown NJ 07748. (732)671-3888. **E-mail:** felice.mikelberg@verizon.net. **Contact:** Felice Mikelberg.

ADDITIONAL INFORMATION "Experienced editor/writer. Enthusiastic communications expert, providing enticing copy that tells a succinct story. More than 20 years of writing and editing for business and community publications. Meticulous grammarian with a sense of humor who understands the needs of today's readers. Clients include national and regional magazines and newspapers, book publishers, Web sites, and international businesses." See previous experience at http://www.the-efa.org/members/data/resumes/mikelbergf.pdf.

MEGAN FAIR MILLER

Russellville KY. **E-mail:** mfmiller3000@gmail.com. **Contact:** Megan Fair Miller, editor/proofreader.

ADDITIONAL INFORMATION Years in field: 16. Years as a freelancer: 10. "I am a versatile and experienced editor, copy editor, and proofreader. I've worked as an editor, associate editor, production editor, copy editor, proofreader for packagers and publishers such as Byron Preiss Visual Publications, Viking Children's Books/Puffin, Random House/Knopf

Juvenile, on children's fiction and nonfiction, adult trade nonfiction, science fiction, business textbooks, computer science textbooks, textbook and instructional guide support materials, and interactive educational products. I also have substantial experience in book compositing, web production, project management, and desktop design and publishing." See previous experience at www.the-efa.org/members/data/resumes/millermf.pdf.

ROBIN H. MIURA

Smithfield NC. (919)634-1989. **E-mail:** rmiura@embarqmail.com. **Contact:** Robin H. Miura.
ADDITIONAL INFORMATION Years in field: 12. Years as freelancer: 9. Experienced editor with almost a decade of in-house and freelance experience for major publishers. Clients include Algonquin Books, Oxford University Press, Duke University Press, University of North Carolina Press, Stenhouse Publishers, and individual authors. "I especially enjoy working on adult fiction and scholarly trade books, and I also specialize in education and psychology titles."

M.J. HINKO

23 Tejano Canyon Road, Sandia Park NM 87047. (505)281-4655. **E-mail:** mjhinko@aol.com. **Contact:** M.J. Hinko.
ADDITIONAL INFORMATION 8 years in the field. Proofreader and copy editor with experience working in a wide variety of fields. Specialties include educational, psychological, and scientific publishing (including educational/psychological assessments and supporting materials), marketing materials (print ads, catalogs, PowerPoint presentations) and proposals. Clients include Riverside Publishing. See www.the-efa.org/members/data/resumes/hinkom.pdf.

MONIFA COLTHURST

Multilingual Editing & Proofreading Services, Toronto CA. (416)960-3154. **E-mail:** wordsgalore@rogers.com. **Website:** www.wordsgalore.net. **Contact:** Monifa Colthurst, BA, BEd, MEd.
ADDITIONAL INFORMATION With 10 years in the field, 5 as a freelancer, Monifa Colthurst has strong communication and organizational skills. "I am detail-oriented and approachable. I have copyedited and proofread manuscripts, websites, theses, cover letters, resumes, and press releases in English, French and Spanish. My educational background includes a B.A. (Hons) from the University of Toronto (French, Spanish, Sociology), a B.Ed. from Brock University

(Adult Education), and an M.Ed. from the University of Calgary (Adult Education). I have also completed editing courses at the Editors' Association of Canada (EAC), George Brown College and the University of Waterloo."

MONOCLE EDITING

Woodbridge VA. **E-mail:** bibliophile80@yahoo.com. **Contact:** Barbie L. Halaby.
ADDITIONAL INFORMATION Years in field: 9. Years as a freelancer: 4. "I come from a five-year background with Arcadia Publishing, the leading local history publisher in the United States, which allowed me to work with literally thousands of different history titles. My freelance career has been focused on nonfiction, scholarly manuscripts, both monographs and contributed volumes, published by such companies as Routledge, Cambria Press, Continuum, and Palgrave Macmillan, as well as repeat editing of the prestigious journal University of Toronto Quarterly. My work with these publishers has received high praise from on-staff editors and authors alike, and my consistency has ensured long-lasting relationships with staff editors and publishers. My passion has always been to preserve the nuances of language so that writers can express their ideas better. I firmly believe copyediting is of the utmost importance during these times when first impressions are often the only impression, and an author's or company's reputation must be preserved. Each manuscript (whether a few hundred words or a few hundred pages) will benefit significantly from the careful craftsmanship I provide." See previous experience at www.the-efa.org/members/data/resumes/halabybl.pdf.

JESSICA MORELAND

22 Audry Lane, Westford VT 05494. (802)355-3408. **E-mail:** info@jessicamoreland.com. **Contact:** Jessica Moreland.
ADDITIONAL INFORMATION Years in field: 8. Years as freelancer: 8. "Jessica Moreland is an award-winning freelance writer, editor, and book designer from Vermont. She finds it extremely rewarding to work one-on-one with authors, and her best recommendations are from happy clients. Jessica graduated Magna Cum Laude from Brigham Young University in English with an emphasis in editing, and she received an MFA in Creative Writing from the University of Massachusetts-Boston.

J.L. MORENO WRITING, EDITING & RESEARCH

When Clarity Counts, 4820 West Flint St., Chandler AZ 85226. (480)540-7637. **E-mail:** jlmoreno@whenclaritycounts.com. **E-mail:** jlmoreno@q.com. **Website:** www.whenclaritycounts.com. **Contact:** Jerryll L. Moreno, M.A..

ADDITIONAL INFORMATION J.L. Moreno is an independent publishing professional and academic editorproviding production management, editing, proofing, and design thattransform information into knowledge and connects content with scholarsworldwide. While working toward her certification in scholarly publishing, Jerryll received a Scholarly Publishing Endowment for excellence in the program, and she has since delivered award winning production and design on collaborations with Left Coast Press and the World Archaeological Congress. Jerryll is a member of the Left Coast Press freelance team and the book review editor for Kiva: The Southwestern Journal of Anthropology and History. As both a production manager and an editor, she has overseen and edited books in archaeology, higher education, numerous interdisciplinary titles, and an enormous amount of grey matter in the environmental sciences. Currently, Jerryll works closely with authors, typesetters, indexers, publishers, and acquisition managers to provide a wide variety of publishing expertise. As a publishing professional, she believes that negotiating best practices and competing interests is critical to successfully transform information into knowledge, create quality content, and build lasting relationships with authors and presses.

GRACE A. MORSBERGER

4826 Langdrum Ln., Chevy Chase MD 20815. (301)656-2724 (tel./fax); (202)468-6433 (cell). **E-mail:** morsbergerg@gmail.com. **Contact:** Grace Anne Morsberger.

ADDITIONAL INFORMATION "Academic editor and proofreader with over ten years of experience. Specializing in complex, multiauthor volumes, ensuring a consistency in style and language throughout. Adept at polishing the prose of non-native speakers of English. Can review translations from Russian or German for accuracy and flow, and can also translate from those languages into English. I also have extensive experience with smaller projects such as concert programs and newsletters. Special areas of expertise include 18th- through 20th-century history and culture, art history, and literature." Experience: 7 years as Managing Editor, Dumbarton Oaks, Washington, D.C. Grace earned a Ph.D. in Slavic Languages and Literatures, Univ. of California, Berkeley, 1997. See previous experience at www.the-efa.org/members/data/resumes/morsbergerg.pdf.

LORETTA MOWAT

E-mail: loretta.mowat@verizon.net. **Contact:** Loretta Mowat.

ADDITIONAL INFORMATION "Years in field: 20. Years as freelancer: 16. Full-time freelance copy editor and proofreader since 1996. Experience with many different kinds of text: financial, fiction and nonfiction, legal, reference, and more."

MUCHMORE, INC.

Quality editorial services since 1998, P.O. Box 373, Perry Kansas 66073. (785)550-1715. **E-mail:** nicole_muchmore@yahoo.com. **Website:** www.muchmore-inc.com. **Contact:** Nicole Muchmore.

ADDITIONAL INFORMATION Nicole Muchmore has been a full-time freelance copy editor for 15 years, with a focus on scientific and academic publishing. "I have had long and productive relationships with publishing houses such as Nature Publishing and Oxford University Press, among others." Nicole's specialty subjects include biological and genetic sciences, and medical specialties such as urology. She is skilled at editing the science research reports of English-as-second-language authors. For more information see www.the-efa.org/members/data/resumes/muchmorens.pdf.

THE MUIR WORKSHOP

Tryon NC. (864)431-2983. **E-mail:** chris@muirworks.com. **Website:** muirworks.com. **Contact:** Chris Pelton.

ADDITIONAL INFORMATION Chris Pelton has been in the field for 15 years and is the founder and principal of The Muir Workshop. He is an accomplished writer, researcher, and editor with experience in the U.S. and Ireland. "At The Muir Workshop, we provide writing, proofreading, copy editing, research, and web and document design services to individuals, companies, and nonprofit organizations. We specialize in working collaboratively with our clients to craft well-organized, clearly written and polished reports, articles, books, documents, and other publications." Chris holds an M.A. in Sociology (Political Economy) and a B.A. in Environmental Sociology from the University of Tennessee and is also a published poet and songwriter.

MY LITERARY COACH™

9764 Gates Ave., Cleveland OH 44105. (888)317-7270. **Fax:** (888)317-0342. **E-mail:** info@myliterarycoach. com. **Website:** www.myliterarycoach.com. **Contact:** Timothy Staveteig. Estab. 2009.

ADDITIONAL INFORMATION My Literary Coach is a newer, full-service literary agency, which selects clients whose work—mostly nonfiction and some fiction—we think we can successfully place with royalty-paying publishers.We adhere to the Association of Authors' Representatives, Inc., Canon of Ethics, which provides for compensation for agreed upon services and reimbursement for pass-along charges. Our passion is 'getting authors published well.' Our website offers numerous free links. See website or contact for additional information.

AMBER NEFF

Chicago IL. **E-mail:** aneff@uchicago.edu. **Contact:** Amber Neff. Estab. 2002.

ADDITIONAL INFORMATION Amber Neff has been working in editing and publishing since 2002 and freelancing for 8 years. Her rates for proofreading begin at $20/hr.

LISA NEFF EDITORIAL SERVICES

150 Hart Ln., Springfield PA 19064. (610)328-0768. **E-mail:** neffeditorial@gmail.com. **Contact:** Lisa Neff.

ADDITIONAL INFORMATION Lisa Neff has edited medical manuscripts for 20 years, 12 of them freelancing. She states her goals include: editing pre-pubilcation ESL journal manuscripts for foreign authors; editing medical books; and editing and writing patient education materials. Her experience includes the fields of ESL medical editing as well as regular editing of nursing, psychology, and environmental manuscripts. She received thorough training in-house at W. B. Saunders, Philadelphia, in all aspects of medical journal production, including manuscript, first and second pages, bluelines, and advanced-copy review. She has some book-production experience as well. See previous experience at www.the-efa.org/members/data/resumes/neffl.pdf.

MICHELLE NESBIT

Rockford TN. (865)982-0905.

ADDITIONAL INFORMATION "I have spent the last 10 years honing my writing and editing skills. I have published a book in the industry that I worked and in my spare time have written and/or ghostwritten numerous articles for publication on the web, in magazines and newspapers. I have also managed other writers and edited their work before release to publication." See previous experience at www.the-efa.org/members/data/resumes/nesbitm.pdf.

THE NEW YORK BOOK EDITOR

E-mail: nybookeditor@hotmail.com. **Website:** www.nybookeditor.blogspot.com. **Contact:** Erin Niumata. Estab. 2004.

ADDITIONAL INFORMATION "We have provided valuable proofreading, copy editing, critiques and much more. We have worked with many best-selling authors as well as first-time writers. Additional editors: Foster Niumata, Mira Park, Tracy Cartwright and more."

NINGER MEDICAL COMMUNICATIONS, LLC

(201)635-5006. **Fax:** (201)635-9781. **Website:** www.ningermedcom.com. **Contact:** Laura J. Ninger.

ADDITIONAL INFORMATION Laura J. Ninger, ELS, is a full-time independent contractor with more than 20 years of experience in medical editing and writing, including 14 years as a freelancer. Her clients include medical communications companies, medical societies, MD and PhD authors, major universities, medical publishers, and other institutions. Ms. Ninger's services range from copyediting to substantive editing and from abstracting to report writing, and also include fact checking, project management, creation of slides and notes, and other projects. She communicates on clinical topics aimed at physician or consumer audiences. See her website for a list of her services, a bibliography of editing and writing projects, and client testimonials. She is a certified Editor in the Life Sciences (ELS), and has earned an Editing/Writing Core Curriculum Certificate and an Advanced Curriculum Certificate from the American Medical Writers Association.

NOLA EDITING

Gail Naron Chalew, 6310 Fontainebleau Dr., New Orleans LA 70125. (504)864-0266. **E-mail:** nolaeditor@gmail.com. **Contact:** Gail Naron Chalew.

ADDITIONAL INFORMATION Gail Chalew has spent 25 years in the field; 23 years freelancing. "Substantive editing of academic works and dissertations, with a focus on the social sciences, humanities, and Judaica; particularly skilled in working with material written by non-native English speakers. Edited books for Cambridge University Press, Stanford University Press, Elsevier, Greenwood, Lawrence Erlbaum, and Temple University Press, as well as dissertations in the social sciences and library science." "A graduate of the Baltimore Institute for Jewish Communal Service in which she earned a Masters of Social Work and a Masters of Jewish History, Gail has worked both in the editing field and in Jewish journalism. Since, 1989, she has been editor of the Journal of Jewish Communal Service, a professional journal distributed internationally to people working for Jewish agencies. From 2000 to early 2005, Gail was the editor of The New Orleans Jewish News, the Jewish newspaper for the New Orleans community." Education: 1973: B.A. in anthropology, Vassar College, Poughkeepsie, New York; 1975: M.S.W., University of Maryland School of Social Work, Baltimore, Maryland; 1975: M.A. in Jewish History, Baltimore Hebrew University, Baltimore; Professional memberships: American Jewish Press Association, Editorial Freelancers Association. See resume: www.the-efa.org/members/data/resumes/chalewgn.pdf.

CHRIS OLSEN PROFESSIONAL WRITING & EDITING SERVICES

11 Hidden Hills Dr., Stony Point NY 10980. (973)652-6776. **E-mail:** chrisolseneditorial@gmail.com. **Contact:** Chris Olsen.

ADDITIONAL INFORMATION Chris Olsen has been in the field for 20 years. His services include: Writing, Ghostwriting, Technical Writing, Copy Editing, Line Editing, and Proofreading. "I have superb writing and editing skills, and my high level of professionalism drives me to turn over final products that are impeccable every time. I am accustomed to both short-term deadlines and long-term project planning, and I can often provide quick turnaround on small projects. I am versed in Chicago Manual, AP style, AMA style, Mac and PC platforms, MS Word/Tracking Changes, HTML, Photoshop, and Quark. My job is to make you happy while I make you look great!" See previous experience at www.the-efa.org/members/data/resumes/olsenc.pdf.

JIM O'NEAL

3848 Cass St., Apt. 1, Omaha NE 68131. (402)415-8076. **E-mail:** jimoneal@cox.net. **Contact:** Jim O'Neal.

ADDITIONAL INFORMATION Award winning author Jim O'Neal has been a professional writer and editor for 26 years. He has worked in various roles at the Rocky Mountain News, the Suburban Journals of Greater St. Louis, the Cedar Rapids Gazette and the Omaha World-Herald. "Jim's clients get just what they want, whether it's a light edit to correct only demonstrable errors, a strong edit to produce flawless copy, or a consultative edit in which he provides a list of suggestions and recommendations for a rewrite by the author. His goal is achieving excellence as defined by the client. His rates—per page or by the hour, depending on the project—are in line with Midwestern standards." See rèsumè at www.the-efa.org/members/data/resumes/onealj.pdf.

PATRICIA A. ONORATO

58 Prentice St., Waltham MA 02451. (781)790-1813. **E-mail:** patonorato@msn.com. **Contact:** Patricia A. Onorato.

ADDITIONAL INFORMATION "Experienced freelance proofreader and copyeditor with meticulous attention to detail, respect for deadlines, and thorough understanding of grammar, spelling, and language usage. Types of projects include reference books in the humanities and social sciences, dissertations, training materials, and newsletters. Experience with electronic and hard copy manuscripts." Clients include (1983-present) Anatolia College, Board of Trustees, Boston, MA; proofread quarterly newsletter, copyedited grant proposals. Charles Scribner's Sons, Reference Books, New York, NY. Dictionary of American History (copyediting). Scribner's American Writers Series (proofreading). Education: School of the Museum of Fine Arts, Boston, MA—Diploma, Fine Arts (Artist's Books and Mixed Media), 1996; Wheaton College, Norton, MA, B.A.—Art History, *cum laude*, 1982. See more information at http://www.the-efa.org/members/data/resumes/onoratopa.pdf.

FRANCES OSTENDORF

Seekonk MA. (401)316-1616. **E-mail:** fran.ostendorf@gmail.com. **Contact:** Frances Ostendorf.

ADDITIONAL INFORMATION Frances Ostendorf has been in the field 30 years; 20 as a freelancer: "Attention to detail makes me the ideal candidate for your next project. A well-edited product delivered on time will keep you coming back for more! I am a flexible, versatile editor with a variety of communications skills including story development, layout, writing, copy editing, proofreading and publication production. I have experience with books, papers, newspaper and magazine articles, recipes and food articles, newsletters, brochures and marketing materials. No project is too big or to small. Accuracy and ability to multi-task are among my strengths. My wide range of computer skills include Quark, Word and Excel on PC and Mac platforms."

ROBYN J. OXBORROW

Reno NV 89503. (775)910-1137. **E-mail:** roxborrow@gmail.com. **Contact:** Robyn J. Roxborrow.

ADDITIONAL INFORMATION Robyn J. Roxborrow has spent 3 years in the field, 1 year as freelancer. Robyn is a freelance writer and editor based in Reno, NV. "I understand that deadlines and priorities can change fast, and take a calm approach when working closely with my employers to get the the job done." Robyn acquired a B.A. in English writing and a minor in photography in 2009. She interned at the University of Nevada Press where she learned about book publishing. She enjoys helping others to develop their ideas into a story or work of art. For more info, see www.the-efa.org/members/data/resumes/oxborrowrj.pdf.

PAGE TURNER EDITING

Oakland CA. (510)655-7301. **E-mail:** deniseleto@att.net. **Contact:** Denise Michelle Leto.

ADDITIONAL INFORMATION "Currently, I am a freelance substantive and developmental editor. For 10 years I was a Senior Editor at the University of California, Berkeley. During the last 15 years, I have edited work by faculty and post-doctoral scholars for university presses, non-fiction professional and trade authors, and work by creative writers, such as personal essays, novels, and poetry for literary journals and publishers. I earned a Masters in Fine Arts at Saint Mary's College of California. Prior to that, I graduated Valedictorian and Phi Beta Kappa in Legal Studies and Social Policy from UC Berkeley. I have edited writing from a range of disciplines and genres: environmental science, psychology, sociology, literary scholarship as well as the creative arts. I am a published poet and author."

ROB PALLADINO

11401 Hornsby St., Austin TX 78753. (512)300-0085; (512)217-6318. **E-mail:** robpalladino@austin.rr.com. **Contact:** Roberto Palladino.

ADDITIONAL INFORMATION Robert Palladino has 17 years of experience. "My editing style allows the copy to flow and have punch, while keeping the writer's original ideas in tact. I view my style as very much an enhancement to the piece at hand and that is what I try to do at all times. I have experience with AP, Chicago and WIT. I also use Word and can use InDesign and, in the past, have user experience with Quark. My resume has all my information and you are welcome to get in touch." See www.the-efa.org/members/data/resumes/palladinoro.pdf.

PAPER TYGER

E-mail: editor@papertyger.net. **Website:** www.papertyger.net. **Contact:** Juliet Ulman. Estab. 2009.

ADDITIONAL INFORMATION "Quality freelance fiction and narrative nonfiction editorial services from a seasoned senior editor with eleven years of experience at Bantam Books." Services: Substantive or structural editing, proofreading. Cost: Charges an hourly rate for developmental and line editing, and per-page rate for proofreading; contact for price quote. "First time clients will receive a one-time discount of 10% on the final invoice." See website for additional information.

BARBARA J. PARKER

13 Burnham Pl., Fair Lawn NJ 07410. (201)475-1525. **E-mail:** bjp100@optimum.net. **Contact:** Barbara J. Parker.

ADDITIONAL INFORMATION "I have enjoyed a varied career as a writer and editor, including work for newspapers, non-profit organizations, trade organizations, pharmaceutical firms, educational publishers, magazines, newsletters and Web sites. I'm looking for assignments that will best use my skills and professional background and that will match one of my many interests. I have written about everything from the arts and literature to finance and business and have served as a feature writer, magazine editor, newspaper and reporter. I have a particular interest in putting my abilities to work for an environmental organization, but I am open to all suitable freelance opportunities. For details, See previous experience at www.the-efa.org/members/data/resumes/parkerbj.pdf.

LORI PAXIMADIS

20515 Bunker Hill Dr., Fairview Park OH 44126. **E-mail:** lori@loripax.com. **Website:** loripax.com. **Contact:** Lori Paximadis, principle. Estab. 1991. Offers copyediting, line editing, developmental editing, proofreading, and project management.

KIM ALAN PEDERSON

29 Front St., #2, Marblehead MA 01945-3261. **Fax:** (866)254-5556. **E-mail:** kap@editheads.com. **Contact:** Kim Alan Pederson. Estab. 1996.

ADDITIONAL INFORMATION Kim Alan Pederson has spent 19 years in the field: 13 years as freelancer. Prior to freelancing as editor and writer, Kim was a Senior Editor at Charles River Associates, an internationally recognized economics consulting firm with offices in Boston, Washington, D.C., London, and many other locations. Please see rèsumè for full details.

PENULTIMATE EDITORIAL SERVICES

#27-4520 Gallagher's Lookout, Kelowna BC V1W 3Z8 Canada. (778)478-0877. **E-mail:** info@penultimateword.com. **Website:** www.penultimateword.com. **Contact:** Arlene Prunkl, editor.

ADDITIONAL INFORMATION "I specialize in working with first-time, self-publishing authors." Services include manuscript consultation, developmental editing, structural and stylistic editing, copyediting, proofreading, writing and rewriting, indexing, research, and fact checking/reference checking. Cost: $45US/hour for proofreading and copyediting; $50US/hour for substantive editing, structural editing, consultation, critique, or indexing. Receive free estimate through online submission form. See the website for additional information.

LAURA PERKINS

Baltimore MD. **E-mail:** laura@siriusthoth.com. **Contact:** Laura Perkins.

ADDITIONAL INFORMATION Laura Perkins is an adept proofreader and copy-editor with 5 years of publishing experience. She has proofread and contributed editorial input for 9 editions of a set of technical manuals, while employed as a technical writer. Familiar with all stages of the publishing process, from first draft to galleys, bluelines, and bound book. "Seeking freelance work in the world of literary publishing." See previous experience at www.the-efa.org/members/data/resumes/perkinsl.pdf.

CAROL ANNE PESCHKE

Greenbank WA. (360)678-0761. **Fax:** (360)222-3732. **E-mail:** CAPeschk@aol.com. **Contact:** Carol Anne Peschke.

ADDITIONAL INFORMATION Carol Anne Peschke has 20 years in the field, 16 as a freelancer. Copyediting, rewriting, and proofreading of STM academic and professional publications, specializing in environmental science and healthcare. Electronic manuscript coding, cold reads, design surveys, permission tracking, author contact, and other production and editorial services. Copyeditor of *The American Journal of Psychology* since 1997. Carol Anne Peschke is skilled at editing translated and second-language manuscripts. "As former editing manager of a full-service house, I have in-depth knowledge of prepress production. I work independently and have earned a reputation in the industry for fast, efficient, thorough editing." See more information at www.the-efa.org/members/data/resumes/peschkec.pdf.

DIANE PINIARIS

2621 Palisade Ave., Apt. 14E, Bronx NY 10463. (718)548-7859. **E-mail:** dianepiniaris@gmail.com. **Contact:** Diane Piniaris.

ADDITIONAL INFORMATION Diane has been in the field for over 30 years. "My specialty is ELT (EFL/ESL) writing/editing - I have written a series of highly successful ELT test preparation textbooks for the Greek market for University of Michigan Proficiency (ECPE) and Competency (ECCE) exams. Previously, I worked for 5 years at Oxford University Press as an ELT developmental editor and I have over 20 years of ELT classroom experience. Before getting into ELT, I was in trade publishing (4 years with Scribners in the late 1960s-early 1970s and 5 years with Paddington press, a now-defunct Anglo-America publisher based in London)."

TERESE PLATTEN

2404 State Route 295, Canaan NY 12029. **E-mail:** tplatten@freelance-editorial-services.com. **Website:** www.freelance-editorial-services.com. **Contact:** Terese Platten.

ADDITIONAL INFORMATION Terese B. Platten has been serving as a freelance editor since 1994 with more than 25 years of experience in both book publishing and institutional publications. She is conversant in Chicago, AMA, APA, and Bluebook manuals of style. "Editorial: Copyedit and proofread nonfiction and educational text, journals, and newsletters, electronically and on hard copy. Proofread fiction. Typemark and code for composition. Check and style references, AMA, APA, Chicago, Bluebook, or house style. Write and proofread press releases and fact check." See more info at www.the-efa.org/members/data/resumes/plattent.pdf.

DANARAE POMEROY EDITORIAL SERVICES

139 Turner Circle, Greenville SC. (864)834-7549. **E-mail:** INFO@dana-rae.com. **Website:** www.dana-rae.com. **Contact:** DanaRae Pomeroy. Estab. 1987.

ADDITIONAL INFORMATION A complete line of editorial services offered by a published author with twenty-three years of professional experience in the editorial field. DanaRae provides analysis and critique, content editing, line editing, revisions, rewrites, ms preparation for submission. Welcomes both fiction and nonfiction mss. Please see website for details.

HILARY POWERS

385 Palm Ave., #5A, Oakland CA 94610. (510)834-1066. **E-mail:** hilary@powersedit.com. **Website:** www.powersedit.com. **Contact:** Hilary Powers.

ADDITIONAL INFORMATION Hilary Powers has a journalism degree from Stanford. She has spent almost 20 years as a freelance editor. Hilary can help with editing from the lightest of copyediting to polishing developmental work, and radical revision for tone and focus. See more information at http://www.the-efa.org/members/data/resumes/powersh.pdf.

PROFESSIONAL EDITING

Greensboro NC. (336)288-0482. **E-mail:** marciahorowitz@bellsouth.net. **Contact:** Marcia R. Horowitz.

ADDITIONAL INFORMATION Marcia has been in the publishing field for 15 years, 6 as freelancer. "SUBJECT AREAS: Business, leadership, management development, social sciences, humanities. SERVICES: Developmental editing—idea stage to publication, copyediting, book-proposal writing, ghostwriting, publication project management. TRACK RECORD: Helped authors publish over thirty books, wrote magazine and newsletter articles, edited articles for major professional journals, ghostwrote chapters and major parts of books, helped prospective authors write successful book proposals."

PRO NOVEL EDITING SERVICES

3805 Burke, Cheyenne WY 82009. (307)772-1741. **Fax:** (501)325-0305. **E-mail:** proediting@earthlink.net. **Website:** www.pronovelediting.com. **Contact:** Michael McIrvin, founding writer and editor. Estab.

2003. Pro Novel Editing Services can provide the following for fiction writers of all skill levels: line editing, developmental (content) editing, novel manuscript critiques, and query letters.

ADDITIONAL INFORMATION Pro Novel Editing Services can also facillitate the following for self-publishers: book layout in the appropriate program files required by your POD company, book cover design, conversion to all digital formats, e-book layout and design, and website design.

PROOFED TO PERFECTION EDITING SERVICES

PO Box 71851, Durham NC 27722. (919)732-8565. **E-mail:** inquiries@proofedtoperfection.com. **Website:** www.proofedtoperfection.com. **Contact:** Pamela Guerrieri.

ADDITIONAL INFORMATION Pamela works with all genres of fiction, both secular and inspirational, in the capacity of a proofreader, content editor, developmental editor, and ghostwriter. Her genres are any type of fiction and narrative and educational non-fiction, as well as inspirational books. Pamela currently does contract editing work for several major publishing houses and editorial firms as a manuscript evaluator and content editor.

SHERI QUIRT

Seattle WA. (206)450-8796. **E-mail:** sheri@sheriquirt.com. **Website:** www.sheriquirt.com. **Contact:** Sheri Quirt.

ADDITIONAL INFORMATION Sheri Quirt is a copy editor, substantive editor, and proofreader versed in Chicago and AP style. Sheri earned a Certificate in Editing from the University of Washington and spent two years at *The Seattle Times*, copy editing and writing for NWsource.com, the newspaper's online guide to local shopping and entertainment.

JAYA JOHNY RAMCHANDANI

29 C Sagar Sangeet, Colaba, Mumbai 400005 India. (91) 9967967693. **E-mail:** jayar@siriusinteractive.co.in. **Website:** http://siriusinteractive.co.in. **Contact:** Jaya Johny Ramchandani.

ADDITIONAL INFORMATION "Editorial consultant with over 6 years experience in science editing (over 1,000 mss) for ESL authors (from Japan, Korea, China, Taiwan, India, Finland, Italy, and Switzerland). Background in author services for journal submission, editor quality and training, translation and editing quality management systems, process reengineering, content management, and website development and strategy." Languages: English (Native), Hindi, German (Elementary), Dutch (Elem.). BSc, Physics (+Computer Science), St. Xavier's College, Mumbai, India. See more information at www.the-efa.org/members/data/resumes/ramchandanijj.pdf.

JENNIFER RAPPAPORT

New York NY. **E-mail:** jennifer.rappaport@gmail.com. **Contact:** Jennifer Rappaport, copy editor, proofreader, and translator.

ADDITIONAL INFORMATION With 12 years in the field and 5 as freelancer, Jennifer Rappaport provides English-language copyediting and proofreading services for book publishers, organizations, and individual authors. She edits on hard copy and electronically. She knows the Chicago Manual of Style. Recent Clients include: Oxford University Press, The New Press, Bloomsbury USA, Duke University Press, University of Chicago Press, Penguin, St. Martin's Press, The Overlook Press. Her editorial specialties are: scholarly and trade nonfiction books, nonprofit projects. She is also a French-to-English translator. Her translation specialties are academic and historical documents.

MYTHILI RAVI

Edison NJ. **E-mail:** himyths@yahoo.com. **Contact:** Mythili Ravi.

ADDITIONAL INFORMATION "Mythili Ravi is an independent writing and editing professional with more than 20 years of experience in serving corporate as well as individual clients across geographies and industries. She started her career as an ESL (English as a Second Language) teacher. Mythili has worked with academics for textbooks on a range of subjects from mathematics to social science; research analysts and business writers for reports and articles published in reputed periodicals; industry experts for books on entrepreneurship, foreign exchange, international finance, personal finance, risk management, and regulatory compliance; professional chefs for books on specialty cuisine; anthropologists and theologians for books on cultural history, philosophy, religion, and spirituality; scientists for theses and articles published in prestigious journals; and literary writers for novels and anthologies of poetry/prose/short stories. Mythili has a master's degree in English, a diploma in Publishing, and a certificate in Journalism."

WENDY M. RAYMONT

2500 Q St., NW #121, Washington DC 20007. (202)812-8182. **E-mail:** wraymont@mac.com. **Contact:** Wendy Raymont.

ADDITIONAL INFORMATION "Years in field: 5. Years as freelancer: 1. Wendy Marcus Raymont is a trained lawyer and mediator with a long-time interest in conflict resolution. She also has considerable editing and researching experience beginning with a four-year stint as researcher/fact-checker for the Law Section of *Time* magazine." She earned a degree from Smith College and Harvard Law School.

CYNTHIA A. READ

26 Calam Ave., Ossining NY 10562. (914)944-0124; (914)841-2925. **Contact:** Cynthia A. Read.

ADDITIONAL INFORMATION With 35 years in the business, Cynthia's skills include writing, project management from concept development to final publication, developmental and line editing, copyediting, proofreading, and photo research. Works with novice and academic, scientific, and professional authors, specializing in translating complicated concepts for general readers. Cynthia is editor-in-chief of *The Corgi Cryer*, a quarterly magazine. She was an in-house editor of the journal *Cerebrum: The Dana Forum on Brain Science*, of the Annual Report, and for the grants program in neuroscience and immunology, author of BrainWeb, and managing editor of publications (all for the Dana Foundation). She has extensive experience as a freelance editor and writer for other nonprofit organizations, such as the Albert and Mary Lasker Foundation, the Overbrook Foundation, Funders Concerned About AIDS, and the LEAD Program in Business. See Cynthia Read's resume at www.the-efa.org/members/data/resumes/readca.pdf.

REAL WRITERS APPRAISAL SERVICE AND EDITORIAL CONSULTANCY

P.O. Box 170, Chesterfield S40 1FE United Kingdom. **E-mail:** info@real-writers.com. **Website:** www.real-writers.com. **Contact:** Lynne Patrick, Coordinator.

ADDITIONAL INFORMATION "Our appraisal and editorial service is available to anyone. Send us your manuscript and we will provide comprehensive feedback on anything from a haiku to a family saga. We also edit manuscripts for conventional or self-publication." Accepts online submissions. Cost: basic fee of £30 per hour covers a full professional evaluation of prose, poetry, or script of any length, or £20 per hour for detailed copy editing. Introductory packages also available

ADRIENNE M. REBELLO

44 DeSimone Dr., Marlborough MA 01752. (508)481-8541. **E-mail:** arebello@aol.com. **Contact:** Adrienne M. Rebello.

ADDITIONAL INFORMATION "After 20 years of freelance copy editing, I have a great deal of experience in many subject areas, reading levels, and editing levels. I am sensitive to scheduling needs, and am flexible and dependable. My early years as a technical writer gave me invaluable insight into the process of book creation and production as well, and I am comfortable working with project managers, editorial staff, and authors." Adrienne holds a B.A. in Psychology, Univ. of Massachusetts, Amherst, MA and a Massachusetts Education Certificate, K-8. See previous experience at www.the-efa.org/members/data/resumes/rebelloam.txt.

RECOMMENDED READER

Tucson AZ. (520)327-3312. **E-mail:** sc@recommended-reader.net; mossdreams@live.com. **Contact:** Susan Elizabeth Campbell, proofreader/editor.

ADDITIONAL INFORMATION Years in field: 10. "Susan Campbell is a freelance proofreader and copyeditor specializing in scholarly, literary, and scientific work (including the social sciences) for university presses and other institutions. She has worked on titles for Harvard University Press, Oregon State University Press, Penn State Press, Cedars-Sinai Medical Center LA, the Arizona Department of Game and Fish, the Arizona-Sonora Desert Museum, astronomers of the UA Vatican Observatory, and the University of Arizona Press (where she completed her editorial internship), among others. Susan is a meticulous and focused editor and proofreader, always on time, with particular reading experience and education in horticulture, agriculture, natural history, botany, and ornithology, as well as the social sciences, biology, ethnobotany, ethnoarchaeology, and astronomy. For UA Press she has also worked on dozens of titles in fiction, history, memoir, and poetry. She is conversant in CMS, APA, and AP style. Clients note she is flexible, intelligent, and easy to work with." See previous experience at www.the-efa.org/members/data/resumes/campbellse.pdf.

JEAN REDMOND

Columbus OH. (614)486-9906. **E-mail:** jredmond.edit@gmail.com. **Contact:** Jean Redmond.

ADDITIONAL INFORMATION Jean Redmond has been in the field for 25 years; 12 years as a freelancer. 20 years of experience as a technical editor of scientific research articles, primarily in physical and applied chemistry and chemical engineering. "I have a degree in chemistry with a minor in physics, and in the course of my work I have also extensively edited mathematical material (e.g., variables, arrays, and equations). I have edited online using XML and specifically MathML for mathematical and chemical expressions. I have also copy edited master's level material, including a report for a capstone project in elementary education and the literature review for a seminary thesis. I have extensive experience with Microsoft Word, including developing style sheets and applying styles. I have also used MS Word to create newsletters to be converted into PDF file format. I have used Microsoft Publisher to design and lay out a cookbook." See resume: www.the-efa.org/members/data/resumes/redmondje.pdf.

WENDY REIS EDITING AND PROOFREADING

Stratford ON N5A 5L9 Canada. **E-mail:** wendyreisediting@gmail.com. **Website:** www.wendyreisedit-ingandproofreading.com; www.wendyreisediting.wordpress.com. **Contact:** Wendy Reis.

ADDITIONAL INFORMATION "I do a mandatory 2000 word sample edit before accepting a project. (This applies to first time clients only.) I need to know if your work is ready for a professional edit. This will also give you valuable feedback." Editing: $50 per hour with a 1 hour minimum. By the quarter hour ($12.50) after that. Large projects require a $200 deposit.

BARBARA RESCH

5310 Meadowgreen Dr., Colorado Springs CO 80919. (719)548-0612. **Website:** www.the-efa.org/members/data/resumes/reschb.pdf. **Contact:** Barbara Resch.

ADDITIONAL INFORMATION 15 Years in the field; 8 years as freelancer. Experience in substantive editing, copyediting, production editing/manuscript coding, reading-level determination/adjustment, proofreading and a focus on K–12 science curricula and young-adult nonfiction books. Permissions identification. Special interest in Chinese language and culture, among others.

MIKE REVZIN

1927 N. Akin Dr., Atlanta GA 30345. (404)633-0817. **E-mail:** atlmjr@aol.com. **Contact:** Mike Revzin.

ADDITIONAL INFORMATION 35 years in the field. Mike Revzin has edited and written numerous scripts for CNN's high-profile shows and anchors. "I spent eight years in Asia and have an indepth knowledge of that part of the world, especially China. I edited a book on doing business in China and write training materials for people who are going there for business. I also worked in Germany for 2 years and currently edit business news for a Swedish company." For more information, see www.the-efa.org/members/data/resumes/revzinm.pdf.

MICHAEL J. RICCA

(917)270-6645. **E-mail:** major318@yahoo.com. **Website:** www.linkedin.com/in/michaelricca. **Contact:** Michael J. Ricca.

ADDITIONAL INFORMATION Michael is an editor, proofreader, writer, and researcher. His "clients and employers include New York City-based: PR, Ad, and, Info agencies, Corporations, Publishers, packagers, books, and publications in: trade, public, healthcare, financial, reference, social sciences, professional basketball, arts, music, and audio; Security, Government, U.S. Census Bureau." Performed the final editorial proofreading, editing, and signoff of: *The Good Housekeeping Cookbook*, for Hearst Corporation.

RIGHT TOUCH EDITING

Haverhill MA. (978)996-0389. **E-mail:** erin.brenner@gmail.com. **Website:** www.righttouchediting.com. **Contact:** Erin Brenner.

ADDITIONAL INFORMATION Erin Brenner has been in the field for 16 years, 5 years as a freelancer. Her skills include line/substantive editing, copyediting, fact-checking, proofreading, training proofreaders and editors, creating and maintaining style guides, developing and documenting publishing processes for online publication, HTML coding, and posting content online. Erin holds a M.A. in English, Northeastern University and a B.A. in English, Salem State College. See previous experience at www.the-efa.org/members/data/resumes/brennerec.txt.

DEBORAH A. RING

Professional Writing & Editing Services, 198 Chapmans Ave., Warwick RI 02886. **E-mail:** ring@wordbirdonline.com. **Contact:** Deborah A. Ring, writer/editor.

ADDITIONAL INFORMATION Deborah Ring has 17 years in the field, 7 years as a freelancer. Deborah is a full-time freelancer providing professional copyediting, proofreading, and writing services to publishers of academic, reference, and professional books and journals. Her areas of speciality include literature, history, arts, humanities, business and economics, and social sciences.

JUDITH ROBEY

1721 Scott St., Conway AR 72034. (501)205-1681. **E-mail:** judith-robey@sbcglobal.net. **Contact:** Judith Robey.

ADDITIONAL INFORMATION "My background as an academic, publishing and teaching intensive writing classes, was great preparation for my second career as a freelance copy editor and proofreader. Since 2005 I have edited and proofread for academic clients (in business, linguistics, history, German and Russian literature, art, and art history) and university presses (Northern Illinois University Press, Yale University Press, Macmillan). A Ph.D. in Russian Literature (Indiana University) with a double major in Russian and German (University of Virginia), I have specialized in academic prose and foreign language-related materials. I have also freelanced as an abstractor of Russian history journal articles. This work has honed my ability to make prose precise and succinct." See previous experience at www.the-efa.org/members/data/resumes/robeyj.pdf.

ARLENE W. ROBINSON

E-mail: bettyboopwrites@aol.com. **Contact:** Arlene W. Robinson.

ADDITIONAL INFORMATION "Arlene W. Robinson has developed and edited 400+ full-length mss in a variety of genres since 1996. Her clients include: Women's fiction author Angie Daniels; Award-winning YA author Hannah R. Goodman; College-success guide author Josh Richardson, and Sue Dent, whose first novel, *Never Ceese*, earned a spot on the 2007 Stoker Award's preliminary ballot." "Arlene welcomes new or published authors as clients, and enjoys helping journalistic, business and academic writers transform their writings into marketable, polished products for mainstream readers. She also takes pride in helping non-native-English writers to produce top notch fiction and nonfiction works." "For many full-length manuscripts, Arlene offers a no-cost, no-obligation evaluation of at least the first two pages. If she feels the manuscript is ready to be edited, she does a brief sample edit at no charge. This allows her to quote a more accurate fee for the editing, and allows her client-to-be to get a better idea of her editing and critiquing style. If she doesn't believe your manuscript is ready for professional services, she will refer you to some helpful free or low-cost resources to help you hone your writing skill." To see if your ms qualifies for a free evaluation, send your excerpt of the first 5-10 pages by email attachment, MS Word or RTF format preferred. See www.the-efa.org/members/data/resumes/robinsonarw.pdf.

VELANY BRENDEN RODRIGUES

E-mail: velany@gmail.com. Contact: Velany Brenden Rodrigues.

ADDITIONAL INFORMATION Velany Rodrigues is a language professional who has spent 8 years in the field. He specializes in Copy editing text written by ESL as well as EFL authors; writing Web content; writing articles on a wide range of topics (as a features editor); writing features and articles for special-interest magazines; Coaching students who wish to learn various forms of writing. "As a copy editor, Ive edited several hundred manuscripts, newsletters, fiction texts (even poetry!), advertising copy, etc."

AMANDA ROOKER

102 Yearling Ct., Yorktown VA 23693. (757)240-4241. E-mail: amanda@amandarooker.com. Website: www.amandarooker.com. Contact: Amanda Rooker. Estab. 2007.

ADDITIONAL INFORMATION Offers full-service custom editing and publishing packages for nonfiction authors and professionals, including critique and consultation, project management, developmental editing, copyediting, proofreading, electronic publishing, and press-ready book design (Adobe InDesign). "We specialize in helping professionals translate their expertise into a polished, publishable, true-to-self manuscript to meet their professional goals, and are passionate advocates for writers and independent publishing." Member, Editorial Freelancers Association. Cost: free phone consultation for project fee estimates (please provide sample).

BEV KATZ ROSENBAUM

Canada. E-mail: bevrosenbaum@yahoo.ca. Website: www.bevkatzrosenbaum.com. Contact: Bev Katz Rosenbaum.

ADDITIONAL INFORMATION Offers mss critiques. Former in-house editor at Harlequin.

STEVE ROSSMAN

Baltimore MD. E-mail: topeditor4u@yahoo.com; srossman@bdlcommunications.com. Website: http://srossman.bdlcommunications.com. Contact: Steve Rossman.

ADDITIONAL INFORMATION Copy editor/proofreader with extensive experience. Strong research, writing, organizational, and computer skills. Skilled in reviewing and editing collateral materials, magazines, novels, and nonfiction. "Working in the publishing, academic, and medical industries for more than 14 years, Steve is an editor and proofreader specializing in fiction and educational workbooks as well as dissertations and magazines. Working with companies, such as H. M. Rowe Company and Nautical & Aviation Publishing, his ongoing clients include Kennedy Krieger Institute, Johns Hopkins University, and TBC. He also does light proofreading to detailed editing of dissertations, particularly for graduate students and professionals who need help with English grammar and usage." Proficient: MS Word, MS Word tracking, WordPerfect, Excel. Growing knowledge of Site Executive, MAC OS X Tiger, Apple, including FlightCheck Professional, QuarkXPress, Adobe InDesign CS3, and Dreamweaver.

ROTH EDITORIAL SERVICES

Lebanon PA. E-mail: kristin@rotheditorial.com. Website: www.rotheditorial.com. Contact: Kristin Roth.

ADDITIONAL INFORMATION "I graduated summa cum laude from Lebanon Valley College with a BA in English communications and Spanish, and I have worked with several internationally acclaimed publishing houses, including Brill, Cambria Press, Palgrave Macmillan, and Parragon. While my experience in the publishing industry runs the gamut from the preliminary developmental stage to typesetting, my absolute passion is editing, whether it be proofreading, copy editing, or substantive editing. I have edited books on a variety of topics including history, technology, health, education, literature, philosophy, sociology, and Asian studies. I am proficient in both

APA and Chicago styles and am skilled at quickly learning and applying whatever university or publishing-house style your work is required to follow." Visit www.rotheditorial.com for more information.

MAGGIE RYAN

7029 Sutherland Ave., St. Louis MO 63109. (314)647-2144. **E-mail:** maggiesnow@sbcglobal.net. **Contact:** Maggie Edelmann Ryan.

ADDITIONAL INFORMATION Maggie Ryan has been in the field for 7 years, 1 year as a freelancer. "I am a freelance proofreader and editor with considerable professional and educational writing, proofreading and editorial experience. Currently, I am responsible for writing and editing grants, press releases, newsletters and e-communications, case-for-support documents, direct mail pieces, donor acknowledgement letters and other constituent communications. While attending Saint Louis University, I took several journalism and editing courses and received the highest grade in the class in Introduction to Journalism, Editing and Editorial and Opinion Writing." For more information see www.the-efa.org/members/data/resumes/ryanmag.pdf.

SANDYEW PRE-PUBLISHING SERVICES

Providence RI. (401)338-9092. **E-mail:** alcyew@gmail.com. **Contact:** Alice Yew. Estab. 2008.

ADDITIONAL INFORMATION Alice Yew has worked 5 years in the field as a freelancer. Edits or proofreads books, journal articles and websites of any subject matter. Education: BA Mathematics, MSc Applied Mathematics, PhD Applied Mathematics. Skills: copyediting, proofreading. Subjects: mathematics, physics, environmental studies, engineering, education, Chinese. Clients include Pearson, Hodder, Wiley, Harcourt, Oxford University Press, Cambridge University Press. "Given my former 10-year career as an academic mathematician, I especially welcome opportunities to work on texts with mathematical, scientific, or educational content and typescripts in LaTeX."

LINDA SCHMUKLER

Brooklyn NY. **E-mail:** lkatsch@earthlink.net. **Contact:** Linda Schmukler. Estab. Linda Schmukler has almost 2 decades experience in the field of children's books, working on all genres: proofreading and copy editing, working both in and out of house, including 11 years as a production editor at Scholastic. Freelance clients have included Scholastic, Random House, HarperCollins, Avon, and an independent author. She has worked in Quark, now in InDesign. Her skills include Word, Excel, and database use and design. Her other areas of experience/expertise include Italian, fine arts, and theater. See more info at www.the-efa.org/members/data/resumes/schmuklerl.pdf..

EILEEN K. SCHOFIELD

Hartsdale NY. (914)725-6872. **Contact:** Eileen K. Schofield.

ADDITIONAL INFORMATION Years in field: 25; Years as freelancer: 7. Eileen earned a "B. A. in Biology, Clark Univ. and M. A. in Botany, Columbia University. Work and publications in several areas of botany at Harvard Univ., Ohio State Univ., and New York Botanical Garden. Full-time scientific editing of journal articles, reports, and books in about 20 subjects at Kansas State University. Since 2001, freelance copyediting, mainly botanical books for New York Botanical Garden Press and recently Columbia University Press."

SCRIBE CONSULTING

29488 Woodward Ave., Suite 426, Royal Oak MI 48073. **E-mail:** info@scribe-consulting.com; jennifer@scribe-consulting.com. **Website:** www.scribe-consulting.com. **Contact:** Jennifer Baum, founder. Estab. 2010.

ADDITIONAL INFORMATION "Scribe Consulting offers editing and proofreading services for writers at all levels. Before even considering submitting your work, you should invest in a professional edit and critique. It may mean the difference between rejection and success!" Costs of services varies. E-mail for free sample edit and price quote.

SCRIBENDI INC.

405 Riverview Drive, Suite 304, Chatham ON N7M 5J5 Canada. (519)351-1626. **Website:** www.scribendi.com. Estab. 1997.

ADDITIONAL INFORMATION "Editing and proofreading are so much more than language correction. We believe that quality revision services directly contribute not just to the success of a project but also to the success of an individual." Services offered: critique, editing, proofreading of mss, query letters and packages, synopsis and outline creation.

BRETTE SEMBER

Clarence NY. (716)759-1706. **E-mail:** Brette@BretteSember.com. **Website:** www.brettesember.com. **Contact:** Brette Sember.

ADDITIONAL INFORMATION Years as a freelancer: 11. "Brette Sember B.A., J.D., is an experienced author, freelancer, ghostwriter, book doctor, blogger, indexer, and copyeditor. She writes often about food, travel, travel shopping, parenting, divorce, business, law, books, lifestyle, pregnancy, health, education, learning skills, women's and family issues, adoption, reproductive technology, finance, writing, children's books, senior issues, and more. She is the author of more than 40 books and many ebooks. As a ghostwriter and book doctor, Brette has worked on a variety of projects and topics including project management, college textbooks, test-taking skills, self-tutoring, adoption, business, virtual assistants, conversation starters, and many more. As an indexer and copyeditor, she has worked on over 300 titles."

FRAN SEVERN

6397 Oliver Road, Salisbury MD 21801. (443)782-2462 (bus); (443)260-2390 (c). **Fax:** (443)782-2464. **E-mail:** fran@fransevern.com. **Website:** www.fransevern.com. **Contact:** Fran Severn.

ADDITIONAL INFORMATION "Years in field: 20. Years as freelancer: 27. Writer, editor, publisher, producer, blogger, technical writer, university instructor (mass communications), special events coordinator, voice-over artist, on-air anchor/reporter/DJ, still and video photographer. My skills are varied and—after nearly three decades in the field of communications—they are well-honed. I do more than edit copy. With my background, I see the complete picture and how well your material connects with your audience. When more than one approach is used, I know how to integrate them for the more effective, most efficient program and results. And if 'all' you want is line or copy editing, I love red ink." "The first call and consultation are free. This gives you a chance to define your needs and gives me information so I can develop a plan that's cost-effective and successful for you. Within a week, you'll have a detailed proposal, including price, timeline, and specific documents and services I'll deliver. The price includes the draft document(s) and two re-writes, if needed. Simple projects, like copy editing or proofreading existing documents, are priced at a flat rate, based on the number of pages. Complex or on-going projects are billed on an hourly rate. Legitimate non-profits and charities receive a 25% discount." See previous experience at http://www.the-efa.org/members/data/resumes/severnf.pdf.

SGWORDPLAY

Montclair NJ. (973)509-1471. **E-mail:** sgwordplay@gmail.com. **Contact:** Susan Greene.

ADDITIONAL INFORMATION Susan Greene is "an accomplished and imaginative writer, editor, and researcher whose expertise and passion is in the arts and humanities." "During 32 years with the Music & Art Department of Pearson, Greene wrote, edited and supervised the creative inception and production of over 500 publications that include books and online materials. A savvy development editor, she also broke lucrative creative ground for this department, as well as for Language Arts and Social Studies, by guiding the unfolding of product in new genres and markets." Susan has been freelancing for 1 year. For more information, see her LinkedIn profile or email her for her resume.

DANA LYNNE SINGFIELD

Lytaker, New York NY. **Website:** http://lytaker.com. **Contact:** Dana Lynne Singfield.

ADDITIONAL INFORMATION Dana Lynne Singfield has spent 20 years in this field; 15 as a freelancer. She is a skilled editor and writer with experience in newspapers, magazines, advocacy journalism, Web, and book editing. Her rèsumè states she is an "Accomplished developer of multimedia solutions for corporate training organizations, with proven skill in each phase of the training development life cycle, including concept design, writing, editing and programming, integration of deliverables into learning management systems, and anticipation and troubleshooting of customer queries." Wendy was educated at Oberlin College Oberlin College with a dual major in English / Judaic and Near Eastern Studies with Hebrew language focus. See rèsumè at www.the-efa.org/members/data/resumes/singfielddl.pdf.

MIKE SIROTA WRITING SERVICES

1611-A S. Melrose Dr., #107, Vista CA 92081. (619)807-7975. **Fax:** (760)295-0967. **E-mail:** mike.sirota@yahoo.com. **Website:** www.mikesirota.com. **Contact:** Mike Sirota.

ADDITIONAL INFORMATION Services offered include comprehensive manuscript evaluation, line editing, and consulting and mentoring.

ELIZABETH SMITH

Brooklyn NY. (917)974-1879 (cell). **E-mail:** esmithwrite@gmail.com. **Contact:** Elizabeth Smith.

ADDITIONAL INFORMATION "Available for writing, editing, copyediting, and proofreading of print or online projects. Experienced in fiction (literary, romance, science fiction and fantasy, suspense, young adult, and children's) and nonfiction (history, biography, fashion and style, pop culture, architecture and design, art, and art techniques). Also experienced in calendar editing, copyediting, and proofreading for wall, engagement, and boxed formats. Organized, creative, dependable, and interested in developing projects for children, teens, or adults. Familiar with InDesign and writing for Web-based publications. Over 5 years experience as editor, copyeditor, and proofreader. Also available as writing coach and mentor. Clients: Harry N. Abrams, Inc., Rizzoli International Publications, Penguin, Harlequin, Random House, Inc., Museum of Modern Art." See previous experience at www.the-efa.org/members/data/resumes/smithe.pdf.

KIMBERLY M. SMITH

Jacksonville FL. (904)742-7359. **E-mail:** kmsmithwrites@yahoo.com. **Contact:** Kimberly Smith.

ADDITIONAL INFORMATION "I have a Master's degree in English and have taught English and creative writing to writers of all ages. "With twenty years of experience writing, editing, and proofreading, I have created business documents, organizational reports, press releases, fiction, and poetry for small businesses, educational and non-profit organizations, literary magazines, and college and university students. I live and work in Jacksonville, Florida and enjoy an open and flexible schedule, which enables me to work around any project's schedule and produce a quick turn-around time. You will find my assistance helpful, courteous, and fresh with ideas."

SNOWDEN EDITORIAL SERVICES

E-mail: susan7snowden@hotmail.com. **Website:** www.snowdeneditorial.com. **Contact:** Susan Snowden.

ADDITIONAL INFORMATION "At Snowden Editorial Services we focus primarily on books, both fiction and nonfiction; but we also edit book proposals, short stories, essays, articles, newsletters, promotional materials, Web copy, and more." Services offered: manuscript analysis, line editing, proofreading, consulting, coaching, and private workshops and classes. Cost: e-mail for current rate sheet.

COLLEEN SNYDER EDITORIAL SERVICES

72 Blue Valley Road, Linden VA 22642. (540)636-7785 (voice/fax). **E-mail:** csnyder123@comcast.net. **Contact:** Colleen Snyder.

ADDITIONAL INFORMATION Colleen Snyder has been in the field for 27 years and has exhibited comprehensive writing and editing skills, as evidenced by her teaching experience and writing samples. She is accurate, complete, and on time. Colleen holds a B.A. English, Salisbury State College, Salisbury, Maryland; M.A. Literature and Language, American University, Washington, D.C.; Certificate in Teaching English as a Second Language, American University, Washington, D.C. Continuing Education in Grant Writing through The Writers Center, Bethesda, Maryland. For more information see http://www.the-efa.org/members/data/resumes/snydercg.pdf.

JAN SOKOL

Overland Park KS. (913)381-8552. **Contact:** Jan Sokol.

ADDITIONAL INFORMATION Jan Sokol has more than a decade of experience in written communications. Her work has included writing editorial copy for publications, developing bid proposals, refining academic writing, and editing articles for newspapers and newsletters. Jan is skilled "in promoting clarity and a logical flow of ideas, with particular strength in synthesizing information from a variety of sources." She is experienced in the following areas: Biomedical, Pharmaceutical, Mental Health, Adult Education, Liberal Arts, Compliance, Quality Control."

RACHEL SOMERSTEIN

108 Trinity Place, Syracuse NY 13210. (917)538-4105. **E-mail:** rachel.somerstein@gmail.com. **Contact:** Rachel Somerstein.

ADDITIONAL INFORMATION "Rachel has six years of experience as a writer and editor for magazines, books, and the Web. Her work has appeared in ARTnews, n+1, Next American City, and PBS.org, among other publications. She writes most frequently about art and urban planning. As a development editor and copywriter, Rachel works with nonprofit and cultural organizations, the federal government, financial-services companies, and independent authors. Rachel holds an M.F.A. in creative writing from NYU and a B.A., *cum laude*, from Cornell University. She also teaches at NYU's Stern School of Business. PUBLICATION COURSES: University of Chicago, "Manuscript Editing"; Simon Fraser University, "Magazine Editing"; EEI Training Division, "Developmental Editing" and "Copyediting." " See previous experience at www. the-efa.org/members/data/resumes/somersteinr.pdf.

SPELLKNOCKER ENTERPRISES

6516 Cavalier Dr., Alexandria VA 22307. **E-mail:** amrush71@gmail.com. **Website:** http://nairda.net/editor. html. **Contact:** Adrian Rush.

ADDITIONAL INFORMATION "My editing has consistently won accolades from supervisors, clients, and peers alike. In a profession in which the relationship between writers and editors often feels adversarial, I'm proud to have built up a tremendous amount of respect and trust among writers. I listen to their concerns, and I empower them to sharpen their craft by explaining things to them in a clear and approachable manner." Adrian Rush is the sole proprietor of this online editing service licensed in the state of Washington. Current clients include Cactus Communications, Demand Studios, and the University of Washington"s Creative Communications department. Former clients include Indiana University-Purdue University Indianapolis. Freelanced for the Indiana University Foundation at IUPUI from 2000 to 2003. Samples and recommendations available. For more information, see www.the-efa.org/members/data/resumes/rusha.pdf.

JAN SPOOR

Tacoma MD. **E-mail:** jan.spoor@wybesse.net. **Contact:** Jan Spoor.

ADDITIONAL INFORMATION "Mr. Spoor has worked in the defense and security sector for over 15 years, serving as technical writer, editor, researcher, analyst, database developer, and trainer under contract to the National Counterterrorism Center, the Department of Defense, the Department of Commerce, and the Office of National Drug Control Policy, among others. He has also worked as an in-house copy-editor, proofreader, publication manager, website designer and maintainer, and indexer for professional associations, environmental research organizations, and academic publishers. He began working part-time as a freelance editor and proofreader in 2007."

SPRINGLEY EDITORIAL SERVICES

Gina Springer Shirley, 4715 Alta Loma Dr., Austin TX 78749. (512)947-5586. **E-mail:** gina@springley. net. **Website:** www.springley.net. **Contact:** Gina E. Springer Shirley, writer/editor/translator.

ADDITIONAL INFORMATION Years in the field: 14. Years as a freelancer: 6. Gina E. Springer Shirley, MA, is a writer and editor of educational materials and an English/Spanish translator. During a ten-year career in educational publishing, Ms. Springer Shirley has written and edited supplemental and intervention programs in the subjects of English, Reading, Language Arts, and ELL/ESL. Some of the programs she has developed include Oxford Picture Dictionary for the Content Areas, Elements of Reading: Fluency, Elements of Reading: Phonics & Phonemic Awareness, and Critical Reading: Differentiated Instruction Across Genres. She remains connected to students and their needs by tutoring and mentoring K - 12 students. See previous experience at www.the-efa.org/members/data/resumes/springershirleyg.pdf.

DAWN MCILVAIN STAHL

Monticello IL. (217)898-4125. **E-mail:** purplepenning@gmail.com. **Contact:** Dawn McIlvain Stahl, editor.

ADDITIONAL INFORMATION Years in field: 12. "With more than ten years freelance and in-house experience as an editor and proofreader, I specialize in skilled editing and clear, respectful, and helpful communication with authors, freelancers, and clients. I offer copyediting and proofreading. My experience includes scholarly monographs and texts, magazines, marketing and promotional materials, websites, film projects, fictional narratives, and four-color, college-level textbooks." See previous experience at www.the-efa.org/members/data/resumes/mcilvaind.pdf.

FRED STANTON

94 Geiser Road, Wynantskill NY 12198. (518)283-1864. **E-mail:** fredstanton1@gmail.com. **Contact:** Fred Stanton.

ADDITIONAL INFORMATION Fred Stanton is a copy editor, proofreader, indexer, and technical writer with over 33 years of experience in the field, 13 as a freelancer. With a strong background in the sciences (B.S. in physics, M.S. in molecular biology), he has copy edited the United Nations International Labour Organization's *Encyclopaedia of Occupational Safety & Health*, monographs in molecular biology, and the *Journal of Biomolecular Techniques*. He has also copy edited books on history, labor, and African-American studies, as well as business newsletters. His desktop publishing skills include formatting and page design in Adobe InDesign. Fred is also a poet and songwriter. See more information at http://www.the-efa.org/members/data/resumes/stantonf.pdf.

STEELE EDITING

1926 Meandering Way, McKinney TX 75071. (972)984-8514. **E-mail:** frank@steele-editing.com. **Website:** www.steele-editing.com. **Contact:** Frank Steele, owner. Estab. 2011. Offers professional proofreading, copyediting, and indexing at a reasonable price.

ADDITIONAL INFORMATION "I have more than 30 years experience in publishing. I specialize in general nonfiction, religious/spiritual material, self-help/motivational material, children's books, and I'm open to almost anything."

WILLIAM H. STEVENSON

109 Parkview Dr., Meridianville AL 35759. (256)823-9017; (256)541-0139. **E-mail:** whsteve3@gmail.com. **Contact:** William H. Stevenson.

ADDITIONAL INFORMATION "Bill began his career as a scientist and ended as a free lance writer. A chemist by training, he worked for 25 years on a variety of projects in industry and as a government contractor,writing more than 20 scientific and technical publications. During this time he also published a number of free lance magazine articles on topics ranging from the chemistry of sunscreens to a profile of FBI undercover agent Robert Wittman, "the world's greatest art recovery detective." He is now a full time free lance writer and editor." He states, "When reading science and history books I am often struck by the poor quality of the editing and, in particular, the fact checking. I would like to contact publishers and any others who have a need for an editor with a wide experience in works of science, history and literature." See previous experience at www.the-efa.org/members/data/resumes/stevensonwh.pdf.

KRISTEN STIEFFEL

Orlando FL. (407)928-7801. **E-mail:** kristen@kristenstieffel.com.

ADDITIONAL INFORMATION Kristen Stieffel is a writer and writing coach specializing in line editing and copyediting. She works primarily in the Christian submarket but has also edited books for the general market. Topic areas of expertise include fiction, especially speculative fiction, business, history, and Bible study.

SUMMER AFTERNOON EDITING CO.

2585 N. River Road, Sylva NC 28779. (828)586-0829. **E-mail:** jenny@summerafternoonediting.net. **Website:** http://summerafternoonediting.net. **Contact:** Jenny Bennett.

ADDITIONAL INFORMATION "I am a highly analytical, detail-oriented editor with a combined 33 years of experience in the areas of copyediting, proofreading, writing, and journalism. The diversity of my skills is demonstrated in my current mix of clients: I edit with pencil on paper for university press clients, with "Track Changes" in Word for the Asian Development Bank, and with Adobe Acrobat for an environmental organization." See www.the-efa.org/members/data/resumes/bennettj.pdf for more information.

SWANSON EDITORIAL SERVICES, INC.

1729 SE 36th Ave., Portland OR 97214. (503)239-7194. **E-mail:** kris@swansoneditorial.com. **Contact:** Kristin Swanson, owner. "In business for the last 20 years as a consultant and freelance writer, developmental editor, andproject/production manager in the area of K-12 and college textbook publishing. Co-author of Nexos, an introductory college Spanish textbook, published by Cengage Learning."

ADDITIONAL INFORMATION Kristin Swanson has been a freelancer for 21 years working as a writer and editor in the areas of foreign language and ELL educational publishing. Fluent in Spanish and able to work in French and Italian (but not fluent in those languages). Also works as a project manager for editorial and production projects. Has working knowledge of html. Projects include textbooks, workbooks, teacher materials, web activities, testing materials, and information packets such as author guidelines and FAQ sheets. Checks Spanish translations and translates from Spanish into English. She has been the managing editor of an educational journal and is familiar with conventions of scholarly publishing. See previous experience at www.the-efa.org/members/data/resumes/swansonk.pdf.

TEXABLE COMMUNICATIONS

P.O. Box 41023, Austin TX 78704. (512)522-4515. **E-mail:** contact@texable.com. **Website:** www.texable.com. **Contact:** Jeff Iezzi.

ADDITIONAL INFORMATION Years as freelancer: 8. "As an experienced author, editor, and translator, I have a proven track record of developing effective communication materials. During the last 15 years,

I have worked on a wide variety of online and print publications—corporate websites, marketing brochures, product handbooks, and style guides. My native language is American English, and I speak, read, and write fluent German."

TEXT UNVEXED

136 Lebanon St. #1, Malden MA 02148. **E-mail:** mj@textunvexed.com. **Website:** www.textunvexed.com. **Contact:** Marijane Leonard.

ADDITIONAL INFORMATION "Marijane Leonard brings her keen eye for detail, passion for clarity and consistency, and desire for excellence to clients across a variety of industries. Her editorial experience comprises work in newspaper, magazine, nonprofit, academic and education publishing. She is as comfortable editing fourth-grade readers as she is computer science research. Marijane is a graduate of the Missouri School of Journalism with a degree in editing. In addition to working as a freelance editor, my experience includes time as the managing editor of a magazine, a staff editor at a major textbook publisher and a content manager at an educational content development house."

RUTH E. THALER-CARTER

2500 East Avenue, Suite 7K, Rochester NY 14610. (585)248-8464 (home); (585)248-8464 (business). **Fax:** (585)248-3638. **E-mail:** ruth@writerruth.com. **Website:** www.writerruth.com. **Contact:** Ruth E. Thaler-Carter.

ADDITIONAL INFORMATION Ruth Thaler-Carter is an award-winning freelancer writer, editor, proofreader, desktop publisher and speaker who has a business called "I can write about anything!" She specializes in articles for and about associations and nonprofits, and in all aspects of newsletters, from concept through publication, including training and critiques. She is a fast, effective, accurate writer, editor and proofreader with a lively writing voice, wide-ranging network of resources, and sharp eye for details." She teaches freelancing, editing/prooofreading and website classes, both online and in person, for several professional organizations. She also holds an annual conference for freelancers through Communication Central (www.communication-central.com).

AMY THOMPSON EDITING

Council Bluffs IA. (402)660-7109. **E-mail:** amy@amythompsonediting.com; amythompsonediting@gmail.com. **Website:** www.amythompsonediting.com. **Contact:** Amy Thompson, owner.

ADDITIONAL INFORMATION Years in field: 25. Years as a freelancer: 1. "I bring years of experience, published works and satisfied clients to the table. From young adult and youth novels to blog and website editing to annual reports, you can be confident that the skills and thoroughness I can provide will always be in your best interest. I believe that forming a partnership with clients is essential to the successful completion of any project. Together, we can create a finished product that you will be proud of and that will shine through the murk and the clutter. I am thorough, accurate, creative and can offer fast turnaround when necessary. I am also a writer. I love the written word and the flow of thoughts and images that can be shared ... words that can bring me to laughter and tears and words that can share information, teach me something and make me think. I believe my writing brings another element to all projects that I undertake and, once again, helps you make your work shine." See previous experience at www.the-efa.org/members/data/resumes/thompsonal.pdf.

TIGERXGLOBAL

Owensboro KY. (270)302-0036. **E-mail:** maria@tigerxeditor.com. **Website:** www.tigerxglobal.com. **Contact:** Maria D'Marco.

ADDITIONAL INFORMATION "TigerXglobal offers experienced, knowledgeable, insightful editing services for every type of written work. Your manuscript receives personalized attention through every step of your edit with comprehensive reviews that bring your work to its fullest potential. TigerX edits ensure clarity, maximize your unique style, and reveal opportunities to strengthen your story, message, or concept. Query to determine which editing service, or blend of services, best suits your needs. Editing can be stand-alone or combined services, including proofreading, style/language edits, continuity reviews, fact-checking, and full developmental edits. An initial consult is performed free of charge to determine your specific needs. A proposal or quote will be supplied from the information gained in this preliminary consult." Maria D'Marco has been in the field for 30 years. Contact her using the form on her website.

THE TOBIN TOUCH, LLC

Arlington Heights IL. (773)368-3079. **Fax:** (773)283-7852. **E-mail:** stacey.tobin@thetobintouch.com. **Web-**

site: www.thetobintouch.com. **Contact:** Stacey C. Tobin, PhD., ELS. Estab. 2003.

ADDITIONAL INFORMATION Stacey Tobin is an "independent PhD medical and scientific writer and board-certified editor in the life sciences, with a background in cellular and molecular physiology research and 14-years' experience in writing, editing, formatting, and submitting peer-reviewed journal articles, invited reviews, editorials, and textbook chapters, as well as preparing abstracts and posters for presentation at professional conferences." She also reviews NIH and NSF grant applications for content organization, continuity, and formatting. Stacey has a B.Sc. (biology, chemistry minor); M.S. (molecular physiology); Ph.D. (neurobiology and physiology). Her subjects are: reproductive medicine, obstetrics and gynecology, oncology, cardiology, diabetes and metabolism, endocrinology, and HIV/AIDS. Stacey Tobin is the owner of The Tobin Touch, LLC, April 2003 - present. Recent assignments include writing and editing for the National Institutes of Health and National Cancer Institute grant applications, invited reviews, and peer-reviewed manuscripts for publication in national journals and international meeting proceedings, as well as creating meeting abstracts and posters. See her resume at www.the-efa.org/members/data/resumes/tobins.pdf.

TOP COPY EDITING SERVICES

Greenbelt MD. **E-mail:** markfarrell@topcopyediting.com. **Website:** www.topcopyediting.com. **Contact:** Mark Farrell.

ADDITIONAL INFORMATION Provides copyediting, proofreading, transcription, and desktop publishing services for all written material, including: Manuscripts, newsletters, proposals, published and nonpublished articles, research papers, term papers. Style guides used: Associated Press Stylebook, The Chicago Manual of Style, Government Printing Office Style Manual, APA, In-house manuals by request. Mark earned an M.A., American Studies, Boston College, 1989; B.A., American Studies, Stonehill College, 1985. PROFESSIONAL EXPERIENCE: Editor (contract), U.S. Department of Commerce, Office of Inspector General, Office of Audit & Evaluation, Washington, D.C., April to August 2010.

TOPNOTCH LIFE & CAREER COACHING

P.O. Box 1185, Merchantville NJ 08109. (856)488-0366. **Website:** http://topnotchlifeandcareercoaching.com. **Contact:** Dr. Mary Ann Diorio. Estab. 2002.

ADDITIONAL INFORMATION Writing coach—offers goal setting, accountability, editorial insights. Charges $120/hour.

TO THE POINT EDITING

1360 Edmund Court NE, Atlanta GA 30306. (678)982-6388. **Website:** www.the-efa.org/dir/membershipinfo.php?mid=13224. **Contact:** Leslie Lapides, owner/operator. Estab. 2011.

ADDITIONAL INFORMATION "Everyone needs an editor—even editors. My goal is for your manuscripts to reflect yoru voice, not mine. My job is to help clarify and bring out what you want to say in the best and clearest way. Naturally, I will also correct any spelling, grammar, and punctuation mistakes."

TRIPLE THREAT FREELANCING, LLC

164 Oak Ave., Malaga NJ 08328. (609)238-2536. **E-mail:** tara.ronda@gmail.com. **Contact:** Tara Ronda, owner. Estab. 2011. Offers complete range of editorial services, including content editing and placement, proofreading, copyediting, and formatting.

TRITTIN EDITING

Saint Paul MN. **E-mail:** sheryl@trittinediting.com. **Website:** www.trittinediting.com. **Contact:** Sheryl Trittin. Estab. 2000.

ADDITIONAL INFORMATION Sheryl Trittin has over 12 years of experience in the field, 10 as a freelancer. Sheryl possesses a B.A. degree in literature and environmental science and has completed graduate-level courses in editing and nonfiction writing. She is currently enrolled in the Professional Sequence in Editing certificate program at UC Berkeley. Trittin Editing offers professional editing services, specializing in copyediting and proofreading. Writing, fact checking, and other related services are available.

VALERIE JOY TURNER

Boonton NJ. **E-mail:** vjt@valeriejoyturner.com. **Website:** http://valeriejoyturner.com. **Contact:** Valerie Turner.

ADDITIONAL INFORMATION Valerie Turner offers a variety of editing services from proofreading and light editing to substantive editing, writing, and reviewing translations. She specializes in works on Middle Eastern history, Islamic studies, and Arabic translations. She holds a Certificate in Editing from the University of Chicago, a Master of Arts in Middle Eastern Studies, and a Bachelor of Arts in Islamic History. She is a native English speaker, with advanced

Arabic (reading, writing, and speaking), and familiarity with Persian and French. She is experienced using various Arabic transliteration systems. See Valerie's website for pay rates.

PHILIP TURNER BOOK PRODUCTIONS LLC

New York NY. **E-mail:** philipsturner@gmail.com. **Website:** http://philipsturner.com. **Contact:** Philip Turner, editing, representation, consulting.

ADDITIONAL INFORMATION Offers line editing of proposals and manuscripts for agents, authors, and publishers. Nonfiction and selected fiction. Services include proposal editing, book proposal development, and line-editing. Cost: Rates given upon review of material. Contact for rates. See http://philipsturner.com or www.publishersmarketplace.com for additional information.

TWELVE POINT BOLD

(484)201-8183. **E-mail:** elizabeth@twelvepointbold.com. **Website:** www.twelvepointbold.com. **Contact:** Elizabeth C. Goldberg.

ADDITIONAL INFORMATION "Twelve Point Bold offers expert copyediting, project editing, and ghostwriting services tailored to meet your goals and deadlines. I edit and write nonfiction prose: academic papers and theses, scholarly articles and books, legal documents, business documents, journalistic articles, speeches and presentations, marketing materials, newsletters, correspondence, proposals, and memoirs. I have a bachelor's degree from Harvard University and a M.A. in journalism from NYU. Prior to launching Twelve Point Bold, I worked for 10 years as a professional writer and editor in New York City. In academia, business, and journalism, my approach to writing is always the same: make it clean, make it clear, make it in on time." See more info at www.the-efa.org/members/data/resumes/goldbergec.pdf.

TWO SONGBIRDS PRESS

(916)837-3017. **E-mail:** robin@twosongbirdspress.com. **Website:** http://www.twosongbirdspress.com. **Contact:** Robin Martin, founder/editor.

ADDITIONAL INFORMATION Robin Martin has spent 11 years in the field; 7 years as a freelancer. "On the editing staff of an internationally-acclaimed literary magazine, Robin evaluates manuscripts for publication. With professionally trained writing skills and strong editorial judgment, she is able to identify the elements of a powerful and effective story and to articulate the strengths and weaknesses of a piece. She performs substantive, line, and developmental edits, determining content, acquiring permissions and establishing and meeting the publication schedule of a non-profit organization." Recent awards, honors and affiliations include: First Place Bazzanella Award for Expository Prose in 2008; First place Literary Insight Award in 2007. MA English (Writing) California State University, Sacramento; BA English (Summa Cum Laude) Rutgers College.

ELIZABETH ANN TYSON

87 Pierce Road, Watertown MA 02472. (617)924-7715. **E-mail:** ba_tyson@comcast.net. **Contact:** Elizabeth Ann Tyson.

ADDITIONAL INFORMATION Experienced editor/proofreader with book publishing experience. Elizabeth has been in the field for 40 years. See more info at www.the-efa.org/members/data/resumes/tysonea.pdf.

JILL B. UHLFELDER

Brooklyn NY. (347)599-1704. **E-mail:** jbuedit@aol.com. **Contact:** Jill B. Uhlfelder, writer/developmental editor/copyeditor/proofreader.

ADDITIONAL INFORMATION "In addition to having a range of experience writing and editing a variety of documents, I am able to provide a rule of grammar and style for every editorial change I make—a skill that has been helpful to professionals for whom writing is a critical part of their responsibilities." Jill Uhlfelder holds a B.A. degree in English, with honors, New School for Social Research—New York, NY. She has been in the field for 30 years. See her resume at www.the-efa.org/members/data/resumes/uhlfelderjb.pdf.

VERSATILE MULTIMEDIA SERVICES

Tucson AZ. (520)990-9582. **E-mail:** lmarkowitz@aol.com. **Website:** www.lauramarkowitz.com. **Contact:** Laura Markowitz. "Versatile, award-winning, multimedia editor, writer, reporter and producer for print, broadcast and online media."

ADDITIONAL INFORMATION "Check out my resume for details about my editing experience, and visit my website to hear some of the stories I reported and produced for Tucson's NPR and PBS affiliates, and to read selected writing clips. Feel free to give me a call or email me to discuss your project. Do you need fresh web content? Help with your memoir? A new brochure? Final eyes on a grant proposal? I'm versatile, deadline-driven and a good listener, and I look forward to helping you. My areas of expertise include psychology, mental health, health, psychotherapy, family therapy, self-help, the environment, Buddhism, diversity, civil rights, civil discourse, literature, education and the Southwest—-but my interests range far and wide."

BRANDY VICKERS

Cincinnati OH. **E-mail:** brandyvickers@gmail.com. **Contact:** Brandy Vickers.

ADDITIONAL INFORMATION "Brandy Vickers is a versatile freelance editor with 14 years of experience in the book industry. Her editorial services include copyediting, proofreading, fact checking, and substantive editing. A former in-house editor for a trade publisher, she is also experienced in drafting catalog copy, cover copy, and reader's guide discussion questions. She is familiar with Chicago Manual (CMS), Council of Science Editors (CSE), American Psychological Association (APA), and American Medical Association (AMA) style guidelines. Areas of interest: STEMM (Science, Technical, Engineering, Mathematics, and Medical) editing, academic editing for ESL (English as a Second Language) authors, food writing, fiction, and literary nonfiction. Electronic Editing Software: Microsoft Word, Adobe Acrobat, Adobe InDesign, Adobe InCopy, InMath, MathType. (She also works in hard copy.)"

VMP WRITING SERVICES

332 Secretariat Way, Frankfort KY 20601. (502)320-4165. **E-mail:** vpopera@aol.com. **Contact:** Vicki M. Pettus.

ADDITIONAL INFORMATION Vicki M. Pettus has been in the field for 33 years, 2 as a freelancer. She earned a B.S. in journalism from Virginia Commonwealth University, and an M.A. in education (teaching) from the University of Kentucky. She has written technical reports, brochures, and legislative summaries. Vicki Pettus is an adjunct professor at Kentucky State University, teaching English as a Second Language (English grammar and writing for foreign students) and writing composition classes for American students. She does freelance work on technical reports or white paper. Want an article about your business, publication-ready for a newspaper or magazine? She offers Power-Point training presentations, speeches "that will captivate your audience," and fast turn-around on small editing or rewriting tasks. A full resume, with references, is available upon request.

MARGARET MILLER VOLPE

Volpe Editorial Services, Falls Church VA. (703)403-4709. **Contact:** Margaret Miller Volpe.

ADDITIONAL INFORMATION Margaret Volpe is a writer and editor with 10 years experience with booklets, articles, organizational history, website content, fundraising materials, brochures, magazines, newsletters, and more. "Deadline-and detail-oriented with a reputation for accuracy and consistency in style." She specializes in non-profit and membership organizations.

ROSANNE N. WAGGER

(415)595-3348. **E-mail:** waggerrn@yahoo.com. **Contact:** Rosanne N. Wagger.

ADDITIONAL INFORMATION Rosanne Wagger has 10 years of experience as a freelance writer, editor (Developmental and Copy), proofreader, researcher-fact checker and project manager, and more than 20 years of experience in technical communications, project management and localization development in the pharmaceutical, biotechnology, environmental, semiconductor, computer and publishing industries. She has worked successfully with all levels of management, scientific and technical staff and external agencies. She is a "forward thinker, self-starter, effective project leader and dynamic team player" who stays within budget. Rosanne has the technical abilities to work in PC, Macintosh, and UNIX operating systems; Windows XP Pro; Adobe PageMaker, FrameMaker+SGML, Photoshop, Illustrator, Acrobat PDF files; Microsoft Office Suite (Excel, PowerPoint, Visio, Word); Livelink, RoboHelp, WinHelp; Information Mapping; Good Manufacturing Practices (GMP). She earned a BSc in Education and Human Services, Boston Univ., Boston, MA. See previous experience at www.the-efa.org/members/data/resumes/waggerr.pdf.

ROBERT GABRIEL (GABE) WAGGONER

207 14th Place NE, Washington DC 20002. (202)569-8472. **E-mail:** gwaggoner@gmail.com. **Website:** www.gwaggoner.com.

ADDITIONAL INFORMATION Robert Gabriel Waggoner is a full-time freelance science writer and editor who has been in the field for 12 years. His work consists of editing biomedical text for journals, books, and monographs (BELS certified); "I am trained in the physical sciences and work with astronomy/astrophysics and quantum physics as well. I enjoy working both directly with authors and with publishers."

RICKY WEISBROTH

(415)864.0518. **E-mail:** ricky.weisbroth@gmail.com. **Website:** www.editor.rickyweisbroth.com. **Contact:** Ricky Weisbroth.

ADDITIONAL INFORMATION "My job, as a Freelance Editor, is to help you translate ideas and experiences into a manuscript that will engage the reader and I have to say, it is a job I love." Services offered include developmental editing, copy editing, ms critique, proofreading, major revision, ghostwriting, and collaboration.

RACHEL WEISMAN

40 Hawk Hill Lane, East Chatham NY 12060. (518)392-1454. **E-mail:** weiswrite@aol.com. **Contact:** Rachel Weisman.

ADDITIONAL INFORMATION Rachel Weisman has skills in writing; developmental editing, substantive editing, copyediting; proofreading. Rachel has worked for 10 years in these fields: health, medical research, medical business, arts education, social services; some engineering. She follows guidelines with CMS, AMA, APA, GPO, AP. "She is clear, concise, collaborative, and creative. On- time, on-budget." For more info see www.the-efa.org/members/data/resumes/weismanr.pdf.

TAMSIN WILLARD

2 Edmarth Place, Hastings-on-Hudson NY 10706. (914)231-7637. **E-mail:** tamsinthw@gmail.com. **Contact:** Tamsin Willard, editor.

ADDITIONAL INFORMATION Years as freelancer: 14. "Editor, copyeditor, and proofreader with 23 years of experience in areas ranging from financial services to pharmaceutical advertising to general-interest periodicals. My experience includes: structural editing and copyediting of research reports written for dissemination to institutional investors; copyediting reports from medical conferences; proofreading advertisements, direct mail pieces, and packaging for products such as Tylenol and Imodium; proofreading magazine articles and book reviews. My clients have included both top-tier and boutique financial firms (Credit Suisse First Boston and Institutional Research Group, among others), as well as Harper's Magazine and pharmaceutical advertising agency Kallir, Philips, Ross. I am accustomed to meeting tight deadlines

while preserving quality and accuracy, and I understand the importance of tact and mutual respect in working with authors, with other editors, and with support and legal staff. I edit both on hard copy and using the Track Changes feature of Microsoft Word 2007. My areas of interest include history (especially 15th century England), politics, literature, theater, film, and popular science." See previous experience at www.the-efa.org/members/data/resumes/willardt.pdf.

EMILY WILLINGHAM

Austin TX. (512)329-0955 (v). **E-mail:** ejwillingham@austin.rr.com. **Contact:** Emily Jane Willingham.

ADDITIONAL INFORMATION Emily Jane Willingham, Ph.D has more than a decade of experience as a writer and editor, especially in health, science, and medicine. She has a B.A. in English and a PhD in biological sciences. Emily's experience covers a variety of editing and writing projects; she is the author of the *Complete Idiot's Guide to College Biology*, published June 2010. Her editing clients include: Plexus Publishing/Info Today, since January 2003; Hot Science writer, San Francisco Edit, since January 2005; Scientific editor, Asuragen Biotech, since June 2008; Grant writer for Med-IQ, since August 2009; Fact checker, Loh Down on Science/California Institute of Technology, since February 2010; Broadcast writer for Kaplan, since March 2010; Content author/'editor, MCAT. Her specialties are: biological sciences, medical sciences, general science, history, and English literature. For more information go to www.the-efa.org/members/data/resumes/willinghame.pdf.

ELIZABETH WITHERSPOON, PHD, APR

Durham NC. **E-mail:** elizabeth@ewitherspoon.com. **Website:** www.ewitherspoon.com. **Contact:** Elizabeth M. Witherspoon.

ADDITIONAL INFORMATION With 20+ years in the field, Elizabeth Witherspoon is an experienced, versatile writer, editor, public relations and marketing specialist. She has written and edited business and lifestyle magazine features, worked in corporate, government and nonprofit communications and taught journalism, public relations and business communications at the university level. Holds MBA with an emphasis in marketing; writes and edits for business (white papers, reports, etc.) and a PhD in mass communication with emphasis in PR, health communications and the role of new technology. Published academically; will copyedit or provide more extensive editing for academic publication. Able to reshape complex or jargon-laden documents for lay audiences. "Clear and concise language on message is my trademark." Blog: Communication Cent$ at www.commcents.wordpress.com.

TRISHA J. WOOLDRIDGE

A Novel Friend, Auburn MA. (508)757-4778. **E-mail:** info@anovelfriend.com. **Website:** www.anovelfriend.com. **Contact:** Trisha J. Wooldridge.

ADDITIONAL INFORMATION Trisha J. Wooldridge has spent 5 years as a professional freelancer and member of the Editorial Freelancers Association. Trisha writes for a number of magazines and e-zines about food, wine, horses, academic essay composition, bath and body products, Goth bands, and business savvy for genre geeks. She has also edited business books, novels, online composition courses, and the text for the massive multiplayer online role-playing game (MMORPG), DUNGEONS & DRAGONS STORMREACH."

WORD COLLABORATIVE

Atlanta GA. (678)612-7463. **E-mail:** jennifer@wordcollaborative.com. **Website:** www.wordcollaborative.com. **Contact:** Jennifer Yankopolus, editor.

ADDITIONAL INFORMATION "I work with writers of any experience level or background to make their first drafts or last drafts ready for publication, whether a book, memoir, novel, or essay. I specialize in working with first-time authors—providing sensitive feedback and guidance throughout the entire writing and editing process. Besides architecture and design, I have experience with business, general nonfiction, fiction, and history topics, as well as self-published titles."

WORDCRAFT EDITING & WRITING SERVICES

40 Genung Circle, Ithaca NY 14850. (607)277-3641; (607)592-7846. **E-mail:** wordcrft@twcny.rr.com. **Website:** www.wordcraftithaca.com. **Contact:** William E. Barnett, Ph.D.. Estab. 1998.

ADDITIONAL INFORMATION Established by William Barnett, "WordCraft specializes in scholarly editing, research, and writing in all academic fields as well as in popular writing of every conceivable kind. Dr. Barnett has edited, proofread, or adapted for republication dozens of articles in the fields of hospitality management and marketing, real estate finance,

and food and beverage management, along with hundreds of articles, dissertations, and books in many other academic fields including economics, psychology and other social sciences, several humanities disciplines, and science." He has worked in the field for 15 years, 12 years as a freelancer.

WORDCRAFTER

50 7th Ave., Sea Cliff NY 11579. (516)674-0415. **E-mail:** wordcrafter47@yahoo.com. **Contact:** Joslyn Pine.

ADDITIONAL INFORMATION "As a seasoned publishing professional and full-time freelancer, my skills include writing and rewriting, line/substantive and developmental editing, copyediting and proofreading, as well as manuscript evaluation. Adult fiction is my specialty, while the mystery/crime/thriller genre is my subspecialty. My client list includes two publishers (ongoing) as well as a growing list of individual writers. Please refer to my project list and testimonials on the Editorial Freelancers Association website: http://www.the-efa.org."

WORDCRAFT.PRO

Le Clos Bel Air 15G, 7 Rue Des Genets, Aix En Provence 13080 France. (33)(0)662-60-3395. **E-mail:** p.gillespie@wordcraft.pro. **Website:** www.wordcraft.pro. **Contact:** Peter Gillespie, agent-proprietor. Estab. 2005. An editorial services company with multicultural roots. "We adapt communications for intended audiences in academic and research fields and work from French into English and vice-versa, from English into French. Our presence in France (on the Mediterranean rim in the Marseille area) makes us an attractive partner for authors and publishers seeking representation among French publishing circles."

ADDITIONAL INFORMATION Translation and editorial services are determined by the project and rates will vary based on the complexity of the original and the extent to which content needs to be rewritten. Work is quoted on the basis of a standard 1,500-character folio, including spaces. A folio is equivalent of 250 words.

WORD FOR WORD EDITORIAL SERVICES

161 Prospect Place, Brooklyn NY 11238. (718)638-4592. **E-mail:** wordforword05@gmail.com. **Contact:** Claire Petrie.

ADDITIONAL INFORMATION Claire Petrie has been in the field for 14 years and works mostly for trade-book publishers. Her work, in both copy editing and proofreading, covers practically every field—biography, social history, all genres of fiction, memoirs, art and architectural history—and much more. "My work is appreciated by editors and is considered probing and meticulous With a long career as a reference librarian, I am a thorough and intuitive fact-checker. I have a working knowledge of Italian, French, and German, which I have, both by request or incidentally, found extremely useful, especially in fiction." See previous experience at www.the-efa.org/members/data/resumes/petriec.pdf.

WORD PILL EDITING SERVICE

2202 Ewing Ave, Evanston IL 60201. (847)918-1996. **E-mail:** matt@wordpill.com. **Website:** http://word-pillediting.com. **Contact:** Matt Ellis, founder/editor. Estab. 2009.

ADDITIONAL INFORMATION "Word Pill is primarily an editing service for writers of fiction and nonfiction. I specialize in developmental and line editing for genre and literary fiction and narrative nonfiction, but am also experienced in writing by those whose first language is not English. I am ideal for writers who want to work toward a more efficient, forceful second draft." Cost: "Standard fee is slightly over a penny/word, but ESL work is more expensive."

WORDSART NONFICTION BOOK EDITING

(914)376-6892. **E-mail:** info@WordsArt.biz. **Website:** www.dlamont.com. **Contact:** Daveda Lamont.

ADDITIONAL INFORMATION Services offered include comprehensive editing, line and copy editing, development, revisions, rewriting, and reorganization of nonfiction mss.

WORDS BY DESIGN

304 West 75th St., #3, New York NY 10023. (212)787-3974. **E-mail:** gamut@mratcliffe.com. **Website:** www.mratcliffe.com. **Contact:** Mary Ratcliffe.

ADDITIONAL INFORMATION "For more than 20 years as a freelance writer, graphic designer, and editor, I have been creating materials that engage and hold readers' attention: newsletters, brochures, feature articles, Web sites, fundraising appeals, direct mail promotion, product collaterals, press kits, news releases, op-ed pieces, award-winning business-to-business advertising, and more. Samples of my work in all of these areas can be seen on my Web site: www.mratcliffe.com. Persuasive fundraising copy (response rates as high as 11%) and easy-to-read prose that demystifies industry-specific jargon, making

technical information accessible to lay readers, are particular strengths. Clients include major corporations, trade associations, nonprofit organizations, start-up companies, trade and consumer publications, retail services, advertising and public relations agencies."

WORDSWORTH EDITORIAL SERVICES

59 Harvey Ct., Irvine CA 92617. (949)357-0941 for. **E-mail:** laura.a.long@cox.net. **Website:** www.wordsortheditorial.com. **Contact:** Laura Ann Long.

ADDITIONAL INFORMATION Editorial services, including copyediting, proofreading, fact checking, manuscript preparation for eBook publication, grant writing, copy writing. "Crystal clear written communication is our goal at Wordsworth Editorial Services. Well written ideas and expertly edited documents have maximum impact, gain your readers' trust, and win the results you seek. Wordsworth Editorial Services provides personalized copy writing, copy editing, and proofreading services for business and individuals. When it's worth saying right, Wordsworth Editorial Services is your personalized editorial partner."

WORDWEAVE EDITORIAL AND GRAPHICS SERVICES

244 Toucan, Rochester Hills MI 48309. (248)289-1121. **Fax:** (248)289-6067. **E-mail:** jdsimecek@gmail.com. **Contact:** John Dana Simecek.

ADDITIONAL INFORMATION English/Writing Teacher with writing, editing, publishing experience; excellent portfolio; freelancing for 15 years. Earned M.A. with High Honors, Eastern Michigan University, English Department's Written Communication Program, Double Focus: Composition Pedagogy and Professional Writing; B.A. with High Honors, Madonna University, Double Major: Professional Writing and Journalism; Minor: Public Relations; B.A. with Distinction, Wayne State University, Double Major: Sociology and Political Science; Minor: English, Professional Development. Professional Memberships: National Council of Teachers of English. See previous experience at www.the-efa.org/members/data/resumes/simecekjd.pdf.

WORD WONK PRINT AND WEB PRODUCTIONS

(347)684-2006. **E-mail:** tracygrenier@gmail.com. **Website:** www.wordwonkeditor.com. **Contact:** Tracy Grenier.

ADDITIONAL INFORMATION "I have more than 10 years of experience in print and web publishing. I have been involved in a variety of projects in different capacities from simple copyediting and proofreading to development of complete elementary school English Language Arts programs. I have worked alone and as a team member. I am looking for full time or freelance work where I can use my skills to make a positive contribution for my employer and/or its clients." See previous experience at www.the-efa.org/members/data/resumes/greniert.pdf.

TECCA L. WRIGHT

Durham NC. (919)620-8648. **Fax:** (866)779-0151. **E-mail:** tecca@mindspring.com. **Contact:** Tecca Wright.

ADDITIONAL INFORMATION "Partners with clients to achieve writing, editing or marketing objectives. Recent projects have included developing scientific posters, editing literature reviews, formatting manuscripts for journal submission, creating a report from a statistical analysis plan, editing training manuals and the coordinating PowerPoint presentations, and developing websites. Clients are in the pharmaceutical, healthcare, intercultural communication, and outdoor advertising industries." See previous experience at www.the-efa.org/members/data/resumes/wrightt.pdf.

WRITE AWAY EDITING

P.O. Box 325, Dayton OH 45401. (937)252-5435. **E-mail:** nancybrooks@writeawayediting.net. **Contact:** Nancy Brooks.

ADDITIONAL INFORMATION "I provide professional copy editing, proofreading, writing, and developmental editing. For 3 years I designed, wrote, and edited a newsletter for a multistate organization. On the publications team at an organizational headquarters for 8 years, I taught classes to train other copy editors and was a leader of editorial teams. My clients include a consulting company that specializes in corporate training and documentation materials, a global scholarly book publisher, a corporation that specializes in government proposals, and a corporation whose publications include nonprofit sector research reports as well as craft books." "Keen awareness of author's style and careful to preserve it in editing. Experienced with SharePoint Server, Microsoft Exchange Server/Outlook, ftp, Word, PowerPoint, Visio, OpenOffice, Wacom Bamboo pen tablet. All Internet/network activities securely encrypted using VPN." See

previous experience at www.the-efa.org/members/data/resumes/brooksn.pdf.

WRITECAT COMMUNICATIONS

Santa Barbara CA. **E-mail:** writecat@cox.net. **Website:** www.writecat.com. **Contact:** Catherine Viel. Estab. 2006.

ADDITIONAL INFORMATION "A full-time freelancer with over 20 years' experience, Catherine M. Viel provides high-quality writing and editing services to publishers, businesses, individuals, and corporate clients. Ms. Viel's background includes marketing communications, technical writing, document design, translation/localization, and document control facilitation. She has also worked as a university teaching assistant, a legal secretary, and an administrative assistant to the president of a savings and loan. Clients range from corporations such as Medtronic Neurosurgery and NovaCoast IT Professional Services to smaller businesses like Dutcher Design and Casa Del Mar Inn. She has edited and proofread over 30 books. DeVorss & Co. Publishing is an ongoing client." Areas of expertise include: Microsoft Word, Track Changes onscreen editing, Adobe Acrobat, Adobe InDesign, Adobe Illustrator. Copyediting certificate from Univ. of California, Santa Barbara. Catherine earned a B.A. in Literature, School of Creative Studies at UC Santa Barbara.

WRITER'S RESOURCE

Laine Cunningham, (866)212-9805. **E-mail:** consultant@writersresource.us. **Website:** www.writersresource.us. **Contact:** Laine Cunningham. Estab. 1994.

ADDITIONAL INFORMATION From Creation to Contract: Editor and publishing consultant helps you capture attention from top publishers and agents. Ghostwritten/rewritten nearly 200 projects. 20 years of experience with queries, book proposals and development. Quoted on CNN and international media. Fiction and nonfiction. Publishing blog: writersresourceblog.com.

WRITING MATTERS

Denver CO. **E-mail:** brenda@writing-matters.com. **Website:** www.writing-matters.com. **Contact:** Brenda Gillen.

ADDITIONAL INFORMATION "Writing Matters, a Denver, Colorado-based business, was established to provide one-stop writing, editing and proofreading services. We provide more personalized service than a large agency or editing mill, while offering affordable rates and outstanding attention to detail. Brenda Gillen has more than 20 years experience as a writer and editor. Her skills in researching, interviewing, writing, editing and proofreading have been honed through work for colleges and universities, newspapers, advertising and marketing firms, an engineering company and an environmental law firm." Member of the Society of Professional Journalists, National Federation of Press Women, Colorado Press Women, Lighthouse Writers Workshop, Editorial Freelancers Association and Freelancers Union. "Brenda earned a Bachelor of Arts from the University of West Florida and a Master of Liberal Studies and a certificate in Creative Writing from the University of Denver. She moved from the South to Colorado in 1998, and has lived in Denver since 2004. Her resources include a network of graphic designers, photographers, writers and editors." "Brenda is available to write nonfiction articles, particularly on the subjects of renewable energy, green living, arts, education, nonprofits and entrepreneurs."

X-HEIGHT STUDIO

83 High St., Milford MA 01757. (508)478-3897; (508)478-6077. **Fax:** (508)478-6077. **E-mail:** cecile@x-heightstudio.com. **Website:** www.x-heightstudio.com. **Contact:** Cecile Kaufman. Estab. 1999.

ADDITIONAL INFORMATION X-Height Studio was founded by Cecile Kaufman. She was educated at Massachusetts College of Art and the Univ. of California at Berkeley, and received her B.A. with honors in Comparative Literature. Cecile has 23 years' experience in publishing. She began as a freelance proofreader for HarperCollins in San Francisco. Later she worked as a book designer and production manager at Waite Group Press, an imprint of Macmillan Computer Publishing, where Cecile managed the process from copyediting manuscripts to interacting with printers.

CAROL M. YEH

2449 Harpoon Dr., Stafford VA 22554. (540)657-2612. **E-mail:** cmyeh102@mac.com. **Contact:** Carol M. Yeh.

ADDITIONAL INFORMATION "My specialty is writing for the everyday person, although I am equally comfortable writing for formal situations, such as the conferring of honorary degrees and corresponding with government officials. I especially enjoy organizing complex material into user-friendly documents, including interpreting data into useable information. I have written training manuals for technology-averse employees on topics such as budgeting, financial software and endowment accounting. My combination of a hard science and marketing education allows me to distill difficult technical information to easily understood narrative. My clients appreciate my attention to detail and commitment to quality. I have worked in AP, APA and Chicago styles and readily incorporate a client's unique culture into the style, such as disabilities-sensitive language." See previous experience at www.the-efa.org/members/data/resumes/yehcm.pdf.

THE YP PUBLISHING

253-4025 Dorchester Road, Niagara Falls ON L2E7K8 Canada. (905) 341-0997. **E-mail:** info@theyppublishing.com. **Website:** www.theyppublishing.com. **Contact:** Yvonne Wu, media strategist, author/speaking assistant. Estab. 2008.

ADDITIONAL INFORMATION Services offered include virtual book tours, Amazon bestseller campaigns, online book promotion, websites, manuscript preparation, book proposals, ebook conversion, print coordination, and social media support.

ENID R. YURMAN

340 Hartert Dr., Idaho Falls ID 83404. (208)521-5725; (208)524-6374. **E-mail:** enid.yurman@gmail.com. **Contact:** Enid Yurman.

ADDITIONAL INFORMATION More than 20 years' experience providing copyediting, technical editing, electronic editing, proofreading, fact checking. "Since 2006, I've been working on technical editing and writing assignments for the Idaho National Laboratory, a U.S. Department of Energy facility. I've written grant proposals, procedures, marketing materials, website content, short biographies, and human interest features. Editing and writing results: Meeting deadlines with clear, concise writing that flows, delivers intended message, and is tailored to targeted audience. Same results with editing, while preserving author's style and voice. Subject matter: Environmental and nuclear engineering and research; soil conservation; children's advocacy, parenting, health and fitness." See work history at www.the-efa.org/members/data/resumes/yurmane.pdf.

KATHLEEN ZANDER

6406 John St., Crystal Lake IL 60014. (815)477-2406. **E-mail:** ktzander@gmail.com. **Contact:** Kathleen Zander.

ADDITIONAL INFORMATION Kathleen Zander has been in the field 13 years, 11 as a freelancer. "My specialty is editorial quality control for college textbook projects, with expertise in copy editing, permissions protection, and design consistency. I have experience across numerous disciplines including social and hard sciences, mathematics, finance, language, and graphic arts, with intensive health and medical focus honed through projects for the American Medical Association, the National Association for Mental Illness, and various textbooks on nursing and psychology. A grammar and usage hawk with an excellent ear for language idioms and style, I expedite any level of edit, from correcting punctuation to standardizing voice across multiple authors. Past experience in content development includes editing submissions for academic journals; writing proposals, reports, and abstracts for aerospace and technology-research think tanks; and creating corporate newsletters and press releases. For the unique needs of projects with large numbers of visuals, I launched The Right Picture (trpic.com), a photo research business geared to the textbook industry. Besides thorough research and licensing, it features an innovative online photo gallery (trpic.info) that produces operating efficiencies, speed of response, and major cost savings for the client." See Kathleen's portfolio at www.the-efa.org/members/data/resumes/zanderk.pdf.

FREELANCE DESIGNERS

///

People really shouldn't judge a book by its cover, but one of the hard truths of publishing is that readers do, in fact, make purchasing decisions based off the covers of books. A poorly designed book cover can doom the best manuscripts to obscurity. On the other hand, a well-designed cover can sometimes help less than worthy books enjoy wonderful sales. The smart self-publisher excels at every level. That includes working to put the best cover on the best manuscript possible.

Finding the right designer for your project can make the difference between success and failure. One knock against self-publishing that still persists is that self-published books are of lesser quality. By using freelance designers, you can work to overcome that specific hurdle in the self-publishing process by giving potential readers a beautiful cover and interior design to admire.

However, there are a variety of freelance design services available with different pricing structures. It's important to remember that sometimes you get what you pay for, and it's possible to pay (or overpay) for services you don't really need. The "How Much Should I Charge?" pay rate chart should help with determining an appropriate fee with your freelance designer.

Beyond determining a fair rate, self-publishers need to know what type of design assistance they need. For instance, do you just need someone to design a book cover? Do you need illustration or photography assistance? Could you use help with fonts and interior layout and formatting?

Each service may have a different fee and a different amount of time required to complete the work. In determining freelance rates, you'll need to know the hourly rate and time requirement to assign a fair fee that will result in quality work. Setting unfair expectations is bad for the freelancer, but it also puts your project at risk, because you're counting on the freelancers to give their best.

KEEP IN MIND

Starting locally will allow you to research each company carefully and learn about their past performance and make it easier to have face-to-face discussions about the design. Realize that any face-to-face time and time on the phone may be considered "billable hours" by your freelancer. Be sure to agree on all such fees and get it in writing before starting work. It will help ensure a more professional working relationship and provide both sides with more security.

Going local is not a requirement. In fact, you may find that going with another designer outside of your area is more affordable or provides you with a freelancer who has better qualifications. Always ask for previous experience and consider checking references, especially if you're investing a lot of money in the design process. After all, you want to make sure your money will be money well spent.

SHAILA ABDULLAH

8408 Dulac Dr., Austin TX 78729. (512)924-7674. **E-mail:** info@myhouseofdesign.com. **Website:** www.myhouseofdesign.com. **Contact:** Shaila Abdullah, owner. Estab. 1995. Offers web, multimedia, and print services.

ADDITIONAL INFORMATION Services for web & multimedia include websites, content management systems, Wordpress sites, landing pages, book launch campaigns, e-mail campaigns, e-newsletters, social media pages, web banners and ads, multimedia demos, presentations, and online courses. Services for print include book covers, book interiors, book design, e-book design, flyers and sell sheets, postcards, posters, business cards, stationery, ads, brand, and identity.

ACCURATE WRITING & MORE

16 Barstow Lane, Hadley MA 01035. (413)586-2388. **E-mail:** shel@greenandprofitable.com. **Website:** www.frugalmarketing.com. **Contact:** Shel Horowitz, owner. Estab. 1982. Offers book marketing and book shepherding services.

ADDITIONAL INFORMATION For book marketing, develops marketing strategy and individualized marketing plans for authors, books, and book series. For book shepherding, helps make the decision to publish traditionally, self-publish, e-publish, or publish through a subsidy publisher.

ART OF ALEXANDRIA

118 E. California Ave., Columbus OH 43202. **E-mail:** artist.ally@gmail.com. **Website:** www.artofalexandria.com. **Contact:** Alexandria Anderson, owner/freelance illustrator. Estab. 2012. Art of Alexandria provides a variety of freelance illustration services, including classic people and pet portraiture, mural painting, children's illustration, fantasy illustration, book, magazine and editorial illustration, character design, stuffed animal design, web design and custom-made jewelry and character sculpture available in both traditional and digital mediums.

ADDITIONAL INFORMATION "I work with you every step of the way to ensure your hand-crafted creation is of the highest quality, made to enchant and delight for all ages."

BELLE ETOILE STUDIOS

112 Reton Ct., Cary NC 27513. **E-mail:** michael@belleetoilestudios.com. **Website:** www.belleetoilestudios.com. **Contact:** Michael Trudeau, editorial manager/co-owner. Estab. 2009. Belle Etoile is a 2-person publishing services studio from principals Michael Trudeau and Jamie Kerry.

ADDITIONAL INFORMATION "We offer design, production, and editorial to book-publishing houses and self-publishing authors." Editorial services include developmental editing, substantive editing, copyediting, proofreading, fact-checking, editorial project management, copywriting, and manuscript review and consultation. Design and production services include typesetting/page layout, book cover design, book interior design, book production management, logo design, branding, general graphic design, and e-book creation (design). "We work primarily with literary fiction, genre fiction, general nonfiction, and poetry. Our genre fiction experience includes titles in crime, fantasy and science fiction, horror, mystery and suspense, romance, young adult, and more. Our trade nonfiction experience includes titles in autobiography and biography, cultural studies and social sciences, ecology, health, history, humor, memoir, politics, sports, the occult, and more."

JOE BIEL DESIGN

636 SE 11th Ave., Portland OR 97214. (503)232-3666. **Fax:** (888)503-0599. **E-mail:** joe@microcosmpublishing.com. **Website:** microcosmpublishing.com. **Contact:** Joe Biel, designer. Estab. 1995. Specializes in one and two color design interiors and two and four color book covers.

ADDITIONAL INFORMATION "We've designed hundreds of books over the life of a teenager, and we'd be happy to consider designing your book. Rates are based on how much affinity we have for your job, your budget, and how much time is presently available but can be tailored to fit any reasonable budget."

BOOK COMPLETION

2407 California St. SE, Huntsville AL 35801. **E-mail:** cara@bookcompletion.com. **Website:** bookcompletion.com. **Contact:** Cara Stein, owner. Estab. 2012. Services include weaving and melding content into a manuscript; editing and polishing manuscripts; designing cover to match branding, attract readers, and convey the feel and message of book's content; designing an interior layout to go with the cover and help communicate the message; producing the book as a PDF e-book for sale or distribution on your website; producing the book as an e-book in Kindle and e-pub formats for sale on Amazon, Barnes & Noble, etc.; and producing the book for print.

ADDITIONAL INFORMATION "We do the whole process, from writing and editing to layout and design. The result will be an attractive, professional book that showcases your work. Let us be your one-stop shop to get your book finished and fabulous!"

THE BOOK DOCTOR IS IN

San Pedro CA 90732. (310)346-8852. **E-mail:** sjaaronson@gmail.com. **Website:** thebookdoctorisin. com. **Contact:** Stacey Aaronson, owner/professional book doctor. Estab. 2011. Offers market analysis program, professional editing, artistic book cover design, standout book layout and design, writing services, superb e-book design, custom graphics creation, publishing facilitation, engaging promo materials, creative website design, attentive communication, and handholding and cheerleading.

ADDITIONAL INFORMATION "I take you by the hand as a self-publishing author and transform your manuscript into the book you've dreamed of--from impeccable editing and proofreading to engaging, audience-targeted cover and professional interior design--rivaling or exceeding a traditional house publication."

WYNNE BROWN LLC

2733 W. Hilltop Road, Portal AZ 85632. (520)558-1131. **E-mail:** wynnebrown@mac.com. **Website:** www.wynnebrown.com. **Contact:** Wynne Brown, owner. Estab. 2012. Wynne Brown has spent 35 years as a freelance graphic designer, writer, and editor. Design services include book design, presentations, brochures, newsletters, technical illustrations, logo development.

ADDITIONAL INFORMATION She also spent 6 years as a copy editor at a mid-sized daily newspaper and has edited books, magazine articles, and academic publications. She is comfortable with Associated Press, Chicago Manual of Style, and American Psychological Association stylebooks.

CALLIGRAPHY BY MICHAEL NOYES

0 E. 4th St., #18, Richmond VA 23224. (804)943-1522. **E-mail:** michael@michaelnoyes.com. **Website:** www. michaelnoyes.com. **Contact:** Michael Noyes, owner. Estab. 1997. Primarily a graphic designer, specializing in text layout, typography, and calligraphy.

ADDITIONAL INFORMATION "I use Adobe Photoshop and Illustrator primarily in corporate brand-ing, logos, brochures, and book covers. Wordpress is my preferred web authoring platform. My calligraphy designs may be seen online."

CAROUSEL PHOTOGRAPHY & DESIGN

95 Lloyd St., Lively ON P34 1C1 Canada. **E-mail:** christine@carouselphotodesign.com. **Website:** www. carouselphotodesign.com. **Contact:** Christine Lewis, owner. Estab. 2009.

ADDITIONAL INFORMATION Offers book/cover layout and design, websites, and marketing materials.

KERI CHRISTIAN

204 Falkirk Court, Fredericksburg VA 22046. (916)905-7074. **E-mail:** keric@kerichristian.com. **Website:** kerichristian.com. **Contact:** Keri Christian, designer. Estab. 2005.

ADDITIONAL INFORMATION "I offer a variety of services including web design/development, graphic design, hosting services, online marketing with Google AdWords, AdSense, PPC campaigns, and SEO."

CORIS DESIGNS

153 Somerside Rd. SE, Medicine Hat AB T1B 0N4 Canada. **E-mail:** corey_majeau@hotmail.com. **Website:** www.facebook.com/CorisDesigns. **Contact:** Corey Majeau, freelance designer. Estab. 2003. Offers book cover designs (both e-book and paperback), e-book formatting, logo designs, website designs.

ADDITIONAL INFORMATION "I use the latest design software and vector imaging."

CREATIVELINK

POB 318, Hammondsport NY 14840. **E-mail:** info@ creativelinkgraphics.com. **Website:** creativelinkgraphics.com. **Contact:** Anne Kiley, sole proprietor. Estab. 1995. Creativelink is a complete design service; check website for portfolio.

ADDITIONAL INFORMATION Offers innovative, production-oriented book design services for authors wanting to self-publish, but who want their books to look as individual as they are themselves. Also complete writing and editorial service.

DADIVAN BOOKS

3104 E. Camelback Road #160, Phoenix AZ 85016. (347)291-1779. **Fax:** (928)268-9181. **E-mail:** dadivanbooks@gmail.com. **Website:** www.dadivanbooks. com. **Contact:** Bootsie Martinez, editor. Estab. 1989. "We are professional writers, editors, and publishers with over a century of combined experience in the publishing world."

ADDITIONAL INFORMATION Dadivan Books also offers complete self-publishing from soup-to-nuts, including economical subsidy publishing services. "We specialize in helping authors achieve their individual dreams, whether that dream is improving a manuscript through proofreading or editing, preparing a manuscript in e-publishing formats, preparing a manuscript in paperback layout, designing the perfect cover, or fulfilling another editorial need, including ghostwriting and book doctoring. All services are available a la carte or as part of an economical package."

DESIGN CAT STUDIO

4400 E. Maplewood St., Gilbert AZ 85297. (480)710-5212. **E-mail:** caitlinproctor@designcatstudio.com. **Website:** www.designcatstudio.com. **Contact:** Caitlin Proctor, owner/graphic designer/expert book designer. Estab. 2010.

ADDITIONAL INFORMATION Offers custom book cover design/layout, custom interior formatting/layout, digital formattting/layout, branding, logo design, consulting, marketing materials.

DGA MEDICAL COMMUNICATIONS

2700 Maple Ave., Bristol PA 19007. (215)498-1859. **E-mail:** deb@dgamedcom.com. **Website:** www.dgamedcom.com. **Contact:** Debbie Anderson, medical writer/instructional designer. Estab. 2012.

ADDITIONAL INFORMATION Services offered include advisory board meetings, case studies, PowerPoint presentations, e-learning courses, sales training materials, annotated guides, brochures, company leave-behinds, video scripts and vignettes, call guides, webinars, video newsletters, e-books, newsletters, articles, briefs, advertisements, assessments, website content, abstracts, posters, reports, outlines, and more.

LAURYL EDDLEMON GRAPHIC DESIGN

7404 Rockberry Cove, Austin TX 78750. **E-mail:** lauryl.eddlemon@gmail.com. **Website:** www.lauryleddlemon.com. **Contact:** Lauryl Eddlemon. Estab. 2004. Lauryl Eddlemon is an Austin-based freelance designer specializing in print design with a focus on publications.

ADDITIONAL INFORMATION Services include book design, magazine editorial design, corporate identity, annual reports, point-of-sale pieces, brochures/flyers, newsletters, posters, and advertisements.

EDEN CREATIVE MARKETING

(972)979-8130. **Fax:** (866)365-2055. **E-mail:** edencreative@verizon.net. **Website:** www.edencreativemarketing.com. **Contact:** Jessica LaBeau, owner. Estab. 1994. Specializes in historical novels, city books, and memoirs.

ADDITIONAL INFORMATION Offers book design/production, brochures, author promotional sheets, business cards, advertising/branding messages.

EMBREE LITERARY SERVICES

138 W. Alta Green, Port Hueneme CA 93041. (805)985-1113. **E-mail:** maryembree@gmail.com. **Website:** www.maryembree.com. **Contact:** Mary Embree, owner/manager. Estab. 1990. Mary Embree is an author, freelance editor, literary consultant, seminar and workshop presenter, and public speaker. Since 1990, she has helped writers with their book manuscripts from first to final draft, guiding and editing their book projects according to professional book publishing standards. Her services include writing and editing book proposals, query letters to literary agents and book publishers, and preparing manuscripts for presentation.

ADDITIONAL INFORMATION If authors choose to self-publish, she guides them through the entire process, such as registering their copyright and getting ISBNs, barcodes, and Library of Congress Control numbers. Embree and her associates desing and typeset interior pages of the book as well as eye-catching book covers, providing print-ready PDF files.

ERIAKO ASSOCIATES

1380 Morningside Way, Venice CA 90291. (310)392-6537. **E-mail:** eriakoassociates@gmail.com. **Contact:** Erika Fabian, CEO. Estab. 1982. Offers design, editing, and overseeing entire publishing process. Erika Fabian of Eriako Associates is an international book designer as well as writer and editor. She has personally written 22 books, some published by the likes of Putnam, Ballantine, and Harlequin. Her books have also been translated and published in several languages.

ADDITIONAL INFORMATION "We cover essentially all phases of publishing for books, brochures, and advertising materials. We also do professional photography of authors, and for the material if it needs photo illustration."

FILAMENT CREATIVE

1024 SW Main St. #730, Portland OR 97205. (509)844-4251. **E-mail:** ryan@filament-creative.com. **Website:** www.filament-creative.com. **Contact:** Ryan Peinhardt, graphic designer. Estab. 2011. **ADDITIONAL INFORMATION** Offers graphic design and book design.

GAL-FRIDAY PUBLICITY

308-1114 Howie Ave., Coquitlam BC V3J 1V1 Canada. (604)366-7846. **E-mail:** rachel@gal-fridaypublicity.com. **Website:** www.gal-fridaypublicity.com. **Contact:** Rachel Sentes, founder/publicist. Estab. 2009. Offers business and book publicity, e-book publicity/publishing, media kit creation and design, editing, manuscript consultations, ghostwriting, Wordpress websites, copy editing, proposal writing, and literary agent and publishing consultations. **ADDITIONAL INFORMATION** "We have worked in all aspects of the book industry behind and in front of the scenes."

TINA GARCIA

Riverview FL 33578. **E-mail:** tinagarcia100@gmail.com. **Website:** www.tina-garcia.com. **Contact:** Tina Garcia, graphic designer. Estab. 2003. **ADDITIONAL INFORMATION** Offers e-book and cover design, brochure and flyer designer, logos and stationery, packaging design, audio and video editing, news infographics and interactives.

GET BETTER GRAPHICS

778 Michigan Ave., Adrian MI 49221. **E-mail:** cameo@groundcontrol.us. **Website:** www.getbettergraphics.com. **Contact:** Cameo Anderson. Estab. 1996. **ADDITIONAL INFORMATION** "I paint illustrations/book cover art. They are delivered digitally as high res files sized to your requirements. I specialize in illustrations for YA books as I prefer fun and imaginative (sci fi, fantasy, and animals) over dark or serious pieces. You'll be dealing directly with me, the artist, and not with a manager. Together, we'll make sure you get a piece of art you love!"

GLYPHICS

1026 21st St., Apt. B, Santa Monica CA 90403. (602)670-3114. **E-mail:** terry@glyphicsdesign.com. **Website:** glyphicsdesign.com. **Contact:** Terry Duffy, owner. Estab. 1985. **ADDITIONAL INFORMATION** "We do branding, book design, packaging, museum exhibit panel design, illustration."

GRATZER GRAPHICS LLC

Union Ridge Dr., Adamstown MD 21710. (301)874-3131. **E-mail:** design@gratzergraphics.com. **Website:** gratzergraphics.com. **Contact:** Colleen Gratzer, principal/graphic designer. Estab. 2003. Offers print, web, and logo design. **ADDITIONAL INFORMATION** Services include print ads, annual reports, banner ads, book covers, book layout, brochures, circulation, direct mail, directories, HTML e-mails, logos/identity packages, magazines, media kits, print newsletters, postcards, posters, banners, rebranding, social media design, trade show/event displays, and websites.

GREYSIGHT STUDIOS

100 Lynbrook Circle, Syracuse NY 13214. (315)497-7278. **E-mail:** support@greysightstudios.com. **Website:** greysightstudios.com. **Contact:** Willie Putmon Jr., owner. Estab. 1996. **ADDITIONAL INFORMATION** Offers layout design, logo design, web design, video editing, mobile development, brochures, magazine design/layout, print ads, complete identity packages, flyers, posters, promotional materials, mail inserts, web promotions, image enhancement/corrections/manipulation, image background removal.

DARLENE HAWVER

E-mail: hawver.darlene@gmail.com. **Website:** darlenehawver.com. **Contact:** Darlene Hawver, graphic designer. Estab. 2009. Offers graphic design services. **ADDITIONAL INFORMATION** Services include book covers, editorial design, publication design, logos, stationery, newsletters, posters, and more.

THE HELP

648 Rivenhurst St., Bremerton WA 98310. (360)440-5795. **E-mail:** admin@thehelpbyastrids.com. **Website:** www.thehelpbyastrids.com. **Contact:** Marie Astrid Stanek, owner/manager. Estab. 2008. The Help is a fast growing virtual assistance agency. **ADDITIONAL INFORMATION** Services provided include administrative support, writing and translation, and multimedia and graphic design.

IDEAS TO IMAGES

5256 Aero Dr., Unit 3, Santa Rosa CA 95403. (707)542-4301. **E-mail:** ideas@sonic.net. **Website:** ideas-to-images.com/samples. **Contact:** Gary Palmatier, owner. Estab. 1984.

ADDITIONAL INFORMATION "I design, illustrate, compose, and manage cover-to-cover book projects from manuscript through printing. I work closely with authors/publishers to design a cover and interior suited to the target market. If desired, I also hire and supervise editorial freelancers (copyeditors, proofreaders, and indexers) and liaise with printers (delivering preflighted PDF files and reviewing proofs)."

INDIEMOBI

Website: indiemobi.wordpress.com. **Contact:** Rebecca Long, owner. Estab. 2012.

ADDITIONAL INFORMATION Solo/freelance company that offers formatting for e-books and Createspace. "Friendly and fast turnaround service with affordable prices."

JESSIE SK DESIGN

5264 Erskine Way SW, Seattle WA 98136. **E-mail:** jessiesk@gmail.com. **Website:** jessiesk.dunked.com. **Contact:** Jessie Summa-Kusiak, designer. Estab. 1996.

ADDITIONAL INFORMATION Offers print design, web design, logo and ID design, illustration.

AMBER JONES CONSULTING

6301 Stonewood Dr., Plano TX 75024. **E-mail:** amber@amberjonesconsulting.com. **Website:** www.amberjonesconsulting.com. **Contact:** Amber Jones, owner/freelance graphic designer. Estab. 2013.

ADDITIONAL INFORMATION "With 6+ years of experience in the marketing/digital space and 10 years as a graphic designer, I offer clients a 'one-stop shop' for all of their marketing needs, including graphic design, web design, online marketing strategy development, and copywriting."

KELLEY & HALL BOOK PUBLICITY

5 Briar Lane, Marblehead MA 01945. (617)680-1976. **E-mail:** jocelyn@kelleyandhall.com. **Website:** www.kelleyandhall.com. **Contact:** Jocelyn Kelley, partner. Estab. 2004. Kelley & Hall is a literary publicity company that is dedicated to helping authors and publishers with their promotion, marketing, and media relations.

ADDITIONAL INFORMATION "We create effective book buzz as well as author recognition that will increase book sales. We help writers build their author brand. Book marketing and book promotion are the cornerstones of Kelley & Hall."

LENTINI DESIGN

1626 Virginia Road, Los Angeles CA 90019. (323)766-8090. **E-mail:** hilary@lentinidesign.com. **Website:** www.lentinidesign.com. **Contact:** Hilary Lentini, owner. Estab. 1990.

ADDITIONAL INFORMATION Services include branding development, marketing pieces/deliverables, web development/deliverables, social media.

MAUREEN LILLA

77 State Road, Plymouth MA 02360. **E-mail:** mlilla777@aol.com. **Contact:** Maureen Lilla, principle. Estab. 1986. Offers developmental editing for authors, professionals, and business writers; development of query letters and book proposals; writing and ghostwriting; book doctoring; book and book cover design.

ADDITIONAL INFORMATION Client list available upon request.

DICK MARGULIS CREATIVE SERVICES

284 W. Elm St., New Haven CT 06515. (203)389-4413. **E-mail:** dick@dmargulis.com. **Website:** www.dmargulis.com. **Contact:** Dick Margulis, owner. Estab. 2004. Offers high-quality printed and electronic books for discerning clients. Thoughtful editing, appropriate design, expert production, comprehensive project management, for publishers of all sizes and for all kinds of books.

ADDITIONAL INFORMATION "If you are an author, agent, publisher, or other organization considering a book project, I'd like the opportunity to quote on the services you need. I have been involved in both editing and typography in one way or another for over half a century; my experience is broad and deep."

NIC MCD LLC

1601 Highview Dr., Des Moines IA 50315. (319)621-8877. **E-mail:** nic@nicmcd.com. **Website:** nicmcd.com. **Contact:** Nic McDougal, illustrator/designer. Estab. 2011. Emerging artist and recent grad from the Minneapolis College of Art and Design.

ADDITIONAL INFORMATION "My business offers self-published authors the opportunity to bring their ideas to life! I offer cover artwork, interior layouts, and a variety of marketing collateral, including video book trailers and web design."

BRIAN MIHOK DESIGN

31 Berkley Place #2, Buffalo NY 14209. **E-mail:** brian@brianmihok.com. **Website:** design.brianmihok.com. **Contact:** Brian Mihok, book designer. Estab.

2010. Offers complete book design services, which includes cover, wrap, and inside layouts.

ADDITIONAL INFORMATION "My design skills are flexible but my approach tends toward modern, clean, and striking. Prices for designs vary but are available for all budgets. I believe a design should be an extension of the manuscript itself, offering the tone and spirit of the book in visual form. Really, it should stop a book browser in her tracks! Bottom line is your book deserves a great design, and I'd love to make it for you."

KATE MOORE GRAPHIC + WEB DESIGN

Vancouver BC Canada. **E-mail:** howdy@katemoore. ca. **Website:** www.katemoore.ca. **Contact:** Kate Moore, owner/designer. Estab. 2006.

ADDITIONAL INFORMATION "I specialize in book design and website design that use Wordpress as a content management system. I believe that design should make things clear, have purpose and show you or your company in the best possible light. I strive for clarity in both my design and communication. Good design should enhance your message and never distract from it."

MURPHY DESIGN

1216 Arch St., 2C, Philadelphia PA 19107. (215)977-7093. **Website:** www.murphydesign.net. Estab. 1985. Rosemary Murphy is an experienced graphic designer.

ADDITIONAL INFORMATION Murphy works in a collaborative style and would be interested in designing book covers, lettering, logos, graphic illustration for print or web and information graphics.

MYSTICAL PRESS PUBLISHING

340 S. Lemon Ave. #4462, Walnut CA 91789. **E-mail:** arial@mysticalpress.com. **Website:** www.mysticalpress.com. **Contact:** Arial Burnz, owner/graphic designer. Estab. 2010. Arial is an award-winning cover artist and has been creating graphic art since 1999.

ADDITIONAL INFORMATION Experienced as an author, editor, and cover artist, Arial is well-versed in the publishing industy and is able to produce eye-catching graphic design for e-book and print book covers, website and blog banners, internet ad banners and icons, ads for print and digital magazines, and more.

BINA NAYAK

D-104, Lake Pleasant, Powai, Mumbai Maharashtra 400076 India. (91)99209-99179. **E-mail:** binanayak@

gmail.com. **Website:** www.binanayak.com. **Contact:** Bina Nayak, designer. Estab. 2003.

ADDITIONAL INFORMATION "I have an advertising background. I have worked in several creative agencies like Leo Burnett and Ogilvy. I was Head of Design at The Walt Disney Company India from 2010-2012 and presently work as a consultant."

SHEN PLUM ILLUSTRATION

70 Empire Ave., Toronto ON M4M 2L4 Canada. **E-mail:** shen.plum@gmail.com. **Website:** www.shen-plum.com. **Contact:** Shen Plum. Offers illustration, art, drawing, illustrative font/typeface, cover art.

PRO NOVEL EDITING SERVICES

3805 Burke, Cheyenne WY 82009. (307)772-1741. **Fax:** (501)325-0305. **E-mail:** proediting@earthlink. net. **Website:** www.pronoveledting.com. **Contact:** Michael McIrvin, founding writer and editor. Estab. 2003. Pro Novel Editing Services can provide the following for fiction writers of all skill levels: line editing, developmental (content) editing, novel manuscript critiques, and query letters.

ADDITIONAL INFORMATION Pro Novel Editing Services can also facillitate the following for self-publishers: book layout in the appropriate program files required by your POD company, book cover design, conversion to all digital formats, e-book layout and design, and website design.

JODY ROGINSON CREATIVE SERVICES

6444 E. Spring St. #312, Long Beach CA 90815. **Website:** jodyroginson.com. **Contact:** Jody Roginson, owner. Estab. 2000.

ADDITIONAL INFORMATION Offers graphic, cover and page design, page composition and illustration. Print coordination and e-publication formatting or consultation is available as well.

THERESA ROSENACKER DESIGN

2845 Minot Ave., Cincinnati OH 45209. (513)312-8992. **E-mail:** theresa@theresarosenacker.com. **Website:** www.theresarosenacker.com. **Contact:** Theresa Rosenacker, principal. Estab. 2013.

ADDITIONAL INFORMATION Offers print and digital design services, specializing in small business in non-profit.

RPARTEKO DESIGNS

740 Westview Dr., Apt. 47, Ossian IN 46777. (260)255-9544. **E-mail:** parteko.rachel@gmail.com. **Website:**

facebook.com/RPartekoDesigns. **Contact:** Rachel Parteko, graphic artist. Estab. 2008.

ADDITIONAL INFORMATION Offers book cover design, book formatting and layout, business cards, flyers, brochures, banner and logo design, T-shirt design, hand-drawn pictures/illustrations, and Facebook cover page/marketing.

ALICE SHAPIRO

4965 W. Ridge Dr., Douglasville GA 30135. **Website:** www.aliceshapiro.com/bookcovers.html. **Contact:** Alice Shapiro, digital artist. Estab. 2011.

ADDITIONAL INFORMATION Offers original digital art designs for children and adult book covers. 50% deposit and balance upon completion. References provided upon request.

JULES STEWART INDEPENDENT GRAPHIC DESIGN

4033 Louisiana #6, San Diego CA 92104. **E-mail:** julesstewartdesign@gmail.com. **Website:** julesstewart.carbonmade.com. **Contact:** Jules Stewart, designer. Estab. 2008. Modern but adaptable, clean design style.

ADDITIONAL INFORMATION Offers digital illustration and design of logos, promotional materials, posters, business cards, resumes, and more.

JEANNE STOCK DESIGN

Kempton PA 19529. **E-mail:** jeannestock@jstockdesign.com. **Website:** jstockdesign.com. **Contact:** Jeanne Stock, owner. Estab. 1980. Prior experience: publication art director/designer for regional and national publications and book designer.

ADDITIONAL INFORMATION Offers design services from concept through production for print projects; specializing in publication design and graphic logos. "I believe that a good outcome requires communication. Creative energy, attention to detail and hard work as well as good design. Every job is equally important and receives my complete attention from start to finish."

SUNNY BAY ARTS

15 Simcoe Terrace SW, Calgary AB T3H 4S6 Canada. (403)252-0792. **E-mail:** sunnybayarts@yahoo.ca. **Website:** www.sunnybayarts.ca. **Contact:** Barbori G. Streibl, co-owner. Estab. 2011. Sunny Bay Arts sells stock photography and artwork.

ADDITIONAL INFORMATION Please enquire about logo design and book cover design services.

TYSON TAYLOR

P.O. Box 19527, Lenexa KS 66285. **E-mail:** tyson.nicole@gmail.com. **Website:** www.tysontaylordesigner.com. **Contact:** Tyson Taylor, freelance designer. Estab. 2007.

ADDITIONAL INFORMATION "I provide graphic and web design services to authors, small business owners, and nonprofit organizations in the areas of business identity, book covers, and other graphics."

STEPHEN TIANO

638 Fresh Pond Ave., #314, Calverton NY 11933. (631)284-3842. **E-mail:** steve@tianobookdesign.com. **Website:** www.tianobookdesign.com. **Contact:** Stephen Tiano, freelance book designer, page compositor and layout artist. Estab. 1992. Offers interior and cover book design and layout.

ADDITIONAL INFORMATION "I create sample interior pages (including all master pages and stylesheets). We discuss the sample pages to get a sense of what works and what might stand some improvement. Then, I make all adjustments and changes until you approve. Upon approval of sample pages, I finalize them into a template. Next, I resample any art (photos) that are less than 300 dpi and correct for color (balance/contrast of black & white), scale to size. Finally (for the interior), I make formatted, balanced interior pages from provided final text files imported into the approved template and place all art appropriately. I create and provide the final, cross-platform, printer-ready PDFs--during the work process, when I send pages to you for review, they will be PDFs to screen resolution for easy e-mailing--after accounting for any necessary specifications for PDFs your printer requires."

TREEHOUSE PUBLISHING GROUP LLC

8734 Norcross Dr., St. Louis MO 63126. (314)363-4546. **E-mail:** authorservices@treehousepublishinggroup.com. **Website:** treehousepublishinggroup.com. **Contact:** Kristina Makansi, managing partner. Estab. 2013. Treehouse Publishing Group offers a full menu of a la carte author services as well as assisted self-publishing under our Treehouse imprint.

ADDITIONAL INFORMATION "At TPG, we believe that every project is as unique as the author who created it. That's why we individually tailor each package--from developmental edits to book layouts to website design--to suit your specific goals."

TURNING HEADS

73-1104 Nuuanu Place, G204, Kailua Kona HI 96740. (562)437-1443. **E-mail:** vic_warren@hotmail.com. **Website:** www.vicwarren.com. **Contact:** Vic Warren, owner. Estab. 1999. Portfolio available upon request.

ADDITIONAL INFORMATION "Sophisticated design and marketing concepts should be more than hot-off-the-desktop formulas using the latest typeface with plenty of bars and borders. They need to build on the unique strengths of a specific product strategy. And they must be responsive to sound business objectives such as sales schedules and budgets. Vic Warren has been solving communication problems for eyars, creating indelible images in words and pictures for an array of successful and smart clients. He's best known for creating the Eskimo corporate image for Alaska Airlines. Branding and corporate image are two of his strengths, and, since joining the writing profession, has designed award-winning book covers as well."

2FACED DESIGN

Heritage Commons Office Park, 11 Middlesex Ave., Suite 10A, Wilmington MA 01887. **Website:** www.2faceddesign.com. **Contact:** Kristie Langone, director. Estab. 2008. Offers e-book covers, front cover design, full cover design, full jacket design, and manuscript and copyediting. "We're 2Faced. Not like Dr. Jekyll and Mr. Hyde. We're multifaceted with strengths in writing and design. We're wordsmiths who use concept and imagery to convey powerful emotions."

ADDITIONAL INFORMATION "Think of us as the set designers of your story, or the photographers at your book's school photo. We'll provide visual messages, concepts, and ideas; covers that trigger a strategic response to position your book in front of your audience. We give authors and publishers a suite of different options when it comes to their covers--from digital to print."

SUZANNE WESLEY FREELANCE WRITING & DESIGN

2964 Terri Lee Court, Terre Haute IN 47805. (812)877-4204. **E-mail:** suzanne@suzannewesley.com. **Web-** site: www.suzannewesley.com. **Contact:** Suzanne Wesley, owner/creative director. Estab. 2009.

ADDITIONAL INFORMATION Offers design and copy writing services for the creation of book covers (print or digital), business cards, flyers, postcards, one sheets, bookmarks, web ads, print advertisements, posters, Facebook or blog headers, newsletters, brochures, annual reports, e-mail, and more.

SUSAN WOOLLIS

E-mail: design@suddenlink.net. **Contact:** Susan Woollis, freelance graphic designer. References available upon request.

ADDITIONAL INFORMATION "I've worked in the print industry since 1996 and solely in the graphics department since 2002. I understand deadlines, book layout/prepress, setting up files correctly, and presenting a professional-looking product. I freelance design in the evenings and on weekends only."

WRITING AS A GHOST

310 W. 39th St., Vancouver WA 98660. (360)566-2781. **Fax:** (360)989-3980. **E-mail:** denise@writingmyownbook.com. **Website:** writingmyownbook.com. **Contact:** Denise Rutledge, account manager. Estab. 2006. Writing as a Ghost offers freelance design, coaching and editorial services as a package and as individual services.

ADDITIONAL INFORMATION Design services include layout and design and manuscript preparation for POD publishing, Kindle and Smashwords submission. Coaching services include research and manuscript development, including assistance with developing market competitive approach to topic. Editing services range from simple proof reading and copy editing to substantive editing. Denise Rutledge approaches the written word as a combination of crafted words and visual message.

INDEPENDENT PUBLICISTS

///

One part of the self-publishing process is creating the product you plan to sell. In the case of self-publishing, that product is a book (either in print or digital form). Another part is raising awareness about your product and sharing how it will imrpove the lives of anyone who buys it.

One way to improve awareness is by working to get good publicity for yourself and your project. For some self-publishers, independent publicists help fill this need by using their media savvy and years of media experience and connections to land interviews for their clients.

Finding the right publicist for your project can enhance your book's chances of success. Since many traditional book retailers won't shelve self-published books, it's up to the self-publisher to find less traditional paths to raising book awareness.

However, all publicists are not created equal. Search for one that specializes in your subject area. Ask for references and find out if previous clients felt satisfied with their investment in independent publicists.

To help determine a fair rate, self-publishers need to know what type of publicity assistance they need and how rates will be determined. For instance, are you paying the publicist on a flat scale regardless of results? Are you paying for number of contacts they make? Or are you paying for actual interviews and reviews?

Know what rates you're paying and why you're paying them. Setting unfair expectations is bad for the freelancer, but it also puts your project at risk, because you're counting on the freelancers to give their best. At the same time, you want to make sure you're getting a fair return on your investment.

Starting locally will allow you to research each company carefully and learn about their past performance and make it easier to have face-to-face discussions about the project. Realize that any face-to-face time and time on the phone may be considered "billable hours" by your freelancer. Be sure to agree on all such fees and get it in writing before starting work. It will help ensure a more professional working relationship and provide both sides with more security.

Going local is not a requirement. In fact, it may be impossible to find an independent publicist in your state. That said, always ask for previous experience and consider checking references, especially if you're investing a lot of money in the publicity process. After all, you want to make sure your money will be money well spent.

ACCURATE WRITING & MORE

16 Barstow Lane, Hadley MA 01035. (413)586-2388. **E-mail:** shel@greenandprofitable.com. **Website:** www.frugalmarketing.com. **Contact:** Shel Horowitz, owner. Estab. 1982. Offers book marketing and book shepherding services.

ADDITIONAL INFORMATION For book marketing, develops marketing strategy and individualized marketing plans for authors, books, and book series. For book shepherding, helps make the decision to publish traditionally, self-publish, e-publish, or publish through a subsidy publisher.

STEPHANIE BARKO, LITERARY PUBLICIST

16100 Crystal Hills, Austin TX 78737. **E-mail:** steffercat@austin.rr.com. **Website:** www.stephaniebarko.com. **Contact:** Stephanie Barko, founder. Estab. 2006.

ADDITIONAL INFORMATION Offers book promotion for professionally edited indie and traditionally published adult nonfiction and historical fiction within one year of release.

JULIA DRAKE PUBLIC RELATIONS

1186 Aztec, Topanga CA 90290. (323)304-2433. **E-mail:** info@juliadrakepr.com. **Website:** www.juliadrakepr.com. **Contact:** Julia Drake, CEO/founder. Estab. 2009. Julia Drake Public Relations is a boutique literary publicity company that has worked with over 100 clients from NY Times bestselling authors to first-time self-published authors.

ADDITIONAL INFORMATION Drake has appeared as a speaker on many industry panels, including the Independent Writers Association of California, UCLA, the Women's National Book Association, and the Lambda Literary Foundation.

GAL-FRIDAY PUBLICITY

308-1114 Howie Ave., Coquitlam BC V3J 1V1 Canada. (604)366-7846. **E-mail:** rachel@gal-fridaypublicity.com. **Website:** www.gal-fridaypublicity.com. **Contact:** Rachel Sentes, founder/publicist. Estab. 2009. Offers business and book publicity, e-book publicity/publishing, media kit creation and design, editing, manuscript consultations, ghostwriting, Wordpress websites, copy editing, proposal writing, and literary agent and publishing consultations.

ADDITIONAL INFORMATION "We have worked in all aspects of the book industry behind and in front of the scenes."

KELLEY & HALL BOOK PUBLICITY

5 Briar Lane, Marblehead MA 01945. (617)680-1976. **E-mail:** jocelyn@kelleyandhall.com. **Website:** www.kelleyandhall.com. **Contact:** Jocelyn Kelley, partner. Estab. 2004. Kelley & Hall is a literary publicity company that is dedicated to helping authors and publishers with their promotion, marketing, and media relations.

ADDITIONAL INFORMATION "We create effective book buzz as well as author recognition that will increase book sales. We help writers build their author brand. Book marketing and book promotion are the cornerstones of Kelley & Hall."

LAUNCH PUBLICITY

64 Rhinestone Terrace, San Rafael CA 94903. (415)686-0668. **E-mail:** steve@launchpublicity.com. **Website:** www.launchpublicity.com. **Contact:** Steve Keyser, publicist. Estab. 2006. Launch Publicity is a performance-based PR firm specializing in media relations.

ADDITIONAL INFORMATION "We don't bill by the hour or hide behind fat retainers. We're totally focused on bringing value to our clients by making them more visible and relevant in today's continually evolving media driven world."

PAULA MARGULIES COMMUNICATIONS

8145 Borzoi Way, San Diego CA 92129. (858)538-2047. **Fax:** (858)538-8445. **E-mail:** paula@paulamargulies.com. **Website:** www.paulamargulies.com. **Contact:** Paula Margulies, publicist/owner. Estab. 1992. Paula Margulies represents all kinds of authors and works on an hourly basis.

ADDITIONAL INFORMATION She writes press releases and places them on the newswires, creates media kits, sets up book tours and speaking appearances, schedules radio, television, print, and web interviews, sets up blog and social media tours, and handles all types of exposure opportunities related to book promotion.

MYERS PRODUCTIONS

P.O. Box 4201, Scottsdale AZ 85261. **E-mail:** psmyers1@cox.net. **Contact:** Patricia Myers, president. Estab. 1985. Offers writing, editing, press releases, publicity, public relations.

ADDITIONAL INFORMATION Specializes in business and personality profiles, food, dining, nightlife, music, travel, books, and local history.

LAUREN ROSENBERG PUBLIC RELATIONS

Santa Monica CA. (310)393-9114. **E-mail:** lauren@lrpr.com. **Website:** lrpr.com. **Contact:** Lauren Rosenberg, publicist/owner. Estab. 1996. LRPR is a national marketing communications and public relations firm. **ADDITIONAL INFORMATION** "We specialize in representing luxury consumer businesses, those appealing to a customer with a higher-income bracket, but we have also successfully represented businesses appealing to the general public. In addition, we represent authors and entertainers." Services include publicity, marketing, event planning, advertising/branding, image consulting, and personal publicity.

CYNDI A. SUMMERS

2279 Yorkshire Rd., Birmingham MI 48009. (586)945-8775. **E-mail:** cyndisummers@prodigy.net. **Website:** linkedin.com/pub/cyndi-summers/9/75/8bb. **Contact:** Cyndi A. Summers, publicist/editor. Estab. 1998. Offers publicity and/or editing services. **ADDITIONAL INFORMATION** Specializes in socially and culturally progressive initiatives.

USAGENCY CREATIVE ARTISTS

Division of USAGENCY, Inc., P.O. Box 111, 224 Saint Louis St., Lewisburg PA 17837. **Fax:** (570)523-8722. **E-mail:** usagency@usagency.com. **Contact:** Richard W. Gathman, CEO. Estab. 1988. **ADDITIONAL INFORMATION** Offers advertising, marketing, public relations services.

XPRESS PRESS NEWS SERVICE

4741 Sarazen Dr., Hollywood FL 33021. (954)989-3338. **E-mail:** tkoening@xpresspress.com. **Website:** www.xpresspress.com. **Contact:** Tina Koenig, owner. Estab. 1986. Offers press release writing, press release distribution, pitching, development of content and scheduling calendars for Twitter, Facebook, Pinterest and other social media outlets. **ADDITIONAL INFORMATION** "We've always had a heavy focus on tech and can be a lifeline to authors who are not tech savvy and/or have no interest in handling this aspect of their PR and marketing."

CONFERENCES

//

Conferences provide self-publishers with a great opportunity to accomplish a few things. First, conferences are designed to help writers improve their craft and knowledge of the publishing business. In fact, some conferences are even designed to help self-publishers specifically.

Second, conferences are great networking opportunities. You may find freelance editors and designers here to help with your project. Or you may find bloggers who can help promote your book through guest posts, interviews, or reviews. And you might also find new readers that will buy copies on the spot.

Finally, conferences do one thing exceptionally well for writers of all skill levels and experience: They help give a jolt of excitement and energy. This enthusiasm should not be discounted, because it helps spur new ideas, innovation, and success.

KEEP IN MIND

Starting locally will allow you to save money on travel and other expenses (such as food, paying for a hotel, etc.). However, you may decide that paying more for your confernce experience is worth it if you're receiving the type of instruction and/or making the connections you need the most. Keep in mind that your conference expenses may actually be considered a business expense and a tax deduction. Consult your account to confirm.

Once you decide upon a conference to attend, make a conference plan. This plan will include directions to the event, contact information for organizers (in case you can't find your way), a list of which panels and/or sessions you wish to attend (don't wait until the day of the event to figure this out), and any other tasks you'd like to accomplish.

Leave the door open to be spontaneous with your schedule and take advantage of unexpected opportunities, but having a plan will make sure you don't feel cheated out of an incredible experience after the event is over.

One more important note: Bring business cards to the event and keep them somewhere that's easy for you to dispense. Any person you speak with should receive your card, even the nice person who sat next to you at lunch, because you never know who will present you with your first or next lucky break.

ABROAD WRITERS CONFERENCES

17363 Sutter Creek Rd., Sutter Creek CA 95685. (209)296-4050. **E-mail:** abroadwriters@yahoo. com. **Website:** www.abroad-crwf.com/index.html. "Abroad Writers Conferences are devoted to introducing our participants to world views here in the United States and Abroad. Throughout the world we invite several authors to come join us to give readings and to participate on a panel. Our discussion groups touch upon a wide range of topics from important issues of our times to publishing abroad and in the United States. Our objective is to broaden our cultural and scientific perspectives of the world through discourse and writing." Conferences are held throughout the year in various places worldwide. See website for scheduling details. Conference duration: 7-10 days. "Instead of being lost in a crowd at a large conference, Abroad Writers' Conference prides itself on holding small group meetings where participants have personal contact with everyone. Stimulating talks, interviews, readings, Q&A's, writing workshops, film screenings, private consultations and social gatherings all take place within a week to ten days. Abroad Writers' Conference promises you true networking opportunities and full detailed feedback on your writing."

COSTS Prices start at $2,750. Discounts and upgrades may apply. Particpants must apply to program no later than 3 months before departure. To secure a place you must send in a deposit of $1000. Balance must be paid in full twelve weeks before departure. See website for pricing details.

ADDITIONAL INFORMATION Agents participate in conference. Application is online at website.

ALABAMA WRITERS' CONCLAVE

137 Sterling Dr, Hueytown AL 35023. **Website:** www. alabamawritersconclave.org. **Contact:** Richard Modlin, President. Estab. 1923. The Alabama Writers' Conclave was organized in 1923 and has been in continuing existence since. Through the years, the Conclave has moved its conferences around the state to provide writers everywhere better access to its resources.The Conclave is today one of the oldest continuing writers' organization in the United States. Writers, aspiring writers and supporters of the writing arts may join. Sharing information, developing ideas, honing skills, and receiving practical advice are hallmarks of the annual meeting. Dates: July 12-14.

COSTS Fees for conference are $150 (member)/$175 (nonmember), includes 2 meals. Critique fee $25 (member)/$30 (nonmember). Membership $25.

ACCOMMODATIONS Special conference rates.

ADDITIONAL INFORMATION "We have major speakers and faculty members who conduct intensive, energetic workshops. Our annual writing contest guidelines and all other information is available at www.alabamawritersconclave.org."

AMERICAN CHRISTIAN WRITERS CONFERENCES

P.O. Box 110390, Nashville TN 37222-0390. (800)219-7483. **Fax:** (615)834-7736. **E-mail:** acwriters@aol.com. **Website:** www.acwriters.com. **Contact:** Reg Forder, director. Estab. 1981. ACW hosts dozens of annual two-day writers conferences and mentoring retreat across America taught by editors and professional freelance writers. These events provide excellent instruction, networking opportunities, and valuable one-on-one time with editors. Annual conferences promoting all forms of Christian writing (fiction, nonfiction, scriptwriting). Conferences are held between March and November during each year.

COSTS Costs vary based on conference. Prices also depend on whether it is a conference or a mentoring retreat.

ACCOMMODATIONS Special rates are available at the host hotel (usually a major chain like Holiday Inn).

ADDITIONAL INFORMATION Send a SASE for conference brochures/guidelines.

ART WORKSHOPS IN GUATEMALA

4758 Lyndale Ave. S., Minneapolis MN 55419-5304. (612)825-0747. **E-mail:** info@artguat.org. **Website:** www.artguat.org. **Contact:** Liza Fourre, director. Estab. 1995. Annual. Workshops held year-round. Maximim class size: 10 students per class.

COSTS See website. ncludes tuition, lodging, breakfast, ground transportation.

ACCOMMODATIONS All transportation and accommodations included in price of conference.

ADDITIONAL INFORMATION Conference information available now. For brochure/guidelines visit website, e-mail or call. Accepts inquiries by e-mail, phone.

ASJA WRITERS CONFERENCE

American Society of Journalists and Authors, 1501 Broadway, Suite 403, New York NY 10036. (212)997-0947. **Fax:** (212)937-2315. **E-mail:** asjaoffice@asja.org;

director@asja.org. **Website:** www.asja.org/wc. **Contact:** Alexandra Owens, executive director. Estab. 1971. Annual conference held in April. Conference duration: 3 days. Average attendance: 600. Covers nonfiction. Held at the Roosevelt in New York. Speakers have included Arianna Huffington, Kitty Kelley, Barbara Ehrenreich, Stefan Fatsis.

COSTS $200+, depending on when you sign up (includes lunch). Check website for updates.

ACCOMMODATIONS The hotel holding our conference always blocks out discounted rooms for attendees.

ADDITIONAL INFORMATION Brochures available in February. Registration form is on the website. Inquire by e-mail or fax. Sign up for conference updates on website.

ASPEN SUMMER WORDS LITERARY FESTIVAL & WRITING RETREAT

Aspen Writers' Foundation, 110 E. Hallam St., #116, Aspen CO 81611. (970)925-3122. **Fax:** (970)925-5700. **E-mail:** info@aspenwriters.org. **Website:** www.aspenwriters.org. **Contact:** Natalie Lacy, programs coordinator. Estab. 1976. ASW is one part laboratory and one part theater. It is comprised of two tracks— the Writing Retreat and the Literary Festival — which approach the written word from different, yet complementary angles. The Retreat features introductory and intensive workshops with some of the nation's most notable writing instructors and includes literature appreciation symposia and professional consultations with literary agents and editors. The Writing Retreat supports writers in developing their craft by providing a winning combination of inspiration, skills, community, and opportunity. The Literary Festival is a booklover's bliss, where the written word takes center stage. Since 2005, each edition of the Festival has celebrated a particular literary heritage and culture by honoring the stories and storytellers of a specific region. Annual conference held the fourth week of June. Conference duration: 5 days. Average attendance: 150 at writing retreat; 300+ at literary festival.

COSTS Check website each year for updates.

ACCOMMODATIONS Discount lodging at the conference site will be available. 2013 rates to be announced. Free shuttle around town.

ADDITIONAL INFORMATION Check website for details on when to buy tickets and passes. Aspen Summer Words runs between June 16-21, 2013.

ASSOCIATION OF WRITERS & WRITING PROGRAMS ANNUAL CONFERENCE

Association of Writers & Writing Programs, George Mason University, 4400 University Drive, MSN 1E3, Fairfax VA 22030-4444. (703)993-4317. **Fax:** (703)993-4302. **E-mail:** conference@awpwriter.org. **Website:** www.awpwriter.org. **Contact:** Anne Le, conference coordinator. Estab. 1992. Each year, AWP holds its Annual Conference & Bookfair in a different city to celebrate the authors, teachers, writing programs, literary centers, and independent publishers of that region. The conference typically features hundreds of readings, lectures, panel discussions, and forums, as well as hundreds of book signings, receptions, dances, and informal gatherings. More than 11,000 writers and readers attended our 2013 conference, and over 700 exhibitors were represented at our bookfair. AWP's is now the largest literary conference in North America.

ADDITIONAL INFORMATION Upcoming conference locations include Seattle (2014), Minneapolis (2015), Los Angeles (2016), and Washington, D.C. (2017).

ATLANTIC CENTER FOR THE ARTS

1414 Art Center Ave., New Smyrna Beach FL 32168. (386)427-6975. **Fax:** (386)427-5669. **E-mail:** program@atlanticcenterforthearts.org. **Website:** www.atlanticcenterforthearts.org. Internship and residency programs. A Florida artist-in-residence program in which artists of all disciplines work with current prominent artists in a supportive and creative environment.

ACCOMMODATIONS $850; $25 non-refundable application fee. Financial aid is availableParticipants responsible for all meals.Accommodations available on site. See website for application schedule and materials.

AUSTIN FILM FESTIVAL & CONFERENCE

1801 Salina St., Suite 210, Austin TX 78702. (512)478-4795; (800)310-FEST. **Fax:** (512)478-6205. **Website:** www.austinfilmfestival.com. **Contact:** Erin Hallagan, conference director. Estab. 1994. "Built around one of the most prestigious screenwriting contests in the country, the Conference attracts groundbreaking producers, agents, managers, and development execs, as well as countless working screenwriters and filmmakers. The speakers converging in Austin every October range from established A-listers like Steven Zaillian,

Ron Howard, Judd Apatow, Caroline Thompson, Susannah Grant and John Lee Hancock to upstart writers and filmmakers who have just broken into the industry. The Conference is famous, like its host city, for a culture of progressive ideas, big heart and zero pretensions. You won't just watch your heroes speak from a podium — we want you to get up close and personal — so panels are designed for intimacy and interaction, workshops are hands-on dream opportunities for writers and filmmakers, and parties are grand and fun without the velvet ropes. AFF's combination of high-caliber talent with access is unmatched by any other film festival or conference." Runs in the final week of October each year.

COSTS Austin Film Festival offers 4 Badge levels for entry into the October festival, which also features access to the conference, depending on the Badge level. Go online for offers, and to view the different options with available with each badge.

ACCOMMODATIONS Discounted rates on hotel accommodations are available to attendees if the reservations are made through the Austin Film Festival office.

ADDITIONAL INFORMATION The Austin Film Festival furthers the art and craft of filmmaking by inspiring and championing the work of screenwriters, filmmakers, and all artists who use the language of film to tell a story. The Austin Film Festival is considered one of the most accessible festivals, and Austin is the premier town for networking because when industry people are here, they are relaxed and friendly. The Austin Film Festival holds annual screenplay/teleplay and film competitions, as well as a Young Filmmakers Program. Check online for competition details and festival information. Inquire via e-mail or fax.

AUSTIN INTERNATIONAL POETRY FESTIVAL

P.O. Box 26455, Austin TX 78755. (512)777-1888. **E-mail:** lynn@aipf.org. **E-mail:** james@aipf.org. **Website:** www.aipf.org. **Contact:** Ashley S. Kim, festival director. Estab. 1993. Annual Austin International Poetry Festival (AIPF) April 11-14, is open to the public. This four-day citywide, all-inclusive celebration of poetry and poets has grown to become "the largest non-juried poetry festival in the U.S." The festival will include up to 20 live local readings, youth anthology read, 20 poetry workshops, 5 open mics, 5 music and poetry presentations, two anthology competions and complete readings, two poetry slams, an all-night

open mic and a poetry panel symposium. API projects over 250 registered poets from the international, national, state, and local areas

ACCOMMODATIONS Includes anthology submission fee, program bio, scheduled reading at one of AIPF's 15 venues, participation in all events, 1 catered meal, workshop participation, and more.

ADDITIONAL INFORMATION Offers multiple poetry contests as part of festival. Guidelines available on website. Registration form available on website. "Largest non-juried poetry festival in the U.S.!"

BACKSPACE AGENT-AUTHOR SEMINAR

P.O. Box 454, Washington MI 48094-0454. (732)267-6449. **Fax:** (586)532-9652. **E-mail:** chrisg@bksp.org. **E-mail:** karendionne@bksp.org. **Website:** www.bksp.org. **Contact:** Karen Dionne. Estab. 2006. Main conference duration: May 23-25. Average attendance: 100. Panels and workshops designed to educate and assist authors in search of a literary agent to represent their work. Only agents will be in program. Past speakers have included Scott Hoffman, Dan Lazar, Scott Miller, Michael Bourret, Katherine Fausset, Jennifer DeChiara, Sharlene Martin and Paul Cirone.

COSTS All 3 days: May 23-25; includes Agent-Author Seminar, Conference Program, Book Signing & Cocktail Reception, Donald Maass workshop—$720. **Backspace Members Receive a $100 discount on a 3-day registration! First 2 days**: May 23-24; includes Agent-Author Seminar, Conference Program, Book Signing & Cocktail Reception—$580. **Friday only**: May 24; Two-track conference program with literary agents, editors and authors. Includes keynote address, booksigning and cocktail reception—$275. **Saturday only**: May 25; Back-to-back craft workshops with bestselling author Jonathan Maberry in the morning and literary agent Donald Maass in the afternoon—$200.

ACCOMMODATIONS Held in the Radisson Martinique, at 49 West 32nd Street, New York, NY 10001. Telephone: (212) 736-3800. Fax: (212) 277-2702. You can call to book a reservation, based on a two-person occupancy.

ADDITIONAL INFORMATION The Backspace Agent-Author Seminar offers plenty of face time with attending agents. This casual, no-pressure seminar is a terrific opportunity to network, ask questions, talk about your work informally and listen from the people who make their lives selling books.

BALTIMORE COMIC-CON

Baltimore Convention Center, One West Pratt St., Baltimore MD 21201. (410)526-7410. **E-mail:** press@baltimorecomiccon.com. **Website:** www.baltimorecomiccon.com. **Contact:** Marc Nathan. Estab. 1999. Annual. September 7-8, 2013. Conference, "promoting the wonderful world of comics to as many people as possible." The Baltimore Comic-Con welcomes the return of The Harvey Awards: "The Harvey Awards are one of the comic book industry's oldest and most respected awards. The Harveys recognize outstanding achievements in over 20 categories, ranging from Best Artist to the Jack Kirby Hall of Fame. They are the only industry awards both nominated by and selected by the full body of comic book professionals."

ACCOMMODATIONS Does not offer overnight accommodations. Provides list of area hotels or lodging options.

ADDITIONAL INFORMATION For brochure, visit website.

BLOCKBUSTER PLOT INTENSIVE WRITING WORKSHOPS (SANTA CRUZ)

Santa Cruz CA **E-mail:** contact@blockbusterplots.com. **Website:** www.blockbusterplots.com. **Contact:** Martha Alderson M.A. (also known as the Plot Whisperer), instructor. Estab. 2000. Held 4 times per year. Conference duration: 2 days. Average attendance: 20. Workshop is intended to help writers create an action, character, and thematic plotline for a screenplay, memoir, short story, novel, or creative nonfiction. Site: Conference hall.

COSTS $95 per day.

ACCOMMODATIONS Provides list of area hotels and lodging options.

ADDITIONAL INFORMATION Brochures available by e-mail or on website. Accepts inquiries by e-mail.

BLOODY WORDS MYSTERY CONFERENCE

E-mail: chair@bloodywords.com. **Website:** www.bloodywords.com. **Contact:** Cheryl Freedman, chair. Estab. 1999. "This is a conference for both readers and writers of mysteries, the only one of its kind in Canada. We also run The Mystery Cafe, a chance to get to know a dozen or so authors, hear them read and ask questions (half hour each)."

COSTS $195 (includes the banquet and all panels, readings, dealers' room and workshop).

ACCOMMODATIONS Offers block of rooms in hotel; list of optional lodging available. Check website for details.

ADDITIONAL INFORMATION Sponsors short mystery story contest—5,000 word limit; judges are experienced editors of anthologies; fee is $5 (entrants must be registered). Also sponsors The Bony Blithe Award for light mysteries; see website for details. Conference information is available now. For brochure, visit website. Accepts inquiries by e-mail and phone. Agents and editors participate in conference.

BLUE RIDGE MOUNTAIN CHRISTIAN WRITERS CONFERENCE

No public address available, 1-800-588-7222. **E-mail:** ylehman@bellsouth.net. **Website:** ridgecrestconferencecenter.org/event/blueridgemountainchristianwritersconference. Annual conference held in May (May 19-May 23). Conference duration: Sunday through lunch on Thursday. Average attendance: 400. A training and networking event for both seasoned and aspiring writers that allows attendees to interact with editors, agents, professional writers, and readers. Workshops and continuing classes in a variety of creative categories are also offered.

COSTS $320, meal package is $141.50 per person (12 meals beginning with dinner Sunday and ending with lunch on Thursday)

ACCOMMODATIONS $59 per night (Standard Acomodations), and $64-69 per night (Deluxe Accomadations), depending on rooms. Located at LifeWay Ridgecrest Conference Center, 1 Ridgecrest Drive, Ridgecrest, NC 28770.

ADDITIONAL INFORMATION The event also features a contest for unpublished writers and ms critiques prior to the conference.

BOOMING GROUND ONLINE WRITERS STUDIO

Buch E-462, 1866 Main Mall, UBC, Vancouver BC V6T 1Z1 Canada. **Fax:** (604)648-8848. **E-mail:** contact@boomingground.com. **Website:** www.boomingground.com. **Contact:** Robin Evans, director. Writer mentorships geared toward beginner, intermediate, and advanced levels in novel, short fiction, poetry, nonfiction, and children's writing, and more. **Open to students.** Online mentorship program—students work for 6 months with a mentor by e-mail, allowing up to 120-240 pages of material to be created. Program cost: $500 (Canadian). Site: online and by e-mail.

BREAD LOAF WRITERS' CONFERENCE

Middlebury College, Middlebury College, Middlebury VT 05753. (802)443-5286. **Fax:** (802)443-2087. **E-mail:** ncargill@middlebury.edu. **E-mail:** blwc@middlebury.edu. **Website:** www.middlebury.edu/blwc. **Contact:** Michael Collier, Director. Estab. 1926. Annual conference held in late August. Conference duration: 11 days. Offers workshops for fiction, nonfiction, and poetry. Agents, editors, publicists, and grant specialists will be in attendance.

COSTS $2,714 (includes tuition, housing).

ACCOMMODATIONS Bread Loaf Campus in Ripton, Vermont.

ADDITIONAL INFORMATION Conference Date: August 14-24. Location: mountain campus of Middlebury College. Average attendance: 230.

BYRDCLIFFE ARTS COLONY

34 Tinker St., Woodstock NY 12498. (845)679-2079. **Fax:** (845)679-4529. **E-mail:** airdirector@woodstockguild.org. **Website:** www.woodstockguild.org. Estab. 1991. Offers 1-month residencies June-September. Open to composers, writers, and visual artists. Accommodates 15 at 1 time. Personal living quarters include single rooms, shared baths, and kitchen facilities. Offers separate private studio space. Composers must provide their own keyboard with headphone. Activities include open studio and readings for the Woodstock community at the end of each session. The Woodstock Guild, parent organization, offers music and dance performances and gallery exhibits.

COSTS $600/month; fellowships available. Residents are responsible for own meals and transportation.

ADDITIONAL INFORMATION Deadline: March 15. Online application; visit woodstockguild.org for submission guidelines. Download application fee and online payment from website.

CALIFORNIA CRIME WRITERS CONFERENCE

Co-sponsored by Sisters in Crime/Los Angeles and the Southern California Chapter of Mystery Writers of America, **E-mail:** sistersincrimela@gmail.com. **Website:** www.ccwconference.org. Estab. 1995. Biennial. Conference held in June. Average attendance: 200. Two-day conference on mystery and crime writing. Offers craft, forensic and career-buildings sessions, 2 keynote speakers, author, editor, and agent panels and book signings. Breakfast and lunch both days included.

ADDITIONAL INFORMATION Conference information is available at www.ccwconference.org.

CAPE COD WRITERS CENTER ANNUAL CONFERENCE

P.O. Box 408, Osterville MA 02655. **E-mail:** writers@capecodwriterscenter.org. **Website:** www.capecodwriterscenter.org. **Contact:** Nancy Rubin Stuart, executive director. Duration: 5 days; first week in August. Offers workshops in fiction, commercial fiction, nonfiction, poetry, writing for children, humor, memoir, pitching your book, screenwriting, digital communications, getting published, ms evaluation, mentoring sessions with faculty. Held at Resort and Conference Center of Hyannis, Hyannis, MA.

COSTS Vary, depending on the number of courses selected.

CAT WRITERS' ASSOCIATION ANNUAL WRITERS CONFERENCE

66 Adams St., Jamestown NY 14701. (716)484-6155. **E-mail:** dogwriter@windstream.net. **Website:** www.catwriters.org. **Contact:** Susan M. Ewing, president. The Cat Writers' Association holds an annual conference at varying locations around the U.S. The agenda for the conference is filled with seminars, editor appointments, an autograph party, networking breakfast, reception and annual awards banquet, as well as the annual meeting of the association. See website for details.

CELEBRATION OF SOUTHERN LITERATURE

Southern Lit Alliance, 3069 S. Broad St., Suite 2, Chattanooga TN 37408-3056. (423)267-1218 or (800)267-4232. **Fax:** (423)267-1018. **E-mail:** srobinson@southernlitalliance.org. **Website:** www.southernlitalliance.org. **Contact:** Susan Robinson. "The Celebration of Southern Literature stands out because of its unique collaboration with the Fellowship of Southern Writers, an organization founded by towering literary figures like Eudora Welty, Cleanth Brooks, Walker Percy, and Robert Penn Warren to recognize and encourage literature in the South. The 2013 celebration marked 24 years since the Fellowship selected Chattanooga for its headquarters and chose to collaborate with the Celebration of Southern Literature. Up to 50 members of the Fellowship will participate in this year's event, discussing hot topics and reading from their latest works. The Fellowship will also award 11 literary prizes and induct 2 new members, making this event the place to discover up-and-coming voices in Southern literature. The Southern Lit Alliance's Celebration of Southern Literature attracts more than 1,000 readers and writers from all over the U.S. It strives to maintain an informal atmosphere where conversations will thrive, inspired by a common passion for the written word. The Southern Lit Alliance (formerly The Arts & Education Council) started as 1 of 12 pilot agencies founded by a Ford Foundation grant in 1952. The Alliance is the only organization of the 12 still in existence. The Southern Lit Alliance celebrates southern writers and readers through community education and innovative literary arts experiences."

CLARION WEST WRITERS WORKSHOP

P.O. Box 31264, Seattle WA 98103-1264. (206)322-9083. **E-mail:** info@clarionwest.org. **Website:** www.clarionwest.org. "Contact us through our webform." **Contact:** Leslie Howle, workshop director. Clarion West is an intensive 6-week workshop for writers preparing for professional careers in science fiction and fantasy, held annually in Seattle WA. Usually goes from mid-June through end of July. Conference duration: 6 weeks. Average attendance: 18. Held near the University of Washington. Deadline for applications is March 1. Instructors are well-known writers and editors in the field.

COSTS $3,600 (for tuition, housing, most meals). Limited scholarships are available based on financial need.

ACCOMMODATIONS Workshop tuition, dormitory housing and most meals: $3,600. Students stay on-site in workshop housing at one of the University of Washington's sorority houses. "Students write their own stories every week while preparing critiques of all the other students' work for classroom sessions. This gives participants a more focused, professional approach to their writing. The core of the workshop remains speculative fiction, and short stories (not novels) are the focus." Conference information available in Fall. For brochure/guidelines send SASE, visit website, e-mail or call. Accepts inquiries by e-mail, phone, SASE. Limited scholarships are available, based on financial need. Students must submit 20-30 pages of ms with 4-page biography and $40 fee ($30 if received prior to February 10) for applications sent by mail or e-mail to qualify for admission.

ADDITIONAL INFORMATION This is a critique-based workshop. Students are encouraged to write a story every week; the critique of student material produced at the workshop forms the principal activity of the workshop. Students and instructors critique mss as a group. Conference guidelines are available for a SASE. Visit the website for updates and complete details.

CRESTED BUTTE WRITERS CONFERENCE

P.O. Box 1361, Crested Butte CO 81224. **E-mail:** coordinator@conf.crestedbuttewriters.org. **Website:** www.crestedbuttewriters.org/conf.php. **Contact:** Barbara Crawford or Theresa Rizzo, co-coordinators. Estab. 2006.

COSTS $330 nonmembers; $300 members; $297 Early Bird; The Sandy Writing Contest Finalist $280; and groups of 5 or more $280.

ACCOMMODATIONS The conference is held at The Elevation Hotel, located at the Crested Butte Mountain Resort at the base of the ski mountain (Mt. Crested Butte, CO). The quaint historic town lies nestled in a stunning mountain valley 3 short miles from the resort area of Mt. Crested Butte. A free bus runs frequently between the 2 towns. The closest airport is 30 miles away, in Gunnison CO. Our website lists 3 lodging options besides rooms at the Event Facility. All condos, motels and hotel options offer special conference rates. No special travel arrangements are made through the conference; however, information for car rental from Gunnison airport or the Alpine Express shuttle is listed on the conference FAQ page.

ADDITIONAL INFORMATION "Our conference workshops address a wide variety of writing craft and business. Our most popular workshop is Our First Pages Readings—with a twist. Agents and editors read opening pages volunteered by attendees-with a few best selling authors' openings mixed in. Think the A/E can identify the bestsellers? Not so much. Each year one of our attendees has been mistaken for a bestseller and obviously garnered requests from some on the panel. Agents attending: Carlie Webber—CK Webber Associates and TBDs. The agents will be speaking and available for meetings with attendees through our Pitch and Pages system. Editors attending: Christian Trimmer, senior editor at Disney Hyperion Books, and Jessica Williams of Harper Collins. Award-winning authors: Mark Coker, CEO of Smashwords; Kristen Lamb, social media guru, Kim Killion, book cover designer; Jennifer Jakes; Sandra

Kerns; and Annette Elton. Writers may request additional information by e-mail."

EAST TEXAS CHRISTIAN WRITERS CONFERENCE

The School of Humanities, Dr. Jerry L. Summers, Dean, Scarborough Hall, East Texas Baptist University, 1 Tiger Dr., Marshall TX 75670. (903)923-2083. **E-mail:** jhopkins@etbu.edu; contest@etbu.edu. **Website:** www.etbu.edu/News/CWC. **Contact:** Sally Roden, humanities secretary. Estab. 2002. Annual conference; held October 25-26, 2013. Duration: 2 days (Friday and Saturday). Average attendance: 160. Site: East Texas Baptist University. "Primarily, we are interested in promoting quality Christian writing that would be accepted in mainstream publishing." Past conference themes were Back to Basics, Getting Started in Fiction, Writers & Agents, Writing Short Stories, Writing for Newspapers, The Significance of Style, Writing Fillers and Articles, Writing Devotionals, Blogging for Writers, Christian Non-Fiction, Inspirational Writing, E-Publishing, Publishing on Demand, and Editor, and Author Relations. Conference offers contact, conversation, and exchange of ideas with other aspiring writers; outstanding presentations and workshop experiences with established authors, agents, editors, and publishers; potential publishing and writing opportunities; networking with other writers with related interests; promotion of both craft and faith; and one-on-one consultations with agents, editors, and publishers. Past conference speakers/workshop leaders were Marlene Bagnull, Bill Keith, Mary Lou Redding, Marie Chapian, Vickie Phelps, Michael Farris, Pamela Dowd, Donn Taylor, Terry Burns, Donna Walker-Nixon, Lexie Smith, Marv Knox, Jim Pence, Andrea Chevalier, and Cecil Murphey. Offers an advanced track, a beginner's track, and a teen track. There is a writing contest with cash awards for grand prize and 1st-, 2nd- and 3rd-place winners. Partial scholarships available for students only.

ACCOMMODATIONS Visit website for a list of local hotels offering a discounted rate.

WRITERS IN PARADISE

Eckerd College, 4200 54th Ave. South, St. Petersburg FL 33711. (727) 864-7994. **Fax:** (727) 864-7575. **E-mail:** cayacr@eckerd.edu. **Website:** www.writersinparadise.com. **Contact:** Christine Koryta, conference coordinator. Estab. 2005. Annual. January. Conference duration: 8 days. Average attendance: 84 maximum. Workshop. Offers college credit. "Writers in Paradise Conference offers workshop classes in fiction (novel and short story), poetry, and nonfiction. Working closely with our award-winning faculty, students will have stimulating opportunities to ask questions and learn valuable skills from fellow students and authors at the top of their form. Most importantly, the intimate size and secluded location of the Writers in Paradise experience allows you the time and opportunity to share your mss, critique one another's work, and discuss the craft of writing with experts and peers who can help guide you to the next level." Site: "Located on 188 acres of waterfront property in St. Petersburg, Florida, Eckerd College is a private, coeducational college of liberal arts and sciences. In 2013, lectures were given on the craft of writing by Ann Patchett, Daniel Woodrell, Michael Koryta, and Sterling Watson. Faculty also led discussions during morning sessions of informal round tables and formal panel discussions on craft. [2013] faculty and guest faculty included: Andre Dubus III (*House of Sand and Fog*), Michael Koryta (*So Cold the River*), Dennis Lehane (*The Given Day*), Laura Lippman (*I'd Know You Anywhere*), Seth Fishman (literary agent), Johnny Temple (Akashic Books), Stewart O'Nan (*The Odds*), David Yoo (*Girls for Breakfast*), Tom Franklin (*Crooked Letter, Crooked Letter*), Beth Ann Fennelly (*Unmentionables*), Josh Kendall (editor), Ann Hood (*The Red Thread*), Les Standiford (*Bringing Adam Home*), Sterling Watson (*Sweet Dream Baby*), and more."

COSTS 2013 tuition fee: 700.

ACCOMMODATIONS Block of rooms at area hotel with free shuttle to and from conference; $582.24.

ADDITIONAL INFORMATION Application materials are required of all attendees. Acceptance is based on a writing sample and a letter detailing your writing background. Submit 1 short story (25 page max) or the opening 25 pages of a novel-in-progress, plus a 2-page synopsis of the book. Deadline for application materials is December 1. "Writers in Paradise is a conference for writers of various styles and approaches. While admission is selective, the admissions committee accepts writers with early potential as well as those with strong backgrounds in writing." Information available in August. For brochure, send SASE, call, e-mail. Agents participate in conference. Editors participate in conference. "The tranquil seaside landscape sets the tone for this informal gathering of writers, teachers, editors and literary agents. After 8 days of workshopping and engagement with peers and professionals in your field, you will leave this unique opportunity with solid ideas about how to find an agent and get published, along with a new and better understanding of your craft."

EVANSTON WRITERS WORKSHOP "IN THE TRENCHES WITH THE WRITER" CONFERENCE

Evanston Writers Workshop, P.O. Box 6322, Evanston IL 60204-6322. (224)999-0201. **E-mail:** info@evanstonwritersworkshop.org; coleen@evanstonwritersworkshop.org. **Website:** www.evanstonwritersworkshop.org. **Contact:** Coleen Goodson, CAO. Held annually for 3 days in late summer or early fall. Average attendance: 75.

COSTS $175 for members; $200 for non-members; $50 master class

ACCOMMODATIONS Special rate of $136 at the Orrington Hotel.

FESTIVAL OF FAITH AND WRITING

Department of English, Calvin College, 1795 Knollcrest Circle SE, Grand Rapids MI 49546. (616)526-6770. **E-mail:** ffw@calvin.edu. **Website:** festival.calvin.edu. Estab. 1990. Biennial festival held in April. Conference duration: 3 days. The festival brings together writers, editors, publishers, musicians, artists, and readers to discuss and celebrate insightful writing that explores issues of faith. Focuses on fiction, nonfiction, memoir, poetry, drama, children's, young adult, academic, film, and songwriting. Past speakers have included Joyce Carol Oates, Salman Rushdie, Patricia Hampl, Thomas Lynch, Leif Enger, Marilynne Robinson and Michael Chabon. Agents and editors attend the festival.

COSTS Consult festival website.

ACCOMMODATIONS Shuttles are available to and from local hotels. Shuttles are also available for overflow parking lots. A list of hotels with special rates for conference attendees is available on the festival website. High school and college students can arrange on-campus lodging by e-mail.

ADDITIONAL INFORMATION Online registration opens in October. Accepts inquiries by e-mail and phone. Next festival is April 10-12, 2014.

FLATHEAD RIVER WRITERS CONFERENCE

P.O. Box 7711, Kalispell MT 59904-7711. (406)881-4066. **E-mail:** answers@authorsoftheflathead.org. **Website:** www.authorsoftheflathead.org/conference.asp. Estab. 1990. Two day conference packed with energizing speakers. After a focus on publishing the past two years, this year's focus is on writing, getting your manuscripts honed and ready for your readers. Highlights include two agents will review 12 manuscripts one-on-one with the first 24 paid attendees requesting this opportunity, a synopsis writing workshop, a screenwriting workshop, and more.

COSTS Contact for cost information, not currently listed on website.

ACCOMMODATIONS Rooms are available at a discounted rate.

ADDITIONAL INFORMATION Watch website for additional speakers and other details. Register early as seating is limited.

FLORIDA CHRISTIAN WRITERS CONFERENCE

2344 Armour Ct., Titusville FL 32780. (386)295-3902. **E-mail:** FloridaChristianWritersConf@gmail.com. **Website:** floridacwc.net. Estab. 1988. Annual conference held in March (February 26-March 2). Conference duration: 4 days. Average attendance: 275. "The Florida Christian Writers Conference 2014 meets under the stately oaks of Lake Yale Conference Center near Leesburg, Florida. The conference is designed to meet the needs of beginning writers to published authors. This is your opportunity to learn more about the publishing industry, to build your platform, and to follow God's leading to publish the message He has given you."

COSTS $575 (includes tuition, meals).

ACCOMMODATIONS We provide a shuttle from the Orlando airport. $725/double occupancy; $950/single occupancy.

ADDITIONAL INFORMATION "Each writer may submit 2 works for critique. We have specialists in every area of writing. Brochures/guidelines are available online or for a SASE."

GENEVA WRITERS CONFERENCE

Geneva Writers Group, Switzerland. **E-mail:** info@GenevaWritersGroup.org. **Website:** www.genevawritersgroup.org. Estab. 1993. Biennial conference held at Webster University in Bellevue/Geneva,Switzerland. Conference duration: 2.5 days, welcoming more than

200 writers from around the world. Speakers and presenters have included Peter Ho Davies, Jane Alison, Russell Celyn Jones, Patricia Hampl, Robert Root, Brett Lott, Dinty W. Moore, Naomi Shihab Nye, Jo Shapcott, Wallis Wilde Menozzi, Susan Tiberghien, Jane Dystel, Laura Longrigg, and Colin Harrison.

THE GLEN WORKSHOP

Image, 3307 Third Ave. W., Seattle WA 98119. (206)281-2988. **Fax:** (206)281-2335. **E-mail:** glenworkshop@imagejournal.org. **Website:** glenworkshop.com. Estab. 1995. A pair of annual workshops. Conference duration: 1 week. Workshop focuses on fiction, poetry, spiritual writing, playwriting, screenwriting, songwriting, and mixed media. Writing classes combine general instruction and discussion with the workshop experience, in which each individual's works are read and discussed critically. Glen West held at St. John's College in Santa Fe, NM from July 28-August 4and Glen East held Mt. Holyoke College in South Hadley, MA from June 9-16. The Glen Workshop combines an intensive learning experience with a lively festival of the arts. It takes place in the stark, dramatic beauty of the Sangre de Cristo mountains and within easy reach of the rich cultural, artistic, and spiritual traditions of northern New Mexico. Lodging and meals are included with registration at affordable rates. A low-cost "commuter" rate is also available for those who wish to camp, stay with friends, or otherwise find their own food and lodging.

COSTS See costs online. A limited number of partial scholarships are available.

ACCOMMODATIONS Offers dorm rooms, dorm suites, and apartments.

ADDITIONAL INFORMATION Like *Image*, the Glen is grounded in a Christian perspective, but its tone is informal and hospitable to all spiritual wayfarers. Depending on the teacher, participants may need to submit workshop material prior to arrival (usually 10-25 pages).

GOTHAM WRITERS' WORKSHOP

WritingClasses.com, 555 Eighth Ave., Suite 1402, New York NY 10018. (212)974-8377. **Fax:** (212)307-6325. **E-mail:** dana@write.org. **Website:** www.writingclasses.com. **Contact:** Dana Miller, director of student relations. Estab. 1993. Online classes are held throughout the year. There are 4 terms of NYC classes, beginning in January, April, June/July, and September/October. Offers craft-oriented creative writing courses in general creative writing, fiction writing, screenwriting, nonfiction writing, article writing, stand-up comedy writing, humor writing, memoir writing, novel writing, children's book writing, playwriting, poetry, songwriting, mystery writing, science fiction writing, romance writing, television writing, article writing, travel writing, business writing and classes on freelancing, selling your screenplay, how to blog, nonfiction book proposal, and getting published. Also, the Workshop offers a teen program, private instruction, and mentoring program. Classes are held at various schools in New York City as well as online at www.writingclasses.com. Agents and editors participate in some workshops.

COSTS $420/10-week workshops; $159 for the four-week online selling seminars and $125 for one-day intensive courses; $299 for 6-week creative writing and business writing classes.

ADDITIONAL INFORMATION "Participants do not need to submit workshop material prior to their first class." Sponsors a contest for a free 10-week online creative writing course (valued at $420) offered each term. Students should fill out a form online at www.writingclasses.com to participate in the contest. The winner is randomly selected. For brochure send e-mail, visit website, or call. Accepts inquiries by e-mail and phone.

THE GREAT AMERICAN PITCHFEST & SCREENWRITING CONFERENCE

Twilight Pictures, 12400 Ventura Blvd., #735, Studio City CA 91604. (877)255-2528. **E-mail:** info@pitchfest.com. **Website:** www.pitchfest.com. Conference duration: 3 days (2-day conference, 1-day pitchfest). "Our companies are all carefully screened, and only the most credible companies in the industry are invited to hear pitches. They include agents, managers, and production companies."

COSTS Saturday is free, with a full day of industry classes, workshops, and panels, all led by industry professionals. The Sunday Pitchfest is $250; Saturday is free. The Friday/Saturday master classes are $50.

ACCOMMODATIONS All activities will be held at the Burbank Marriott Hotel & Convention Center, 2500 N. Hollywood Way, Burbank, CA 91505.

ADDITIONAL INFORMATION 2013 dates: May 31-June 2.

GREATER LEHIGH VALLEY WRITERS GROUP 'THE WRITE STUFF' WRITERS CONFERENCE

3650 Nazareth Pike, PMB #136, Bethlehem PA 18020-1115. **E-mail:** writestuffchair@glvwg.org. **Website:** www.glvwg.org. **Contact:** Donna Brennan, chair. Estab. 1993.

COSTS Members: $110 (includes Friday evening session and all Saturday workshops, 2 meals, and a chance to pitch to an editor or agent); non-members: $130. Late registration: $145. Pre-conference workshops require an additional fee.

ADDITIONAL INFORMATION "The Writer's Flash contest is judged by conference participants. Write 100 words or less in fiction, creative nonfiction, or poetry. Brochures available in January by SASE, or by phone, e-mail, or on website. Accepts inquiries by SASE, e-mail or phone. Agents and editors attend conference. For updated info refer to the website. Greater Lehigh Valley Writers Group hosts a friendly conference and gives you the most for your money. Breakout rooms offer craft topics, business of publishing, editor and agent panels. Book fair with book signing by published authors and presenters."

GREEN LAKE CHRISTIAN WRITERS CONFERENCE

W2511 State Road 23, Green Lake Conference Center, Green Lake WI 54941-9599. (920)294-3323. **E-mail:** program@glcc.org. **E-mail:** janet.p.white@gmail.com. **Website:** glcc.org. **Contact:** Janet White, Conference Director. Estab. 1948. Conference duration: 1 week (August 18-23). Attendees may be well-published or beginners, may write for secular and/or Christian markets. Leaders are experienced writing teachers. Attendees can spend 11.5 contact hours in the workshop of their choice: fiction, nonfiction, poetry, inspirational/devotional. Seminars include specific skills: marketing, humor, songwriting, writing for children, self-publishing, writing for churches, interviewing, memoir writing, the magazine market. Evening: panels of experts will answer questions. Social and leisure activities included. GLCC is in south central WI, has 1,000 acres, 2.5 miles of shoreline on Wisconsin's deepest lake, and offers a resort setting.

COSTS Short Track (Two Days): $65 per person. Full Track: Writers' - $225 per person; Artists' - $40 per person.

ACCOMMODATIONS Hotels, lodges and all meeting rooms are a/c. Affordable rates, excellent meals.

ADDITIONAL INFORMATION Brochure and scholarship info from website or contact Jan White (920-294-7327). To register, call 920-294-3323.

GREEN MOUNTAIN WRITERS CONFERENCE

47 Hazel St., Rutland VT 05701. (802)236-6133. **E-mail:** ydaley@sbcglobal.net. **E-mail:** yvonnedaley@me.com. **Website:** vermontwriters.com. **Contact:** Yvonne Daley, director. Estab. 1999. "Annual conference held in the summer. Covers fiction, creative nonfiction, poetry, journalism, nature writing, essay, memoir, personal narrative, and biography. Held at an old dance pavillion on on a remote pond in Tinmouth, Vermont. Speakers have included Stephen Sandy, Grace Paley, Ruth Stone, Howard Frank Mosher, Chris Bohjalian, Joan Connor, Yvonne Daley, David Huddle, David Budbill, Jeffrey Lent, Verandah Porche, Tom Smith, and Chuck Clarino."

COSTS $600 before June 30; $650 after June 30. Partial scholarships are available.

ACCOMMODATIONS "We have made arrangements with a major hotel in nearby Rutland and two area bed and breakfast inns for special accommodations and rates for conference participants. You must make your own reservations."

ADDITIONAL INFORMATION Participants' mss can be read and commented on at a cost. Sponsors contests. Conference publishes a literary magazine featuring work of participants. Brochures available in January on website or for SASE, e-mail. Accepts inquiries by SASE, e-mail, phone. "We offer the opportunity to learn from some of the nation's best writers at a small, supportive conference in a lakeside setting that allows one-to-one feedback. Participants often continue to correspond and share work after conferences." Further information available on website, by e-mail or by phone.

THE TYRONE GUTHRIE CENTRE

Annaghmakerrig, Newbliss, County Monaghan Ireland. (353)(047)54003. **Fax:** (353)(047)54380. **E-mail:** info@tyroneguthrie.ie. **Website:** www.tyroneguthrie.ie. Estab. 1981. Offers year-round residencies. Artists may stay for anything from 1 week to 3 months in the Big House, or for up to 6 months at a time in one of the 5 self-catering houses in the old farmyard. Open to artists of all disciplines. Accommodates 13 in the big house and up to 7 in the farmyard cottages. Personal living quarters include bedroom with bathroom en suite. Offers a variety of workspaces. There is a music room for composers and musicians with a Yamaha C3M-PE conservative grand piano, a performance studio with a Yamaha upright, a photographic darkroom and a number of studios for visual artists, one of which is wheelchair accessible. At certain times of the year it is possible, by special arrangement, to accommodate groups of artists, symposiums, master classes, workshops and other collaborations.

COSTS Irish and European artists: €300/week for the big house; €150 for self-catering cottages; others pay €600 per week, all found, for a residency in the Big House and €300 per week (plus gas and electricity costs) for one of the self-catering farmyard houses. To qualify for a residency, it is necessary to show evidence of a significant level of achievement in the relevant field.

ADDITIONAL INFORMATION Application forms and guidelines are available on the website. Accepts inquiries via telephone, fax, or e-mail. Submit application form with CV to be reviewed by the selection committee of board members at quarterly meetings.

HAIKU NORTH AMERICA CONFERENCE

1275 Fourth St. PMB #365, Santa Rosa CA 95404. **E-mail:** welchm@aol.com. **Website:** www.haikunorthamerica.com. **Contact:** Michael Dylan Welch. Biannual conference held August 14-18 on board the historic Queen Mary ocean liner, permanently docked in Long Beach, California. Haiku North America (HNA) is the largest and oldest gathering of haiku poets in the United States and Canada. There are no membership fees and HNA provides breaking news and interaction at the HNA blog. All haiku poets and interested parties are welcome. It is a long weekend of papers, panels, workshops, readings, performances, book sales, and much socialization with fellow poets, translators, scholars, editors, and publishers. Both established and aspiring haiku poets are welcome.

ACCOMMODATIONS Typically around $200, including a banquet and some additional meals. Accommodations at discounted hotels nearby are an additional cost. Information available on website as details are finalized closer to the conference date.

HIGHLAND RIDGE FILM FESTIVAL

150 W. Beau St., Suite 214, Washington PA 15301. (724)344-2857. **E-mail:** HRCDCevents@gmail.com. **Website:** washpaelmstreet.org/events. **Contact:** Kar-

en Fleet, coordinator. Estab. 2012. Highland Ridge is a non-profit organization. This is a fundraiser where all monies will be used for the community. "Small independent filmmakers, grade kids, and high school kids' from our area. Encouraging script writing. See website for details."

HIGHLAND SUMMER CONFERENCE

Box 7014, Radford University, Radford VA 24142-7014. (540)831-5366. **Fax:** (540)831-5951. **E-mail:** tburriss@radford.edu; rbderrick@radford.edu. **Website:** www.radford.edu/content/cehd/home/departments/appalachian-studies.html.. **Contact:** Dr. Theresa Burriss, Ruth Derrick. Estab. 1978. The Highland Summer Writers' Conference is a one-week lecture-seminar workshop combination conducted by well-known guest writers. It offers the opportunity to study and practice creative and expository writing within the context of regional culture. The course is graded on Pass/Fail basis for undergraduates and letter grades for graduate students. It may be taken twice for credit. The class runs Monday through Friday 9 a.m.-noon and 1:30-4:30 p.m., with extended hours on Wednesday, and readings and receptions by resident teachers on Tuesday and Thursday evening in McConnell Library 7:30-9:30 p.m. The evening readings are free and open to the public.

ACCOMMODATIONS "We do not have special rate arrangements with local hotels. We do offer accommodations on the Radford University campus in a recently refurbished residence hall."

ADDITIONAL INFORMATION Conference leaders typically critique work done during the one-week conference, and because of the one-week format, students will be asked to bring preliminary work when they arrive at the conference, as well as submit a portfolio following the conference. Brochures/guidelines are available in March by request.

HIGHLIGHTS FOUNDATION FOUNDERS WORKSHOPS

814 Court St., Honesdale PA 18431. (570)253-1122. **Fax:** (570)253-0179. **E-mail:** klbrown@highlightsfoundation.org. **E-mail:** jo.lloy@highlightsfoundation.org. **Website:** highlightsfoundation.org. **Contact:** Kent L. Brown, Jr.. Estab. 2000. Offers more than three dozen workshops per year. Conference duration: 3-7 days. Average attendance: limited to 10-14. Genre specific workshops and retreats on children's writing: fiction, nonfiction, poetry, promotions. "Our

goal is to improve, over time, the quality of literature for children by educating future generations of children's authors." Highlights Founders' home in Boyds Mills, PA.

COSTS Prices vary based on workshop. Check website for details.

ACCOMMODATIONS Coordinates pickup at local airport. Offers overnight accommodations. Participants stay in guest cabins on the wooded grounds surrounding Highlights Founders' home adjacent to the house/conference center.

ADDITIONAL INFORMATION Some workshops require pre-workshop assignment. Brochure available for SASE, by e-mail, on website, by phone, by fax. Accepts inquiries by phone, fax, e-mail, SASE. Editors attend conference. "Applications will be reviewed and accepted on a first-come, first-served basis, applicants must demonstrate specific experience in writing area of workshop they are applying for—writing samples are required for many of the workshops."

HIGHLIGHTS FOUNDATION WRITERS WORKSHOP AT CHAUTAUQUA

814 Court St., Honesdale PA 18431. (570)253-1192. **Fax:** (570)253-0179. **E-mail:** klbrown@highlightsfoundation.org. **E-mail:** jo.lloyd@highlightsfoundation.org. **Website:** highlightsfoundation.org. Estab. 1985. Average attendance: 100. Workshops are geared toward those who write for children at the beginner, intermediate, and advanced levels. Offers seminars, small group workshops, and one-on-one sessions with authors, editors, illustrators, critics, and publishers. Workshop site is the picturesque community of Chautauqua, New York. Speakers have included Bruce Coville, Candace Fleming, Linda Sue Park, Jane Yolen, Patricia Gauch, Jerry Spinelli, Eileen Spinelli, Joy Cowley and Pam Munoz Ryan.

ACCOMMODATIONS We coordinate ground transportation to and from airports, trains, and bus stations in the Erie, Pennsylvania and Jamestown/Buffalo, NY area. We also coordinate accommodations for conference attendees.

ADDITIONAL INFORMATION "We offer the opportunity for attendees to submit a ms for review at the conference. Workshop brochures/guidelines are available upon request."

HOFSTRA UNIVERSITY SUMMER WRITING WORKSHOPS

University College for Continuing Education, 250 Hofstra University, Hempstead NY 11549-2500. (516)463-7200. **Fax:** (516)463-4833. **E-mail:** ce@hofstra.edu. **Website:** hofstra.edu/academics/ce. **Contact:** Colleen Slattery, Senior Associate Dean. Estab. 1972. Hofstra University's 2-week Summer Writers Program, a cooperative endeavor of the Creative Writing Program, the English Department, and Hofstra University Continuing Education (Hofstra CE), offers 8 classes which may be taken on a noncredit or credit basis, for both graduate and undergraduate students. Led by master writers, the Summer Writing Program operates on the principle that true writing talent can be developed, nurtured and encouraged by writer-in-residence mentors. Through instruction, discussion, criticism and free exchange among the program members, writers begin to find their voice and their style. The program provides group and individual sessions for each writer. The Summer Writing Program includes a banquet, guest speakers, and exposure to authors such as Oscar Hijuelos, Robert Olen Butler (both Pulitzer Prize winners), Maurice Sendak, Cynthia Ozick, Nora Sayre, and Denise Levertov. Often agents, editors, and publishers make presentations during the conference, and authors and students read from published work and works in progress. These presentations and the conference banquet offer additional opportunities to meet informally with participants, master writers and guest speakers. Average attendance: 65. Conference offers workshops in short fiction, nonfiction, poetry, and occasionally other genres such as screenplay writing or writing for children. Site is the university campus on Long Island, 25 miles from New York City.

COSTS Check website for current fees. Credit is available for undergraduate and graduate students. Choose one of 9 writing genres and spend two intensive weeks studying and writing in that genre.

ACCOMMODATIONS Free bus operates between Hempstead Train Station and campus for those commuting from New York City on the Long Island Rail Road. Dormitory rooms are available.

ADDITIONAL INFORMATION Students entering grades 9-12 can now be part of the Summer Writers Program with a special section for high school students. Through exercises and readings, students will learn how to use their creative impulses to improve their fiction, poetry and plays and learn how to create cleaner and clearer essays. During this intensive 2-week course, students will experiment with memoir, poetry, oral history, dramatic form and the short story, and study how to use character, plot, point of view and language.

HOW TO BE PUBLISHED WORKSHOPS

P.O. Box 100031, Irondale AL 35210-3006. **E-mail:** mike@writing2sell.com. **Website:** www.writing2sell. com. **Contact:** Michael Garrett. Estab. 1986. Workshops are offered continuously year-round at various locations. Conference duration: 1 session. Average attendance: 10-15. Workshops to "move writers of category fiction closer to publication." Focus is not on how to write, but how to get published. Site: Workshops held at college campuses and universities. Themes include marketing, idea development, characterization, and ms critique. Special critique is offered, but advance submission is not required. Workshop information available on website. Accepts inquiries by e-mail.
COSTS $79-99.

INDIANA UNIVERSITY WRITERS' CONFERENCE

464 Ballantine Hall, 1020 E. Kirkwood Ave., Bloomington IN 47405-7103. (812)855-1877. **Fax:** (812)855-9535. **E-mail:** writecon@indiana.edu. **Website:** www.indiana.edu/~writecon. **Contact:** Bob Bledsoe, director. Estab. 1940. Annual. Conference/workshops held in May. Average attendance: 115. "The Indiana University Writers' Conference believes in a craft-based teaching of fiction writing. We emphasize an exploration of creativity through a variety of approaches, offering workshop-based craft discussions, classes focusing on technique, and talks about the careers and concerns of a writing life." 2013 faculty: Alix Lambert, Scott Hutchins, Nathaniel Perry, Lloyd Suh.
COSTS 2013: Workshop, $550/week; classes only, $300/week.
ACCOMMODATIONS Information on accommodations available on website.
ADDITIONAL INFORMATION Fiction workshop applicants must submit up to 25 pages of prose. Registration information available for SASE, by e-mail, or on website. Spaces still available in all workshops and classes for 2013.

INTERNATIONAL CREATIVE WRITING CAMP

111-11th Ave.SW, Minot ND 58701-6081. (701)838-8472. **Fax:** (701)838-1351. **E-mail:** info@internationalmusiccamp.com. **Website:** www.internationalmusiccamp.com. **Contact:** Joseph Alme, interim director. Writer and illustrator workshops geared toward beginner, intermediate and advanced levels. **Open to students.** Sessions offered include those covering poems, plays, mystery stories, essays. Workshop held June 23-29, 2013. Registration limited to 40. The summer camp location at the International Peace Garden on the Border between Manitoba and North Dakota is an ideal site for creative thinking. Excellent food, housing, and recreation facilities are available.
COSTS Before May 1, $375; after May 1—$390. Write for more information.

IOWA SUMMER WRITING FESTIVAL

The University of Iowa, C215 Seashore Hall, University of Iowa, Iowa City IA 52242. (319)335-4160. **Fax:** (319)335-4743. **E-mail:** iswfestival@uiowa.edu. **Website:** uiowa.edu/~iswfest. Estab. 1987. Annual festival held in June and July. Conference duration: Workshops are 1 week or a weekend. Average attendance: Limited to 12 people/class, with over 1,500 participants throughout the summer. "We offer courses across the genres: novel, short story, poetry, essay, memoir, humor, travel, playwriting, screenwriting, writing for children, and women's writing. Held at the University of Iowa campus." Speakers have included Marvin Bell, Lan Samantha Chang, John Dalton, Hope Edelman, Katie Ford, Patricia Foster, Bret Anthony Johnston, Barbara Robinette Moss, among others.
COSTS $590 for full week; $305 for weekend workshop. Housing and meals are separate.
ACCOMMODATIONS Accommodations available at area hotels. Information on overnight accommodations available by phone or on website.
ADDITIONAL INFORMATION Brochures are available in February. Inquire via e-mail or on website.

JACKSON HOLE WRITERS CONFERENCE

PO Box 1974, Jackson WY 83001. (307)413-3332. **E-mail:** nicole@jacksonholewritersconference.com. **Website:** jacksonholewritersconference.com. Estab. 1991. Annual conference held June 27-29. Conference duration: 4 days. Average attendance: 110. Covers fiction, creative nonfiction, and young adult and offers ms critiques from authors, agents, and editors. Agents in attendance will take pitches from writers. Paid manuscript critique programs are available.

COSTS $365 if registered by May 12. Accompanying teen writer: $175. Pre-Conference Writing Workshop: $150.

ADDITIONAL INFORMATION Held at the Center for the Arts in Jackson, Wyoming and online.

KENYON REVIEW WRITERS WORKSHOP

Kenyon College, Gambier OH 43022. (740)427-5207. **Fax:** (740)427-5417. **E-mail:** kenyonreview@kenyon.edu; writers@kenyonreview.org. **Website:** www.kenyonreview.org. **Contact:** Anna Duke Reach, director. Estab. 1990. Annual 8-day workshop held in June. Participants apply in poetry, fiction, or creative nonfiction, and then participate in intensive daily workshops which focus on the generation and revision of significant new work. Held on the campus of Kenyon College in the rural village of Gambier, Ohio. Workshop leaders have included David Baker, Ron Carlson, Rebecca McClanahan, Meghan O'Rourke, Linda Gregorson, Dinty Moore, Tara Ison, Jane Hamilton, Lee K. Abbott, and Nancy Zafris.

COSTS $1,995; includes tuition, room and board.

ACCOMMODATIONS The workshop operates a shuttle to and from Gambier and the airport in Columbus, Ohio. Offers overnight accommodations. Participants are housed in Kenyon College student housing. The cost is covered in the tuition.

ADDITIONAL INFORMATION Application includes a writing sample. Admission decisions are made on a rolling basis. Workshop information is available online at www.kenyonreview.org/workshops in November. For brochure send e-mail, visit website, call, fax. Accepts inquiries by SASE, e-mail, phone, fax.

KEY WEST LITERARY SEMINAR

718 Love Lane, Key West FL 33040. (888)293-9291. **E-mail:** mail@kwls.org. **Website:** www.kwls.org. "The mission of KWLS is to promote the understanding and discussion of important literary works and their authors; to recognize and support new voices in American literature; and to preserve and promote Key West's literary heritage while providing resources that strengthen literary culture." The annual seminar and writers' workshop program are held in January. Scholarships are available to teachers, librarians, and students. Awards are given to emerging writers. See website for details.

COSTS $545/seminar; $450/writers' workshops.

ACCOMMODATIONS A list of nearby lodging establishments is made available.

KILLER NASHVILLE

P.O. Box 680759, Franklin TN 37068-0686. (615)599-4032. **E-mail:** contact@killernashville.com. **Website:** www.killernashville.com. Jaden Terrell, Exec. Dir. **Contact:** Clay Stafford. Estab. 2006. Annual. Next events: Aug. 22-25. Conference duration: 3 days. Average attendance: 200+. Conference designed for writers and fans of mysteries and thrillers, including fiction and nonfiction authors, playwrights, and screenwriters. There are many opportunities for authors to sign books. Killer Nashville's 2013 writers conference will have over 60 sessions, 2 guests of honor, agent / editor / publisher roundtables, 7 distinct session tracks (general writing, genre specific writing, publishing, publicity & promotion, forensics, screenwriting, sessions for fans), 12 breakout sessions for intense study, special sessions, manuscript critiques (fiction, nonfiction, short story, screenplay, marketing, query), realistic mock crime scene for you to solve, networking with bestselling authors, agents, editors, publishers, attorneys, publicists, representatives from law and emergency services, mystery bingo, authors' bar, wine tasting event, two cocktail receptions, guest of honor dinner and awards program, prizes, free giveaways, free book signings, and more.

COSTS Early Bird Registration: $160 (February 16); Advanced Registration: $170 (May 1); $180 for three day full registration.

ACCOMMODATIONS The Hutton Hotel has all roomas available for the Killer Nashville Conference.

ADDITIONAL INFORMATION Additional information about registration is provided online.

KUNDIMAN POETRY RETREAT

P.O. Box 4248, Sunnyside NY 11104. **E-mail:** info@kundiman.org. **Website:** www.kundiman.org. **Contact:** June W. Choi, executive director. Held annualy June 19-23 at Fordham University's Rose Hill campus. "Opento Asian American poets. Renowned faculty will conduct workshops and provide one-on-one mentorship sessions with fellows. Readings and informal social gatherings will also be scheduled. Fellows selected based on sample of 6-8 poems and short essay answer.

Applications should be received between December 15-February 1."

COSTS $350.

ACCOMMODATIONS Room and board is free to accepted Fellows.

ADDITIONAL INFORMATION Additional information, guidelines, and online application available on website.

LA JOLLA WRITERS CONFERENCE

P.O. Box 178122, San Diego CA 92177. (858)467-1978. **E-mail:** akuritz@san.rr.com. **Website:** www.lajollawritersconference.com. **Contact:** Jared Kuritz, director. Estab. 2001. Annual conference held in October/November. Conference duration: 3 days. Average attendance: 200. "In addition to covering nearly every genre, we also take particular pride in educating our attendees on the business aspect of the book industry by having agents, editors, publishers, publicists, and distributors teach classes. Our conference offers 2 types of classes: lecture sessions that run for 50 minutes, and workshops that run for 110 minutes. Each block period is dedicated to either workshop or lecture-style classes. During each block period, there will be 6-8 classes on various topics from which you can choose to attend. For most workshop classes, you are encouraged to bring written work for review. Literary agents from prestigious agencies such as The Andrea Brown Literary Agency, The Dijkstra Agency, The McBride Agency and Full Circle Literary Group have participated in the past. The conference creates a strong sense of community, and it has seen many of its attendees successfully published."

COSTS Information available online.

LAS VEGAS WRITERS CONFERENCE

Henderson Writers' Group, 614 Mosswood Dr., Henderson NV 89015. (702)564-2488; or, toll-free, (866)869-7842. **E-mail:** marga614@mysticpublishers.com. **Website:** www.lasvegaswritersconference.com. Annual. Held in April. Conference duration: 3 days. Average attendance: 150 maximum. "Join writing professionals, agents, industry experts, and your colleagues for 3 days in Las Vegas as they share their knowledge on all aspects of the writer's craft. While there are formal pitch sessions, panels, workshops, and seminars, the faculty is also available throughout the conference for informal discussions and advice. Plus, you're bound to meet a few new friends, too. Workshops, seminars, and expert panels will take

you through writing in many genres including fiction, creative nonfiction, screenwriting, journalism, and business and technical writing. There will be many Q&A panels for you to ask the experts all your questions." Site: Sam's Town Hotel and Gambling Hall in Las Vegas.

COSTS $400 before December 31, $450 until conference, and $500 at the door. One day registration is $275.

ADDITIONAL INFORMATION Sponsors contest. Agents and editors participate in conference.

LEAGUE OF UTAH WRITERS' ANNUAL WRITER'S CONFERENCE

Dianne Hardy, League of Utah Writers, 420 W. 750 N., Logan UT 84321. **E-mail:** writerscache435@gmail.com. **Website:** www.luwriters.org/index.html. **Contact:** Tim Keller, president; Irene Hastings, president-elect; Caroll Shreeve, secretary. The League of Utah Writers is a non-profit organization dedicated to offering friendship, education, and encouragement to the writers of Utah. New members are always welcome. Writer workshops geared toward beginner, intermediate or advanced. Annual conference.

LOVE IS MURDER

E-mail: hanleyliz@wideopenwest.com. **Website:** loveismurder.net. Annual conference held in February for readers, writers, and fans of mystery, suspense, thriller, romantic suspense, dark fiction, and true crime. Features bestselling headliners, plus ms critiques; editors/agents participate in pitch sessions. Attorneys, criminal justice experts, forensic scientists, physicians, private investigators, computer forensic experts, weapons experts, and more give demos.

COSTS Full conference including panels, discussions, entertainment and all meals: $369.

ACCOMMODATIONS Held at InterContinental Chicago O'Hare. You can register for a room through the website.

ADDITIONAL INFORMATION Banquet and Lovey Awards for best first novel, historical novel, series, crime-related nonfiction, private investigator/police procedural, paranormal/science fiction/horror, traditional/amateur sleuth, suspense thriller, romance/fantasy, and short story.

THE MACDOWELL COLONY

100 High St., Peterborough NH 03458. (603)924-3886. **Fax:** (603)924-9142. **E-mail:** admissions@macdowellcolony.org. **Website:** www.macdowellcolony.org.

Estab. 1907. Open to writers, playwrights, composers, visual artists, film/video artists, interdisciplinary artists and architects. Applicants submit information and work samples for review by a panel of experts in each discipline. Application form submitted online at www.macdowellcolony.org/apply.html.

COSTS Travel reimbursement and stipends are available for participants of the residency, based on need. There are no residency fees.

MAGNA CUM MURDER

Magna Cum Murder Crime Writing Festival, The E.B. and Bertha C. Ball Center, Ball State University, Muncie IN 47306. (765)285-8975. **Fax:** (765)747-9566. **E-mail:** magnacummurder@yahoo.com; kennisonk@aol.com. **Website:** www.magnacummurder.com. Estab. 1994. Annual conference held in October. Average attendance: 300. Festival for readers and writers of crime writing. Held in The Columbia Club, Indianapolis, IN. Usually 30-40 mystery writers are in attendance and there are presentations from agents, editors and professional writers. The website has the full list of attending speakers.

COSTS Check website for updates.

MENDOCINO COAST WRITERS CONFERENCE

1211 Del Mar Dr., Fort Bragg CA 95437. (707)937-9983. **E-mail:** info@mcwc.org. **Website:** www.mcwc.org. Estab. 1988. Annual conference held in July. Average attendance: 80. Provides workshops for fiction, nonfiction, and poetry. Held at a small community college campus on the northern Pacific Coast. Workshop leaders have included Kim Addonizio, Lynne Barrett, John Dufresne, John Lescroart, Ben Percy, Luis Rodriguez, and Ellen Sussman. Agents and publishers will be speaking and available for meetings with attendees.

COSTS $525+ (includes panels, meals, 2 socials with guest readers, 4 public events, 3 morning intensive workshops in 1 of 6 subjects, and a variety of afternoon panels and lectures).

ACCOMMODATIONS Information on overnight accommodations is made available.

ADDITIONAL INFORMATION Emphasis is on writers who are also good teachers. Registration opens March 15. Send inquiries via e-mail.

MIDWEST WRITERS WORKSHOP

Ball State University, Department of Journalism, Muncie IN 47306. (765)282-1055. **E-mail:** midwest-writers@yahoo.com. **Website:** www.midwestwriters.org. **Contact:** Jama Kehoe Bigger, director. Annual workshop held in late July. Writer workshops geared toward intermediate level. Topics include most genres. Faculty/speakers have included Joyce Carol Oates, George Plimpton, Clive Cussler, Haven Kimmel, James Alexander Thom, Wiliam Zinsser, Phillip Gulley, and children's writers Rebecca Kai Dotlich, April Pulley Sayre, Peter Welling, Claire Ewert, and Michelle Medlock Adams. Workshop also includes agent pitch sessions ms evaluation and a writing contest. Registration tentatively limited to 125.

COSTS $135-360. Most meals included.

ADDITIONAL INFORMATION Offers scholarships. See website for more information.

MONTEVALLO LITERARY FESTIVAL

Sta. 6420, University of Montevallo, Montevallo AL 35115. (205)665-6420. **Fax:** (205)665-6422. **E-mail:** murphyj@montevallo.edu. **Website:** www.montevallo.edu/english. **Contact:** Dr. Jim Murphy, director. Estab. 2003. Takes place annually, April 12.

COSTS Readings are free. Readings, plus lunch, reception, and dinner is $20. Master Class only is $30. Master Class with everything else is $50.

ACCOMMODATIONS Offers overnight accommodations at Ramsay Conference Center on campus. Call (205)665-6280 for reservations. Free on-campus parking. Additional information available at www.montevallo.edu/cont_ed/ramsay.shtm.

ADDITIONAL INFORMATION To enroll in a fiction workshop, contact Bryn Chancellor (bchancellor@montevallo.edu). Information for upcoming festival available in February For brochure, visit website. Accepts inquiries by mail (with SASE), e-mail, phone, and fax. Editors participate in conference. "This is a friendly, relaxed festival dedicated to bringing literary writers and readers together on a personal scale." Poetry workshop participants submit up to 5 pages of poetry; e-mail as Word doc to Jim Murphy (murphyj@montevallo.edu) at least 2 weeks prior to festival.

MONTROSE CHRISTIAN WRITERS' CONFERENCE

218 Locust St., Montrose PA 18801. (570)278-1001 or (800)598-5030. **Fax:** (570)278-3061. **E-mail:** info@montrosebible.org. **Website:** montrosebible.org. Estab. 1990. "Annual conference held in July. Offers workshops, editorial appointments, and professional critiques. We try to meet a cross-section of writing

needs, for beginners and advanced, covering fiction, poetry, and writing for children. It is small enough to allow personal interaction between attendees and faculty. Speakers have included William Petersen, Mona Hodgson, Jim Fletcher, and Terri Gibbs." Held in Montrose, from July 21-24.

COSTS Tuition is $175.

ACCOMMODATIONS Will meet planes in Binghamton, NY and Scranton, PA. On-site accomodations: room and board $305-350/conference; $60-70/day including food (2009 rates). RV court available.

ADDITIONAL INFORMATION "Writers can send work ahead of time and have it critiqued for a small fee." The attendees are usually church related. The writing has a Christian emphasis. Conference information available in April. For brochure send SASE, visit website, e-mail, call or fax. Accepts inquiries by SASE, e-mail, fax, phone.

JENNY MCKEAN MOORE COMMUNITY WORKSHOPS

English Department, George Washingtion University, 801 22nd St. NW, Rome Hall, Suite 760, Washington DC 20052. (202) 994-6180. **Fax:** (202) 994-7915. **E-mail:** tvmallon@gwu.edu. **Website:** www.gwu.edu/~english/creative_jennymckeanmoore.html. **Contact:** Thomas Mallon, director of creative writing. Estab. 1976. Workshop held each semester at the university. Average attendance: 15. Concentration varies depending on professor—usually fiction or poetry. The Creative Writing department brings an established poet or novelist to campus each year to teach a writing workshop for GW students and a free community workshop for adults in the larger Washington community. Details posted on website in June, with an application deadline at the end of August or in early September.

ADDITIONAL INFORMATION Admission is competitive and by ms.

MOUNT HERMON CHRISTIAN WRITERS CONFERENCE

PO Box 413, Mount Hermon CA 95041. **E-mail:** info@mounthermon.org. **Website:** mounthermon.org. Estab. 1970. Annual professional conference (always held over the Palm Sunday weekend, Friday noon through Tuesday noon). Average attendance: 450. Sponsored by and held at the 440-acre Mount Hermon Christian Conference Center near San Jose, California in the heart of the coastal redwoods, we are a broad-ranging conference for all areas of Christian writing, including fiction, nonfiction, fantasy, children's, teen, young adult, poetry, magazines, inspirational and devotional writing. This is a working, how-to conference, with Major Morning tracks in all genres (including a track especially for teen writers), and as many as 20 optional workshops each afternoon. Faculty-to-student ratio is about 1 to 6. The bulk of our more than 70 faculty members are editors and publisher representatives from major Christian publishing houses nationwide. Speakers have included T. Davis Bunn, Debbie Macomber, Jerry Jenkins, Bill Butterworth, Dick Foth and others.

COSTS Registration fees include tuition, all major morning sessions, keynote sessions, and refreshment breaks. Room and board varies depending on choice of housing options. Costs vary from $617 to $1565 based on housing rates.

ACCOMMODATIONS Registrants stay in hotel-style accommodations. Meals are buffet style, with faculty joining registrants. See website for cost updates.

ADDITIONAL INFORMATION "The residential nature of our conference makes this a unique setting for one-on-one interaction with faculty/staff. There is also a decided inspirational flavor to the conference, and general sessions with well-known speakers are a highlight. Registrants may submit 2 works for critique in advance of the conference, then have personal interviews with critiquers during the conference. All conference information is online by December 1 of each year. Send inquiries via e-mail. Tapes of past conferences are also available online."

NAPA VALLEY WRITERS' CONFERENCE

Napa Valley College, 1088 College Ave., St. Helena CA 94574. (707)967-2900. **Website:** www.napawritersconference.org. **Contact:** John Leggett and Anne Evans, program directors. Estab. 1981. Established 1981. Annual weeklong event, July 28-August 2. Location: Upper Valley Campus in the historic town of St. Helena, 25 miles north of Napa in the heart of the valley's wine growing community. Excellent cuisine provided by Napa Valley Cooking School. Average attendance: 48 in poetry and 48 in fiction. "Serious writers of all backgrounds and experience are welcome to apply." Offers poets workshops, lectures, faculty readings, ms critiques, and meetings with editors. "Poetry session provides the opportunity to work both on generating new poems and on revising previously written ones."

COSTS Total participation fee is $900.

ADDITIONAL INFORMATION The conference is held at the Upper Valley Campus of Napa Valley College, located in the heart of California's Wine Country. During the conference week, attendees' meals are provided by the Napa Valley Cooking School, which offers high quality, intensive training for aspiring chefs. The goal of the program is to provide each student with hands-on, quality, culinary and pastry skills required for a career in a fine-dining establishment. The disciplined and professional learning environment, availability of global externships, low student teacher ratio and focus on sustainability make the Napa Valley Cooking School unique.

NATCHEZ LITERARY AND CINEMA CELEBRATION

P.O. Box 1307, Natchez MS 39121-1307. (601)446-1208. **Fax:** (601)446-1214. **E-mail:** carolyn.smith@colin.edu. **Website:** www.colin.edu/nlcc. Estab. 1990. Annual conference held in February. Conference duration: 5 days. Conference focuses on all literature, including film scripts. Each year's conference deals with some general aspect of Southern history. Speakers have included Eudora Welty, Margaret Walker Alexander, William Styron, Willie Morris, Ellen Douglas, Ernest Gaines, Elizabeth Spencer, Nikki Giovanni, Myrlie Evers-Williams, and Maya Angelou.

NATIONAL WRITERS ASSOCIATION FOUNDATION CONFERENCE

10940 S. Parker Rd., #508, Parker CO 80138. (303)841-0246. **E-mail:** natlwritersassn@hotmail.com. **Website:** www.nationalwriters.com. **Contact:** Sandy Whelchel, executive director. Estab. 1926. Annual conference held the second week of June in Denver. Conference duration: 1 day. Average attendance: 100. Focuses on general writing and marketing.

COSTS Approximately $100.

ADDITIONAL INFORMATION Awards for previous contests will be presented at the conference. Brochures/guidelines are online, or send an SASE.

THE NEW LETTERS WEEKEND WRITERS CONFERENCE

University of Missouri-Kansas City, 5101 Rockhill Rd., Kansas City MO 64110-2499. (816)235-1168. **Fax:** (816)235-2611. **E-mail:** newletters@umkc.edu. **Website:** http://cas.umkc.edu/ce/. **Contact:** Robert Stewart, director. Estab. 1970s (as The Longboat Key Writers Conference). Annual conference held in late June.

Conference duration: 3 days. Average attendance: 75. The conference brings together talented writers in many genres for seminars, readings, workshops, and individual conferences. The emphasis is on craft and the creative process in poetry, fiction, screenwriting, playwriting, and journalism, but the program also deals with matters of psychology, publications, and marketing. The conference is appropriate for both advanced and beginning writers. The conference meets at the university's beautiful Diastole Conference Center. Two- and 3-credit hour options are available by special permission from the director, Robert Stewart.

COSTS Participants may choose to attend as a noncredit student or they may attend for 1 hour of college credit from the University of Missouri-Kansas City. Conference registration includes Friday evening reception and keynote speaker, Saturday and Sunday continental breakfast and lunch.

ACCOMMODATIONS Registrants are responsible for their own transportation, but information on area accommodations is available.

ADDITIONAL INFORMATION Those registering for college credit are required to submit a ms in advance. Ms reading and critique are included in the credit fee. Those attending the conference for noncredit also have the option of having their ms critiqued for an additional fee. Brochures are available for a SASE after March. Accepts inquiries by e-mail and fax.

NIMROD ANNUAL WRITERS' WORKSHOP

800 S. Tucker Dr., Tulsa OK 74104. (918)631-3080. **E-mail:** nimrod@utulsa.edu. **Website:** www.utulsa.edu/nimrod. **Contact:** Eilis O'Neal, managing editor. Estab. 1978. Annual conference held in October. Conference duration: 1 day. Offers one-on-one editing sessions, readings, panel discussions, and master classes in fiction, poetry, nonfiction, memoir, and fantasy writing. Speakers have included Myla Goldberg, B.H. Fairchild, Colum McCann, Molly Peacock, Peter S. Beagle, Robert Olen Butler, and Marvin Bell. Full conference details are online in August.

COSTS Approximately $50. Lunch provided. Scholarships available for students.

ADDITIONAL INFORMATION *Nimrod International Journal* sponsors *Nimrod* Literary Awards: The Katherine Anne Porter Prize for fiction and The Pablo Neruda Prize for poetry. Poetry and fiction prizes: $2,000 each and publication (1st prize); $1,000 each and publication (2nd prize). Deadline: must be post-marked no later than April 30.

NORTH CAROLINA WRITERS' NETWORK FALL CONFERENCE

P.O. Box 21591, Winston-Salem NC 27120. (336)293-8844. **E-mail:** mail@ncwriters.org. **Website:** www.ncwriters.org. Estab. 1985. Annual conference held in November in different NC venues. Average attendance: 250. This organization hosts 2 conferences: 1 in the spring and 1 in the fall. Each conference is a weekend full of workshops, panels, book signings, and readings (including open mic). There will be a keynote speaker, a variety of sessions on the craft and business of writing, and opportunities to meet with agents and editors.

COSTS Approximately $250 (includes 4 meals).

ACCOMMODATIONS Special rates are usually available at the Conference Hotel, but conferees must make their own reservations.

ADDITIONAL INFORMATION Available at www.ncwriters.org.

NORWESCON

100 Andover Park W. PMB 150-165, Tukwila WA 98188-2828. (425)243-4692. **Fax:** (520)244-0142. **E-mail:** info@norwescon.org. **Website:** www.nor-wescon.org. Estab. 1978. Annual conference held on Easter weekend. Average attendance: 2,800. General multi-track convention focusing on science fiction and fantasy literature with wide coverage of other media. Tracks cover science, socio-cultural, literary, publishing, editing, writing, art, and other media of a science fiction/fantasy orientation. Agents will be speaking and available for meetings with attendees.

ACCOMMODATIONS Conference is held at the Doubletree Hotel Seattle Airport.

ADDITIONAL INFORMATION Brochures are available online or for a SASE. Send inquiries via e-mail.

ODYSSEY FANTASY WRITING WORKSHOP

P.O. Box 75, Mont Vernon NH 03057. **E-mail:** jcavelos@sff.net. **Website:** www.odysseyworkshop.org. Saint Anselm College 100 Saint Anselm Drive, Manchester, New Hampshire, 03102. Estab. 1996. Annual workshop held in June (through July). Conference duration: 6 weeks. Average attendance: 16. A workshop for fantasy, science fiction, and horror writers that combines an intensive learning and writing experience with in-depth feedback on students' mss. Held on the campus of Saint Anselm College in Manchester, New Hampshire. Speakers have included George R.R. Martin, Elizabeth Hand, Jane Yolen, Harlan Ellison, Melissa Scott and Dan Simmons.

COSTS In 2012: $1,900 tuition, $790 housing (double room), $1,580 (single room); $35 application fee, $400-600 food (approximate), $550 processing fee to receive college credit.

ADDITIONAL INFORMATION Students must apply and include a writing sample. Application deadline April 8. Students' works are critiqued throughout the 6 weeks. Workshop information available in October. For brochure/guidelines, send SASE, e-mail, visit website, or call. Accepts inquiries by SASE, e-mail, phone.

OKLAHOMA WRITERS' FEDERATION, INC. ANNUAL CONFERENCE

3800 Bonaire Place, Edmond OK 73013. **Website:** www.owfi.org. **Contact:** Linda Apple, president. Annual conference. Held first weekend in May each year. Writer workshops geared toward all levels. **Open to students.** "Forty seminars, with 30 speakers consisting of editors, literary agents and many best-selling authors. Topics range widely to include craft, marketing, and all genres of writing." Writing facilities available: book room, autograph party, 2 lunch workshops. "If writers would like to participate in the annual writing contest, they must become members of OWFI. You don't have to be a member to attend the conference." See website for more information.

COSTS $150 before March 15; $175 after March 15; $70 for single days; $25 for lunch workshops. Full tuition includes 2-day conference (all events except lunch workshops) and 2 dinners, plus 110-minute appointment with an attending editor or agent of your choice (must be reserved in advance).

OZARK CREATIVE WRITERS, INC. CONFERENCE

P.O. Box 424, Eureka Springs AR 72632. **E-mail:** ozarkcreativewriters@gmail.com. **Website:** www.ozarkcreativewriters.org. Open to professional and amateur writers, workshops are geared to all levels and all forms of the creative process and literary arts. Sessions sometimes include songwriting, with presentations by best-selling authors, editors, and agents. The OCW Conference promotes writing by offering competition in all genres. The annual event is held on the second full weekend in October at the Inn of the Ozarks, in the resort town of Eureka Springs, Arkansas. Approximately 200 attend each year; many also enter the creative writing competitions.

PACIFIC COAST CHILDREN'S WRITERS WHOLE-NOVEL WORKSHOP

P.O. Box 244, Aptos CA 95001. **Website:** www.childrenswritersworkshop.com. Estab. 2003. "Our seminar ofers semi-advanced through published adult writers an editor and/or agent critique on their full novel or 15-30 page partial. A concurrent workshop is open to students age 14 and up, who give adults target-reader feedback. Focus on craft as a marketing tool. Team-taught master classes (open clinics for manuscript critiques) explore such topics as "Story Architecture and Arcs." Continuous close contact with faculty, who have included Andrea Brown, agent, and Simon Boughton, currently VP/executive editor at 3 Macmillan imprints. **Past seminars**: October 7-9, 2011 and October 5-7, 2012. Registration limited to 12 adults and 6 teens. For the most critique options, submit sample chapters and synopsis with e-application by mid May; open until filled. **Content:** Character-driven novels with protagonists ages 11 and older. Collegial format; 90 percent hands-on. Our faculty critiques early as well as optional later chapters, plus synopses. Our pre-workshop anthology of peer manuscripts maximizes learning and networking. Several enrollees have landed contracts as a direct result of our seminar. **Details:** visit our website and e-mail us via the contact form."

WILLIAM PATERSON UNIVERSITY SPRING WRITER'S CONFERENCE

English Department, Atrium 232, 300 Pompton Rd., Wayne NJ 07470. (973)720-3067. **Fax:** (973)720-2189. **E-mail:** liut@wpunj.edu. **Website:** wpunj.edu/cohss/departments/english/writers-conference/. Annual conference held each spring (April 13). Conference duration: 1 day. Average attendance: 100-125. Small writing workshops and panels address topics such as writing from life, getting your work in print, poetry, playwriting, fiction, creative nonfiction, and book and magazine editing. Sessions are led by William Paterson faculty members and distinguished guest writers and editors of verse and prose. Speakers have included Francine Prose, David Means, Alison Lurie, Russell Banks, Terese Svoboda, and Anthony Swofford.

COSTS $55 (includes lunch).

PHILADELPHIA WRITERS' CONFERENCE

P.O. Box 7171, Elkins Park PA 19027-0171. (215) 619-7422. **E-mail:** dresente@mc3.edu. **E-mail:** info@pwcwriters.org. **Website:** www.pwcwriters.org. **Contact:** Dana Resente. Estab. 1949. Annual. Conference held June 7-9. Average attendance: 160-200. Conference covers many forms of writing: novel, short story, genre fiction, nonfiction book, magazine writing, blogging, juvenile, poetry.

COSTS Advance registration is $205; walk-in registration is $225. The banquet and buffet are $40 each. Master classes are $50.

ACCOMMODATIONS Holiday Inn, Independence Mall, Fourth and Arch Streets, Philadelphia, PA 19106-2170. "Hotel offers discount for early registration."

ADDITIONAL INFORMATION Sponsors contest. "Length is generally 2,500 words for fiction or nonfiction. 1st Prize, in addition to cash and certificate, gets free tuition for following year." Also offers ms critique. Accepts inquiries by e-mail and SASE. Agents and editors attend conference. Visit us on the web for further agent and speaker details."

PHOTOGRAPHERS' FORMULARY

P.O. Box 950, 7079 Hwy 83 N, Condon MT 59826-0950. (800)922-5255. **Fax:** (406)754-2896. **E-mail:** lynnw@blackfoot.net; formulary@blackfoot.net. **Website:** www.photoformulary.com; www.workshopsinmt.com. **Contact:** Lynn Wilson, workshop program director. Photographers' Formulary workshops include a wide variety of alternative processes, and many focus on the traditional darkroom. Located in Montana's Swan Valley, some of the best wilderness lands in the Rocky Mountains. See website for details on costs and lodging. Open to all skill levels. Workshops held frequently throughout the year. See website for listing of dates and registration.

PIMA WRITERS' WORKSHOP

Pima College, 2202 W. Anklam Rd., Tucson AZ 85709. (520)206-6084. **Fax:** (520)206-6020. **E-mail:** mfiles@pima.edu. **Contact:** Meg Files, director. Writer conference geared toward beginner, intermediate and advanced levels. **Open to students.** The conference features presentations and writing exercises on writing and publishing stories for children and young adults, among other genres. Annual conference. Workshop held in May. Cost: $100 (can include ms critique). Participants may attend for college credit. Meals and accommodations not included. Features a dozen authors, editors, and agents talking about writing and publishing fiction, nonfiction, poetry, and stories for children. Write for more information.

POETRY WEEKEND INTENSIVES

40 Post Ave., Hawthorne NJ 07506. (973)423-2921. **Fax:** (973)523-6085. **E-mail:** mariagillan@verizon. net. **Website:** www.mariagillan.com; www.mariagillan.blogspot.com. **Contact:** Maria Mazziotti Gillan, executive director. Estab. 1997. Usually held 2 times/year in June and December. Average attendance: 26.
COSTS $425, including meals. Offers a $25 early bird discount. Housing in on-site facilities included in the $425 price.
ACCOMMODATIONS Location: generally at St. Marguerite's Retreat House, Mendham, NJ; also several other convents and monasteries.
ADDITIONAL INFORMATION Individual poetry critiques available. Poets should bring poems to weekend. Registration form available for SASE or by fax or e-mail. Maria Mazziotti Gillan is the director of the Creative Writing Program of Binghamton University-State University of New York, exec. director of the Poetry Center at Passaic County Community College, and edits Paterson Literary Review. Laura Boss is the editor of *Lips* magazine. Fifteen professional development credits are available for each weekend.

ROCKY MOUNTAIN FICTION WRITERS COLORADO GOLD

Rocky Mountain Fiction Writers, P.O. Box 735, Confier CO 80433. **E-mail:** conference@rmfw.org. **Website:** www.rmfw.org. Estab. 1982. Annual conference held in September. Conference duration: 3 days. Average attendance: 350. Themes include general novel-length fiction, genre fiction, contemporary romance, mystery, science fiction/fantasy, mainstream, young adult, and historical fiction. Speakers have included Jodi Thomas, Bernard Cornwell, Terry Brooks, Dorothy Cannell, PatriciaGardner Evans, Diane Mott Davidson, Constance O'Day, Connie Willis, Clarissa Pinkola Estes, Michael Palmer, Jennifer Unter, Margaret Marr, Ashley Krass, and Andren Barzvi. Approximately 8 editors and 5 agents attend annually.
COSTS Available online.
ACCOMMODATIONS Special rates will be available at conference hotel.
ADDITIONAL INFORMATION Editor-conducted workshops are limited to 8 participants for critique,

with auditing available. Pitch appointments available at no charge. Friday morning master classes available. New for 2013: Writers' retreat available immediately following conference; space is limited.

RT BOOKLOVERS CONVENTION

55 Bergen St., Brooklyn NY 11201. (718)237-1097 or (800)989-8816, ext. 12. **Fax:** (718)624-2526. **E-mail:** jocarol@rtconvention.com. **E-mail:** nancy@rt-bookreviews.com. **Website:** rtconvention.com. Annual conference held May 1-5. 2013 Convention will be in Kansas City at the Sheraton Kansas City Hotel at Crown Center. Features 125 workshops, agent and editor appointments, a book fair, and more.
COSTS See website for pricing and other information.
ACCOMMODATIONS Rooms available at a nearby Sheaton and Westin. Check online to reserve a room.

SAGE HILL WRITING EXPERIENCE

Box 1731, Saskatoon SK S7K 3S1 Canada. (306)652-7395. **E-mail:** sage.hill@sasktel.net. **Website:** sagehillwriting.ca. **Contact:** Philip Adams, Executive Director. Annual workshops held in late July/August and May. Conference duration: 10-14 days. Average attendance: 40/summer program; 8/spring program. Sage Hill Writing Experience offers a special working and learning opportunity to writers at different stages of development. Top-quality instruction, low instructor-student ratio, and the beautiful Sage Hill setting offer conditions ideal for the pursuit of excellence in the arts of fiction, poetry and playwriting. The Sage Hill location features individual accommodations, in-room writing areas, lounges, meeting rooms, healthy meals, walking woods, and vistas in several directions. Classes being held (may vary from year to year) include: Introduction to Writing Fiction & Poetry, Fiction Workshop, Writing Young Adult Fiction Workshop, Poetry Workshop, Poetry Colloquium, Fiction Colloquium, Novel Colloquium, Playwriting Lab, Fall Poetry Colloquium, and Spring Poetry Colloquium. Speakers have included Nicole Brossard, Steven Galloway, Robert Currie, Jeanette Lynes, Karen Solie and Colleen Murphy.
COSTS Summer program: $1,295 (includes instruction, accommodation, meals). Fall Poetry Colloquium: $1,495. Scholarships and bursaries are available.
ACCOMMODATIONS Located at Lumsden, 45 kilometers outside Regina.
ADDITIONAL INFORMATION For Introduction to Creative Writing, send a 5-page sample of your writ-

ing or a statement of your interest in creative writing and a list of courses taken. For workshop and colloquium programs, send a résumé of your writing career and a 12-page sample of your work, plus 5 pages of published work. Guidelines are available for SASE. Inquire via e-mail or fax.

SAN DIEGO STATE UNIVERSITY WRITERS' CONFERENCE

SDSU College of Extended Studies, 5250 Campanile Dr., San Diego State University, San Diego CA 92182-1920. (619)594-2517. **Fax:** (619)594-8566. **E-mail:** sdsuwritersconference@mail.sdsu.edu. **Website:** ces.sdsu.edu/writers. Estab. 1984. Annual conference held in January/February. Conference duration: 2 days. Average attendance: 375. Covers fiction, nonfiction, scriptwriting and e-books. Held at the Doubletree Hotel in Mission Valley. Each year the conference offers a variety of workshops for the beginner and advanced writers. This conference allows the individual writer to choose which workshop best suits his/her needs. In addition to the workshops, editor reading appointments and agent/editor consultation appointments are provided so attendees may meet with editors and agents one-on-one to discuss specific questions. A reception is offered Saturday immediately following the workshops, offering attendees the opportunity to socialize with the faculty in a relaxed atmosphere. Last year, approximately 60 faculty members attended.

COSTS Approximately $365-485

ACCOMMODATIONS Attendees must make their own travel arrangements.

SAN FRANCISCO WRITERS CONFERENCE

1029 Jones St., San Francisco CA 94109. (415)673-0939. **Fax:** (415)673-0367. **E-mail:** Barabara@sfwriters.org. **Website:** sfwriters.org. **Contact:** Barbara Santos, marketing director. Estab. 2003. "Annual conference held President's Day weekend in February. Average attendance: 400+. Top authors, respected literary agents, and major publishing houses are at the event so attendees can make face-to-face contact with all the right people. Writers of nonfiction, fiction, poetry, and specialty writing (children's books, cookbooks, travel, etc.) will all benefit from the event. There are important sessions on marketing, self-publishing, technology, and trends in the publishing industry. Plus, there's an optional 4-hour session called Speed Dating for Agents where attendees can meet with 20+

agents. Speakers have included Jennifer Crusie, Richard Paul Evans, Jamie Raab, Mary Roach, Jane Smiley, Debbie Macomber, Firoozeh Dumas, Zilpha Keatley Snyder, Steve Berry, Jacquelyn Mitchard. More than 20 agents and editors participate each year, many of whom will be available for meetings with attendees."

COSTS Early price (until September) is $575. Check the website for pricing on later dates.

ACCOMMODATIONS The Intercontinental Mark Hopkins Hotel is a historic landmark at the top of Nob Hill in San Francisco. The hotel is located so that everyone arriving at the Oakland or San Francisco airport can take BART to either the Embarcadero or Powell Street exits, then walk or take a cable car or taxi directly to the hotel.

ADDITIONAL INFORMATION "Present yourself in a professional manner and the contact you will make will be invaluable to your writing career. Brochures and registration are online."

SAN FRANCISCO WRITING FOR CHANGE CONFERENCE

1029 Jones St., San Francisco CA 94109. (415)673-0939. **E-mail:** Barbara@sfwriters.org. **Website:** SFWritingforChange.org. **Contact:** Barbara Santos, marketing director; MIchael Larsen, director. Estab. 2004. Biannual conference held in early fall 2014 at a location to be announced. Average attendance: 200.

COSTS TBA; early discounts available. Includes over 20 workshops, keynote address, editor, and agent consultations.

ACCOMMODATIONS Check website for event details, accommodations, directions, and parking.

ADDITIONAL INFORMATION "The limited number of attendees (150) and excellent presenter-to-attendee ratio make this a highly effective and productive conference. The presenters are major names in the publishing business, but take personal interest in the projects discovered at this event each year." Guidelines available on website, e-mail, and fax.

SANGRIA SUMMIT: A MILITARY WRITERS' CONFERENCE

23376 E. Fifth Place, Unit 204, Aurora CO 80018. (772)418-2380. **E-mail:** isaac@cubillos.com. **Website:** www.sangriasummit.com. **Contact:** Isaac Cubillos, director. Estab. 2012. Annual conference held for two days in September. "Drawing from successful writers in the military genre, the conference will connect established writers with aspiring writers seeking to develop their craft in this niche market. The format will consist of an intensive workshop led by established writers of fiction and non-fiction books – historical, biographical, memoirs, current affairs. Beyond the workshop there will be panel discussions on writing, self-publishing, traditional publishing, selling your book and author readings."

COSTS $195 before Aug. 12, 2012; $250 afterward. $35 for editor/agent critique. Special dinners with authors $25. Cost includes: workshop, author panels, all program material, special books, two lunches.

ACCOMMODATIONS "The conference will be in meeting rooms at the Denver Marriott City Place."

SANTA BARBARA WRITERS CONFERENCE

27 W. Anapamu St., Suite 305, Santa Barbara CA 93101. (805)568-1516. **E-mail:** info@sbwriters.com. **Website:** www.sbwriters.com. Estab. 1972. Annual conference held June 8-13. Average attendance: 200. Covers fiction, nonfiction, journalism, memoir, poetry, playwriting, screenwriting, travel writing, young adult, children's literature, humor, and marketing. Speakers have included Ray Bradbury, William Styron, Eudora Welty, James Michener, Sue Grafton, Charles M. Schulz, Clive Cussler, Fannie Flagg, Elmore Leonard, and T.C. Boyle. Agents will appear on a panel; in addition, there will be an agents and editors day that allows writers to pitch their projects in one-on-one meetings.

COSTS Conference registration is $550 on or before March 16 and $625 after March 16.

ACCOMMODATIONS Hyatt Santa Barbara.

ADDITIONAL INFORMATION Register online or contact for brochure and registration forms.

SASKATCHEWAN FESTIVAL OF WORDS

217 Main St. N., Moose Jaw SK S6J 0W1 Canada. **Website:** www.festivalofwords.com. Estab. 1997. Annual 4-day event, third week of July (2013 dates: July 18-21). Location: Moose Jaw Library/Art Museum complex in Crescent Park. Average attendance: about 4,000 admissions. "Canadian authors up close and personal for readers and writers of all ages inmystery, poetry, memoir, fantasy, graphic novels, history, and novel. Each summer festival includes 60 events within 2 blocks of historic Main Street. Audience favorite activities include workshops for writers, audience readings, drama,performance poetry, concerts, panels, and music."

ACCOMMODATIONS Information available at www.templegardens.sk.ca, campgrounds, and bed and breakfast establishments. Complete information about festival presenters, events, costs, and schedule also available on website.

SASKATCHEWAN FESTIVAL OF WORDS AND WORKSHOPS

217 Main St. N., Moose Jaw SK S6H 0W1 Canada. **E-mail:** word.festival@sasktel.net. **Website:** www.festivalofwords.com. **Contact:** Donna Lee Howes. Writer workshops geared toward beginner and intermediate levels. **Open to students.** Readings that include a wide spectrum of genres—fiction, creative nonfiction, poetry, songwriting, screenwriting, playwriting, dramatic reading with actors, graphic novels, Great Big Book Club Discussion with author, children's writing, panels, independent film screening, panels, slam poetry, interviews and performances. Annual festival. Workshop held third weekend in July. Cost of workshop varies from $10 for a single reading to $200 for a full pass (as of 2011). Trivia Night Fun ticket is extra. Visit website for more information.

SCBWI–CANADA EAST

Canada. **E-mail:** araeast@scbwicanada.org; raeast@scbwicanada.org. **Website:** www.scbwicanada.org/east. **Contact:** Lizann Flatt, regional advisor. Writer and illustrator events geared toward all levels. Usually offers one event in spring and another in the fall. Check website Events pages for updated information.

SCBWI COLORADO/WYOMING (ROCKY MOUNTAIN); EVENTS

E-mail: denise@rmcscbwi.org; todd.tuell@rmcscbwi.org. **Website:** www.rmcscbwi.org. **Contact:** Todd Tuell and Denise Vega, co-regional advisors. SCBWI Rocky Mountain chapter (CO/WY) offers special events, schmoozes, meetings, and conferences throughout the year. Major events: Fall Conference (annually, September); Summer Retreat, "Big Sur in the Rockies" (bi- and triannually). More info on website.

BOISE REGIONAL CONFERENCE FOR UTAH/SOUTHERN IDAHO SCBWI

ID **E-mail:** neysajensen@msn.com. **Contact:** Sydney Husseman, Regional Advisor; Neysa Jensen, Assis. Regional Advisor. "One day workshop focuses on the craft of writing, as well as getting to know an editor. One-on-one critiques available for an additional fee. Event held in Boise, Idaho every spring."

SCBWI—MIDATLANTIC; ANNUAL FALL CONFERENCE

P.O. Box 3215, Reston VA 20195. **E-mail:** scbwimidatlantic@gmail.com. **Website:** www.SCBWI-MidAtlantic.org. **Contact:** Sydney Dunlap and Erin Teagan, conference co-chairs; Ellen Braaf, regional advisor. For updates and details visit website. Registration limited to 200. Conference fills quickly. Cost: $115 for SCBWI members; $145 for nonmembers. Includes continental breakfast. Lunch is on your own. (The food court at the Ballston Common Mall is two blocks away.)

SCBWI—NEW JERSEY; ANNUAL SUMMER CONFERENCE

SCBWI-New Jersey: Society of Children's Book Writers & Illustrators, New Jersey NJ **Website:** www.newjerseyscbwi.com. **Contact:** Kathy Temean, regional advisor. This weekend conference is held in the beginning of June in Princeton, NJ. Multiple one-on-one critiques; "how to" workshops for every level, first page sessions, agent pitches and interaction with the faculty of editors, agents, art director and authors are some of the highlights of the weekend. On Friday attendees can sign up for writing intensives or register for illustrators' day with the art directors. Published authors attending the conference can sign up to participate in the bookfair to sell and autograph their books; illustrators have the opportunity to display their artwork. Attendees have the option to participate in group critiques after dinner on Saturday evening and attend a mix and mingle with the faculty on Friday night. Meals are included with the cost of admission. Conference is known for its high ratio of faculty to attendees and interaction opportunities.

SCBWI—NEW JERSEY; FIRST PAGE SESSIONS

New Jersey NJ **E-mail:** njscbwi@newjerseyscbwi.com; kathy@newjerseyscbwi.com; laurie@newjerseyscbwi.com. **Website:** www.newjerseyscbwi.com. Held 4 times a year in Princeton, NJ. Two editors/agents give their first impression of a first page and let participants know if they would read more. These sessions are held late afternoon during the week and are limited to 30 people. Attendees can choose to have dinner with the editors after the session. Please visit www.newjerseyscbwi.com for more information.

SCBWI—VENTURA/SANTA BARBARA; FALL CONFERENCE

Simi Valley CA 93094-1389. **E-mail:** alexisinca@aol.com. **Website:** www.scbwicencal.org. **Contact:** Alexis O'Neill, regional advisor. Estab. 1971. Writers' conference geared toward all levels. Speakers include editors, authors, illustrators and agents. Fiction and nonfiction picture books, middle grade and YA novels, and magazine submissions addressed. Annual writing contest in all genres plus illustration display. Conference held October 26, 2013 at California Lutheran University in Thousand Oaks, California in cooperation with the CLU Graduate School of Education. For fees and other information, e-mail or visit website.

SCBWI WINTER CONFERENCE ON WRITING AND ILLUSTRATING FOR CHILDREN

8271 Beverly Blvd., Los Angeles CA 90048. (323)782-1010. **Fax:** (323)782-1892. **E-mail:** scbwi@scbwi.org. **Website:** www.scbwi.org. **Contact:** Stephen Mooser. Estab. 2000. (formerly SCBWI Midyear Conference), Society of Children's book Writers and Illustrators. Annual. Conference held in February. Average attendance: 1,000. Conference is to promote writing and illustrating for children: picture books; fiction; nonfiction; middle grade and young adult; network with professionals; financial planning for writers; marketing your book; art exhibition; etc. Site: Manhattan.

COSTS See website for current cost and conference information.

ADDITIONAL INFORMATION SCBWI also holds an annual summer conference in August in Los Angeles. See the listing in the West section or visit website for details.

THE SCHOOL FOR WRITERS SUMMER WORKSHOP

The Humber School for Writers, Humber Institute of Technology & Advanced Learning, 3199 Lake Shore Blvd. W., Toronto ON M8V 1K8 Canada. (416)675-6622. **E-mail:** antanas.sileika@humber.ca; hilary.higgins@humber.ca. **Website:** www.creativeandperformingarts.humber.ca/content/writers.html. The School for Writers Summer Workshop has moved to the fall with the International Festival of Authors. Workshop the last week in October through first week in November. Conference duration: 1 week. Average attendance: 100. New writers from around the world gather to study with faculty members to work on their novels, short stories, poetry, or creative nonfiction. Agents and editors participate in conference. Include a work-in-progress with your registration. Faculty has included Martin Amis, David Mitchell, Rachel

Kuschner, Peter Carey, Roddy Doyle, Tim O'Brien, Andrea Levy, Barry Unsworth, Edward Albee, Ha Jin, Julia Glass, Mavis Gallant, Bruce Jay Friedman, Isabel Huggan, Alistair MacLeod, Lisa Moore, Kim Moritsugu, Francine Prose, Paul Quarrington, Olive Senior, and D.M. Thomas, Annabel Lyon, Mary Gaitskill, M. G. Vassanji.

COSTS around $800 (in 2013). Some limited scholarships are available.

ACCOMMODATIONS Nearby hotels are available.

ADDITIONAL INFORMATION Accepts inquiries by e-mail, phone, and fax.

SCHOOL OF THE ARTS AT RHINELANDER UW-MADISON CONTINUING STUDIES

21 N Park St., 7th Floor, Madison WI 53715-1218. (608)262-7389. **E-mail:** lkaufman@dcs.wisc.edu. **Website:** continuingstudies.wisc.edu/lsa/soa/. Estab. 1964. "Each summer for nearly 50 years, more than 250 people have gathered in northern Wisconsin for a week of study, performance, exhibits, and other creative activities. More than 50 workshops in writing, body/mind/spirit; food and fitness; art and folk art; music; and digital media are offered. Participants can choose from any and all 1-, 2-, and 5-day classes to craft their own mix for creative exploration and renewal." Dates: July 20-24. Location: James Williams Middle School and Rhineland High School, Rhinelander, WI. Average attendance: 250.

COSTS Ranges from $20-$300 based on workshops.

ACCOMMODATIONS Informational available from Rhinelander Chamber of Commerce.

SCIENCE FICTION WRITERS WORKSHOP

English Department/University of Kansas, Wesoce Hall, 1445 Jayhawk Blvd., Room 3001, Lawrence KS 66045-7590. (785)864-2508. **E-mail:** cmckit@ku.edu. **Website:** www.sfcenter.ku.edu/SFworkshop.htm. Estab. 1985. Annual. Workshop held June 2-14. The workshop is "small, informal, and aimed at writers on the edge of publication or regular publication." For writing and marketing science fiction and fantasy. Site: Workshop sessions operate informally in a university housing lounge on the University of Kansas campus where most participants also reside. Established in 1985 by James Gunn and currently led by Christopher McKitterick, with guest authors joining for the second week. Writer and editor instructors have included Lou Anders, Bradley Denton, James Gunn, Kij Johnson, John Ordover, Frederik Pohl, Pa-

mela Sargent, and George Zebrowski, and each year the winners of the Campbell and Sturgeon Memorial Awards participate in 1 or more days of the workshop. A novel workshop in science fiction and fantasy is also available at the same time, led by Kij Johnson.

COSTS $500, exclusive of meals and housing.

ACCOMMODATIONS Housing information is available. Several airport shuttle services offer reasonable transportation from the Kansas City International Airport to Lawrence.

ADDITIONAL INFORMATION Admission to the workshop is bysubmission of an acceptable story, usually by May. Two additional stories are submitted by the middle of June. These 3 stories are distributed to other participants for critiquing and are the basis for the first week of the workshop. One story is rewritten for the second week, when students also work with guest authors. See website for guidelines. This workshop is intended for writers who have just started to sell their work or need that extra bit of understanding or skill to become a published writer.

SEWANEE WRITERS' CONFERENCE

735 University Ave., 119 Gailor Hall, Stamler Center, Sewanee TN 37383-1000. (931) 598-1654. **E-mail:** allatham@sewanee.edu. **Website:** www.sewaneewriters.org. **Contact:** Adam Latham. Estab. 1990. Annual conference held July 23 - August 4. Average attendance: 144. "We offer genre-based workshops in fiction, poetry, and playwriting. The conference uses the facilities of Sewanee: The University of the South. The university is a collection of ivy-covered Gothic-style buildings located on the Cumberland Plateau in mid-Tennessee. Editors, publishers, and agents structure their own presentations, but there is always opportunity for questions from the audience." A score of writing professionals will visit. The Conference will offer its customary Walter E. Dakin Fellowships and Tennessee Williams Scholarships as well as awards in memory of Stanley Elkin, Donald Justice, Howard Nemerov, Father William Ralston, Peter Taylor, Mona Van Duyn, and John N. Wall. Additional scholarships have been made possible by Georges and Anne Borchardt and Gail Hochman. Each participant—whether contributor, scholar, or fellow—receives financial support.

COSTS $1,000 for tuition and $700 for room, board, and activity costs

ACCOMMODATIONS Participants are housed in single rooms in university dormitories. Bathrooms are shared by small groups. Motel or B&B housing is available, but not abundantly so.

SHEVACON

PO Box 7622, Roanoke VA 24019. (540)248-4152. **E-mail:** shevacon@shevacon.org. **Website:** www.shevacon.org. **Contact:** Lynn Bither, chairperson. Estab. 1993. Annual conference held in March. Conference focuses on writing, art, and gaming in the science fiction, fantasy, and horror genres.

COSTS Contact Shevacon for rates.

ACCOMMODATIONS There is special rate at the Sheraton Roanoke Hotel & Conference Center, Virginia. "Shuttles from the airport are available; we do not have airline discounts." Offers overnight accomodations; "individuals must make their own reservations." For brochure send SASE or visit website. Accepts inquiries by mail, e-mail or phone.

ADDITIONAL INFORMATION "SheVaCon is celebrating it's 19th year as the largest Multi-Media Science Fiction & Fantasy convention in Southwestern Virginia. We offer many fun events and great programming focusing on sci-fi, fantasy, and horror. Workshops, panel discussions, art show & artist alley, dealer's room, costumed fandom groups, auctions, computer and console gaming, RPG/LARP gaming, Video and Anime screenings.... and so much more!" "There is more parking and we can open sooner on Friday the 4th. Confirmed guests are listed on the website and we are updating regularly."

SILKEN SANDS CONFERENCE

Gulf Coast Chapter RWA, P.O. Box 1815, Ocean Springs MS 39566. (228)875-3864. **E-mail:** info@gccrwa.com. **E-mail:** kelly@authorkellylstone.com. **Website:** www.gccrwa.com. **Contact:** Kelly Stone, president. Estab. 1995. Bi-annual conference. Next one will be held in 2014. Average attendance: 100. Focuses on romance, fiction including paranormal, inspirational, romantic suspense, category.

COSTS To be announced.

ADDITIONAL INFORMATION Brochures available for SASE, e-mail, phone or on website. Accepts inquiries by e-mail. Agents and editors participate in conference. The conference is noted for its relaxed, enjoyable atmosphere where participants can immerse themselves in the total writing experience from the moment they arrive.

SITKA CENTER FOR ART AND ECOLOGY

56605 Sitka Dr., Otis OR 97368. (541)994-5485. **Fax:** (541)994-8024. **E-mail:** info@sitkacenter.org. **Website:** www.sitkacenter.org. **Contact:** Caroline Brooks, program manager. Estab. 1970. Workshop program is open to all levels and is held annually from late May until early October. There is also a residency program October-May. Average attendance: 10-14/workshop. A variety of workshops in the creative process, including book arts and other media. Site: The Center borders a Nature Conservatory Preserve, the Siuslaw National Experimental Forest and the Salmon River Estuary, located just north of Lincoln City, OR.

COSTS Workshops are generally $65-500; they do not include meals or lodging.

ACCOMMODATIONS Does not offer overnight accommodations. Provides a list of area hotels or lodging options.

ADDITIONAL INFORMATION Brochure available in February of each year; request a copy by e-mail or phone, or visit website for listing. Accepts inquiries in-person or by e-mail, phone, fax.

SOCIETY OF CHILDREN'S BOOK WRITERS & ILLUSTRATORS ANNUAL SUMMER CONFERENCE ON WRITING AND ILLUSTRATING FOR CHILDREN

8271 Beverly Blvd., Los Angeles CA 90048-4515. (323)782-1010. **Fax:** (323)782-1892. **E-mail:** scbwi@scbwi.org. **Website:** www.scbwi.org. Estab. 1972. Annual conference held in early August. Conference duration: 4 days. Average attendance: 1,000. Held at the Century Plaza Hotel in Los Angeles. Speakers have included Andrea Brown, Steven Malk, Ashley Bryan, Bruce Coville, Karen Hesse, Harry Mazer, Lucia Monfried, and Russell Freedman. Agents will be speaking and sometimes participate in ms critiques.

COSTS Approximately $450 (does not include hotel room).

ACCOMMODATIONS Information on overnight accommodations is made available.

ADDITIONAL INFORMATION Ms and illustration critiques are available. Brochure/guidelines are available in June online or for SASE.

SOUTH COAST WRITERS CONFERENCE

Southwestern Oregon Community College, P.O. Box 590, 29392 Ellensburg Ave., Gold Beach OR 97444. (541)247-2741. **Fax:** (541)247-6247. **E-mail:** scwc@socc.edu. **Website:** www.socc.edu/scwriters. Estab.

1996. Annual conference held Presidents Day weekend in February. Conference duration: 2 days. Covers fiction, poetry, children's, nature, songwriting, and marketing. William Sullivan is the next scheduled keynote speaker, and presenters include Linda Barnes, Merritt "Biff" Barnes, Judy Cox, Bruce Holbert, Elizabeth Lyon, Carolyn J. Rose, Johnny Shaw, Lauren Sheehan, William Sullivan, and Bob Welch. **ADDITIONAL INFORMATION** See website for cost and additional details.

SPACE (SMALL PRESS AND ALTERNATIVE COMICS EXPO)

Back Porch Comics, P.O. Box 20550, Columbus OH 43220. **E-mail:** bpc13@earthlink.net. **Website:** www.backporchcomics.com/space.htm. Next conference/trade show to be held April 13-14. Conference duration: 2 days. "The Midwest's largest exhibition of small press, alternative, and creator-owned comics." Site: Held at Ramada Plaza Hotel and Conference Center, 4900 Sinclair Rd., Columbus, OH 43229. Over 150 small press artists, writers, and publishers. **COSTS** Admission: $5 per day or $8 for weekend. **ADDITIONAL INFORMATION** For brochure, visit website. Editors participate in conference.

STEAMBOAT SPRINGS WRITERS CONFERENCE

Steamboat Springs Arts Council, Eleanor Bliss Center for the Arts at the Depot, 1001 13th St., Steamboat Springs CO 80487. (970)879-9008. **Fax:** (970)879-8138. **E-mail:** info@steamboatwriters.com. **Website:** www.steamboatwriters.com. **Contact:** Susan de Wardt. Estab. 1982. Annual conference held in mid-July. Conference duration: 1 day. Average attendance: approximately 35. Attendance is limited. Featured areas of instruction change each year. Held at the restored train Depot. Speakers have included Carl Brandt, Jim Fergus, Avi, Robert Greer, Renate Wood, Connie Willis, Margaret Coel, and Kent Nelson. **COSTS** Tuition: $50 early registration, $65 after May 4. **ADDITIONAL INFORMATION** Brochures are available in April for a SASE. Send inquiries via e-mail.

STEAMBOAT SPRINGS WRITERS GROUP

P.O. Box 774284, Steamboat Springs CO 80477. (970)879-8079. **E-mail:** susan@steamboatwriters.com. **Website:** www.steamboatwriters.com. **Contact:** Susan de Wardt, director. Estab. 1982. Group meets year-round on Thursdays, 12-2 p.m. at Arts De-

pot; guests welcome. Annual conference held in July. Conference duration: 1 day. Average attendance: 35. "Our conference emphasizes instruction within the seminar format. Novices and polished professionals benefit from the individual attention and camaraderie which can be established within small groups. A pleasurable and memorable learning experience is guaranteed by the relaxed and friendly atmosphere of the old train depot. Registration is limited." Site: Restored train depot. **COSTS** $50 before May 25, $60 after. Fee covers all seminars and luncheon. **ACCOMMODATIONS** Lodging available at Steamboat Resorts. **ADDITIONAL INFORMATION** Optional dinner and activities during evening preceding conference. Accepts inquiries by e-mail, phone, mail.

STELLARCON

Box F4, Brown Annex, Elliott University Center, UNCG, Greensboro NC 27412. (336)294-8041. **E-mail:** info@stellarcon.org. **Website:** www.stellarcon.com. Estab. 1976. Annual conference held in March. Average attendance: 500. Conference focuses on general science fiction, fantasy, horror with an emphasis on literature, and comics. Held at the Radisson Hotel in High Point, North Carolina. **COSTS** At the door rate for weekend pass: $35. **ACCOMMODATIONS** Make a reservation at the Greensboro - High Point Airport Mariott. Call 336-852-6450 for StellarCon room block reservations.

STONY BROOK SOUTHAMPTON SCREENWRITING CONFERENCE

Stony Brook Southampton, 239 Montauk Highway, Southampton NY 11968. (631)632-5030. **Fax:** (631)632-2576. **E-mail:** southamptonwriters@notes.cc.sunysb.edu. **E-mail:** Carla.Caglioti@stonybrook.edu. **Website:** www.stonybrook.edu/southampton. **Contact:** Carla Caglioti. "The Southampton Screenwriting Conference welcomes new and advanced screenwriters, as well as all writers interested in using the language of film to tell a story. The five-day residential Conference will inform, inspire, challenge, and further participants understanding of the art of the screenplay and the individual writing process. Our unique program of workshops, seminars, panel presentations, and screenings will encourage and motivate attendees under the professional guidance of accomplished screenwriters, educators, and script analysts." Held in two sessions from July 10-28.

COSTS Residential $1495, Non-Residential $1300.

ADDITIONAL INFORMATION Space is limited.

STORY WEAVERS CONFERENCE

Oklahoma Writer's Federation, (405)682-6000. E-mail: president@owfi.org. **Website:** www.OWFI.org. **Contact:** Linda Apple, president. Oklahoma Writer's Federation, Inc. is open and welcoming to writers of all genres and all skill levels. Our goal is to help writers become better and to help beginning writers understand and master the craft of writing.

COSTS Cost is $150 before April. $175 after April. Cost includes awards banquet and famous author banquet. Three extra sessions are available for an extra fee: How to Self-Publish Your Novel on Kindle, Nook, and iPad (and make more money than being published by New York), with Dan Case; When Polar Bear Wishes Came True: Understanding and Creating Meaningful Stories, with Jack Dalton; How to Create Three-Dimensional Characters, with Steven James.

ACCOMMODATIONS The site is at the Embassy Suite using their meeting halls. There are very few stairs and the rooms are close together for easy access.

ADDITIONAL INFORMATION "We have 20 speakers, five agents, and nine publisher/editors for a full list and bios, please see website."

SUMMER WRITING PROGRAM

Naropa University, 2130 Arapahoe Ave., Boulder CO 80302. (303)245-4600. **Fax:** (303)546-5287. **E-mail:** swpr@naropa.edu. **Website:** www.naropa.edu/swp. **Contact:** Kyle Pivarnik, administrative coordinator. Estab. 1974. Annual. Workshops held July 1-27. Workshop duration: 4 weeks. Average attendance: 250. Offers college credit. Accepts inquiries by e-mail, phone."With 13 workshops to choose from each of the 4 weeks of the program, students may study poetry, prose, hybrid/cross-genre writing, small press printing, or book arts." Site: "All workshops, panels, lectures and readings are hosted on the Naropa University main campus. Located in downtown Boulder, the campus is within easy walking distance of restaurants, shopping, and the scenic Pearl Street Mall."

COSTS In 2013: $500/week, $2,000 for all 4 weeks (non-credit students).

ACCOMMODATIONS Housing is available at Snow Lion Apartments. Additional info is available on the housing website: www.naropa.edu/student-life/housing/index.php.

ADDITIONAL INFORMATION Writers can elect to take the Summer Writing Program for noncredit, graduate, or undergraduate credit. The registration procedure varies, so consider whether or not you'll be taking the SWP for academic credit. All participants can elect to take any combination of the first, second, third, and/or fourth weeks. To request a catalog of upcoming program or to find additional information, visit www.naropa.edu/swp. Naropa University alsowelcomes participants with disabilities. Contact Andrea Rexilius at (303)546-5296 or arexilius@naropa.edu before May 15 to inquire about accessibility and disability accommodations needed to participate fully in this event.

SUNSHINE COAST FESTIVAL OF THE WRITTEN ARTS

5511 Shorncliffe Ave., Rockwood Centre, Box 2299, Sechelt BC V0N 3A0 Canada. (604)885-9631 or (800)565-9631. **Fax:** (604)885-3967. **E-mail:** info@writersfestival.ca. **E-mail:** jane@writersfestival.ca. **Website:** www.writersfestival.ca. Estab. 1983. Annual festival held August 15-18. Average attendance: 3,500. The festival does not have a theme. Instead, it showcases 25 or more Canadian writers in a variety of genres each year. Held at the Rockwood Centre. Speakers have included Jane Urquhart, Sholagh Rogers, David Watmough, Zsuzsi Gartner, Gail Bowen, Charlotte Gray, Bill Richardson, P.K. Page, Richard B. Wright, Madeleine Thien, Ronald Wright, Michael Kusugak, and Bob McDonald.

COSTS Check online for prices — tickets go on sale in late May.

ACCOMMODATIONS A list of hotels is available.

ADDITIONAL INFORMATION The festival runs contests during the event. Prizes are books donated by publishers. Brochures/guidelines are available. Visit the website for current updates and details.

SURREY INTERNATIONAL WRITERS' CONFERENCE

SIWC, P.O. Box 42023 RPO Guildford, Surrey BC V3R 1S5 Canada. **E-mail:** kathychung@siwc.ca. **Website:** www.siwc.ca. **Contact:** Kathy Chung, conference coordinator. Writing workshops geared toward beginner, intermediate, and advanced levels. More than 70 workshops and panels, on all topics and genres. Blue Pencil and Agent/Editor Pitch sessions included. Annual Conference held every October. Different conference price packages available. Check our website for more information.

TAOS SUMMER WRITERS' CONFERENCE

Department of English Language and Literature, MSC 03 2170, 1 University of New Mexico, Albuquerque NM 87131-0001. (505)277-5572. **Fax:** (505)277-2950. **E-mail:** taosconf@unm.edu. **Website:** www.unm.edu/~taosconf. **Contact:** Sharon Oard Warner. Estab. 1999. Annual conference held July 14-21. Offers workshops in novel writing, short story writing, screenwriting, poetry, creative nonfiction, travel writing, historical fiction, memoir, and revision. Participants may also schedule a consultation with a visiting agent/editor.

COSTS Weeklong workshop registrations are $650.

ACCOMMODATIONS Held at the Sagebrush Inn and Conference Center.

THRILLERFEST

P.O. Box 311, Eureka CA 95502. **E-mail:** infocentral@thrillerwriters.org. **Website:** www.thrillerfest.com. **Contact:** Kimberley Howe, executive director. Grand Hyatt New York, 109 E. 42nd St., New York, NY 10017. Estab. 2006. Annual. July 10-13 in Manhattan. Conference duration: 4 days. Average attendance: 900. Workshop/conference/festival. "A great place to learn the craft of writing the thriller. Classes taught by NYT best-selling authors. A fabulous event for fans/readers to meet and spend a few days with their favorite authors and packed with terrific programming." Speakers have included David Morrell, James Patterson, Sandra Brown, Ken Follett, Eric Van Lustbader, David Baldacci, Brad Meltzer, Steve Martini, R.L. Stine, Steve Berry, Kathleen Antrim, Douglas Preston, Gayle Lynds, Harlan Coben, Lee Child, Lisa Scottolini, Katherine Neville, Robin Cook, Andrew Gross, Kathy Reichs, Brad Thor, Clive Cussler, Donald Maass, MJ Rose, and Al Zuckerman. Two days of the conference are CraftFest, where the focus is on the craft of writing, and 2 days are ThrillerFest, which showcase the author-fan relationship. Also featured: AgentFest—a unique event where authors can pitch their work face-to-face to 50 top literary agents, and the International Thriller Awards and Banquet.

COSTS Price will vary from $300-1,100, depending on which events are selected. Various package deals are available offering savings, and Early Bird pricing is offered beginning August of each year.

ACCOMMODATIONS Grand Hyatt in New York City.

TMCC WRITERS' CONFERENCE

Truckee Meadows Community College, 5270 Neil Rd., Reno NV 89502. (775)829-9010. **Fax:** (775)829-9032. **E-mail:** wdce@tmcc.edu. **Website:** wdce.tmcc.edu. Estab. 1991. Annual conference held April 27. Average attendance: 150. Conference focuses on strengthening mainstream/literary fiction and nonfiction works and how to market them to agents and publishers. Site: Truckee Meadows Community College in Reno, Nevada. "There is always an array of speakers and presenters with impressive literary credentials, including agents and editors." Speakers have included Chuck Sambuchino, Sheree Bykofsky, Andrea Brown, Dorothy Allison, Karen Joy Fowler, James D. Houston, James N. Frey, Gary Short, Jane Hirschfield, Dorrianne Laux, and Kim Addonizio.

COSTS $119 for a full-day seminar; $32 for a 10-minute one-on-one appointment with an agent or editor.

ACCOMMODATIONS The Silver Legacy, in downtown Reno, offers a special rate and shuttle service to the Reno/Tahoe International Airport, which is less than 20 minutes away.

ADDITIONAL INFORMATION "The conference is open to all writers, regardless of their level of experience. Brochures are available online and mailed in January. Send inquiries via e-mail."

TONY HILLERMAN WRITER'S CONFERENCE

1063 Willow Way, Santa FE NM 87505. (505)471-1565. **E-mail:** wordharvest@wordharvest.com. **Website:** www.wordharvest.com. **Contact:** Jean Schaumberg, co-director. Estab. 2004. Annual. November 7-9, 2013. Conference duration: 3 days. Average attendance: 100. Site: Hilton Santa Fe Historic Plaza. First day: Author/teacher Margaret Coel, focuses on the art of writing to create great characters. Other programs focus on creating memorable plots and the business of writing. "We'll honor the winner of the $10,000 Tony Hillerman Prize for best first mystery at a lunch with keynote speaker Craig Johnson, a *New York Times* best-selling author. A 'flash critique' session, open to any interested attendee, will add to the fun and information. Author attendees will also have a chance to talk about their new books at teh new Book/New Author Breakfast."

COSTS Previous year's costs: $395 per-registration.

ACCOMMODATIONS Hilton Santa Fe Historic Plaza offers $119 single or double occupancy. November 6-10. Book online with the hotel.

ADDITIONAL INFORMATION Sponsors a $10,000 first mystery novel contest with St. Marttin's Press. Brochures available in July for SASE, by phone, e-mail, and on website. Accepts inquiries by SASE, phone, e-mail. Deadline for the Hillerman Mystery Competition is June 1.

UCLA EXTENSION WRITERS' PROGRAM

10995 Le Conte Ave., #440, Los Angeles CA 90024. (310)825-9415 or (800)388-UCLA. **Fax:** (310)206-7382. **E-mail:** writers@uclaextension.edu. **Website:** www.uclaextension.org/writers. Estab. 1891. "As America's largest and most comprehensive continuing education creative writing and screenwriting program, the UCLA Extension Writers' Program welcomes and trains writers at all levels of development whose aspirations range from personal enrichment to professional publication and production. Taught by an instructor corps of 250 professional writers, the Writers' Program curriculum features 530 annual open-enrollment courses onsite and online in novel writing, short fiction, personal essay, memoir, poetry, playwriting, writing for the youth market, publishing, feature film writing, and television writing, and is designed to accommodate your individual writing needs, ambitions, and lifestyle. Special programs and services include certificate programs in creative writing, feature film writing, and television writing; a four-day Writers Studio which attracts a national and international audience; nine-month master classes in novel writing and feature film writing; an online screenwriting mentorship program; one-on-one script and manuscript consultation services; literary and screenplay competitions; advisors who help you determine how best to achieve your personal writing goals; and free annual public events such as Writers Faire and Publication Party which allow you to extend your writing education and network with the literary and entertainment communities."

COSTS Depends on length of the course.

ACCOMMODATIONS Students make their own arrangements. Out-of-town students are encouraged to take online courses.

ADDITIONAL INFORMATION Some advanced-level classes have ms submittal requirements; see the UCLA Extension catalog or see website.

UMKC WRITERS WORKSHOPS

5300 Rockhill Rd., Kansas City MO 64110. (816)235-2736. **Fax:** (816)235-5279. **E-mail:** wittfeldk@umkc.edu. **Website:** www.newletters.org/writingConferences.asp. **Contact:** Kathi Wittfeld. Mark Twain Workshop will not be held in 2013. New Letters Weekend Writing Conference was held on Friday, Saturday and Sunday, June 28-30,2013 at Diastole. New Letters Writer's Conference and Mark Twain Writer's Workshop are geared toward intermediate, advanced and professional levels. Workshops open to students and community. Annual workshops. Workshops held in Summer. Cost of workshop varies. Write for more information.

UNIVERSITY OF NORTH DAKOTA WRITERS CONFERENCE

Department of English, 110 Merrifield Hall, 276 Centennial Drive, Stop 7209, Grand Forks ND 58202. (701)777-3321. **E-mail:** writersconference@und.nodak.edu. **Website:** www.undwritersconference.org. Estab. 1970. Annual conference held March 19-23. Offers panels, readings, and films focused around a specific theme. Almost all events take place in the UND Memorial Union, which has a variety of small rooms and a 1,000-seat main hall. Past speakers include Art Spiegelman, Truman Capote, Sir Salman Rushdie, Allen Ginsberg, Alice Walker, and Louise Erdrich.

COSTS All events are free and open to the public. Donations accepted.

ACCOMMODATIONS All events are free and open to the public. Accommodations available at area hotels. Information on overnight accommodations available on website.

ADDITIONAL INFORMATION Schedule and other information available on website.

UNIVERSITY OF NORTH FLORIDA WRITERS CONFERENCE

12000 Alumni Dr., Jacksonville FL 32224-2678. (904)620-4200. **E-mail:** sharon.y.cobb@unf.edu. **Website:** www.unfwritersconference.com. **Contact:** Sharon Y. Cobb, conference director. Estab. 2009.

COSTS See website for current registration fees. Full conference attendees receive: workshops, critiques by faculty and fellow students, lunches, Friday wine/cheese reception, and book signings.

ACCOMMODATIONS Nearby accommodations are listed on website. There is free parking provided at the University Center.

UW-MADISON WRITERS' INSTITUTE

21 North Park St., Room 7331, Madison WI 53715. (608)265-3972. **Fax:** (608)265-2475. **E-mail:** lscheer@ dcs.wisc.edu. **Website:** www.uwwritersinstitute.org. **Contact:** Laurie Scheer. Estab. 1989. Annual. Conference usually held in April. Site: Madison Concourse Hotel, downtown Madison. Average attendance: 300. Conference speakers provide workshops and consultations. For information, send e-mail, visit website, call, fax. Accepts inquiries by SASE, e-mail, phone, fax. Agents and editors participate in conference.
COSTS $155-255; includes materials, breaks.
ACCOMMODATIONS Provides a list of area hotels or lodging options.
ADDITIONAL INFORMATION Sponsors contest.

THE VANCOUVER INTERNATIONAL WRITERS & READERS FESTIVAL

202-1398 Cartwright St., Vancouver BC V6H 3R8 Canada. (604)681-6330. **Fax:** (604)681-8400. **E-mail:** info@writersfest.bc.ca. **E-mail:** hwake@writersfest. bc.ca. **Website:** www.writersfest.bc.ca. Estab. 1988. Annual festival held October 22-27. Average attendance: 11,000. The program of events is diverse and includes readings, panel discussions, and seminars. There are lots of opportunities to interact with the writers who attend. Held on Granville Island in the heart of Vancouver. Speakers have included Margaret Atwood, Maeve Binchy, and J.K. Rowling.
ACCOMMODATIONS Local tourist information can be provided upon request.
ADDITIONAL INFORMATION Remember—this is a festival and a celebration, not a conference or workshop. Brochures are available after August for a SASE. Inquire via e-mail or fax, or go online for updates.

VERMONT COLLEGE OF FINE ARTS POSTGRADUATE WRITERS' CONFERENCE

36 College St., Montpelier VT 05602. (802)828-8835. **Fax:** (802)828-8649. **E-mail:** pgconference@vcfa.edu. **Website:** www.vcfa.edu/writing/pwc. Estab. 1996. Annual conference for writers with MFAs or equivalent preparation on the historic campus of Vermont College of Fine Arts. August 12-18. Features intensive small-group workshops taught by an award-winning faculty, plus readings, craft talks, writing exercise sessions and individual consultations. Conference size: 70 participants. Workshops in creative nonfiction, novel, short story, poetry, poetry manuscript and writing for young people.

COSTS Costs: $875 or $995 (Poetry Ms.)/tuition, $330/private room, $180/shared room, $185/meals. Limited scholarships are available.
ACCOMMODATIONS Single or double rooms are available in the VCFA campus dormitories.

VERMONT STUDIO CENTER

P.O. Box 613, 80 Pearl Street, Johnson VT 05656. (802)635-2727. **Fax:** (802)635-2730. **E-mail:** info@ vermontstudiocenter.org. **Website:** www.vermont-studiocenter.org.. **Contact:** Gary Clark, Writing Program Director. Estab. 1984. Founded by artists in 1984, the Vermont Studio Center is the largest international artists' and writers' Residency Program in the United States, hosting 50 visual artists and writers each month from across the country and around the world. The Studio Center provides 4-12 week studio residencies on an historic 30-building campus along the Gihon River in Johnson, Vermont, a village in the heart of the northern Green Mountains.
ACCOMMODATIONS "The cost of a 4-week residency is $3,750. Generous fellowship and grant assistance available. "Accommodations available on site. "Residents live in single rooms in ten modest, comfortable houses adjacent to the Red Mill Building. Rooms are simply furnished and have shared baths. Complete linen service is provided. The Studio Center is unable to accommodate guests at meals, overnight guests, spouses, children or pets."
ADDITIONAL INFORMATION Fellowships application deadlines are February 15, June 15 and October 1. Writers encouraged to visit website for more information. May also e-mail, call, fax.

VIRGINIA CENTER FOR THE CREATIVE ARTS

154 San Angelo Dr., Amherst VA 24521. (434)946-7236. **Fax:** (434)946-7239. **E-mail:** vcca@vcca.com. **Website:** www.vcca.com. Estab. 1971. Offers residencies year-round, typical residency lasts 2 weeks to 2 months. Open to originating artists: composers, writers, and visual artists. Accommodates 25 at one time. Personal living quarters include 22 single rooms, 2 double rooms, bathrooms shared with one other person. All meals are served. Kitchens for fellows' use available at studios and residence. The VCCA van goes into town twice a week. Fellows share their work regularly. Four studios have pianos. No transportation costs are covered. "Artists are accepted into the VCCA without regard for their ability to contribute

financially to their residency. Daily cost is $180 per fellow. We ask fellows to contribute according to their ability."

COSTS Application fee: $30. Deadline: May 15 for October-January residency; September 15 for February-May residency; January 15 for June-September residency. Send SASE for application form or download from website. Applications are reviewed by panelists.

VIRGINIA FESTIVAL OF THE BOOK

Virginia Festival of the Book Foundation for the Humanities, 145 Ednam Dr., Charlottesville VA 22903-4629. (434)924-3296. **Fax:** (434)296-4714. **E-mail:** vabook@virginia.edu; spcoleman@virginia.edu. **Website:** www.vabook.org. **Contact:** Nancy Damon, program director. Estab. 1995. Annual. Held March 20-24. Average attendance: 22,000. Festival held to celebrate books and promote reading and literacy. Open to Students. Readings, panel discussions, presentations and workshops by author, and book-related professionals for children and adults. Most programs are free and open to the public. See website for more information. Applications available online from May through September.

COSTS Most events are free and open to the public. Two luncheons, a breakfast, and a reception require tickets.

ACCOMMODATIONS Overnight accommodations available.

ADDITIONAL INFORMATION "The festival is a 5-day event featuring authors, illustrators, and publishing professionals. Authors must apply to the festival to be included on a panel. Applications accepted only online.

WESLEYAN WRITERS CONFERENCE

Wesleyan University, 294 High St., Room 207, Middletown CT 06459. (860)685-3604. **Fax:** (860)685-2441. **E-mail:** agreene@wesleyan.edu. **Website:** www.wesleyan.edu/writing/conference. Estab. 1956. Annual conference held June 12-16. Average attendance: 100. Focuses on the novel, fiction techniques, short stories, poetry, screenwriting, nonfiction, literary journalism, memoir, mixed media work and publishing. The conference is held on the campus of Wesleyan University, in the hills overlooking the Connecticut River. Features a faculty of award-winning writers, seminars and readings of new fiction, poetry, nonfiction and mixed media forms - as well as guest lectures on a range of topics including publishing. Both new and experienced writers are welcome. Participants may attend seminars in all genres. Speakers have included Esmond Harmsworth (Zachary Schuster Agency), Daniel Mandel (Sanford J. Greenburger Associates), Dorian Karchmar, Amy Williams (ICM and Collins McCormick), Mary Sue Rucci (Simon & Schuster), Denise Roy (Simon & Schuster), John Kulka (Harvard University Press), Julie Barer (Barer Literary) and many others. Agents will be speaking and available for meetings with attendees. Participants are often successful in finding agents and publishers for their mss. Wesleyan participants are also frequently featured in the anthology *Best New American Voices*.

ACCOMMODATIONS Meals are provided on campus. Lodging is available on campus or in town.

ADDITIONAL INFORMATION Ms critiques are available, but not required. Scholarships and teaching fellowships are available, including the Joan Jakobson Awards for fiction writers and poets; and the Jon Davidoff Scholarships for nonfiction writers and journalists. Inquire via e-mail, fax, or phone.

WESTERN RESERVE WRITERS & FREELANCE CONFERENCE

7700 Clocktower Dr., Kirtland OH 44094. (440) 525-7812. **E-mail:** deencr@aol.com. **Website:** www.deannaadams.com. **Contact:** Deanna Adams, director/conference coordinator. Estab. 1983. Biannual. Last conference held September 28, 2013. Conference duration: 1 day or half-day. Average attendance: 120. "The Western Reserve Writers Conferences are designed for all writers, aspiring and professional, and offer presentations in all genres—nonfiction, fiction, poetry, essays, creative nonfiction, and the business of writing, including Web writing and successful freelance writing." Site: "Located in the main building of Lakeland Community College, the conference is easy to find and just off the I-90 freeway. The Fall 2013 conference featured top-notch presenters from newspapers and magazines, along with published authors, freelance writers, and professional editors. Presentations included developing issues in today's publishing and publishing options, turning writing into a lifelong vocation, as well as workshops on plotting, creating credible characters, writing mysteries, romance writing, and tips on submissions, getting books into stores, and storytelling for both fiction and nonfiction writers. Included throughout the day are one-on-one editing consults, Q&A panel, and book sale/author signings."

COSTS Fall all-day conference includes lunch: $95. Spring half-day conference, no lunch: $69.

ADDITIONAL INFORMATION Brochures for the conferences are available by January (for spring conference) and July (for fall). Also accepts inquiries by e-mail and phone. Check Deanna Adams' website for all updates. Editors and agents often attend the conferences.

WILDACRES WRITERS WORKSHOP

233 S. Elm St., Greensboro NC 27401. (336)255-8210. **E-mail:** judihill78@yahoo.com. **Website:** www.wildacreswriters.com. **Contact:** Judi Hill, Director. Estab. 1985. Annual residential workshop held July 6-13. Conference duration: 1 week. Average attendance: 100. Workshop focuses on novel, short story, flash fiction, poetry, and nonfiction. 10 on faculty include Ron Rash, Carrie Brown, Dr. Janice Fuller, Phillip Gerard, Luke Whisnant, Dr. Joe Clark, John Gregory Brown, Dr. Phebe Davidson, Lee Zacharias, and Vicki Lane. **COSTS** The total price for seven days is $690. This price includes workshop fees, one manuscript critique, programs, parties, room, and meals.

ADDITIONAL INFORMATION Include a 1-page writing sample with your registration. See the website for information.

WILLAMETTE WRITERS ANNUAL WRITERS CONFERENCE

2108 Buck St., West Linn OR 97068. (503)305-6729. **Fax:** (503)344-6174. **E-mail:** wilwrite@willamettewriters.com. **Website:** www.willamettewriters.com. **Contact:** Bill Johnson, office manager. Writer workshops geared toward all levels. Emphasizes all areas of writing, including children's and young adult. Opportunities to meet one-on-one with leading literary agents and editors. Workshops held in August. Cost of conference: $230-$430; includes membership.

WILLAMETTE WRITERS CONFERENCE

2108 Buck St., Portland OR 97068. (503)305-6729. **Fax:** (503)344-6174. **E-mail:** wilwrite@willamettewriters.com. **Website:** www.willamettewriters.com. Estab. 1981. Annual conference held in August. Conference duration: 3 days. Average attendance: 600. "Williamette Writers is open to all writers, and we plan our conference accordingly. We offer workshops on all aspects of fiction, nonfiction, marketing, the creative process, screenwriting, etc. Also we invite top-

notch inspirational speakers for keynote addresses. Recent theme was 'Fresh Brewed.' We always include at least 1 agent or editor panel and offer a variety of topics of interest to both fiction and nonfiction writers and screenwriters." Agents will be speaking and available for meetings with attendees. Recent editors, agents, and film producers in attendance have included April Eberhardt, Katheryn Flynn, Robert Guinsler, Laura Mclean, Tooschis Morin.

COSTS Pricing schedule available online.

ACCOMMODATIONS If necessary, arrangements can be made on an individual basis through the conference hotel. Special rates may be available.

ADDITIONAL INFORMATION Brochure/guidelines are available for a catalog-sized SASE.

WINCHESTER WRITERS' CONFERENCE, FESTIVAL AND BOOKFAIR, AND IN-DEPTH WRITING WORKSHOPS

University of Winchester, Winchester Hampshire WA S022 4NR United Kingdom. 44 (0) 1962 827238. **E-mail:** Barbara.Large@winchester.ac.uk. **Website:** www.writersconference.co.uk. **Contact:** Barbara Large. "The 33rd Winchester Writers' Conference, Festival, and Bookfair will be launched by Lord Julian Fellowes, author/scriptwriter, internationally famous for many works, including *Downton Abbey*, in-depth writing workshops June 24-25, 2-13, at the University of Winchester, Winchester, Hampshire S022 4NR. Lord Felloews will give the Keynote Address and will lead an outstanding team of 65 professional writers who will offer during 14 masters' courses, 16 Friday evening-Sunday morning, 55 lectures, and 500 one-to-one appointments to help writers harness their creative ideas into marketable work. Participate by entering some of the 17 writing competitions, even if you can't attend. Over 120 writers have now reported major publishing successes as a direct result of their attendance at past conferences. This leading international literary event offers a magnificent source of information and network of support from tutors who are published writers and industry specialists, a support that continues throughout the year with additional short courses. Enjoy a creative writing holiday in Winchester, the oldest city in England, yet within an hour of London. Tours planned to Jane Austen's home and the Chawton Study Centre for Women's Literature, the haunts of Keats and the 12th century illuminated Winchester Bible. To receive the 66-page conference programme, including all the competition details please contact us:sara.gangai@winchester.ac.uk, 44(0)1962-826367; barbara.large@winchester.ac.uk, 44(0)1962-827238; or write to us at University of Winchester, Winchester, Hampshire SO22 4NR, United Kingdom."

WINTER POETRY & PROSE GETAWAY

18 N. Richards Ave., Ventnor NJ 08406. (888)887-2105. **E-mail:** info@wintergetaway.com. **Website:** www.wintergetaway.com. **Contact:** Peter Murphy. Estab. 1994. Annual January conference at the Jersey Shore. "This is not your typical writers' conference. Advance your craft and energize your writing at the Winter Getaway. Enjoy challenging and supportive workshops, insightful feedback, and encouraging community. Choose from small, intensive workshops in memoir, novel, YA, nonfiction, and poetry."

ACCOMMODATIONS See website or call for current fee information.

ADDITIONAL INFORMATION Previous faculty has included Julianna Baggott, Christian Bauman, Laure-Anne Bosselaar, Kurt Brown, Mark Doty (National Book Award winner), Stephen Dunn (Pulitzer Prize winner), Dorianne Laux, Carol Plum-Ucci, James Richardson, Mimi Schwartz, Terese Svoboda, and more.

WISCONSIN BOOK FESTIVAL

Wisconsin Humanities Council, 222 S. Bedford St., Suite F, Madison WI 53703. (608)262-0706. **Fax:** (608)263-7970. **E-mail:** atjoneschaim@wisc.edu. **Website:** www.wisconsinbookfestival.org. Estab. 2002. Annual festival held November 7-11. Conference duration: 5 days. The festival features readings, lectures, book discussions, writing workshops, live interviews, children's events, and more. Speakers have included Michael Cunningham, Grace Paley, TC Boyle, Marjane Satrapi, Phillip Gourevitch, Myla Goldberg, Audrey Niffenegger, Harvey Pekar, Billy Collins, Tim O'Brien and Isabel Allende.

COSTS All festival events are free.

WISCONSIN REGIONAL WRITERS' ASSOCIATION CONFERENCES

PO Box 085270, Racine Wisconsin 53408-5270. **E-mail:** cfreg@wiwrite.org. **Website:** www.wiwrite.org. Estab. 1948. Annual conferences are held in May 10 and 11 and September. Conference duration: 2-3 days. Provides presentations for all genres, including fiction, nonfiction, scriptwriting, and poetry. Presenters include authors, agents, editors, and publishers. Speak-

ers have included Jack Byrne, Michelle Grajkowski, Benjamin Leroy, Richard Lederer, and Philip Martin. **COSTS** $40-75.

ACCOMMODATIONS Provides a list of area hotels or lodging options. "We negotiate special rates at each facility. A block of rooms is set aside for a specific time period."

ADDITIONAL INFORMATION Award winners receive a certificate and a cash prize. First place winners of the Jade Ring contest receive a jade ring. Must be a member to enter contests. For brochure, call, e-mail or visit website in March/July.

WOMEN WRITERS WINTER RETREAT

Homestead House B&B, 38111 West Spaulding, Willoughby OH 44094. (440)946-1902. **E-mail:** deencr@aol.com. **Website:** www.deannaadams.com. Estab. 2007. Annual. Conference duration: 3 days. Average attendance: 35-40. Retreat. "The Women Writers' Winter Retreat was designed for aspiring and professional women writers who cannot seem to find enough time to devote to honing their craft. Each retreat offers class time and workshops facilitated by successful women writers, as well as allows time to do some actual writing, alone or in a group. A Friday night dinner and keynote kick-starts the weekend, followed by Saturday workshops, free time, meals, and an open mic to read your works. Sunday wraps up with 1 more workshop and fellowship. All genres welcome. Choice of overnight stay or commuting." Site: Located in the heart of downtown Willoughby, this warm and attractive bed and breakfast is easy to find, around the corner from the main street, Erie Street, and behind a popular Arabica coffee house. Door prizes and book sale/author signings throughout the weekend.

COSTS Single room: $315; shared room: $235 (includes complete weekend package, with B&B stay and all meals and workshops); weekend commute: $165; Saturday only: $125 (prices include lunch and dinner).

ADDITIONAL INFORMATION Brochures for the writers retreat are available by December. Accepts inquiries and reservations by e-mail or phone. See Deanna's website for additional information and updates.

WOMEN WRITING THE WEST

8547 E. Araphoe Rd., Box J-541, Greenwood Village CO 80112-1436. **E-mail:** conference@women-writingthewest.org. **Website:** www.womenwritingthewest.org. Held October 11-13 in Kansas City, Missouri. "Women Writing the West is a nonprofit association of writers, editors, publishers, agents, booksellers, and other professionals writing and promoting the women's West. As such, women writing their stories in the American West in a way that illuminates them authentically. In addition, the organization provides support, encouragement, and inspiration to all women writing about any facet of the American West. Membership is open to all interested persons worldwide. Open to students. Cost of membership: Annual membership dues $60. Publisher dues are $60. International dues are $70. In addition to the annual dues, there is an option to become a sustaining member for $100. Sustaining members receive a WWW enamel logo pin, prominent listing in WWW publications, and the knowledge that they are assisting the organization. Members actively exchange ideas on a list e-bulletin board. WWW membership also allows the choice of participation in our marketing marvel, the annual WWW Catalog of Author'sBooks. An annual conference is held every fall. Our WWW newsletter is current WWW activities; features market research, and experience articles of interest pertaining to American West literature and member news. Sponsors annual WILLA Literary Award, which is given in several categories foroutstanding literature featuring women's stories, set in the West. The winner of a WILLA literary Award receives a cash award and a trophy at the annualconference. Contest open to non-members. Annual conference held in third weekend in October. Covers research, writing techniques, multiple genres, marketing/promotion, and more. Agents and editors will be speaking and available for one-on-one meetings with attendees. Conference location changes each year."

COSTS Early Registration: $295 (June 30); Registration (after June 30): $320. Discounts available for members, and for specific days only.

ACCOMMODATIONS See website for location and accommodation details.

WORDS & MUSIC

624 Pirate's Alley, New Orleans LA 70116. (504)586-1609. **Fax:** (504)522-9725. **E-mail:** info@wordsandmusic.org. **Website:** www.wordsandmusic.org. Estab. 1997. Annual conference held November 20-24. Conference duration: 5 days. Average attendance: 300. Presenters include authors, agents, editors and pub-

lishers. Past speakers included agents Deborah Grosvenor, Judith Weber, Stuart Bernstein, Nat Sobel, Jeff Kleinman, Emma Sweeney, Liza Dawson and Michael Murphy; editors Lauren Marino, Webster Younce, Ann Patty, Will Murphy, Jofie Ferrari-Adler, Elizabeth Stein; critics Marie Arana, Jonathan Yardley, and Michael Dirda; fiction writers Oscar Hijuelos, Robert Olen Butler, Shirley Ann Grau, Mayra Montero, Ana Castillo, H.G. Carrillo. Agents and editors critique manuscripts in advance; meet with them one-on-one during the conference.

COSTS See website for a costs and additional information on accommodations. Website will update closer to date of conference.

ACCOMMODATIONS Hotel Monteleone in New Orleans.

WRITE-BY-THE-LAKE WRITER'S WORKSHOP & RETREAT

21 N. Park St., 7th Floor, Madison WI 53715. (608)262-3447. **E-mail:** cdesmet@dcs.wisc.edu. **Website:** www.dcs.wisc.edu/lsa/writing. **Contact:** Christine DeSmet, director. Open to all writers and students; 12 workshops for all levels. Includes 2 Master Classes for full-novel critique. Held the third week of June on UW-Madison campus. Registration limited to 15; fewer in Master Classes. Writing facilities available; computer labs, wi-fi in all buildings and on the outdoor lakeside terrace.

COSTS $345 before May 20; $395 after May 20. Additional cost for Master Classes and college credits. Cost includes instruction, welcome luncheon, and pastry/coffee each day.

ADDITIONAL INFORMATION E-mail for more information. "Registration opens every December for following June. See web pages online."

WRITE! CANADA

The Word Guild, P.O. Box 1243, Trenton ON K8V 5R9 Canada. **E-mail:** info@thewordguild.com. **E-mail:** writecanada@rogers.com. **Website:** www.writecanada.org. Conference duration: 3 days. Annual conference June 14-16 in Guelph, Ontario for writers who are Christian of all types and at all stages. Offers solid instruction, stimulating interaction, exciting challenges, and worshipful community.

WRITE ON THE SOUND WRITERS' CONFERENCE

Edmonds Arts Commission, 700 Main St., Edmonds WA 98020. (425)771-0228. **Fax:** (425)771-0253. **E-**

mail: sarah.cocker@edmondswa.gov. **Website:** www.writeonthesound.com. Estab. 1985. Annual conference held October 4-6. Conference duration: 2.5 days. Average attendance: 200. Features over 30 presenters, a literary contest, ms critiques, a reception and book signing, onsite bookstore, and a variety of evening activities. Held at the Frances Anderson Center in Edmonds, just north of Seattle on the Puget Sound. Speakers have included Elizabeth George, Dan Hurley, Marcia Woodard, Holly Hughes, Greg Bear, Timothy Egan, Joe McHugh, Frances Wood, Garth Stein and Max Grover.

COSTS See website for more information on applying to view costs.

ADDITIONAL INFORMATION Brochures are available in July. Accepts inquiries via phone, e-mail, and fax.

WRITERS@WORK CONFERENCE

P.O. Box 711191, Salt Lake City UT 84171-1191. (801)996-3313. **E-mail:** jennifer@writersatwork.org. **Website:** www.writersatwork.org. Estab. 1985. Annual conference held June 5-9. Conference duration: 5 days. Average attendance: 250. Morning workshops (3-hours/day) focus on novel, advanced fiction, generative fiction, nonfiction, poetry, and young adult fiction. Afternoon sessions will include craft lectures, discussions, and directed interviews with authors, agents, and editors. In addition to the traditional, one-on-one manuscript consultations, there will be many opportunities to mingle informally with agents/editors. Held at the Alta Lodge in Alta Lodge, Utah. Speakers have included Steve Almond, Bret Lott, Shannon Hale, Emily Forland (Wendy Weil Agency), Julie Culver (Folio Literary Management, Chuck Adams (Algonquin Press), and Mark A. Taylor (Juniper Press).

COSTS $675-965, based on housing type and consultations.

ACCOMMODATIONS Onsite housing available. Additional lodging and meal information is on the website.

WRITERS' CONFERENCE AT OCEAN PARK

14 Temple Ave., P.O. Box 7296, Ocean Park ME 04063-7296. (207)934-9068. **Fax:** (207)934-2823. **E-mail:** opa@oceanpark.org. **Website:** www.oceanpark.org. Other addresses: P.O. Box 7146, Ocean Park, ME 04063-7146; P.O. Box 172, Assonet, MA 02702 (mailing address for conference). Estab. 1941. Annual conference held in mid-August. Conference duration: 4 days. Average attendance: 50. "We try to present a balanced and eclectic conference. In addition to time and attention given to poetry, we also have children's literature, mystery writing, travel, fiction, nonfiction, journalism, and other issues of interest to writers. Our speakers are editors, writers, and other professionals. Our concentration is, by intention, a general view of writing to publish with supportive encouragement. We are located in Ocean Park, a small seashore village 14 miles south of Portland. Ours is a summer assembly center with many buildings from the Victorian age. The conference meets in Porter Hall, one of the assembly buildings which is listed in the National Register of Historic Places. Speakers have included Michael C. White (novelist/short story writer), Betsy Shool (poet), Suzanne Strempek Shea (novelist), John Perrault (poet), Josh Williamson (newspaper editor), Dawn Potter (poet), Bruce Pratt (fiction writer), Amy McDonald (children's author), Anne Wescott Dodd (nonfiction writer), Kate Chadbourne (singer/songwriter), Wesley McNair (poet/Maine faculty member), and others. We usually have about 8 guest presenters each year." Publishes writers/editors will be speaking, leading workshops, and available for meetings with attendees.

COSTS $200. The fee does not include housing or meals, which must be arranged separately by conferees.

ACCOMMODATIONS "An accommodations list is available. We are in a summer resort area where motels, guest houses, and restaurants abound."

ADDITIONAL INFORMATION Official summer hours begin in late June, check then for specific dates for 2013 conference. "We have 6 contests for various genres. An announcement is available in the spring. The prizes (all modest) are awarded at the end of the conference and only to those who are registered. Send SASE in June for the conference program."

WRITER'S DIGEST CONFERENCE

F+W Media, Inc., 10151 Carver Road, Suite 200, Blue Ash OH 45242. **E-mail:** jill.ruesch@fwmedia.com. **Website:** www.writersdigestconference.com. The Writer's Digest Conference features an amazing line up of speakers to help writers with the craft and business of writing. The most popular feature of this conference is the agent pitch slam, in which potential authors are given the ability to pitch their books directly to agents. For the 2013 conference, there will be more than 50 agents in attendance. The 2013 conference will be held in New York City on April 5-7. For more details, see the website.

WRITER'S DIGEST CONFERENCE WEST

F+W Media, Inc., 10151 Carver Road, Suite 200, Blue Ash OH 45242. **E-mail:** jill.ruesch@fwmedia.com. **Website:** www.writersdigestconference.com. The Writer's Digest Conference West features an amazing line up of speakers to help writers with the craft and business of writing. The most popular feature of this conference is the agent pitch slam, in which potential authors are given the ability to pitch their books directly to agents. For the 2013 conference, there will be more than 50 agents in attendance. The 2013 conference will be held in Los Angeles in October. For more details, see the website.

WRITERS' LEAGUE OF TEXAS AGENTS CONFERENCE

Writers' League of Texas, 611 S. Congress Ave., Suite 505, Austin TX 78704. (512)499-8914. **Fax:** (512)499-0441. **E-mail:** wlt@writersleague.org. **E-mail:** jennifer@writersleague.org. **Website:** www.writersleague.org. Estab. 1982. Established in 1981, the Writers' League of Texas is a nonprofit professional organization whose primary purpose is to provide a forum for information, support, and sharing among writers, to help members improve and market their writing skills, and to promote the interests of writers and the writing community. The Writers' League of Texas Agents & Editors Conference is for writers at every stage of their career. Beginners can learn more about this mystifying industry and prepare themselves for the journey ahead. Those with completed manuscripts can pitch to agents and get feedback on their manuscripts from professional editors. Published writers can learn about market trends and network with rising stars in the world of writing. No matter what your market, genre, or level, our conference can benefit you.

COSTS Rates vary based on membership and the date of registration. The starting rate (registration through December 15) is $309 for members and $369 for nonmembers. Rate increases by through later dates. See website for details.

ACCOMMODATIONS 2013 event is at the Hyatt Regency Austin, 208 Barton Springs Road, Austin, TX 78704. Check back often for new information.

ADDITIONAL INFORMATION Event held from June 21-23, 2013. Contests and awards programs are offered separately. Brochures are available upon request.

WRITERS' LEAGUE OF TEXAS WORKSHOPS AND SUMMER WRITING RETREAT

611 S. Congress Ave., Suite 130, Austin TX 78704. (512)499-8914. **Fax:** (512)499-0441. **E-mail:** wlt@writersleague.org. **Website:** www.writersleague.org. **Contact:** Sara Kocek, program coordinator. "Classes and workshops provide practical advice and guidance on the craft of writing for writers at all stages of their career." Retreat: Annual Summer Writing Academy in Alpine, TX, is a weeklong writing intensive with five tracks. Special presentations: "The Secrets of the Agents" series of workshops with visiting literary agents. Classes and Workshops: Topics: E-publishing; creative nonfiction; screenwriting; novel writing; short fiction; journaling; manuscript revision; memoir writing; poetry; essays; freelance writing; publicity; author/book websites; and blogging. Instructors include Carol Dawson, Karleen Koen, Kirsten Cappy, Eric Butterman, Cyndi Hughes, Scott Wiggerman, Debra Monroe, Jennifer Ziegler, W.K. Stratton.

WRITERS OMI AT LEDIG HOUSE

55 Fifth Ave., 15th Floor, New York NY 10003. (212)206-6114. **E-mail:** writers@artomi.org. **Website:** www.artomi.org. Residency duration: 2 weeks to 2 months. Average attendance and site: "Up to 20 writers per session—10 at a given time—live and write on the stunning 300 acre grounds and sculpture park that overlooks the Catskill Mountains." Deadline: October 20.

ACCOMMODATIONS Residents provide their own transportation. Offers overnight accommodations.

ADDITIONAL INFORMATION "Agents and editors from the New York publishing community are invited for dinner and discussion. Bicycles, a swimming pool, and nearby tennis court are available for use."

THE WRITERS RETREATS' NETWORK

15 Canusa St., Stanstead QC J0B 3E5 Canada. **Website:** www.writersretreat.com. A worldwide selection of residential retreats opened year-round to writers and authors—most of them offering on-site literary services. The retreats cater to writers of all genres and offer on-site support such as mentoring, work-

shops, editing, book printing, and lodging; some of them offer scholarships. To start and operate a retreat in your area, visit the website and read a few pages of the handbook *A Writers' Retreat: Starting from Scratch to Success!*

WRITERS RETREAT WORKSHOP

P.O. Box 4236, Louisville KY 40204. **E-mail:** wrw04@netscape.net. **Website:** www.writersretreatworkshop.com. Estab. 1987. Annual workshop held June 14-23 at the Villa Maria Retreat and Conference Center in Frontenac, Minnesota. Conference duration: 10 days. Focuses on fiction and narrative nonfiction books in progress (all genres). This is an intensive learning experience for small groups of serious-minded writers. Founded by the late Gary Provost (one of the country's leading writing instructors) and his wife Gail (an award-winning author). The goal is for students to leave with a solid understanding of the marketplace, as well as the craft of writing a novel. Speakers have included Becky Motew, Donald Maass, Jennifer Crusie, Michael Palmer, Nancy Pickard, Elizabeth Lyon, Lauren Mosko (Writer's Digest Books), Adam Marsh (Reece Halsey North), and Peter H. McGuigan (Sanford J. Greenburger Literary Agency).

COSTS $1,750 for returning students and $1,825 for new students. Tuition includes private room, thre meals daily, all 1-1 meetings with staff and agents, and classes.

WRITERS WEEKEND AT THE BEACH

P.O. Box 877, Ocean Park WA 98640. (360)262-0160. **E-mail:** bhansen6@juno.com. **E-mail:** bobtracie@hotmail.com. **Contact:** John Pelkey. Estab. 1992. Annual conference held in March. Conference duration: 2 days. Average attendance: 60. A retreat for writers with an emphasis on poetry, fiction, and nonfiction. Held at the Ocean Park Methodist Retreat Center & Camp. Speakers have included Wayne Holmes, Miralee Ferrell, Jim Whiting, Birdie Etchison, Colette Tennant, Gail Dunham, Linda Clare and Marion Duckworth.

COSTS $199 for full registration before February 17 and $209 after February 17.

ACCOMMODATIONS Offers on-site overnight lodging.

WRITE-TO-PUBLISH CONFERENCE

WordPro Communication Services, 9118 W. Elmwood Dr., Suite 1G, Niles IL 60714-5820. (847)296-3964. **Fax:** (847)296-0754. **E-mail:** lin@writetopublish.com. **Website:** www.writetopublish.com. **Contact:** Lin Johnson, director. Estab. 1971. Annual. Conference held June 4-7, 2013. Average attendance: 250. Conference is focused for the Christian market and includes classes on writing for children. Writer workshops geared toward all levels. Open to students. Site: Wheaton College, Wheaton, IL (Chicago).

COSTS approximately $485; includes conference and banquet.

ACCOMMODATIONS In campus residence halls. Cost is approximately $280-360.

ADDITIONAL INFORMATION Optional ms evaluation available. College credit available. Conference information available in January. For details, visit website, or e-mail brochure@writetopublish.com. Accepts inquiries by e-mail, fax, phone.

WRITING FOR THE SOUL

Jerry B. Jenkins Christian Writers Guild, 5525 N. Union Blvd., Suite 101, Colorado Springs CO 80918. (866)495-5177. **Fax:** (719)495-5181. **E-mail:** contactus@christianwritersguild.com. **Website:** www.christianwritersguild.com/conference. Annual conference held in February. Workshops and continuing classes cover fiction, nonfiction and magazine writing, children's books, and teen writing. The keynote speakers are nationally known, leading authors. The conference is hosted by Jerry B. Jenkins.

COSTS See website for pricing.

ACCOMMODATIONS The Broadmoor in Colorado Springs.

WRITING WORKSHOP AT CASTLE HILL

1 Depot Rd., P.O. Box 756, Truro MA 02666-0756. **E-mail:** cherie@castlehill.org. **Website:** www.castlehill.org. Poetry, Fiction, Memoir workshops geared toward intermediate and advanced levels. **Open to students.** Workshops by Keith Althaus: Poetry; Anne Bernays: Elements of Fiction; Elizabeth Bradfield: Poetry in Plein Air & Broadsides and Beyond: Poetry as Public Art; Melanie Braverman: In Pursuit of Exactitude: Poetry; Josephine Del Deo: Preoccupation in Poetry; Martin Espada: Barbaric Yamp: A Poetry Workshop; Judy Huge: Finding the Me in Memoir; Justin Kaplan: Autobiography. See website under Summer 2011 Writers for dates and more information.

THE HELENE WURLITZER FOUNDATION

P.O. Box 1891, Taos NM 87571. (575)758-2413. **Fax:** (575)758-2559. **E-mail:** hwf@taosnet.com. **Website:** www.wurlitzerfoundation.org. **Contact:** Michael A. Knight, executive director. Estab. 1953. The Foundation's purpose is to provide a quiet haven where artists may pursue their creative endeavors without pressure to produce while they are in residence.

ACCOMMODATIONS "Provides individual housing in fully furnished studio/houses (casitas), rent and utility free. Artists are responsible for transportation to and from Taos, their meals, and the materials for their work. Bicycles are provided upon request."

PROFESSIONAL ORGANIZATIONS

//

AGENTS' ORGANIZATIONS

ASSOCIATION OF AUTHORS' AGENTS (AAA), 5-8 Lower John Street, Golden Square, London W1F 9HA . E-mail: anthonygoff@davidhigham.co.uk. Website: www.agentsassoc.co.uk.

ASSOCIATION OF AUTHORS' REPRESENTATIVES (AAR). E-mail: info@aar-online.org. Website: www.aar-online.org.

ASSOCIATION OF TALENT AGENTS (ATA), 9255 Sunset Blvd., Suite 930, Los Angeles CA 90069. (310)274-0628. E-mail: shellie@agentassociation.com. Website: www.agentassociation.com.

WRITERS' ORGANIZATIONS

ACADEMY OF AMERICAN POETS 584 Broadway, Suite 604, New York NY 10012-5243. (212)274-0343. Fax: (212)274-9427. E-mail: academy@poets.org. Website: www.poets.org.

AMERICAN CRIME WRITERS LEAGUE (ACWL), 17367 Hilltop Ridge Dr., Eureka MO 63205. Website: www.acwl.org.

AMERICAN INDEPENDENT WRITERS (AIW), 1001 Connecticut Ave. NW, Suite 701, Washington DC 20036. E-mail: info@aiwriters.org. Website: www.americanindependentwriters.org.

AMERICAN MEDICAL WRITERS ASSOCIATION (AMWA), 30 West Gude Drive, Suite 525, Rockville MD 20850-4347. (301)294-5303. Fax: (301)294-9006. E-mail: amwa@amwa.org. Website: www.amwa.org.

AMERICAN SCREENWRITERS ASSOCIATION (ASA), 269 S. Beverly Dr., Suite 2600, Beverly Hills CA 90212-3807. (866)265-9091. E-mail: asa@goasa.com. Website: www.asascreenwriters.com.

AMERICAN TRANSLATORS ASSOCIATION (ATA), 225 Reinekers Lane, Suite 590, Alexandria VA 22314. (703)683-6100. Fax: (703)683-6122. E-mail: ata@atanet.org. Website: www.atanet.org.

EDUCATION WRITERS ASSOCIATION (EWA), 2122 P St., NW Suite 201, Washington DC 20037. (202)452-9830. Fax: (202)452-9837. E-mail: ewa@ewa.org. Website: www.ewa.org.

HORROR WRITERS ASSOCIATION (HWA), 244 5th Ave., Suite 2767, New York NY 10001. E-mail: hwa@horror.org. Website: www.horror.org.

THE INTERNATIONAL WOMEN'S WRITING GUILD (IWWG),P.O. Box 810, Gracie Station, New York NY 10028-0082. (212)737-7536. Fax: (212)737-9469. E-mail: dirhahn@aol.org. Website: www.iwwg.com.

MYSTERY WRITERS OF AMERICA (MWA), 1140 Broadway, Suite 1507, New York NY 10001. (212)888-8171. Fax: (212)888-8107. E-mail: mwa@mysterywriters.org. Website: www.mysterywriters.org.

NATIONAL ASSOCIATION OF SCIENCE WRITERS (NASW), P.O. Box 7905, Berkeley, CA 94707. (510)647-9500. E-mail: LFriedmann@nasw.org. website: www.nasw.org.

NATIONAL ASSOCIATION OF WOMEN WRITERS (NAWW), 24165 IH-10 W., Suite 217-637, San Antonio TX 78257. Phone/Fax: (866)821-5829. Website: www.naww.org.

ORGANIZATION OF BLACK SCREENWRITERS (OBS). Golden State Mutual Life Insurance Bldg., 1999 West Adams Blvd., Rm. Mezzanine Los Angeles, CA 90018. Website: www.obswriter.com.

OUTDOOR WRITERS ASSOCIATION OF AMERICA (OWAA), 121 Hickory St., Suite 1, Missoula MT 59801. (406)728-7434. E-mail: krhoades@owaa.org. Website: www.owaa.org.

POETRY SOCIETY OF AMERICA (PSA), 15 Gramercy Park, New York NY 10003. (212)254-9628. website: www.poetrysociety.org. Poets & Writers, 90 Broad St., Suite 2100, New York NY 10004. (212)226-3586. Fax: (212)226-3963. Website: www.pw.org.

ROMANCE WRITERS OF AMERICA (RWA), 114615 Benfer Road, Houston TX 77069. (832)717-5200. Fax: (832)717-5201. E-mail: info@rwanational.org. Website: www.rwanational.org.

SCIENCE FICTION AND FANTASY WRITERS OF AMERICA (SFWA), P.O. Box 877, Chestertown MD 21620. E-mail: execdir@sfwa.org. Website: www.sfwa.org.

SOCIETY OF AMERICAN BUSINESS EDITORS & WRITERS (SABEW), University of Missouri, School of Journalism, 30 Neff Annex, Columbia MO 65211. (602) 496-7862. E-mail: sabew@sabew.org. Website: www.sabew.org.

SOCIETY OF AMERICAN TRAVEL WRITERS (SATW), 7044 S. 13 St., Oak Creek WI 53154. (414)908-4949. Fax: (414)768-8001. E-mail: satw@satw.org. Website: www.satw.org.

SOCIETY OF CHILDREN'S BOOK WRITERS & ILLUSTRATORS (SCBWI), 8271 Beverly Blvd., Los Angeles CA 90048. (323)782-1010. E-mail: scbwi@scbwi.org. Website: www.scbwi.org.

WESTERN WRITERS OF AMERICA (WWA). E-mail: spiritfire@kc.rr.com. Website: www.westernwriters.org.

INDUSTRY ORGANIZATIONS

AMERICAN BOOKSELLERS ASSOCIATION (ABA), 200 White Plains Rd., Suite 600, Tarrytown NY 10591. (914)591-2665. E-mail: info@bookweb.org. Website: www.bookweb.org.

AMERICAN SOCIETY OF JOURNALISTS & AUTHORS (ASJA), 1501 Broadway, Suite 302, New York NY 10036. (212)997-0947. E-mail: director@asja.org. Website: www.asja.org.

ASSOCIATION FOR WOMEN IN COMMUNICATIONS (AWC), 3337 Duke St., Alexandria VA 22314. (703)370-7436. E-mail: info@womcom.org. Website: www.womcom.org.

ASSOCIATION OF AMERICAN PUBLISHERS (AAP), 71 5th Ave., 2nd Floor, New York NY 10003. Or, 50 F St. NW, Suite 400, Washington DC 20001. Website: www.publishers.org.

THE ASSOCIATION OF WRITERS & WRITING PROGRAMS (AWP), Mail Stop 1E3, George Mason University, Fairfax VA 22030. (703)993-4301. Fax: (703)993-4302. E-mail: services@awpwriter.org. website: www.awpwriter.org.

THE AUTHORS GUILD, INC., 31 E. 32nd St., 7th Floor, New York NY 10016. (212)563-5904. Fax: (212)564-5363. E-mail: staff@authorsguild.org. website: www.authorsguild.org.

CANADIAN AUTHORS ASSOCIATION (CAA), P.O. Box 581, Stn. Main Orilla ON L3V 6K5 Canada. (705)653-0323. E-mail: admin@canauthors.org. Website: www.canauthors.org.

CHRISTIAN BOOKSELLERS ASSOCIATION (CBA), P.O. Box 62000, Colorado Springs CO 80962-2000. (800)252-1950. Fax: (719)272-3510. E-mail: info@cbaonline.org. website: www.cbaonline.org.

THE DRAMATISTS GUILD OF AMERICA, 1501 Broadway, Suite 701, New York NY 10036. (212)398-9366. Fax: (212)944-0420. Website: www.dramatistsguild.com.

NATIONAL LEAGUE OF AMERICAN PEN WOMEN (NLAPW), 1300 17th St. NW, Washington DC 20036-1973. (202)785-1997. E-mail: nlapw1@verizon.net. Website: www.americanpen-women.org.

NATIONAL WRITERS ASSOCIATION (NWA), 10940 S. Parker Rd., #508, Parker CO 80134. (303)841-0246. Fax: (303)841-2607. E-mail: natlwritersassn@hotmail.com. Website: www.nationalwriters.com

NATIONAL WRITERS UNION (NWU), 256 West 38th Street, Suite 703, New York, NY 10018. (212)254-0279. Fax: (212)254-0673. E-mail: nwu@nwu.org. Website: www.nwu.org.

PEN AMERICAN CENTER, 588 Broadway, Suite 303, New York NY 10012-3225. (212)334-1660. Fax: (212)334-2181. E-mail: pen@pen.org. Website: www.pen.org.

THE PLAYWRIGHTS GUILD OF CANADA (PGC), 215 Spadina Ave., Suite #210, Toronto ON M5T 2C7 Canada. (416)703-0201. Fax: (416)703-0059. E-mail: info@playwrightsguild.ca. Website: www.playwrightsguild.com.

VOLUNTEER LAWYERS FOR THE ARTS (VLA), One E. 53rd St., 6th Floor, New York NY 10022. (212)319-2787. Fax: (212)752-6575. Website: www.vlany.org.

WOMEN IN FILM (WIF), 6100 Wilshire Blvd., Suite 710, Los Angeles CA 90048. (323)935-2211. Fax: (323)935-2212. E-mail: info@wif.org. Website: www.wif.org.

WOMEN'S NATIONAL BOOK ASSOCIATION (WNBA), P.O. Box 237, FDR Station, New York NY 10150. (212)208-4629. Fax: (212)208-4629. E-mail: publicity@bookbuzz.com. Website: www.wnba-books.org.

WRITERS GUILD OF ALBERTA (WGA), 11759 Groat Rd., Edmonton AB T5M 3K6 Canada. (780)422-8174. Fax: (780)422-2663. E-mail: mail@writersguild.ab.ca. Website: writersguild.ab.ca.

WRITERS GUILD OF AMERICA-EAST (WGA), 555 W. 57th St., Suite 1230, New York NY 10019. (212)767-7800. Fax: (212)582-1909. e-mail: info@wgaeast.org. Website: www.wgaeast.org.

WRITERS GUILD OF AMERICA-WEST (WGA), 7000 W. Third St., Los Angeles CA 90048. (323)951-4000. Fax: (323)782-4800. Website: www.wga.org.

WRITERS UNION OF CANADA (TWUC), 90 Richmond St. E., Suite 200, Toronto ON M5C 1P1 Canada. (416)703-8982. E-mail: info@writersunion.ca. Website: www.writersunion.ca.

GLOSSARY

#10 ENVELOPE. A standard, business-size envelope.

ADVANCE. A sum of money a publisher pays a writer prior to the publication of a book. It is usually paid in installments, such as one-half on signing contract; one-half on delivery of complete and satisfactory manuscript.

AGENT. A liaison between a writer and editor or publisher. An agent shops a manuscript around, receiving a commission when the manuscript is accepted. Agents usually take a 10-15% fee from the advance and royalties.

ARC. Advance reader copy.

ASSIGNMENT. Editor asks a writer to produce a specific article for an agreed-upon fee.

AUCTION. Publishers sometimes bid for the acquisition of a book manuscript that has excellent sales prospects. The bids are for the amount of the author's advance, advertising and promotional expenses, royalty percentage, etc. Auctions are conducted by agents.

AVANT-GARDE. Writing that is innovative in form, style, or subject.

BACKLIST. A publisher's list of its books that were not published during the current season, but that are still in print.

BIMONTHLY. Every two months.

BIO. A sentence or brief paragraph about the writer; can include education and work experience.

BIWEEKLY. Every two weeks.

BLOG. Short for weblog. Used by writers to build platform by posting regular commentary, observations, poems, tips, etc.

BLURB. The copy on paperback book covers or hard cover book dust jackets, either promoting the book and the author or featuring testimonials from book reviewers or well-known people in the book's field. Also called flap copy or jacket copy.

BOILERPLATE. A standardized contract.

BOUND GALLEYS. Prepublication edition of book, usually photocopies of final galley proofs; also known as "bound proofs."

BYLINE. Name of the author appearing with the published piece.

CATEGORY FICTION. A term used to include all types of fiction.

CHAPBOOK. A small booklet usually paperback of poetry, ballads or tales.

CIRCULATION. The number of subscribers to a magazine.

CLIPS. Samples, usually from newspapers or magazines, of a writer's published work.

COFFEE-TABLE BOOK. An heavily illustrated oversize book.

COMMERCIAL NOVELS. Novels designed to appeal to a broad audience. These are often broken down into categories such as western, mystery and romance. See also genre.

CONTRIBUTOR'S COPIES. Copies of the issues of magazines sent to the author in which the author's work appears.

CO-PUBLISHING. Arrangement where author and publisher share publications costs and profits of a book. Also known as cooperative publishing.

COPYEDITING. Editing a manuscript for grammar, punctuation, printing style and factual accuracy.

COPYRIGHT. A means to protect an author's work.

COVER LETTER. A brief letter that accompanies the manuscript being sent to and agent or editor.

CREATIVE NONFICTION. Nonfictional writing that uses an innovative approach to the subject and creative language.

CRITIQUING SERVICE. Am editing service in which writers pay a fee for comments on the salability or other qualities of their manuscript. Fees vary, as do the quality of the critiques.

CV. Curriculum vita. A brief listing of qualifications and career accomplishments.

ELECTRONIC RIGHTS. Secondary or subsidiary rights dealing with electronic/multimedia formats (i.e., the Internet, CD-ROMs, electronic magazines).

ELECTRONIC SUBMISSION. A submission made by modem or on computer disk.

EROTICA. Fiction that is sexually oriented.

EVALUATION FEES. Fees an agent may charge to evaluate material. The extent and quality of this evaluation varies, but comments usually concern salability of the manuscript.

FAIR USE. A provision of the copyright law that says short passages from copyrighted material may be used without infringing on the owner's rights.

FEATURE. An article giving the reader information of human interest rather than news.

FILLER. A short item used by an editor to "fill" out a newspaper column or magazine page. It could be a joke, an anecdote, etc.

FILM RIGHTS. Rights sold or optioned by the agent/author to a person in the film industry, enabling the book to be made into a movie.

FOREIGN RIGHTS. Translation or reprint rights to be sold abroad.

FRONTLIST. A publisher's list of books that are new to the current season.

GALLEYS. First typeset version of manuscript that has not yet been divided into pages.

GENRE. Refers either to a general classification of writing, such as the novel or the poem, or to the categories within those classifications, such as the problem novel or the sonnet.

GHOSTWRITER. Writer who puts into literary form article, speech, story or book based on another person's ideas or knowledge.

GRAPHIC NOVEL. A story in graphic form, long comic strip, or heavily illustrated story; of 40 pages or more.

HI-LO. A type of fiction that offers a high level of interest for readers at a low reading level.

HIGH CONCEPT. A story idea easily expressed in a quick, one-line description.

HONORARIUM. Token payment.

HOOK. Aspect of the work that sets it apart from others and draws in the reader/viewer.

HOW-TO. Books and magazine articles offering a combination of information and advice in describing how something can be accomplished.

IMPRINT. Name applied to a publisher's specific line of books.

JOINT CONTRACT. A legal agreement between a publisher and two or more authors, establishing provisions for the division of royalties the book generates.

KILL FEE. Fee for a complete article that was assigned and then cancelled.

LEAD TIME. The time between the acquisition of a manuscript by an editor and its actual publication.

LITERARY FICTION. The general category of serious, non-formulaic, intelligent fiction.

MAINSTREAM FICTION. Fiction that transcends popular novel categories such as mystery, romance and science fiction.

MARKETING FEE. Fee charged by some agents to cover marketing expenses. It may be used to cover postage, telephone calls, faxes, photocopying or any other expense incurred in marketing a manuscript.

MASS MARKET. Non-specialized books of wide appeal directed toward a large audience.

MEMOIR. A narrative recounting a writer's (or fictional narrator's) personal or family history; specifics may be altered, though essentially considered nonfiction.

MIDDLE GRADE OR MID-GRADE. The general classification of books written for readers approximately ages 9-11. Also called middle readers.

MIDLIST. Those titles on a publisher's list that are not expected to be big sellers, but are expected to have limited/modest sales.

MODEL RELEASE. A paper signed by the subject of a photograph giving the photographer permission to use the photograph.

MULTIPLE CONTRACT. Book contract with an agreement for a future book(s).

MULTIPLE SUBMISSIONS. Sending more than one book or article idea to a publisher at the same time.

NARRATIVE NONFICTION. A narrative presentation of actual events.

NET ROYALTY. A royalty payment based on the amount of money a book publisher receives on the sale of a book after booksellers' discounts, special sales discounts and returns.

NOVELLA. A short novel, or a long short story; approximately 7,000 to 15,000 words.

ON SPEC. An editor expresses an interest in a proposed article idea and agrees to consider the finished piece for publication "on speculation." The editor is under no obligation to buy the finished manuscript.

ONE-TIME RIGHTS. Rights allowing a manuscript to be published one time. The work can be sold again by the writer without violating the contract.

OPTION CLAUSE. A contract clause giving a publisher the right to publish an author's next book.

PAYMENT ON ACCEPTANCE. The editor sends you a check for your article, story or poem as soon as he decides to publish it.

PAYMENT ON PUBLICATION. The editor doesn't send you a check for your material until it is published.

PEN NAME. The use of a name other than your legal name on articles, stories or books. Also called a pseudonym.

PHOTO FEATURE. Feature in which the emphasis is on the photographs rather than on accompanying written material.

PICTURE BOOK. A type of book aimed at preschoolers to 8-year-olds that tells a story using a combination of text and artwork, or artwork only.

PLATFORM. A writer's speaking experience, interview skills, website and other abilities which help form a following of potential buyers for that author's book.

POD. Print on demand.

PROOFREADING. Close reading and correction of a manuscript's typographical errors.

PROPOSAL. A summary of a proposed book submitted to a publisher, particularly used for nonfiction manuscripts. A proposal often contains an individualized cover letter, one-page overview of the book, marketing information, competitive books, author information, chapter-by-chapter outline, and two to three sample chapters.

QUERY. A letter that sells an idea to an editor or agent. Usually a query is brief (no more than one page) and uses attention-getting prose.

REMAINDERS. Copies of a book that are slow to sell and can be purchased from the publisher at a reduced price.

REPORTING TIME. The time it takes for an editor to report to the author on his/her query or manuscript.

REPRINT RIGHTS. The rights to republish a book after its initial printing.

ROYALTIES, STANDARD HARDCOVER BOOK. 10 percent of the retail price on the first 5,000 copies sold; 121/2 percent on the next 5,000; 15 percent thereafter.

ROYALTIES, STANDARD MASS PAPERBACK BOOK. 4-8 percent of the retail price on the first 150,000 copies sold.

ROYALTIES, STANDARD TRADE PAPERBACK BOOK. No less than 6 percent of list price on the first 20,000 copies; 7½ percent thereafter.

SASE. Self-addressed, stamped envelope; should be included with all correspondence.

SELF-PUBLISHING. In this arrangement the author pays for manufacturing, production and marketing of his book and keeps all income derived from the book sales.

SEMIMONTHLY. Twice per month.

SEMIWEEKLY. Twice per week.

SERIAL. Published periodically, such as a newspaper or magazine.

SERIAL FICTION. Fiction published in a magazine in installments, often broken off at a suspenseful spot.

SERIAL RIGHTS. The right for a newspaper or magazine to publish sections of a manuscript.

SHORT-SHORT. A complete short story of 1,500 words.

SIDEBAR. A feature presented as a companion to a straight news report (or main magazine article) giving sidelights on human-interest aspects or sometimes elucidating just one aspect of the story.

SIMULTANEOUS SUBMISSIONS. Sending the same article, story or poem to several publishers at the same time. Some publishers refuse to consider such submissions.

SLANT. The approach or style of a story or article that will appeal to readers of a specific magazine.

SLICE-OF-LIFE VIGNETTE. A short fiction piece intended to realistically depict an interesting moment of everyday living.

SLUSH PILE. The stack of unsolicited or misdirected manuscripts received by an editor or book publisher.

SOCIAL NETWORKS. Websites that connect users: sometimes generally, other times around specific interests. Four popular ones at the moment are MySpace, Facebook, Twitter and LinkedIn.

SUBAGENT. An agent handling certain subsidiary rights, usually working in conjuction with the agent who handled the book rights. The percentage paid the book agent is increased to pay the subagent.

SUBSIDIARY RIGHTS. All right other than book publishing rights included in a book publishing contract, such as paperback rights, book club rights and movie rights. Part of an agent's job is to negotiate those rights and advise you on which to sell and which to keep.

SUBSIDY PUBLISHER. A book publisher who charges the author for the cost to typeset and print his book, the jacket, etc., as opposed to a royalty publisher who pays the author.

SYNOPSIS. A brief summary of a story, novel or play. As part of a book proposal, it is a comprehensive summary condensed in a page or page and a half, single-spaced.

TABLOID. Newspaper format publication on about half the size of the regular newspaper page.

TEARSHEET. Page from a magazine or newspaper containing your printed story, article, poem or ad.

TOC. Table of Contents.

TRADE BOOK. Either a hardcover or softcover book; subject matter frequently concerns a special interest for a general audience; sold mainly in bookstores.

TRADE PAPERBACK. A soft-bound volume published and designed for the general public; available mainly in bookstores.

TRANSLATION RIGHTS. Sold to a foreign agent or foreign publisher.

UNSOLICITED MANUSCRIPT. A story, article, poem or book that an editor did not specifically ask to see.

YA. Young adult books

GEOGRAPHIC INDEX

CANADA

GENERAL INDEX

WRITER'S DIGEST

Is Your Manuscript Ready?

Trust 2nd Draft Critique Service to prepare your writing to catch the eye of agents and editors. You can expect:

- Expert evaluation from a hand-selected, professional critiquer
- Know-how on reaching your target audience
- Red flags for consistency, mechanics, and grammar
- Tips on revising your manuscript and query to increase your odds of publication

Visit **WritersDigestShop.com/2nd-draft** for more information.

THE PERFECT COMPANION TO *GUIDE TO LITERARY AGENTS*

The Writer's Market Guide to Getting Published

Learn exactly what it takes to get your work into the marketplace, get it published, and get paid for it!

Available from **WritersDigestShop.com** and your favorite book retailers.

To get started, join our mailing list: **WritersDigest.com/enews**

FOLLOW US ON:

 Find more great tips, networking and advice by following **@writersdigest**

 And become a fan of our Facebook page! **facebook.com/writersdigest**